HEARING THE OLD TESTAMENT
IN THE NEW TESTAMENT

McMaster New Testament Studies

The McMaster New Testament Studies series, edited by Stanley E. Porter, is designed to address particular themes in the New Testament that are of concern to Christians today. Written in a style easily accessible to ministers, students, and laypeople by contributors who are proven experts in their fields of study, the volumes in this series reflect the best of current biblical scholarship while also speaking directly to the pastoral needs of people in the church today.

Hearing the Old Testament in the New Testament

Edited by

Stanley E. Porter

WILLIAM B. EERDMANS PUBLISHING COMPANY
GRAND RAPIDS, MICHIGAN / CAMBRIDGE, U.K.

© 2006 Wm. B. Eerdmans Publishing Co.
All rights reserved

Published 2006 by
Wm. B. Eerdmans Publishing Co.
2140 Oak Industrial Drive N.E., Grand Rapids, Michigan 49505 /
P.O. Box 163, Cambridge CB3 9PU U.K.

Printed in the United States of America

11 10 09 08 07 06   7 6 5 4 3 2 1

Library of Congress Cataloging-in-Publication Data

Hearing the Old Testament in the New Testament / edited by Stanley E. Porter.
p.   cm.
Includes index.
ISBN-10: 0-8028-2846-9 / ISBN-13: 978-0-8028-2846-0 (pbk.: alk. paper)
1. Bible. N.T. — Relation to the Old Testament.
2. Bible. O.T. — Quotations in the New Testament.
I. Porter, Stanley E., 1956-

BS2387.H36 2006
225.6 — dc22

2006014253

www.eerdmans.com

Contents

CONTENTS

Preface

The 2003 H. H. Bingham Colloquium in New Testament at McMaster Divinity College in Hamilton, Ontario, Canada, was entitled "Hearing the Old Testament through the New: The Use of the Old Testament in the New Testament." The Colloquium, the ninth in a continuing series, attracted not only the speakers whose papers are included here but also a congregation of those interested in hearing and responding to the papers.

One of the distinctives of the Bingham Colloquium at McMaster Divinity College is its provision of an opportunity for selected scholars to present their perspectives on a contemporary New Testament theme of relevance to the larger community of both students and laity. The topic for this Bingham Colloquium, "Hearing the Old Testament through the New," focused upon understanding the Old Testament texts as mediated through the New Testament, and the New Testament texts as they interpreted the Old Testament especially in relation to Jesus Christ. We hope that this volume will be of interest to general readers and serve as a useful textbook for study of an issue that continues to be of high interest. If the response on the day is any indication, the printed volume should provide a greater opportunity for others to participate in this ongoing discussion. The final word is far from having been said on such an important topic.

The Bingham Colloquium is named after Dr. Herbert Henry Bingham, who was a noted Baptist leader in Ontario, Canada. His leadership abilities were recognized by Baptists across Canada and around the world. His qualities included his genuine friendship, dedicated leadership, unswerving Christian faith, tireless devotion to duty, insightful service as a preacher and pastor, and visionary direction for congregation and denomination alike. These qualities endeared him both to his own church members and to believers in other denominations. The Colloquium has been endowed by his daughter as an act of appreciation for her father. We are pleased to be able to continue this tradition.

I am once more very pleased to be able to thank William B. Eerdmans Publishing of Grand Rapids, Michigan, for undertaking the publication of the McMaster New Testament Studies series, of which this volume is the eighth to appear. In particular, I wish to thank Bill Eerdmans, Sam Eerdmans, Michael Thompson, and John Simpson for their help in different but important ways. Previous Colloquia published in this series include the following: *Patterns of Discipleship in the New Testament* (1996), *The Road from Damascus: The Impact of Paul's Conversion on His Life, Thought, and Ministry* (1997), *Life in the Face of Death: The Resurrection Message of the New Testament* (1998), *The Challenge of Jesus' Parables* (2000), *Into God's Presence: Prayer in the New Testament* (2001), *Reading the Gospels Today* (2004), and *Contours of Christology in the New Testament* (2005).

Lastly, I would like to thank a number of people for their particular contributions. I first wish to thank the individual contributors for their efforts to tackle their assignments and present insightful papers of benefit not only to scholars but to all those enquiring after truth in these matters. I would also like to thank those staff at McMaster Divinity College, especially Bonnie Neil and her cadre of student helpers, for creating such a pleasant and supportive environment for the conference. This was my second Colloquium as chair, and my prayer is that this volume, like the previous ones, will help others by bringing to light important insights into God's communication through his written Word, in both the Old and the New Testaments.

STANLEY E. PORTER
McMaster Divinity College
Hamilton, Ontario, Canada

Contributors

James W. Aageson, Professor of Biblical Studies, Concordia College, Moorhead, Minnesota, USA

Craig A. Evans, Payzant Distinguished Professor of Biblical Studies, Acadia Divinity College, Wolfville, Nova Scotia, Canada

Sylvia C. Keesmaat, Adjunct Professor of Biblical Studies and Hermeneutics, Institute for Christian Studies, Toronto, Ontario, Canada

Michael P. Knowles, George F. Hurlburt Associate Professor of Preaching, McMaster Divinity College, Hamilton, Ontario, Canada

Andreas J. Köstenberger, Professor of New Testament and Greek, Southeastern Baptist Theological Seminary, Wake Forest, North Carolina, USA

R. Timothy McLay, Associate Professor of Biblical Studies, St. Stephen's University, St. Stephen, New Brunswick, Canada

Paul Miller, First Grantham United Church, St. Catharines, Ontario, Canada, and McMaster Divinity College, Hamilton, Ontario, Canada

Stanley E. Porter, President, Dean and Professor of New Testament, McMaster Divinity College, Hamilton, Ontario, Canada

Kurt Anders Richardson, McMaster University, Hamilton, Ontario, Canada

Dennis L. Stamps, Ministerial Development Officer for St. Albans Diocese and Residentiary Canon at St. Albans Cathedral and Abbey Church, Hertfordshire, UK, and Visiting Fellow in New Testament and Ancient Rhetoric, University of Chichester, UK

Abbreviations

AB	Anchor Bible
ABRL	Anchor Bible Reference Library
ANTC	Abingdon New Testament Commentaries
ASNU	Acta seminarii neotestamentici upsaliensis
BAIFCS	The Book of Acts in Its First-Century Setting
BBR	*Bulletin for Biblical Research*
BDB	F. Brown, S. R. Driver, and C. A. Briggs, *Hebrew and English Lexicon of the Old Testament*
BETL	Bibliotheca ephemeridum theologicarum lovaniensium
BFCT	Beiträge zur Förderung christlicher Theologie
BGU	*Aegyptische Urkunden aus den Königlichen Staatlichen Museen zu Berlin, Griechische Urkunden.* 15 vols. Berlin, 1895-1983
BIS	Biblical Interpretation Series
BLG	Biblical Languages — Greek
BZNW	Beihefte zur Zeitschrift für die neutestamentliche Wissenschaft
CBQ	*Catholic Biblical Quarterly*
CD	Damascus Code
CGTC	Cambridge Greek Testament Commentaries
CPL	*Clavis partum latinorum.* Edited by E. Dekkers. 2nd ed. Steenbrugis, 1961
CRINT	Compendia rerum iudaicarum ad Novum Testamentum
CSR	*Christian Scholar's Review*
CTR	*Calvin Theological Review*
DSS	Dead Sea Scrolls

EBC	Expositor's Bible Commentary
ETL	*Ephemerides theologicae lovanienses*
FRLANT	Forschungen zur Religion und Literatur des Alten und Neuen Testaments
HBT	*Horizons in Biblical Theology*
HNTC	Harper's NT Commentaries
HSM	Harvard Semitic Monographs
HUT	Hermeneutische Untersuchungen zur Theologie
ICC	International Critical Commentary
IGR	Inscriptiones Graecae ad res Romanas pertinentes
ILS	Inscriptiones Latinae Selectae
IM	*Die Inschriften von Magnesia am Mäander.* Edited by Otto Kern. Berlin, 1900
Int	*Interpretation*
JBL	*Journal of Biblical Literature*
JPTSS	Journal of Pentecostal Theology Supplement Series
JSNT	*Journal for the Study of the New Testament*
JSNTSup	Journal for the Study of the New Testament — Supplement Series
JSOTSup	Journal for the Study of the Old Testament — Supplement Series
JTS	*Journal of Theological Studies*
LD	Lectio divina
LXX	Septuagint
MT	Masoretic Text
NA^{26}	Nestle-Aland, *Novum Testamentum Graece*, 26th edition (1979)
NCB	New Century Bible
NICNT	New International Commentary on the New Testament
NIGTC	New International Greek Testament Commentary
NIV	New International Version
NovTSup	Novum Testamentum, Supplements
NRSV	New Revised Standard Version
NSBT	New Studies in Biblical Theology
NT	New Testament
NTAbh	Neutestamentliche Abhandlungen
NTS	*New Testament Studies*
NTTS	New Testament Tools and Studies
OG	Old Greek
OGIS	*Orientis Graeci Inscriptiones Selectae.* Edited by W. Dittenberger
OT	Old Testament

OTL	Old Testament Library
SB	*Sammelbuch griechischer Urkunden aus Aegypten.* Edited by E. Preisigke et al. Vols. 1- , 1915-
SBL	Society of Biblical Literature
SBLDS	Society of Biblical Literature Dissertation Series
SBLMS	Society of Biblical Literature Monograph Series
SBLSBS	Society of Biblical Literature Sources for Biblical Study
SBS	Stuttgarter Bibelstudien
SBT	Studies in Biblical Theology
SIG	*Sylloge inscriptionum graecarum.* Edited by W. Dittenberger. 4 vols. 3rd ed. Leipzig, 1915-1924
SNT	Studien zum Neuen Testament
SNTSMS	Society for New Testament Studies Monograph Series
SSEJC	Studies in Scripture in Early Judaism and Christianity
STDJ	*Studies on the Texts of the Desert of Judah*
Str-B	Strack, H. L., and P. Billerbeck, *Kommentar zum Neuen Testament aus Talmud und Midrasch.* 6 vols. Munich, 1922-1961
TDNT	Theological Dictionary of the New Testament
TEV	Today's English Version
TNTC	Tyndale New Testament Commentaries
TrinJ	*Trinity Journal*
TZ	*Theologische Zeitschrift*
UBS^3	United Bible Societies *Greek New Testament,* 3rd edition
WBC	Word Biblical Commentary
WUNT	Wissenschaftliche Untersuchungen zum Neuen Testament
ZAW	*Zeitschrift für die alttestamentliche Wissenschaft*
ZNW	*Zeitschrift für die neutestamentliche Wissenschaft*

Introduction:
The Use of the Old Testament
in the New Testament

STANLEY E. PORTER

How do we hear the Old Testament through the New? How does one Scripture echo another? How do we know that the New Testament writer was citing the Old Testament? What versions are the New Testament writers using? What do the New Testament writers mean when they cite the Old Testament? Are we free to understand the Old Testament in the same way as the New Testament writers did? The use of the Old Testament in the New Testament raises a host of exegetical and practical questions — from questions of text type to intertextuality, from questions of allusion to the possibility of illusion, from questions of ancient understanding to modern meaning. The 2003 Bingham Colloquium in New Testament tackled what continues to be one of the most important topics in New Testament studies — but one that also has important implications for all who take the New Testament seriously.[1] These include how one views the relation between the Testaments, how one interprets the Bible today in light of how it has been interpreted in the past, and, perhaps most importantly, how one views Jesus Christ in the light of scriptural witness and fulfillment. The papers in this volume approach these issues from a number of different perspectives, some concentrating upon method and others upon particular biblical writers.[2]

---

1. Those interested in the numerous volumes that address the issue of the use of the Old Testament in the New Testament should consult the individual chapters.

2. I thank the individual contributors for providing abstracts of their own chapters, which I draw freely upon in providing brief summaries of their individual chapters.

Two papers have focused upon foundational issues in such a discussion. The first is by Dennis Stamps on the question of method. This paper helps to set the agenda for all that follows. The first part of the paper provides a brief general survey of the key issues related to the understanding of the use of the Old Testament in the New. Here Stamps looks at such topics as terminology, hermeneutics, and theological questions. He suggests that the multiplicity of interpretative goals in evidence among scholars has made consensus on this issue difficult. The second part of the paper first posits a general definition of rhetoric as persuasive discourse and examines how the use of authoritative tradition in contemporaneous Jewish and Greco-Roman writings is persuasive. Stamps follows this by looking at how the New Testament uses the Old Testament as a rhetorical device. The implication of seeing this usage as a rhetorical device is that assessing the use of the Old Testament in the New Testament is not primarily about determining historical antecedents as interpretative controls or as theological issues that challenge our concept of the Word of God. Instead, it gives freedom to the interpreter to explore the question from the perspective of its "effect" upon the reader, ancient and modern. Stamps concludes by suggesting that if we accept the rhetorical nature of the New Testament's use of the Old Testament then this may have an impact on the way that we as readers critically analyze the historical issues involved and the way that we hear authoritative tradition in the New Testament today.

In the second paper, also foundational for the topic, Timothy McLay investigates the nature of the biblical texts and the concept of Scripture during the period when the New Testament was written. He too defines important terms, such as "Scripture," "canon," and "biblical text," before he examines the nature of the biblical texts that existed in the first and second centuries. By way of illustrating textual diversity, McLay uses the example of Hebrews 1:6. He demonstrates that Odes 2:43 and Hebrews 1:6 are both related to a longer reading of Deuteronomy 32:43 that is preserved in the Old Greek (Septuagint) but that is not in the Masoretic Text or the Qumran document, 4QDeut^q. He also shows that the Old Greek, 4QDeut^q, the Masoretic Text, and Odes 2:43 and Hebrews 1:6 represent four separate and distinct ways that the biblical text was transmitted, and that they all were regarded as Scripture by particular communities at the time. McLay concludes his paper by discussing the ongoing quest for the original biblical text. He notes that unintentional and intentional errors that inevitably occurred while copying the Scriptures, and the fact that there were multiple literary editions for some books of the Bible, contributed to a multiplicity of texts that were identified with a particular book of Scripture. One interested in the issue of the use of the Old Testament in the New would be well advised to consider these larger issues regarding the rhetoric of the texts and even the basis of the quotations that are used. In fact, both of these reemerge in the individual treatments of the biblical material.

After these two important methodologically oriented papers, we turn to the individual books or groups of books in the New Testament. The Gospels are treated first. Michael Knowles, the author of the third paper, tackles Matthew's Gospel. Knowles begins with the assumption that Matthew composed his Gospel in the context of profound social upheaval, overwhelming religious catastrophe, a welter of competing religious visions and candidates for the title of "Messiah," and even uncertainty as to the authoritative text of Scripture — nevertheless, Jesus of Nazareth represented a point of fixity for the author of the Gospel. According to Knowles, Matthew seeks to demonstrate the correlation of ancient prophecy with the advent of the Messiah, as one source or revelation comes to fulfillment in another. In this regard, Matthew depicts his interpretative methodology as taking its cue from the Messiah's own reading of Scripture. Matthean scholars, Knowles notes, tend to favor the evidence of the explicit fulfillment formulas as particularly characteristic of the author of Matthew's Gospel, but these must be juxtaposed, Knowles believes, with Jesus' own use of citation formulas in order to indicate the narrative and theological continuity between them. Matthew does not prioritize one form of reference over another. As a result, textual and typological allusions, and explicit formulas with direct quotations of Scripture (whether cited by Jesus or by Matthew, whatever the literary source and regardless of their messianic potential elsewhere in Second Temple Judaism), are juxtaposed without apparent preference. Matthew, therefore, weaves together a variety of references from a range of sources to create a seamless theological and narrative fabric. Taken together, Knowles believes, these various references to prophetic tradition serve to validate the main features of the Messiah's life, ministry, and teaching — and are validated in return by them. It is not only the texts themselves but larger thematic and historical patterns that come to fruition in Jesus Christ.

The fourth essay, by Craig Evans, begins with a brief review of recent research into the use of the Old Testament in Mark's Gospel. Some scholars have concluded that the evangelist Mark had little interest in the theme of the fulfillment of Scripture. When compared to Matthew's and John's systematic and programmatic use of the Old Testament, and Luke's skillful use of Old Testament language and imagery, Mark's Gospel may well appear to have little interest in Scripture. However, this impression, Evans believes, is misleading. When we examine Mark's Gospel without comparison with the others, the full extent of Mark's use of the Old Testament emerges. In fact, Evans contends that the author of Mark's Gospel may have wished to present Jesus as the fulfillment of prophecy as a conscious and direct challenge to various rumors that were circulating at the time that Jewish prophecy was fulfilled with the ascendancy of Vespasian as emperor. A number of stories were in circulation, perhaps originating with events related to Josephus, which indicated that Vespasian was the fulfillment of Old Testament prophecy regarding Israel and the destruction of the Temple. As Evans shows, much of this attempt to ground events in Scripture probably came out of the intense instability in the Roman Empire, after the suicide of Nero and the deaths of three emperors — Galba, Otho, and Vitellius — in fairly quick succession. On the contrary, Mark says, it is not Vespasian but Jesus who is the "son of God."

Stanley Porter addresses the use of the Old Testament in both Luke and Acts. A number of passages have repeatedly come to the fore in previous studies of the use of the Old Testament in Luke–Acts. Rather than approaching the topic from any number of angles that have been previously used, this essay shifts the critical focus slightly by concentrating upon two instances of usage of the Old Testament that appear near the beginnings of Luke and of Acts and that, Porter believes, are fundamental for establishing their overall purpose. The first instance is Jesus' citing of Isaiah 61:1-2 in Luke 4:18-19 in the Nazareth synagogue. What is implied regarding the figure depicted in the citation of this Isaiah passage, and what is Jesus implying about himself by citing this passage? The second instance is at the beginning of Acts, when Peter stands up and addresses the crowd in order to explain the behavior of his fellow disciples. Here he cites Joel 2:28-32 in Acts 2:17-21, Ps 16:8-11 in Acts 2:25-28, and Ps 110:1 in Acts 2:34-35. The contention here is that exposition of these passages outlines the major themes of the Gospel and Acts and provides a programmatic statement for determining the purpose of each work, as well as unifying them around these common themes.

The treatment of the Gospels is concluded with the paper by Paul Miller on John's Gospel. As Miller notes, scholars who have treated the use of Scripture in John's Gospel have tended to focus their attention on either the explicit formula quotations cited in the Gospel or on the broad biblical themes that are woven into the Johannine narrative. There is merit in each of these approaches. However, in this paper Miller explores a theological typology of vision and witness that underlies John's use of biblical materials to explicate the work of the divine Logos. John's emphasis, according to Miller, is not on a christological use of biblical texts but on the writers of Scripture themselves who saw some aspect of the Logos and testified to him. Their testimony, preserved in Scripture, foreshadows the full manifestation of the Word made flesh in Jesus. To testify to this point, the author of John's Gospel draws on four major representative witnesses: Abraham, Isaiah, Moses, and John the Baptist. As one can see from these four papers on the Gospels and Acts, there is a range of discussion regarding how the authors use the Old Testament, but there is also the common christological emphasis that clearly emerges as central to each Gospel writer.

The next set of papers concerns the Pauline epistles. The Pauline use of the Old Testament is divided into two major parts in this volume, according to the four pillar epistles and the shorter epistles, as well as a brief section on the Pastoral Epistles in a third essay. James Aageson, well known for his work on Paul's use of the Old Testament, notes that the past one hundred years of investigation of this topic suggest that there are five general areas of investigation. The first is the textual traditions reflected in Paul's explicit citations and his manipulation of the biblical texts. The second is comparison of Paul's usage with that of other Jewish interpreters of the period. A third is the prospect that Paul used earlier Christian *testimonia* or *excerpta* and that these influenced his selection of texts. The fourth is the relation of Paul's scriptural quotations and arguments to their larger Old Testament contexts. The fifth and final is the issue of intertextuality and inner biblical exegesis. Rather than being unconnected issues, these are dimensions of Paul's use of Scripture that have received and continue to receive considerable attention. In the first part of his paper, Aageson focuses on certain aspects of the last two issues. In particular, he considers issues related to the Old Testament context of Paul's citations, the character of intertextuality and inner biblical exegesis in Paul's major epistles, and the problem of scriptural echoes. In the second part, he treats the example of 1 Corinthians 10. Acknowledging that recent research has looked to Deuteronomy 32 as the formative basis of Paul's rock imagery,

Aageson wishes to look at a much wider tradition that includes the Old Testament and contemporary and later rabbinic Judaism. When he turns to 1 Corinthians 10, he sees a "symbolic constellation" that allows Paul to connect the rock imagery with Christ, especially in v. 4. The result is a typology in which Paul's Christology is focused upon a particular situation in the church, and hence has ecclesiological relevance.

The second essay devoted to Paul is by Sylvia Keesmaat on the shorter epistles. The letters to the Ephesians, Philippians, Colossians, Thessalonians, and Philemon were written to communities struggling with what it meant to be followers of Jesus at the heart of a world-dominating empire. Keesmaat believes that, since we too are reading these letters in a time of globalization that has clear imperial qualities, the parallels between our time and that of these letters are extensive. Rome proclaimed itself to be ruler of the entire world; hence it is not surprising that throughout these letters Paul draws on the fundamental narratives that shaped Israel's view of history. This includes allusions to Adam in Colossians and Philippians, the prophetic and apocalyptically shaped eschatological coming in judgment and salvation of Ephesians and 1 and 2 Thessalonians, and allusions to the Jubilee and the prophetic ingathering of the Gentiles in Colossians, Philemon, and Ephesians. Paul uses the term "gospel" to describe the mystery of this story of God's faithfulness to the world. This good news is the story line that begins with Israel and comes to its fullest plot resolution in Jesus. This story, rather than the story of Rome, provides the basis for Christian hope. These two papers on Paul's letters take very different approaches to the topic, one focusing upon a particular passage and the other seeing large sweeping themes. Nevertheless, each contributes to the discussion through its approach and its recognition of how not just individual texts but particular themes have relevance to the New Testament writers.

There are also two papers that address the other portions of the New Testament that are often overlooked. In the first of these, Kurt Richardson discusses Job as an exemplar in the epistle of James. James is the only book that provides explicit reference to Job in the entire New Testament. For James, Job is important as an exemplar of faith, particularly in terms of his endurance in the face of trials. Job opens up a particular understanding of one who suffers righteously and not because of divine chastisement. James views trials in terms of training in virtue and the gaining of wisdom in view of God's eschatological promise. Job's life and his endurance sum up the message of James in poignant ways. He stands together with the prophets of the Old Testament and, as such, receives a unique distinction in this New Testament writing.

The second paper, by Andreas Köstenberger, was not delivered at the Bingham Colloquium, but Köstenberger offered to provide it to round out the published volume and provide treatment of several other New Testament books not covered by the other presenters. Although no one had a chance to respond to his paper at the Colloquium, the book clearly benefits from having this additional paper. In this chapter, Köstenberger begins with the Pastoral Epistles of Paul. One of the major passages that he immediately deals with is the use of the Genesis 2 narrative in 1 Tim 2:13. Responding to recent exegesis of this passage, he notes how the Genesis argument forms the basis of Paul's logic. Next, Köstenberger turns to the General Epistles. Returning to James, Köstenberger notes the use of Genesis 15:6 in James 2 as part of a holistic interpretation of the Abraham story that includes both faith and obedience. The book of Hebrews provides a particular challenge. One of the major emphases that Köstenberger addresses is the use of the Old Testament to establish the Son's superiority over other beings. Jude is analyzed in terms of its use of a midrashic exposition of the Old Testament, and 2 Peter, even though it has only a single Old Testament quotation (Prov 26:11 at 2 Pet 2:22), is seen as sharing a common story line with Jude in terms of the Old Testament narrative. First Peter is appreciated for its use of Old Testament passages referring to Israel in terms of the church. Köstenberger also notes that the notoriously difficult passage in 1 Peter 3:19-20 does not cite an explicit Old Testament source, even though it is clearly referring to Old Testament personages, such as Noah. After brief treatment of the Johannine epistles, Köstenberger concludes with discussion of the book of Revelation. The approximately four hundred allusions to the Old Testament provide a challenge for any interpreter. Köstenberger sees these Old Testament allusions functioning in a variety of ways. These include typological identifications between Old Testament images and contemporary figures, by which the Old Testament becomes a means of viewing the present and future.

A new feature of the Bingham Colloquium this year was the provision of a single respondent to all of the papers. Andreas Köstenberger agreed to make a response to the various contributors. Having received the papers in advance (at least, most of them!), he divided his comments on the day into two parts, one following the first five papers, and the other at the end. Here his response is presented as a single paper. Köstenberger's response to each of the essays is useful in helping to focus the issues involved in each essay. As a result, at certain points he endorses the conclusions of the papers, while at others he raises questions that merit further discussion. Sometimes he does both. Each of the presenters had the benefit of hearing Köstenberger's responses on the day of the Colloquium and revising their paper in the light of his comments. But Köstenberger has also had the opportunity to see the papers again and has shaped his comments appropriately. The intention is that this response will have its own integrity as an initial but important response to the papers in this volume, but, more than that, that it will help to direct further response to individual contributions and raise pertinent questions in the minds of readers.

As in previous years, at the time that these papers were first presented in their oral form they generated much stimulating discussion, both from the other contributors and from the general audience. At the end of the session, we again had a panel discussion in which we invited interaction between both the individual contributors and the general audience. This discussion also raised pertinent issues, including a healthy realization that the contributors themselves came from a number of different perspectives, each of which merited a hearing in such a forum. Although various approaches and assumptions are witnessed in these papers, I believe that they represent genuine attempts to come to terms with a number of the major issues that confront any reader of the New Testament today, and that they provide a way forward in considering the issues involved.

The Use of the Old Testament in the New Testament as a Rhetorical Device: A Methodological Proposal

Dennis L. Stamps

Introduction

The topic, the use of the OT in the NT, is a broad and multifaceted issue. At the level of critical New Testament studies, it addresses issues of how one understands the historical context of the NT and how one determines the theological perspective of each NT writer. In a broader perspective, the study of this topic spills over from biblical studies into hermeneutics and theology proper. The brief of this paper is to discuss issues of method. In this short article, one cannot begin to address the myriad of methodological issues. In order to attempt to address a number of the significant issues, the paper is

---

It is a privilege to have been a participant in the 2003 H. H. Bingham Colloquium, and I wish to thank McMaster Divinity College for funding my participation in it. The topic, the use of the Old Testament in the New Testament, is an important issue in NT studies and in theological studies. Three professors from McMaster have made important contributions to this topic. Richard Longenecker's book *Biblical Exegesis in the Apostolic Period* (Grand Rapids: Eerdmans, 1975) remains a classic on the subject. Stanley Porter has written a number of seminal articles on the topic — not least, with regard to method, the important article "The Use of the Old Testament in the New Testament: A Brief Comment on Method and Terminology," in *Early Christian Interpretation of the Scriptures of Israel: Investigation and Proposals* (ed. C. A. Evans and J. A. Sanders; JSNTSup 148; SSEJC 5; Sheffield: Sheffield Academic Press, 1997) 79-96. Michael Knowles has contributed to the complex debate about Matthew's use of the OT in *Jeremiah in Matthew's Gospel: The Rejected-Prophet Motif in Matthaean Redaction* (JSOTSup 68; Sheffield: Sheffield Academic Press, 1993). This paper is indebted to all of them.

organized into three parts. In the first part, there is a brief and general survey of a number of methodological issues, suggesting that the multiplicity of interpretative concerns has clouded consensus and clarity. The second part of the paper explores how an understanding of rhetoric helps one understand the use of authoritative tradition in Jewish, Greco-Roman, and early Christian culture, and thus to understand the way the NT uses the OT as a rhetorical device. The central thesis is that one needs to recognize that use of the OT in the NT is not exclusively a study of the influence of Jewish interpretative methods on the NT writers. Rather, the use of the OT in the NT takes place within a clash of cultures, which was primarily between the emerging Christian culture and the Hellenistic world. If this is the primary context, then we need to understand how the diverse ways the NT uses the OT are persuasive in that collision of cultures. The final, and very brief, third part of the paper suggests that understanding the use of the OT in the NT as a persuasive technique provides a way for the modern reader of the NT and its use of the OT to attend to the historical issues and to attend to the text as a voice speaking to and in the culture or context of the twenty-first century.

Part 1: A Survey of Methodological Issues

The methodological issues related to the use of the OT in the NT are many and complex. In an attempt to bring some kind of order to this general survey, the issues will be discussed under three subheadings: terminology, hermeneutics, and theological issues.

Terminology

What Is the "Old Testament"?

It is methodologically important that scholars are clear about what they are referring to when they speak of the OT with respect to this topic.[1] It is anachronistic to speak of the OT when referring to the perspective of the

---

1. R. B. Hays and J. B. Green, "The Use of the Old Testament by New Testament Writers," in *Hearing the New Testament: Strategies for Interpretation* (ed. J. B. Green; Carlisle: Paternoster Press, 1995) 223-35.

NT writers since the differentiation between old and new had not yet occurred. What is often being studied with regard to the use of the OT in the
NT is how the OT canonical writings are used in the canonical NT. The use
of the term "Hebrew Scriptures" instead of "the OT" does not necessarily
help this situation, for the Greek translation of the OT, the Septuagint
(LXX), was the "bible" for some NT writers.[2] "Jewish sacred writings" is
probably the best way to speak of what the NT writers were citing or referring to as the authoritative textual tradition.[3]

When one begins to examine the nature and extent of Jewish sacred
writings in the first century CE, several issues arise. Historically, the canonical boundaries of the OT were not fixed at the time the NT authors were
writing. While a concept of sacred writings was well established and the
term "the Law and Prophets" was commonly used to designate such, the
precise extent of this corpus was not established.[4] In addition, it appears
that the multifarious nature of Judaism in the first century CE meant that a
particular community often defined its canon.[5] It may be important to
consider the communal context of the NT documents and how this may
have impacted their use of OT texts.[6] It is clear, however, from studies to
date that the majority of quotations in the NT are from what is often referred to as the rabbinical canon. But there are a few citations in the NT of
the apocrypha and pseudepigrapha, and research continues to identify
many other possible references to Jewish writings outside the canon.[7]

2. H. B. Swete, *An Introduction to the Old Testament in Greek* (Cambridge: Cambridge
University Press, 1902) 392: "the LXX is the principal source from which the writers of the
N.T. derived their O.T. quotations."

3. Another term that is often used is "scriptures of Israel," which is slightly more inclusive of the range of texts cited, but it has a slightly political or nationalistic reference that
seems unhelpful. In this paper two terms are used, "citation" and "reference." Citation is any
quotation, however many words, which has verbal correspondence with the textual tradition; reference is any way in which the NT writers invoke the Jewish sacred writers whether
by a quotation or by naming a character or event or by referring to a theme, etc.

4. E. Ulrich, "Hebrew Bible," in *Dictionary of New Testament Background: A Compen-
dium of Contemporary Biblical Scholarship* (ed. C. A. Evans and S. E. Porter; Downers Grove:
InterVarsity, 2000) 455-57.

5. Ulrich, "Hebrew Bible," 457a; see also R. Beckwith, *The Old Testament Canon of the
New Testament Church* (London: SPCK, 1985).

6. For instance, the use of *1 En.* 1:9 in Jude 14-15 may imply a recognition of the authority of this text in this Christian community or at least by this Christian writer.

7. P. J. Hartin, "Apocryphal and Pseudepigraphical Sources in the New Testament," in
Evans and Porter, eds., *Dictionary of NT Background*, 69-71.

Another concern is what textual tradition the NT writers used when citing the sacred Scriptures. The OT text that undergirds most modern OT study is the Hebrew Masoretic text (MT). This text was the foundation for the Jewish rabbinical parties that attempted to regularize the canon.[8] Some NT quotations are from the MT.[9] But a majority of identified OT citations and references are from the Septuagint (LXX).[10] But even this does not regularize the issue, because there are several textual traditions or recensions for the LXX.[11] Also, a few OT citations in the NT seem to be related to the Aramaic targumic traditions.[12] Still other citations seem to be unrelated to any extant OT textual tradition.[13]

All in all, one must be careful to clarify what one means when one attempts to speak of the "OT" that a particular NT writer was using.

What Kind of Citation?

Stanley Porter[14] has demonstrated that, surprisingly, there is a distinct lack of clarity or consensus in the way terms referring to use of the OT in the NT are defined, terms like "quotation," "allusion," and "echo."[15] Most commonly scholars discuss direct or explicit quotations, which are formally marked by an introductory formula of some sort. But scholarly dis-

8. S. Talmon, "The Old Testament Text," in *The Cambridge History of the Bible,* Volume 1: *From the Beginnings to Jerome* (ed. P. R. Ackroyd and C. F. Evans; Cambridge: Cambridge University Press, 1970) 159-99.

9. K. Aland et al., "Index of Allusions and Verbal Parallels," in *The Greek New Testament* (3rd ed., corrected; Stuttgart: UBS, 1983).

10. See note 2 above.

11. S. E. Porter, "Septuagint/Greek Old Testament," in Evans and Porter, eds., *Dictionary of NT Background,* 1101-2.

12. For instance, Ps 68:18 in Eph 4:8 and Lev 22:28 in Luke 6:36. While the targumic tradition was not fixed in the first century CE, the practice of translating and commenting on the reading of the Hebrew text in the first century suggests that this was being done in Aramaic. See B. Chilton, "Targums," in *Dictionary of Jesus and the Gospels* (ed. J. B. Green and S. McKnight; Downers Grove: InterVarsity, 1992) 800-804.

13. R. T. France, *Jesus and the Old Testament* (London: Tyndale, 1982) 240-41, has a detailed study of quotations that differ from both the LXX and the MT in the synoptic Gospels.

14. Porter, "Use of the Old Testament," 80-88.

15. S. Moyise, "Intertextuality and the Study of the Old Testament in the New Testament," in *The Old Testament in the New Testament: Essays in Honour of J. L. North* (ed. S. Moyise; JSNTSup 189; Sheffield: Sheffield Academic Press, 2000) 18-19, provides a useful discussion of the differences between quotation, allusion, and echo.

cussion slips into confusion because some quotations seem to be explicit but without an introductory formula. R. Gundry speaks of formal quotations that, whether formally marked or not, appear to stand apart from the discourse of the text.[16] But the problem is how one determines if a citation stands apart from the textual prose, especially given the way in which original manuscripts had little or no punctuation or even breaks for words. Porter has also demonstrated that conclusions regarding a NT writer's use of the OT by scholars can be skewed by how one defines a quotation. His study of a test case, Phil 1:19, shows that, while scholars acknowledge an OT quotation in this verse, they still conclude that Paul does not cite the OT in Philippians because the quotation is not formally marked or designated.[17]

If it is difficult to determine what a direct, explicit, or formal quotation is, it is even more difficult to define an allusion or echo: all those citations and references that are indirect, implicit, and informal. It would be helpful if scholars could agree on a range of designations for references to the OT and related texts found in the NT, but it is unlikely. As Porter suggests, perhaps scholars should be more diligent about defining their terms.[18] The most helpful categorization of OT references not discussed by Porter is by R. T. France, though he does not fully explain the categories: *verbatim* quotations with introductory formula, *verbatim* quotations without introductory formula, clear verbal allusions, clear references without verbal allusions, possible verbal allusions, and possible references without verbal allusions.[19] Any exhaustive study of the use of the OT in the NT must at some point reckon with the way OT themes, characters, stories, and the like are utilized without any direct citation or verbal allusions.[20]

Further, the matter of discursive style may also be an issue. Can one assess the way in which style of discourse found in the OT and related texts influenced the vocabulary, grammar, and syntax of the NT? Once this issue was focused under the rubric of Semitism, but of course it is now recog-

---

16. R. H. Gundry, *The Use of the Old Testament in St Matthew's Gospel: With Special Reference to the Messianic Hope* (NovTSup 8; Leiden: Brill, 1975) 9.

17. Porter, "Use of the Old Testament," 89-92.

18. Porter, "Use of the Old Testament," 92.

19. France, *Jesus and the OT*, 259-63.

20. I. H. Marshall, "An Assessment of Recent Developments," in *It Is Written: Scripture Citing Scripture; Essays in Honour of Barnabas Lindars* (ed. D. A. Carson and H. G. M. Williamson; Cambridge: Cambridge University Press, 1988) 9-10.

nized as much broader than issues of the impact of Hebrew upon NT Greek, especially when one considers the primary influence of the LXX.[21]

The influence on and use of the OT in the NT goes beyond those instances of verbal citation, and studies need to be clear about the definitions and the limitations or boundaries with which they operate when discussing quotations, allusions, or echoes.

Jewish Background

A majority of scholars focus on Jewish interpretative methods used in the Second Temple and early rabbinic periods as the primary historical background for understanding the use of the OT in the NT. This is understandable for two reasons. First, the Jewish context of early Christianity is without question even if the nature and degree of influence of that context are debatable.[22] Second, the correspondence between the way the NT cites and interprets the OT and Jewish interpretative methods is very evident in a number of instances.[23]

Problems of terminology exist in two areas. First, one has to be precise about what one means by Judaism. The Jewish milieu for the NT writers was not monolithic. The way the different communities (Qumran, Alexandrian, Antiochene, Syrian, Ethiopian) and traditions of Judaism (wisdom, apocalyptic, rabbinic, or pharisaic) interpreted the OT varied.[24]

---

21. S. E. Porter, "The Greek Language of the New Testament," in *Handbook to Exegesis of the New Testament* (ed. S. E. Porter; NTTS 25; Leiden: Brill, 1997) 99-130; M. Wilcox, "Semitic Influence on the New Testament," in Evans and Porter, eds., *Dictionary of NT Background*, 1093-98.

22. Compare the perspectives in works like F. F. Bruce, *New Testament History* (London: Nelson, 1969); J. Neusner, *Judaism in the Beginnings of Christianity* (Philadelphia: Fortress, 1984); A. F. Segal, *Rebecca's Children: Judaism and Christianity in the Roman World* (Cambridge, Mass.: Harvard University Press, 1986); D. R. Schwartz, *Studies in the Jewish Background of Christianity* (Tübingen: J. C. B. Mohr/Paul Siebeck, 1992); and Oskar Skarsaune, *In the Shadow of the Temple: Jewish Influences on Early Christianity* (Downers Grove: InterVarsity, 2002).

23. P. Enns, "Biblical Interpretation, Jewish," in Evans and Porter, eds., *Dictionary of NT Background*, 159-65; J. L. Kugel and R. A. Greer, *Early Biblical Interpretation* (Library of Early Christianity 3; Philadelphia: Westminster, 1986).

24. Helpful discussions can be found in Carson and Williamson, eds., *It Is Written*; M. Fishbane, *Biblical Interpretation in Ancient Israel* (Oxford: Clarendon, 1985); M. J. Mulder, ed., *Mikra: Text, Translation, Reading, and Interpretation of the Hebrew Bible in An-*

Consideration of the variety and differences begins with looking at how the OT interprets the OT and how the different kinds of Jewish intertestamental biblical literature designated as apocryphal and pseudepigraphal, as well as related texts like the Dead Sea Scrolls, interpret the OT. In addition, early Jewish writings from Philo and Josephus and later Jewish writings from Origen and the rabbinic tradition all contribute to the understanding of how Jewish communities and traditions interpreted the OT. The sheer scope and diversity of this literature suggests that one must be careful to avoid generalizations and facile conclusions about the Jewish context out of which NT writers "borrowed" their interpretative practice with regard to the OT. One has to take care not to let the scholarly analysis of NT use of the OT become an exercise in finding a match in the vast array of Jewish practice without giving due attention to distinctions and differences between different Jewish groups. For instance, do individual NT authors demonstrate any identification with a specific Jewish community and/or tradition in the way they interpret the OT?

Second, the way scholars discuss specific Jewish interpretative practices suggests a lack of precision or clarity. In particular, terms like "pesher," "midrash," "typology," and "allegory" are used as labels to identify NT use of the OT as if the very labeling finishes the task of locating the use in its Jewish context. Terms like "pesher" and "midrash" are not actually a specific form of interpretative practice, but generic terms that cover a variety of exegetical practice.[25] Indeed, some NT scholars have used these terms in an iconoclastic manner, not to invoke a Jewish influence, but to describe a NT writer's distinctive, even unique approach in using the OT.[26]

In sum, NT scholars would enhance the study of NT use of the OT by being more precise in defining their terms and in recognizing how the lim-

---

cient Judaism and Early Christianity (CRINT 2/1; Philadelphia: Fortress, 1988); J. M. G. Barclay, *Jews in the Mediterranean Diaspora from Alexander to Trajan (323 BCE–117 CE)* (Edinburgh: T&T Clark, 1996).

25. G. J. Brooke, "Pesharim," in Evans and Porter, eds., *Dictionary of NT Background*, 778-82; G. G. Porton, "Rabbinic Literature: Midrashim," in Evans and Porter, eds., *Dictionary of NT Background*, 889-93.

26. For instance, Gundry's concept of midrash in his commentary on Matthew, R. H. Gundry, *Matthew: A Commentary on His Literary and Theological Art* (Grand Rapids: Eerdmans, 1982). See a response by P. B. Payne, "Midrash and History in the Gospels with Special Reference to R. H. Gundry's *Matthew*," in *Gospel Perspectives: Studies in Midrash and Historiography, Volume 3* (ed. R. T. France and D. Wenham; Sheffield: JSOT Press, 1983) 177-215.

itations of their terms affect any conclusions they draw about the use of the OT in the NT.

Hermeneutics

The use of the OT in the NT is also an interpretative issue. At a historical level, the use of the OT by the NT writers reveals how they understood the nature of sacred writings and thus how they felt able to interpret the OT. At a contemporary level, once one assesses the historical level, what are the implications of the NT writers' interpretation of the OT for interpreting the OT today?[27] Can and should their practice be imitated? Is any imitation tied to their specific methods or can one translate their practice into general interpretative principles? In understanding the methodological issues related to hermeneutics, one needs to look at historical factors, literary dimensions, and interpretative issues.

Historical Factors

The Author or Audience Perspective   With regard to the use of the OT in the NT, one factor is the perspective from which one determines a citation or reference, the original author's or the original reader's/hearer's.[28] The question emerges, When does a citation of or reference to the OT occur, when the author intended to create one or when the audience recognizes one? Determining the author's intention is a slippery interpretative task, but it is legitimate to ask the question especially when the focus of the study is historical.[29] It is easier, for historical purposes, to focus on the author. However, when one begins to examine allusions, it is not always easy to say that those vague one- or two-word allusions were intended. Some al-

---

27. The literature on this is vast, but helpful works include Longenecker's now classic work, *Biblical Exegesis;* also S. Moyise, "Can We Use the New Testament the Way the New Testament Authors Used the Old Testament?" *Die Scriflig* (2002) 643-60.

28. Porter, "Use of the Old Testament," 93.

29. Authorial intention remains a problematic issue in biblical hermeneutics, but a helpful perspective is K. J. Vanhoozer, *Is There a Meaning in This Text? The Bible, the Reader and the Morality of Literary Knowledge* (Grand Rapids: Zondervan, 1998) 43-97, 201-80; see also W. Jeanrond, *Text and Interpretation as Categories of Theological Thinking* (Dublin: Gill and Macmillan, 1988) 33-44.

lusions may come out of the broad milieu of sacred or religious discourse that has been shaped by an author's knowledge of and exposure to Jewish sacred texts. But of course that in and of itself is another level of influence or use.

Assessing the level of audience understanding and perception is virtually impossible. Scholars may feel confident in providing a profile of the original historical recipients, but this is as subjective, or even more so, than reconstructing the historical author. It is understandable why scholars would want to speculate on the Jewish or Gentile make-up of the recipients, as this could have significant impact upon audience perception of the use of the OT. Perhaps more useful is the category of optimal "readers/hearers" who represent the informed reader who responds appropriately to all literary constructs and devices the author uses, that is, who recognizes all the OT citations and references.[30] Yet one must remember that this ideal (or implied) reader is a product within the author's text.[31]

It is peculiar that some scholars when analyzing a NT writer's use of the OT identify citations or references from the perspective of the audience.[32] If one speaks of Paul's use of the OT or Matthew's, it seems best to interpret from the author's point of view, or at least that of their ideal reader.

Assessing Theological Development   The NT writings document a distinctive innovative hermeneutical development that emerged within the complex historical context of first-century Judaism and Hellenism. One of the components of this development was the innovative way Christianity interpreted its inheritance, one dimension being Jewish sacred Scriptures.[33] While studies show dependence and congruity with some Jewish

---

30. S. E. Fish, "Interpreting the *Variorum*," in *Reader-Response Criticism: From Formalism to Post-Structuralism* (ed. J. P. Tompkins; Baltimore: Johns Hopkins University Press, 1980) 174. More common is the concept of implied reader; W. Iser, *The Act of Reading: A Theory of Aesthetic Response* (Baltimore: Johns Hopkins University Press, 1978) 27-38.

31. Helpful discussion of literary theory and the reader in relation to biblical studies is S. D. Moore, *Literary Criticism and the Gospels: The Theoretical Challenge* (New Haven: Yale University Press, 1989) 71-107.

32. Studies that emphasize the audience perspective include: R. B. Hays, *Echoes of Scripture in the Letters of Paul* (New Haven: Yale University Press, 1989); C. D. Stanley, *Paul and the Language of Scripture: Citation Technique in the Pauline Epistles and Contemporary Literature* (SNTSMS 74; Cambridge: Cambridge University Press, 1992).

33. One of the best expositions of this phenomenon is C. F. D. Moule, *The Birth of the New Testament* (3rd ed.; San Francisco: Harper and Row, 1982) 68-106.

exegetical practices, it is acknowledged that there was creative and original interpretation of that inheritance. This distinctive development often has been labeled as christological or christocentric.[34]

There are several ways to understand this development. First, this development is perceived as essentially uniform across the NT corpus; it is what was common to the identity of Christianity. But even if this is true, and recent studies bring this into question,[35] it is still methodologically important to recognize shades of difference between different Christian writers or communities. It is fair to say that the ways in which Paul and Matthew and the author of Revelation interpret Jewish sacred writings differ.[36] If all three can still be identified as christological, one still needs to comment on the distinctive contribution each writer brings to this development in the different way he interprets the inheritance of faith.

Another way to understand this development is by tracing its chronological unfolding as documented in the NT. C. H. Dodd, in his *According to the Scriptures,* posits that the interpretation of the OT in relation to the kerygma was the primary factor in the development of early Christian theology.[37] Dodd suggests that the OT, in particular certain specific areas or "fields" in the OT, provides the substructure by which the NT writers formulated, expanded, and exposited its theology out of the kerygma.

A different yet similarly historical approach is proposed by B. Lindars in *New Testament Apologetic.*[38] Once again, the kerygma represents the crucial first stage of the Christian trajectory, with the events of the resurrection and the passion being central to the early kerygma and other events in the life of Jesus coming at a later stage. According to Lindars one can trace the developing apologetic use of the OT to bolster the kerygma in its various stages, the apologetic support of the resurrection being the first stage.

---

34. D. Juel, *Messianic Exegesis: Christological Interpretations of the Old Testament in Early Christianity* (Philadelphia: Fortress, 1988); Longenecker, *Biblical Exegesis,* 104-5, 205-9; E. E. Ellis, *Paul's Use of the Old Testament* (Grand Rapids: Baker, 1981) 115-16.

35. Hays, *Echoes,* 84-94, sees Paul's use as ecclesiocentric and not christological.

36. S. Moyise, *The Old Testament in the New* (London: Continuum, 2001), provides chapters looking at specific NT writers and their differing use of the OT.

37. C. H. Dodd, *According to the Scriptures: The Sub-structure of New Testament Theology* (London: Nisbet, 1952).

38. B. Lindars, *New Testament Apologetic* (London: SCM, 1961).

While there are strengths and weaknesses to these theses,[39] both provide a historical trajectory by which to evaluate the way early Christianity accessed, utilized, and interpreted the OT that is slightly different from the inductive conclusions of other studies that look at the use in each NT writer. What these studies suggest is that more work needs to be done on how or whether the historical development of Christianity influenced the way the OT was used and interpreted by different OT writers.

Literary Dimensions

In recent biblical studies the terms "intertextuality" and "echo" have become prominent and important, especially as they are used to describe the NT use of the OT.[40] It is helpful to focus on the term "intertextuality," as most use "echo" as a synonymous term.[41] What many wish to convey by using the term is that reference to the OT by NT writers is not measured purely by the transfer of meaning of specific texts from the OT to the NT or by the interpretative meaning the NT author gives to an OT text.[42] Rather, intertextuality recognizes that the relationship between two texts is complex: that which is evoked by a quotation of or allusion to another text is more than meaning; it is a range of "voices" or "textual surfaces."[43] In addition, intertextuality recognizes the role the reader or interpreter brings to discerning the impact or effect of a textual citation or reference — that is, the author does not have complete control over how a reader responds to or makes sense of an embedded reference. The problem is that intertextuality is being used by biblical scholars to discuss a range of phe-

---

39. See the helpful discussion of Dodd and Lindars in Marshall, "Assessment," 2-9.

40. S. Draisma, ed., *Intertextuality in Biblical Writings* (Kampen: Kok, 1989); D. N. Fewell, ed., *Reading Between Texts: Intertextuality and the Hebrew Bible* (Louisville: Westminster John Knox, 1992); G. R. O'Day, "Jeremiah 9:22-23 and 1 Corinthians 1:26-31: A Study in Intertextuality," *JBL* 109 (1990) 259-67; and T. W. Berkley, *From a Broken Covenant to Circumcision of the Heart: Pauline Intertextual Exegesis in Romans 2:17-29* (SBLDS 175; Atlanta: SBL, 2000). Helpful theoretical discussions are found in Moyise, "Intertextuality and the Study of the OT," 14-41; and Moyise, "Intertextuality and Biblical Studies: A Review," *Verbum et Ecclesia* 23 (2002) 418-31.

41. As demonstrated by Porter, "The Use of the OT," 85. Hays, *Echoes*, 14-24, even uses the phrase "intertextual echo."

42. Moyise, "Intertextuality and the Study of the OT," 14-18.

43. Often used to support this understanding is the literary theory of J. Kristeva; see T. Moi, ed., *The Kristeva Reader* (New York: Columbia University Press, 1980) 36.

nomena from source criticism to the way modern readers make connections between a text and their memory of other texts.[44] Porter suggests that the wide range of meanings biblical scholars give to the term "intertextuality" brings an unhelpful vagueness to its use and that scholars should either abandon the term or be more diligent in defining it, listening especially to what literary criticism brings to any such definition.[45]

What the concept of intertextuality does suggest is that how any hearer, past or present, hears the explicit or unconscious reference to another text is part of how one analyses the use of the OT in the NT. Equally, the relationship between an author and a text cited or referred to is more than the meaning in the words that are "borrowed." The influence of some texts extends to the social, cultural, and ideological baggage that gets attached to them.[46]

Interpretative Issues

Another important area that is affected by the study of the use of the OT in the NT is formulating the way the OT is interpreted and applied to the present context. In essence, does the way the NT uses the OT teach anything about the way one should interpret and apply the OT today?

One other dimension to how one understands and applies the NT interpretation of the OT is the cultural gap between the NT writers and interpreters today.[47] Readers and interpreters today no longer share the same worldview and cultural context the NT writers did. They are very distant from the Jewish and Hellenistic contexts of the first century. The

44. Moyise describes five types of intertextuality that biblical scholars are employing; Moyise, "Intertextuality and Biblical Studies," 419-30. I am still trying to figure out what Richard Hays means when he talks about "the silent space framed by the juncture of two texts"; Hays, *Echoes,* 155.

45. Porter, "The Use of the Old Testament," 84-85. Moyise is more positive than Porter about the use of the term: Moyise, "Intertextuality and the Study of the OT," 15-16; Moyise, "Intertextuality and Biblical Studies," 418-31.

46. A helpful exploration of this is V. K. Robbins, *The Tapestry of Early Christian Discourse: Rhetoric, Society and Ideology* (London: Routledge, 1996) 144-91; Robbins, *Exploring the Texture of Texts: A Guide to Socio-Rhetorical Interpretation* (Harrisburg: Trinity Press International, 1996) 71-86; even if one does not fully subscribe to his theory of socio-rhetorical interpretation. See below for a brief discussion of helpful aspects of Robbins's theory.

47. Moyise, "Can We Use," 643-60; Moyise, "The Use of Analogy in Biblical Studies," *Anvil* 18 (2001) 33-42.

Enlightenment-informed, scientific, historical-critical approach to Scripture in a post-Christian context is distinctly different from the way the NT writers understood their interpretative task. Perhaps interpretative theory could change the way one interprets the OT to conform to that of the NT. But can it and should it?

Some argue that interpreters should simply imitate the Jewish exegetical practices the NT writers used in their interpretation of the OT, extending these practices to all parts of the OT.[48] Some argue that the NT writers were not finding new meaning in OT texts but merely applying the intended meaning to their context, and modern interpreters should do the same.[49] Some argue that the NT writers operated as inspired prophets and that interpreters today cannot duplicate their distinctive interpretative stance and practice.[50] Some argue that, though interpreters cannot duplicate the way the NT authors interpreted the OT, one can attempt to imitate the transformative impact their interpretation of the OT produced in their faith community, so scholars likewise should interpret the OT as inheritors of the proclamation and participants in the ongoing eschatological drama of salvation.[51]

The question — what does one learn about how to understand and interpret the OT from the NT? — is an important hermeneutical concern. Does the NT provide a specific methodology, or does it provide principles, or does it represent a unique unrepeatable interpretative occasion? Whatever one decides has important implications.

Theological Issues

The use of the OT in the NT raises a number of important theological issues. The primary issue is ascertaining the relationship between the OT

48. Perhaps implied by K. Snodgrass, "The Use of the Old Testament in the New," in *Interpreting the New Testament: Essays on Methods and Issues* (ed. D. A. Black and D. S. Dockery; Nashville: Broadman and Holman, 2001) 222-24.

49. W. C. Kaiser, *The Uses of the Old Testament in the New Testament* (Chicago: Moody Press, 1985); Kaiser, "The Single Intent of Scripture," in *The Right Doctrine from the Wrong Texts?* (ed. G. K. Beale; Grand Rapids: Baker Books, 1994) 55-69.

50. Longenecker, *Biblical Exegesis*, 205-20; A. T. Hanson, *The Living Utterances of God* (London: Darton, Longman and Todd, 1983) 178-95.

51. Vanhoozer, *Is There a Meaning*, 367-452; Hays, *Echoes*, 178-92.

and the NT,[52] or how one understands the OT as word of God in relation to the NT. This issue impinges upon one's understanding of revelation and inspiration.

One matter relates to the OT text the NT writers used. If one holds to a position of verbal plenary inspiration related to the original autographs, how does one handle the variety of OT texts the NT writers use, from the MT to the LXX to the targums to texts that are not extant in any OT textual tradition? Equally, how does one handle those few instances where the NT writer appears to modify the OT text, possibly to suit the theological point he is trying to make?[53] Then there is the problem of the extent of the authoritative scriptural canon to which the NT refers, particularly the more than a few references to the apocrypha and pseudepigrapha; does this challenge what one understands about the inspired text?

There are several theological strategies to cope with this problem. First, some hold to a concept of single intent that is consistent between the OT and NT, with divergent understanding actually coming down to application, not meaning.[54] Others recognize a form of *sensus plenior*, which recognizes that the inspired meaning of a text in the canon is that which God intended or may divinely reveal through the authority of the church.[55] This fuller sense of the text may extend beyond that which is perceived as the author's intention. For others the issue of continuity and discontinuity is not understood in such rigid terms.[56] In sum, the creative way the NT uses and interprets the OT and the way the NT uses various texts of the OT present a theological challenge to one's understanding of revelation and inspiration.

52. D. L. Baker, *Two Testaments, One Bible: A Study of Some Modern Solutions to the Theological Problems of the Relationship Between the Old and the New Testaments* (Downers Grove: InterVarsity, 1976).

53. A perspective that is thoroughly explored with reference to Paul in Stanley, *Paul and the Language*, 17-28.

54. Kaiser, *The Uses of the OT in the NT*; Kaiser, "The Single Intent," 55-69.

55. R. E. Brown, "The History and Development of the Theory of a Sensus Plenior," *CBQ* 15 (1953) 141-62; R. E. Brown, "The Sensus Plenior in the Last Ten Years," *CBQ* 25 (1963) 262-65; D. J. Moo, "The Problem of Sensus Plenior," in *Hermeneutics, Authority and Canon* (ed. D. A. Carson and J. D. Woodbridge; Grand Rapids: Zondervan, 1986) 179-211.

56. See the summary discussion in Moyise, *The Old Testament in the New*, 131-37.

Summary

The study of the NT use of the OT provokes a number of important issues and questions. At one level, there is the historical-critical question of trying to determine the relationship of the NT writers to the first-century world, particularly the Jewish context, with regard to their use and interpretation of sacred writings — and, just as crucially, trying to understand the intent and purpose of the NT author's use of the OT in a particular instance. These analyses require definition and clarity with regard to the various terms used. At another level, the use of the OT in the NT raises important hermeneutical matters, such as how the NT use of the OT informs modern-day interpretation of the OT. At a third level, theological issues emerge as the modern critic assesses the impact of the use of the OT in the NT on the issue of one Bible, two testaments, and how the NT use of the OT impacts an understanding of inspiration and revelation. The problem, of course, is that one may heuristically look at the issues of terminology, hermeneutics, and theology discretely, but they are linked and interwoven.

Can a biblical scholar who is committed to a certain view of inspiration come to a conclusion other than finding continuity between the OT and NT? Richard Longenecker's important work purports to be exegetically neutral, trying to get an accurate historical picture of how the NT writers were interpreting the OT in relation to their historical context, and then attempting to deal with the theological questions. But the interrelationship between terminology, hermeneutics, and theology means that many studies of the NT use of the OT have multiple interpretative goals. The multiplicity of interpretative goals can potentially cloud the matter of definitions and terms. In addition, consensus is unlikely on this issue as long as there is such diversity of theological perspectives and agendas. Perhaps what one can hope for is that further study will be more precise in defining terms and in declaring the hermeneutical concerns and theological perspective informing a particular study.

Part 2: The New Testament Use of the Old Testament as Rhetorical Device

In the study of the NT use of the OT, the Jewish background and context have been the dominant place where scholars have looked for understanding

23

a NT writer's perspective and practice. This is understandable, and there is more work to be done to understand the important role of the Jewish context for informing this issue. However, the exploration of the Hellenistic context for considering the NT use of the OT has not been as fully explored.[57] Consideration of the Hellenistic context should also include exploration of the use of the OT in early Christian writings. While one needs to be careful not to read back into the NT developments documented in the post-NT writings like the early church fathers, nonetheless these early writings provide further evidence of the developing perspective and practice of early Christian communities, which may shed light on the use of the OT in the NT. In this second part of the paper the Hellenistic context, including the early Christian writings, will be examined, particularly with reference to rhetoric, to see if this can help in evaluating the use of the OT in the NT.

Rhetoric as an Important Concept in the Hellenistic Context

If it is granted that the NT letters are the earliest NT documents, then it must be conceded that at least the Pauline letters were written to communities of faith where the Gentile make-up of the congregation was significant. All of the Pauline letters were written to churches outside Palestine. In addition, when the Gospels are considered, the location of the community of faith for the Gospels is generally suggested as outside Palestine: for Mark, Rome or Syria; for Matthew, Antioch; for Luke, the churches of Paul's mission or Greece or Syria; for John, Ephesus or Syria.[58] Debate over locating the provenance of the other NT epistles is more contested, but once again a majority of scholars locate the recipients of these letters in places outside Palestine. What this suggests, at least, is that the Hellenistic context is a greater influence than one might expect. While certain Jewish Diaspora communities, and hence Jewish Christian communities, may have attempted to maintain rigid cultural and social boundaries, Hengel's massive study *Judaism and Hellenism* has demonstrated that cultural

57. For a general exploration of the usefulness of the Hellenistic context for NT studies, see L. C. A. Alexander, "The Relevance of Greco-Roman Literature and Culture to New Testament Study," in Green, ed., *Hearing the NT,* 109-26.

58. While consensus is not unanimous, discussion of the provenance of each of the Gospels can be found in most NT introductions or individual commentaries, e.g., R. Brown, *An Introduction to the New Testament* (ABRL; New York: Doubleday, 1997).

interpenetration occurred in Palestine itself as well as in the Diaspora.[59] This indicates that it is appropriate to consider the Hellenistic context as an important context for the use of the OT in the NT writings.

While Hellenistic culture has many dimensions, like any culture, one prominent aspect of Hellenistic culture was rhetoric.[60] It formed the basis for the education of most Gentiles, at least among those whose socioeconomic status permitted the luxury of a formal education.[61] As a result of the grounding of culture in rhetoric through education, rhetoric formed the basis for communication in the legal, civic, and social spheres of the Greco-Roman world. It is not surprising, then, that there is demonstrable evidence that Greco-Roman rhetoric even influenced educated Jewish writers in Palestine.[62] It is therefore arguable that rhetoric was a "universal" influence upon communication conventions in the Greco-Roman world, including Palestine.[63]

Defining Rhetoric

It is difficult to state a definition of rhetoric in the first century CE. Aristotle's definition from late 300 BCE was (and remains) influential throughout the history of rhetoric: "the faculty of discovering the possible means of persuasion in reference to any subject whatever."[64] Cicero, in the first century BCE, defined rhetoric as persuasion by speech.[65] Quintilian, in the first century

---

59. M. Hengel, *Judaism and Hellenism: Studies in Their Encounter in Palestine During the Early Hellenistic Period* (one-volume ed.; Philadelphia: Fortress, 1981) 65-106.

60. D. L. Stamps, "Rhetoric," in Evans and Porter, eds., *Dictionary of NT Background*, 953-56.

61. D. F. Watson, "Education: Jewish and Greco-Roman," in Evans and Porter, eds., *Dictionary of NT Background*, 308-11.

62. Hengel, *Judaism and Hellenism*, 65-78, and 102: "knowledge of Greek language and literature, indeed training in rhetoric, were put completely at the service of the defence of the Jewish tradition against the dangers of Hellenistic civilization."

63. G. A. Kennedy, *New Testament Interpretation Through Rhetorical Criticism* (Chapel Hill: University of North Carolina Press, 1984) 9-10; but compare S. E. Porter, "The Theoretical Justification for Application of Rhetorical Categories to Pauline Epistolary Literature," in *Rhetoric and the New Testament: Essays from the 1992 Heidelberg Conference* (ed. S. E. Porter and T. H. Olbricht; JSNTSup 90; Sheffield: JSOT Press, 1993) 100-109.

64. *Rhetorica* 1.2.1.

65. *De Inventione* 1.5.

CE, defined it as a good person speaking well.[66] Even in the case of Quintilian, however, the goal is speaking to influence especially with regard to virtue.[67] Each emphasized a different mode of persuasion: Aristotle emphasized proof; Cicero, arrangement; Quintilian, style. Nevertheless, persuasion is the central element to all ancient conceptions of rhetoric.[68]

The focus on persuasion has remained central to the history of rhetorical study so that modern studies echo ancient definitions.[69] A primary example is the definition of rhetoric by the New Rhetoric school: "to induce or to increase the mind's adherence to the theses presented for its assent."[70] As rhetoric so defined is essentially an action — that is, to persuade — then rhetorical criticism must include not only the analysis of the means of persuasion (a study of the kind of action), but also the analysis of the effects (a study of the effectiveness of the action).

For the purposes of this study, rhetoric may be defined as the ways and means employed in a text to persuade and the effect(s) of those ways and means.

The Use of Authoritative Tradition as Persuasion in the First Century and Early Christian Writings

Jewish Writings

Different kinds of Jewish writings drew upon and interpreted the OT to persuade. The scope of this paper does not allow a detailed analysis but

---

66. *Institutio oratoria* 2.14-15.

67. *Inst.* 2.20.

68. F. M. Young, *Biblical Exegesis and the Formation of Christian Culture* (Cambridge: Cambridge University Press, 1997) 100: "the object of every discourse was persuasion." Persuasion is a broad concept, but it is in contradistinction to the broad concepts of Jewish interpretative practices, which are primarily exposition and application. But Jewish writings are persuasive as well; H. A. Fischel, "Story and History: Observations on Greco-Roman Rhetoric and Pharisaism," in *Essays in Greco-Roman and Related Talmudic Literature* (New York: Ktav, 1977) 443-72.

69. The Middle Ages shifted the emphasis to rhetoric as a form of stylistic ornamentation, seeing rhetoric more as a set of devices and techniques; G. A. Kennedy, *Classical Rhetoric and Its Christian and Secular Tradition from Ancient to Modern Times* (Chapel Hill: University of North Carolina Press, 1980) 161-94.

70. C. Perelman and L. Olbrechts-Tyteca, *The New Rhetoric: A Treatise on Argumentation* (trans. J. Wilkinson and P. Weaver; Notre Dame: University of Notre Dame Press, 1969) 4.

only a few general suggestions with regard to three forms of Jewish writings. Each of these sets of Jewish writings cites the OT as authoritative tradition in a persuasive manner.

First, Philo employed an allegorical approach to his reading of the OT in order to substantiate that Greek philosophical and moral theory was rooted in the ancient authority of Moses and the Pentateuch: "He was thus able to prove to his own satisfaction, and for use in missionary propaganda, that the best Greek thought had been anticipated by Moses."[71]

Second, the rabbinic or pharisaic tradition used complex exegetical procedures to interpret the OT in order to make it applicable to their context, interpretations that do not seem tied to the meaning or sense of the OT context.[72] In this way, they ensured the authority of the OT in new situations, demonstrated the relevance of the OT to contemporary contexts, and validated the religious system they were constructing.

Third, the Dead Sea Scrolls used typology and other exegetical ploys to reveal that OT predictions of events were taking place in the life of their community and in the person of the Teacher of Righteousness.[73] In so doing, they demonstrate that their "sect" was the true messianic fulfillment of OT prophecy.

In all three cases, the OT is used partially to persuade — the interpretation of the OT is used to validate among the members of their community the truthfulness of their community ethos and to convince others of the truth they espouse and proclaim.

Greco-Roman Writings

It is often suggested that authoritative tradition did not operate in the same way in Greco-Roman culture as it did in the Jewish culture.[74] Although this may be true, establishing and citing authoritative tradition was part of Greco-Roman culture.[75]

---

71. C. K. Barrett, "The Interpretation of the OT in the New," in Ackroyd and Evans, eds., *Cambridge History of the Bible*, 395. For a summary of the importance of Philo, and bibliography, see G. E. Sterling, "Philo," in Evans and Porter, eds., *Dictionary of NT Background*, 789-93.

72. Barrett, "Interpretation," 383-86.

73. Barrett, "Interpretation," 386-89.

74. C. D. Stanley, "Paul and Homer: Greco-Roman Citation Practice in the First Century CE," *NovTest* 32 (1990) 48-49, cites the comments by D.-A. Koch in his study *Die Schrift als Zeuge des Evangeliums* (Tübingen: J. C. B. Mohr, 1986) 190.

75. It needs to be emphasized that what is being argued for here is not similarity be-

The importance of tradition is demonstrated by the way certain Greco-Roman literary traditions established an authoritative corpus. One of the impacts of the library at Alexandria was that Alexandrian scholars collected and standardized the classic texts. In particular, by the late second century BCE, Homer's *Iliad* and *Odyssey* were standardized in the critical text known as the Homeric "vulgate."[76] The practice of collecting excerpts of important writings arranged topically in what are known as anthologies or extract collections was widespread in Greco-Roman literary practice primarily for educational or didactic purposes.[77] These anthologies helped to establish the concept of a classical literary canon. In addition, maxims were collected to aid in moral instruction. In the upper stages of a rhetorical education, certain kinds of extract collections were used: the epitome (condensed versions of a larger work); the philosophical handbook and the doxography (collections of philosophical teachings); and rhetorical handbooks (collections of rhetorical theory).[78] There is also evidence of a long tradition from the fourth century BCE to the second century CE of sayings collections and *chreiai* collections.[79] Another example of a totally different literary tradition is the formation of collections of Greek magical papyri, which helped to establish a written tradition that not only preserved spells for reference and posterity but also provided authoritative tradition by the selectivity of what was preserved.[80] It is clear that within Hellenistic culture there was concerted effort to establish and preserve literary and textual traditions for use in other literary traditions.

But how was this authoritative tradition to be used? Rhetorical theory did not have a great deal to say about the practice of citing authoritative tradition either by quotation or allusion, but what is stated is interesting and suggestive.[81] Aristotle briefly discusses witnesses as a form of

---

tween Jewish and Greco-Roman practice. Further work needs to be done to compare the concepts of "authority" and "scripture" in Jewish and Hellenistic culture and tradition.

76. Stanley, "Paul and Homer," 51.

77. M. C. Albl, *"And Scripture Cannot Be Broken": The Form and Function of the Early Christian* Testimonia *Collections* (NovTSup 94; Leiden: Brill, 1999) 73-81.

78. Albl, *"And Scripture,"* 75-77.

79. Albl, *"And Scripture,"* 77-79.

80. H. D. Betz, "The Formation of Authoritative Tradition in the Greek Magical Papyri," in *Jewish and Christian Self-Definition,* Volume Three: *Self-Definition in the Graeco-Roman World* (ed. B. F. Meyer and E. P. Sanders; London: SCM, 1982) 161-70.

81. Young, *Biblical Exegesis,* 99-103; C. D. Stanley, "The Rhetoric of Quotations: An

inartistic proof for forensic (law court) rhetoric (*Rhet.* 1.15.1-3). He expands on witnesses as a form of evidence, speaking of two kinds of witnesses, ancient and recent (*Rhet.* 1.15.13-19). By ancient witnesses, Aristotle means "the poets and men of repute whose judgments are known to all" (*Rhet.* 1.15.13). As an example, he cites appeal to Homer and to ancient proverbs.[82] They are effective because they represent agreed or common judgment. Quintilian also has a brief discussion of the use of quotations.[83] He states that a good orator should have a well-stocked memory to draw upon for oration.[84] In addition, he acknowledges that quoting respected authors gives weight to what one says:

> being able to quote the happy sayings of the various authors [gives them] a power they will find most useful in courts. For phrases which have not been coined merely to suit the circumstances of the lawsuit of the moment carry greater weight and often win greater praise than if they were our own.[85]

Quoting poets is also a way of adorning your eloquence and supporting your argument: "such quotations have the additional advantage of helping the speaker's case, for the orator makes use of the sentiments expressed by the poet as evidence in support of his own statements."[86] Longinus gives credence to quoting the great writers and poets as a form of *mimesis* in which the orator copies the style of past authorities to give inspiration and expressiveness to what he says.[87] Citing tradition played a role in proof or in reinforcing the content: it influenced the hearer to empathy, and it added eloquence to style.

Christopher Stanley has demonstrated that during the first century

---

Essay on Method," in Evans and Sanders, eds., *Early Christian Interpretation*, 45n.1; Albl, "*And Scripture*," 70-73; Barrett, "Interpretation," 377-79.

82. Aristotle also refers to the use of maxims (*Rhet.* 2.21.11) as generally what an orator coins, but he does speak of those which are common and frequently quoted. Maxims are most effective on the lips of the elderly whose experience gives credibility to the maxim. They are also effective because "the hearers are pleased to hear stated in general terms the opinion which they have already specially formed" (*Rhet.* 2.21.15).

83. *Inst. orat.* 1.8; 2.7; 5.36-44.

84. *Inst. orat.* 2.7.

85. *Inst. orat.* 2.7.4.

86. *Inst. orat.* 1.8.12. See also *Inst. orat.* 5.36-44 on quotations and maxims.

87. *On the Sublime* 13.2-3; 14.1.

CE the Homeric epic texts were quoted and interpreted in an authoritative manner similar to the OT in the NT, particularly Paul's use of the OT.[88] He lists six parallel comparisons:

(1) Both the Homeric texts and the sacred Jewish writings functioned as primordial texts and exercised formative influence on communal life and thought.
(2) Both were regarded as revelations of divine truth whose full and correct meaning could be understood only by those attuned to the proper way of reading them.
(3) Both served as sources for their community's views regarding the divine order, the nature of the universe, and the proper behavior of individuals and society.
(4) Both texts were central to the education of children and hence became part of the memory of individuals and the fabric of everyday life.
(5) Both texts were cited in argumentation as authoritative for both the author and the audience.
(6) Both sets of texts were established in a relatively standard text-form in the first century, with some possibility for variation due to the limited availability of other text-type manuscripts.[89]

By examining the use of Homer in four Greek authors who were roughly contemporary with Paul, Stanley shows that the concern for the authoritative text and tradition is very high in Greco-Roman culture, at least with respect to the Homeric texts. In fact, it appears that these four writers were more conservative in their quotation of the Homeric textual tradition than Paul was in his use of the OT.

Early Christian Writings and Hellenistic Culture

We will now turn to examine the post-NT writings. These writings deal with authoritative tradition in some interesting ways.

As noted above, the NT writings, though firmly rooted in a Jewish context since most NT authors seem to be Jewish Christians, are written

88. Stanley, "Paul and Homer," 48-78.
89. Stanley, "Paul and Homer," 51-52.

within and to a Hellenistic context. The process of distinguishing Christianity from Judaism, which is often called a parting of the ways, in at least some terms is as early as Paul's writings if not earlier, given the record of the Pauline mission in Acts.[90] At some point, if not at the same time, Christianity also began to distinguish itself from Greco-Roman culture.[91] The Pauline creedal affirmation of "Jesus is Lord" and the Christianizing of the Greco-Roman household codes are evidence for this. Equally, they are evidence of Christianity being enculturated to its Greco-Roman context and influenced by Hellenism.[92]

The interesting aspect of this clash of cultures is the role the OT played in the argument of early Christian apologists in securing the place of Christianity over both Judaism and Hellenism.[93] In the Hellenistic culture, novelty was not a virtue but usually a superstition; truth was that which was rooted in antiquity. Tacitus (115 CE) charged the followers of Chrestus with following a new superstition. The early Christian apologists utilized Hellenistic conventions — historical, philosophical, and literary — to demonstrate that Christianity was founded on a tradition prior to and superior to that of the Greeks: the OT.[94] For Justin, in his *Hortatory Address to the Greeks* (ca. 150-160 CE), the Jewish Scriptures embodied true philosophy (the universal logos) more effectively than Plato or any other philosophical school; and as Christianity was the rightful heir of this tradition, it was superior to Greco-Roman philosophies. Tatian's *Address to the Greeks* (ca. 160-170 CE) likewise identifies the earliest universal wisdom with Moses and uses a chronological argument to show that Moses was more ancient than even Homer. Theophilus of Antioch (ca. 180 CE) read the Jewish Scriptures and especially Genesis to substantiate the antiquity

---

90. J. D. G. Dunn, *The Partings of the Ways Between Christianity and Judaism and Their Significance for the Character of Christianity* (London: SCM, 1991).

91. A. Cameron, *Christianity and the Rhetoric of Empire: The Development of Christian Discourse* (Berkeley: University of California Press, 1991); A. Harnack, *The Mission and Expansion of Christianity* (Vol. 1; London: Williams and Norgate, 1908).

92. J. L. Kinneavy, *Greek Rhetorical Origins of Christian Faith* (Oxford: Oxford University Press, 1987); W. Jaeger, *Early Christianity and Greek Paideia* (Cambridge, Mass.: Belknap Press, 1961); E. Hatch, *The Influence of Greek Ideas on Christianity* (New York: Harper, 1957).

93. A. J. Droge, *Homer or Moses? Early Christian Interpretation of the History of Culture* (HUT 26; Tübingen: J. C. B. Mohr/Paul Siebeck, 1989). See also Young, *Biblical Exegesis*, chs. 3 and 10.

94. Young, *Biblical Exegesis*, 49-57.

of Moses as being greater than all Greek progenitors and to establish the truthfulness of these ancient texts in providing insights into contemporary Greco-Roman scientific interests.

In order to substantiate the validity of Christianity, these three apologists, using Hellenistic argumentation, demonstrated that the Jewish sacred tradition is older than the Greek tradition and also enshrined the true ancient wisdom and philosophy.[95] The apologists went on to demonstrate that Christianity was the true purveyor of this inheritance. All in all, in this clash of cultures, their use of the OT can be seen as a rhetorical device or technique to persuade the reader of the validity of Christianity.

F. Young goes on to argue that the foundation of the apologists led to the establishment of a thoroughgoing Christian *paideia,* with the OT at the heart of this new classical literary tradition.[96] The establishment of this *paideia* succeeded in subordinating both Jewish and Hellenistic culture. In this cultural takeover, Christianity became the third race *(tertium genus):* "they adopted the literature of the Jews, and claimed access to the primitive and true wisdom which both Judaism and Hellenism had fragmented and distorted."[97] In fact, evidence for the development of this all-pervasive Christian *paideia* may go back as early as Revelation and 1 Clement in the manner in which *mimesis,* at least with regard to style, is at the heart of their use of the OT.

Methodological Implications

It may be helpful to begin to see the NT as part of this clash of cultures and its writings as part of the persuasive agenda of the post-NT writers.[98] For example, Paul's argument that justification by faith is earlier than the Law may be persuasive, not only because it employs some form of Jewish exegetical practice, but because it corresponds to a Hellenistic concern to establish truth in that which is most ancient. Even where the NT uses or

95. This tradition was carried on in the writings of Clement of Alexandria, Origen, and Eusebius.

96. Young, *Biblical Exegesis,* 285-99.

97. Young, *Biblical Exegesis,* 69.

98. An interesting article along this line is J. J. Murphy, "Early Christianity as a 'Persuasive Campaign': Evidence from the Acts of the Apostles and the Letters of Paul," in Porter and Olbricht, eds., *Rhetoric and the NT,* 90-99; also Young, *Biblical Exegesis,* 285-90.

draws upon Jewish interpretative practice, its effectiveness as a persuasive strategy in a Greco-Roman context and among Greco-Roman readers may have depended on the Hellenistic perspective of giving regard to ancient authoritative tradition. Indeed, the non-Jewish members of Christian congregations would be attentive to citing ancient authors, proverbs, and maxims even if their recognition of the source of these quotations and of allusions to Jewish Scriptures was limited and the use of Jewish exegetical practice unrecognized. The non-Jewish recipients of NT writings would recognize the explicit quotations and the *mimesis* of OT style as helping to reinforce the content as well as enjoining the hearer to attend to the argument and to appreciate the eloquence. More work needs to be done to understand how the use of the OT in the NT was persuasive from the perspective of its Hellenistic context.[99]

The term "rhetoric" is helpful at this point. Rhetoric as the ways and means employed in a text to persuade and as an assessment of the intended effect(s) of those ways and means provides a useful means to evaluate the use of the OT in the NT. Further work needs to be done to determine if ancient Greco-Roman rhetorical theory sheds any further light on the use of quotations. But a qualification is necessary: the generic differences between the NT and Greco-Roman rhetorical writings need to be kept in view. With regard to rhetoric, the emphasis on "effect" may permit a more thorough understanding of the original non-Jewish audience perspective or, more precisely, a more accurate caricature of the optimal or ideal historical reader. More importantly, by expanding the understanding of why and how NT writers may have referred to authoritative tradition through such use in Hellenistic culture, scholars may better understand how NT authors, who wrote in a predominately Hellenistic context, used OT references in their texts.

A rhetorical critical approach also allows the biblical critic to draw in other means of assessing the impact of citing and referring to authoritative tradition. V. K. Robbins's theory of socio-rhetorical interpretation provides another means of identifying and evaluating the implications of a text referring to another text or tradition.[100] This kind of intertextuality

99. In response to the conference and the excellent response from Andreas Köstenberger, I want to say that the intent here is not to advocate Hellenistic context over or instead of the Jewish context. I simply suggest that the Hellenistic context has been neglected for understanding the NT use of the OT, and I hope that this paper presents cogent reasons for considering the Hellenistic context alongside the Jewish context.

100. See note 46 for details of the two main books by Robbins in view here.

is the way a text draws in the world outside the text, what Robbins calls intertexture. There are four aspects or dimensions to intertexture: oral-scribal, cultural, social, and historical. "Oral scribal intertexture involves a text's use of any other text outside of itself, whether it is an inscription, the work of a Greek poet, non-canonical apocalyptic material, or the Hebrew Bible."[101] His theory of oral-scribal intertexture suggests five ways in which a text refers to language in another text: recitation, recontextualization, reconfiguration, narrative amplification, and thematic elaboration.[102] Cultural intertexture is the way language in a text refers or alludes to or echoes cultural knowledge: "this kind of knowledge is known only by people inside a particular culture or by a people who have learned about that culture through some kind of interaction with it."[103] Social intertexture is wider than cultural. It is when a text refers to knowledge that is readily observable such as social role (i.e., a soldier), social institution (a household), social code (honor and shame), and social relationship (friendship).[104] Historical intertexture is when a text refers to specific events at specific times in specific locations.[105] While one may have reservations about the complexity of textures that Robbins's theory of socio-rhetorical interpretation introduces into the interpretative task, his theory is helpful in alerting the interpreter to the multiplicity of issues that a citation or reference can invoke. The impact of a reference extends beyond the verbal sense. The persuasive nature and the effect of a reference may be linked to the oral-scribal, cultural, social, and historical intertexture.

C. D. Stanley has surveyed a number of contemporary ways to assess the rhetorical impact of using quotations.[106] Stanley suggests that the use of quotations is a rhetorical act. They are part of a broader argument to convince or persuade others to believe or act in a certain way. He then surveys different ways to evaluate the use of quotations. He looks at modern rhetorical approaches to speeches; linguistic approaches like dramaturgical theory, the Proteus principle, and demonstration theory; and literary approaches. He suggests that H. H. Clark and R. R. Gerrig's demonstration

---

101. Robbins, *Exploring*, 40.
102. Robbins, *Exploring*, 41-58.
103. Robbins, *Exploring*, 58.
104. Robbins, *Exploring*, 62-63.
105. Robbins, *Exploring*, 63-68.
106. Stanley, "Rhetoric," 44-58.

theory is most useful.[107] This theory suggests that (1) direct quotation lends vividness and drama to a discourse by giving the audience an experience of what it might have been like to experience the original event, obviously in a limited and edited manner; (2) direct quotation distances the author from the material by letting the quotation say things the author might be uncomfortable stating in his own words; and (3) direct quotations help to create a sense of solidarity between speaker and audience because they potentially refer to a shared world or perspective.[108] Stanley applies this theory to NT biblical quotations:

> Quotations increase the likelihood of a favourable response to the speaker's message by recalling the common bond that unites speaker and audience. Quotations also allow the speaker to shape the hearer's response by highlighting certain aspects of the authoritative text and minimizing others. Most importantly, quotations lead the audience into a personal encounter with the original text, where a second, more powerful voice speaks on behalf of the quoting author. In short, biblical quotations bring the audience into the presence of God, who typically stands firmly on the side of the speaker.[109]

Stanley's helpful study shows that different interpretative approaches can help the critic to understand and assess the rhetorical, that is, persuasive, act of quoting an authoritative source.

The use of the term "rhetoric" to understand the use of the OT in the NT expands the appreciation of the nature of a quotation to include its persuasive effect. Emphasis on effect enlarges the focus on assessing the use of OT references beyond identifying historical antecedents (primarily Jewish) as the principal or primary means for determining the meaning and significance. This interpretative perspective may open the door to a greater appreciation of the Hellenistic context for understanding the NT use of the OT. It also may lead to a broader understanding of the potential impact an author may have intended by a citation or reference and the potential impact a citation or reference may have had on a designated audi-

---

107. H. H. Clark and R. R. Gerrig, "Quotations as Demonstrations," *Language* 66 (1990) 767-93.
108. Stanley, "Rhetoric," 54-55.
109. Stanley, "Rhetoric," 55-56.

ence. Another implication of seeing the use of the OT in the NT as a rhetorical device is that it may allow critics to draw upon different interpretative approaches or strategies to assess the effect either in the original context or for the modern situation.

The mention of the modern situation moves the discussion to the third and final part of the paper.

Part 3: How Do People Hear the Old Testament in the New Testament Today?

The primary focus on understanding the use of the OT in the NT through its historical context and through the relationship of the quotation to its meaning in the OT has dulled the way one understands how such references impact the modern hearer or reader. It is almost as if one is considered an uninformed hearer or reader of the NT, especially with regard to the NT use of the OT, unless one knows all about first-century Jewish exegetical practices with regard to interpreting sacred writings.[110] One may wish to argue, however, that the meaning that is intended for the hearer today is the one that was intended in the original context. But no matter the validity of that theological stance, the use and impact of the Bible in modern society and culture cannot be limited to that interpretative stance because the majority of modern hearers or readers are not able to excavate that meaning, nor do they wish to.[111] Modern hearers and readers of the NT experience the NT in many different contexts: devotional, liturgical, political, literary, imaginative, critical, etc. The impact of these varieties of contexts means that the modern hearer or reader experiences the use of the OT in the NT in a range of ways.

First of all, the way the NT uses and interprets the OT has influenced the way people hear or read the OT whether in a quotation or from its

---

110. This is not to suggest that a historical perspective is unimportant; no textual interpretation can wholly divorce itself from the implications of history — the history of the author, the history in the text, the history of the text, as well as the history of the reader.

111. For an interesting perspective on this, see D. L. Jeffrey, *People of the Book: Christian Identity and Literary Culture* (Grand Rapids: Eerdmans, 1996). The importance of reader-response theory and its impact on hermeneutics come into play equally here; E. V. McKnight, *Postmodern Use of the Bible: The Emergence of Reader-Oriented Criticism* (Nashville: Abingdon, 1988).

original literary context in the present. In addition, modern culture is no longer an oral culture, so people hear or listen (even read) differently than in the first-century context. Moreover, modern contexts do not share the same cultural, social, and historical texture as the first-century context, so what we hear as quotation, allusion, or echo is different.

All this changes the analysis of the impact that Stanley identifies for biblical quotations as stated in the quotation above (p. 30). From a rhetorical perspective, what is different about the impact or effect of quoting the OT in the NT for the modern hearer or reader based on Stanley's list? First, the common bond that can be established between the author and the modern audience by quoting the OT is diminished. We no longer perceive the OT as the ancient authoritative tradition. Modern understanding of ancient authoritative tradition is much broader than the Jewish sacred writings, and now includes the NT writings as well as the early Christian writings. Second, the NT use of the OT has minimized some aspects of the OT and highlighted other aspects for the modern hearer or reader. One need only look at the number of sermons based on the OT compared to the NT; the OT has taken a secondary position in relation to the NT. Also, the christological perspective of much NT use of the OT has fostered a prophetic or fulfillment perspective for modern hearers or readers so that they read the OT as a "Christian" text. Further, modern hearers or readers do not necessarily hear the OT as a *more* authoritative or powerful voice, but as an ancient precursor to what the NT writer is saying. Quoting the OT gives gravitas to the NT sense by linking it to an older tradition, albeit a tradition with some authority. Nor is the presence of God necessarily invoked by an OT quotation for a modern reader. The Word of God is now firmly resident in the NT voice, and the NT text is perceived as the most recent and up-to-date revelation in the drama of salvation. In sum, a key methodological issue for the study of the NT use of the OT is also the way it impacts the modern hearer or reader, and more work needs to be done in this regard.

In conclusion, by expanding the understanding of the NT use of the OT to include the Hellenistic context and a rhetorical perspective, interpreters may better understand the historical context that shaped the practice of quoting authoritative tradition by the original author, and one may better appreciate the impact this persuasive device has on the modern hearer or reader.

Biblical Texts and the Scriptures for the New Testament Church

R. Timothy McLay

How do we know that the New Testament writer was citing the Old Testament (OT)/Hebrew Bible (HB)? What versions were the New Testament (NT) writers using? These are just two of the many questions that are the subject of this conference volume, but they are the primary questions to be addressed in this paper as we investigate the nature of the biblical texts and the concept of Scripture during the period when the NT was written. Prior to discussing the nature of the biblical texts that existed in the first and second century of our common era, we will begin by defining the terms "Scripture" and "canon." The citation of Scripture in Heb 1:6 will then be examined to illustrate the pluriformity (or the multiple forms) of the biblical text in the time of the early church, and this analysis will be followed by a discussion of the quest for the biblical text.

Defining Scripture and Canon

What we understand by the terms "Scripture" and "canon" is often and easily confused in our contemporary context because what we recognize as Scripture (whatever our denominational affiliation) is included within a recognized canon. Thus, the concept of a canon presupposes the existence

I would like to thank McMaster Divinity College for the funding to participate in the Bingham Colloquium.

of Scripture(s), and that is how these terms should be understood histori-cally.[1] Initially, a faith community deems some particular writings to be Scripture, which basically affirms that those writings are recognized to be authoritative for the faith and practice of the community. In the context of Judaism, the Torah or Law was the first collection of writings that were rec-ognized as having a continuing authority for Judaism and for that reason became recognized as Scripture.[2] The translation of the Torah into Greek circa 250 BCE and the Letter of Aristeas, which was written to defend the authority of the translation, confirm the initial recognition of these Scrip-tures in both languages (at least for some communities within Judaism) at an early date.[3] Over time and in various places other writings were also understood to be authoritative for the Jewish community; therefore, they were accorded the status of Scripture. The term "canon," however, denotes a specific listing and order of books that are understood to be the authori-tative books for a particular faith community. Thus, the creation of a canon by definition requires that it is a later historical development and that it imposes limits on what books are recognized as Scripture.

A Canon in the Early Church?

The distinction between Scripture and canon takes on particular signifi-cance for any examination of the texts that were used by the writers of the NT at the end of the period of what is commonly known as Second Temple Judaism because the canon for the OT/HB had not yet been formed. Though this issue is deserving of a lengthy treatment, we can offer only the

---

1. For an excellent extended discussion and definition of the terms see E. Ulrich, "The Notion and Definition of Canon," in *The Canon Debate* (ed. L. McDonald and J. Sanders; Peabody: Hendrickson, 2002) 21-35.

2. Most early references to the Scriptures such as those by Sirach (38:34–39:1), 4QMMT, and the New Testament refer generally to the Law and the prophets, though the Law may also be qualified by an association with "Moses" (John 1:45; Acts 28:23), or Moses can even be substituted for the Law (Luke 16:29, 31) in the New Testament. Josephus refers to the five books of Moses in *Against Apion* 1.39. J. Vanderkam argues that, though the five books of the Pentateuch were authoritative for the Qumran community, we cannot assume that their references to Torah or Moses referred only to those books. See "Questions of Canon Viewed Through the Dead Sea Scrolls," in McDonald and Sanders, eds., *The Canon Debate*, 91-109.

3. See R. Sollamo, "The Letter of Aristeas and the Origin of the Septuagint," in *X Congress of the IOSCS* (ed. B. Taylor; Atlanta: Scholars Press, 2001) 329-42.

briefest of summaries of some of the most important issues of this discussion here.[4]

It was once commonplace to refer to the establishment of the Jewish canon at the "council of Jamnia" circa 100 CE, but this has proved to be a scholarly fiction, and we do not have any firm evidence for the fixing of the Jewish canon.[5] It has also been argued that for all intents and purposes there was a first-century Hebrew tripartite (or bipartite) canon equivalent to the present-day canon of twenty-four books based on Josephus or other early lists of books by Melito and Origen.[6] So, for example, Josephus mentions twenty-two books: the five books of Moses, thirteen by the prophets after Moses, and four more (by prophets) comprising hymns and practical advice. Beckwith has suggested that we understand Josephus as follows. The five books of Moses refer to the Pentateuch; the thirteen volumes of the prophets are counted as Joshua, Judges, Samuel (I and II count as one), Kings (I and II), Isaiah, Jeremiah-Lamentations, Ezekiel, the twelve Minor Prophets, Daniel, Esther, Ezra-Nehemiah, Job, and Chronicles; and the final four are Psalms, Proverbs, Song of Songs, and Ecclesiastes.[7] However, the view that Josephus's reference to twenty-two books refers to the present-day Jewish canon (equivalent to the Protestant OT) has been severely criticized. First, Josephus's reference to *twenty-two* books is very ambiguous and has been subject to a number of interpretations in order to make his number become equivalent to the present-day canon of *twenty-four* books. Furthermore, Josephus refers to the "prophets after Moses" as having written thirteen books. In other words, Josephus's terminology reflects his view that all of the Jewish Scriptures were written by prophets.[8]

---

4. I have discussed this in greater detail in ch. 5 of *The Use of the Septuagint in New Testament Research* (Grand Rapids: Eerdmans, 2003). For a comprehensive treatment of all matters relating to canon, see the volume edited by McDonald and Sanders, *The Canon Debate*.

5. For a history of the development of the idea that the canon had been fixed, how it has been overturned, and an examination of the evidence, see J. Lewis, "Jamnia Revisited," in McDonald and Sanders, eds., *The Canon Debate*, 146-62.

6. R. Beckwith, *The Old Testament Canon of the New Testament Church* (Grand Rapids: Eerdmans, 1985); E. Ellis, *The Old Testament in Early Christianity: Canon and Interpretation in the Light of Modern Research* (Tübingen: Mohr, 1991).

7. R. Beckwith, "Formation of the Hebrew Bible," *Mikra* (1990) 50-51. For a different configuration, see J. Vanderkam, "Questions of Canon Viewed Through the Dead Sea Scrolls," *BBR* 11 (2001) 269-92.

8. See J. Barton, *Oracles of God* (Oxford: Oxford University Press, 1986) 35-48, for a discussion of the NT evidence and the use of the term "prophets."

Thus, his reference to thirteen prophets after Moses is not to be identified with thirteen books that are part of the prophetic section of the current canon.

Josephus's testimony, then, is not a clear reference to the current Hebrew canon at all. In like manner, other early statements about the Scriptures cannot be interpreted to refer to the specific books of our present canon unless we assume the existence of the canon for which we are attempting to provide evidence. For example, Jesus ben Sira refers to "the study of the law" and "the wisdom of all the ancients" (Sir 39:1), 4QMMT refers to "the book of Moses, the books of the prophets, and of David," and Philo speaks of "laws and oracles delivered through the mouths of the prophets, and psalms and anything else" (*Contempl.* 25).[9] A reasonable conclusion is that "the wisdom of all the ancients," "the books of the prophets," "of David," and "psalms and anything else" are vague references to writings (by prophets) that were deemed to be Scripture, but they do not define a canon. The most that we can say is that there was a canon in the making.

The Scripture(s) in the Early Church

The fuzzy picture of what might have been regarded as the Jewish canon in the second and even the third centuries is reflected in the NT. The NT refers to the Jewish Scriptures in a variety of ways, but "the Law and the Prophets" is the common designation. The frequent references to the "Law and the Prophets" in such places as Matt 5:17; 7:12; and Luke 16:16 may suggest that there were two groupings of Scriptures in the early church, but that does not mean that the specific form and contents of both of these groupings, particularly the Prophets, had been definitely fixed. The most inclusive reference to the Jewish Scriptures in the NT is Luke 24:44, which refers to "the Law of Moses, the Prophets, and the Psalms." Given the elastic use of "prophets" in the NT and by Josephus it would hardly be justified to conclude from this passage that the prophetic books in the Hebrew canon had been determined. Nor would it be justified to interpret "the

---

9. For a more complete discussion of these statements and the NT references to the Scriptures, see C. A. Evans, "The Scriptures of Jesus and His Earliest Followers," in McDonald and Sanders, eds., *The Canon Debate*, 185-95.

Psalms" as an all-inclusive reference to the books now included in the Writings. Rather, Luke 24:44 refers to the Psalms as one of those books that were regarded as Scripture.

Thus, in the period when the NT was written there were authoritative writings associated with the Law (of Moses), those written by Prophets, and other writings (by prophets) that were regarded as Scripture like the Psalms.[10] This is not to suggest that all of the books that later formed the canon of the Hebrew Bible were regarded as Scripture during the NT period, but, as Sundberg demonstrated, there was no unanimity regarding what particular books were considered Scripture in the early church.[11]

The Biblical Text(s) in the Early Church

The use of the terminology "biblical text" can likewise be confusing because we commonly associate the idea of "the text of the Bible" with the complete set of the books of the Bible[12] or the canon, which did not exist during the period when the early church was developing and the NT documents were being written. Yet, scholars also use the term "biblical" as an adjective that defines an area of research. That is, there are biblical texts at Qumran, whose content is defined as relating to those books that are now regarded as part of the canon, as opposed to non-biblical texts. When used as just described, the emphasis in "biblical text" is on the type or category of "text" to which a particular manuscript, scroll, or codex belongs. This judgment about the status of a document as biblical or not is obviously anachronistic because it assumes the later historical distinction of what books were deemed to be part of the Bible; and, for this reason, we might be better served by curtailing its use. However, reference to "biblical texts"

10. Though it is an anachronism to refer to there being a fixed canon, there is ample evidence of both Old and New Testament books being cited as Scripture in the second and third century. For a good discussion of the canonical process and how it has been interpreted by scholars, see J. Barton, *Holy Writings, Sacred Text* (Louisville: Westminster John Knox, 1997) 1-32.

11. Albert C. Sundberg, *The Old Testament of the Early Church* (Cambridge: Harvard University Press, 1964), 56-61, has a useful discussion and a table that demonstrates the differences in the lists of authoritative books according to various writers and councils.

12. For example, in "Notion and Definition," 30, Ulrich notes that the concept of the Bible includes the idea of a collection that is completed.

is intended to mean that there are numerous textual witnesses to any particular book that later became canonized, and we compare these biblical texts using the methods of textual criticism in order to ascertain what we believe to be the most original text for that book of Scripture. We might refer to the most original text that we can reconstruct as the "Biblical Text," but, as we shall see, that is not a straightforward process when considering the witnesses to the Scriptures that became the OT/HB. For the time being it is most important to recognize that there would have been no such thing as a biblical text in the context of the early church, though there would have been a variety of written books (texts) and collections of books (like the Torah) that were accorded the status of Scripture.

The fact that there were texts of Scriptures but no sense of a canon during the early church era had a significant influence on the transmission and content of the Scriptures. We can grasp the implications of the organic nature of the Scriptures within their communities prior to the common era more easily by examining the impact of the developing canonical consciousness. The creation of a canon of books was accompanied by an increased concern for maintaining the particular form of those books. Historically, the means to enable the believing community to do this more effectively emerged concurrently with the development of the codex. With the codex, all of the books that were considered authoritative could be bound together in one volume. As Robert Kraft suggests,

> once it was possible to produce and view (or visualize) "the Bible" under one set of physical covers, the concept of "canon" became concretized in a new way that shapes our thinking to the present day and makes it very difficult for us to recapture the perspectives of earlier times. "The canon" in this sense is the product of fourth-century technological developments.[13]

The process of the fixing of the biblical text, or "standardization," culminated centuries later in the majority texts produced by the Masoretes for the HB and the Byzantine text for the NT.

Prior to the concept of the canon, then, the Scriptures were copied and transmitted within and for the believing community primarily on

---

13. R. Kraft, "The Codex and Canon Consciousness," in McDonald and Sanders, eds., *The Canon Debate*, 233. For a discussion of the codex, see C. H. Roberts and T. C. Skeat, *The Birth of the Codex* (Oxford: Oxford University Press, 1983).

scrolls.[14] Additionally, the Scriptures of the early Christians consisted of original writings and translations in three different languages: Hebrew, Aramaic, and Greek. As we have already noted above, the early translation of the Torah into Greek and the defense of its authority provided the basis for the early church to use the Greek Scriptures. Obviously, the use of the Greek texts would have been more practical for the mission efforts of the church in the Hellenistic world, and this is evident in the NT where the influence of citations from the Greek is so prevalent,[15] though the equivalent status of the Greek Scriptures with the Hebrew Scriptures later became a source of tension in the discussions between Jews and the church fathers.[16] During this time there does not seem to have been a widely held consensus of the specific books or the content of the Scriptures like that which would emerge in later centuries. It is not as though we have explicit testimony to the effect that the Scriptures were regarded as free-floating texts that were shaped to differing degrees by a variety of circumstances and concerns within the communities in which they were used, but the nature of the evidence from the extant witnesses to the biblical texts argues that such was often the case. There are a wide variety of textual variants, ranging from single words or morphemes to whole sentences and paragraphs, when one compares the ancient texts for any book of Scripture.

Hebrews 1:6 and the Texts of Scripture

In order to illustrate the pluriformity of the Scriptures as well as discuss some of the reasons why these textual differences developed within the texts that were read, understood, and copied as holy Scripture for the early church and the writers of the NT, I have selected the citation of Scripture in Heb 1:6. The choice is not random. We will begin our examination by citing

14. For background on the production of writing materials made of papyrus, parchment, and leather see any textbook on textual criticism, such as E. Würthwein, *The Text of the Old Testament* (trans. E. Rhodes; Grand Rapids: Eerdmans, 1979) 7-9.

15. H. B. Swete stated that the LXX is the "principal source from which the NT writers derived their OT quotations," and this view remains generally true. H. B. Swete, *An Introduction to the Old Testament in Greek* (rev. R. Ottley; Cambridge: Cambridge University Press, 1914) 392.

16. M. Müller, *The First Bible of the Church* (JSOTSup 206; Sheffield: Sheffield Academic Press, 1996) 98-123; M. Hengel, *The Septuagint as Christian Scripture* (trans. M. Biddle; Edinburgh: T&T Clark, 2002).

the texts as they are known to us in the NT, Old Greek (OG), and Masoretic text (MT). The English translations that I offer are intentionally rather literal and consequently not all that elegant, but will enable the person with less facility in the biblical languages to follow the argument more easily.

Heb 1:6 NT   καὶ προσκυνησάτωσαν αὐτῷ πάντες ἄγγελοι θεοῦ
                And let all angels of God worship him

OG Deut 32:43   καὶ προσκυνησάτωσαν αὐτῷ πάντες υἱοὶ θεοῦ
                And let all sons of God worship him.

MT Deut 32:43   There is no equivalent in the Hebrew for the reading in the OG.

The first matter to consider is the absence of this passage from the MT and the corresponding suggestion that the passage is related to the passage in OG Deut 32:43. Both of these issues will be addressed throughout the course of this discussion, but looking at the passages in parallel alignment will help us to understand the problem.

	MT Deut 32:43	OG Deut 32:43
1		εὐφράνθητε οὐρανοὶ ἅμα αὐτῷ
2		καὶ προσκυνησάτωσαν αὐτῷ
3		πάντες υἱοὶ θεοῦ
4	הַרְנִינוּ גוֹיִם עַמּוֹ	εὐφράνθητε ἔθνη μετὰ τοῦ λαοῦ αὐτοῦ
5		καὶ ἐνισχυσάτωσαν αὐτῷ πάντες ἄγγελοι θεοῦ
6	כִּי דַם־עֲבָדָיו יִקּוֹם	ὅτι τὸ αἷμα τῶν υἱῶν αὐτοῦ ἐκδικᾶται

	MT Deut 32:43	OG Deut 32:43
1		*Praise, O heavens, together with him,*
2		*and worship him,*
3		*all sons of God.*[17]

---

17. Presumably υἱοὶ θεοῦ is a translation of something like בני האלהים *sons of god* in its source text (cf. Gen 6:2). The Hebrew word בן *son* (as well as the Aramaic equivalent בר) was used in construct with another noun to indicate that an individual or group belonged to a class of beings. See P. Joüon, *A Grammar of Biblical Hebrew* (2 vols.; trans. and rev. T. Muraoka; Rome: Pontifical Biblical Institute, 1991) 129j. Thus, בני האלהים *sons of god* equals the class of divine beings or gods. Therefore, the *Vorlage* of the OG could be trans-

4 *Praise, O nations, his people,*	*Praise, O nations, with his people,*
5	*and let all the angels of God strengthen him,*
6 *for he vindicates the blood of*	*for he vindicates the blood of his children.*
his servants.	

Referring to the Greek text of this portion of Deut 32:43, we see that two clauses begin with the word εὐφράνθητε *praise* in lines 1 and 4; however, there is no equivalent in the MT for lines 1-3 above. Instead, v. 43 in MT begins with the line הַרְנִינוּ גוֹיִם עַמּוֹ *praise, O nations, his people*. If the OG is a faithful translation of a Hebrew text (its *Vorlage*), then the Hebrew passage that the Greek translator had before him was longer than the one currently preserved in the MT. In addition, the OG has another extra clause in the verse (numbered line 5 above) compared to the MT. One is immediately struck by the differences between the Hebrew and Greek texts and how they might be best explained.

If there were not two additions, most scholars would probably readily agree that the initial one is most likely an error in the transmission of the (proto) MT. Due to an error when he read the text *(parablepsis)*, the scribe for the MT passed from a first occurrence of הַרְנִינוּ *praise* (rendered by εὐφράνθητε) in line 1 to the second occurrence of *praise* in line 4 and in the process omitted two whole clauses (our lines 1 to 3), which are preserved in the OG. However, the nature of the addition as well as the presence of the second clause in line 5 may suggest to some that the longer reading in the OG is the result of a double translation or explanatory addition to what was originally only one clause such as we have in the MT. It seems to me that this kind of argument is probably rooted either in an uncritical assumption that the Hebrew text is inherently more trustworthy than a translation or in just plain bias toward the MT.[18] These comments are not intended to denigrate the MT, because it is an important witness to the biblical text. At the same time, the MT is not equivalent to the OT or HB, which has often been assumed in the past. The allegiance that has been shown toward the MT by

---

lated something like *Worship him, all you gods,* which is what is found in one modern translation. We use *sons of God* because υἱοὶ θεοῦ was not a Greek idiom that was equivalent to the Hebrew expression. The Greek reflects formal equivalence.

18. See the comments by E. Tov, who now affirms that we cannot give priority to the MT because it became the accepted rabbinic text, in "The Status of the Masoretic Text in Modern Text Editions of the Hebrew Bible: The Relevance of Canon," in McDonald and Sanders, eds., *The Canon Debate,* 234-51, esp. 240-47.

scholars despite the evidence of the other witnesses is similar in many ways to those who regard the King James version as the only trustworthy English translation. Most assuredly, it is always possible that the Greek translator made additions as he translated a text like the MT, but the question is whether that is likely and what is the best explanation for the available evidence. After all, if the two clauses that are represented in the OG were based on a Hebrew *Vorlage,* the OG would witness to two parallel clauses advocating praise to God, and parallelism is a characteristic of Hebrew. Purely from the content and style of the texts, then, there is no good reason to prefer the MT over the OG. Assuming that we cannot determine an original text in this instance, what reading should we prefer?

It becomes all the more unlikely that the Greek translator arbitrarily added material to his translation when we consider that there are not similar examples of the translator adding clauses elsewhere in the book. Furthermore, the presence of the second addition (line 5) and the similarities of vocabulary in the OG between our lines 1-3 and 4-5 suggest that it is more likely that something has been omitted in the Hebrew text. Though it would be difficult to solve the differences between the MT and OG in this particular verse to everyone's satisfaction, the similarity between πάντες υἱοὶ θεοῦ *all sons of God* or *all you Gods* and πάντες ἄγγελοι θεοῦ *all angels of God* in the OG may offer further evidence that the MT has omitted elements through a series of textual errors rather than indicating that the OG reflects a double translation. It should also be noted that, following the portion of the passage in Deut 32:43 that we have cited above, there is another clause in the OG that is not represented in the MT, though it is represented in one witness from Qumran, 4QDeut^q.

Discerning what might have been the original text of Deut 32:43 is not aided a great deal by the manuscripts of the book that have been discovered among the Dead Sea Scrolls. In fact, one might argue that the reconstruction of Deut 32:43 only becomes more confusing. Though there are thirty-three scrolls of Deuteronomy, of which thirty were found in the eleven caves at Qumran,[19] only 4QDeut^q preserves Deut 32:43. The reading of 4QDeut^q for 32:43 is as follows:[20]

19. See J. Vanderkam and P. Flint, *The Meaning of the Dead Sea Scrolls* (San Francisco: Harper, 2002) 111.

20. For the texts, see E. Ulrich et al., *Qumran Cave 4: IX: Deuteronomy, Joshua, Judges, Kings* (DJD XIV; Oxford: Oxford University Press, 1986), esp. 141 for 4QDeut^q.

1	הרנינו שמים עמו	*Praise, O heavens, his people,*
2	והשתחוו לו כל אלהים	*and worship him, every god,*
3	כי דם בניו יקום	*for he vindicates the blood of his children.*
4	ונקם ישיב לצריו	*He will bring vengeance to his enemies*
5	ולמשנאיו ישלם	*and he will repay his enemies*
6	ויכפר אדמת עמו	*and cleanse the land of his people.*

The passage in 4QDeut^q is interesting because of the way it is both similar to and different from the readings of the same verse that are preserved in the OG and MT. First, we note that like the MT it has only one clause that invokes praise to God. Second, despite the fact that there is only one clause that invokes praise, the admonition והשתחוו לו כל אלהים *and worship him, every god* (or *all gods/divine beings*) is almost identical to OG's καὶ προσκυνησάτωσαν αὐτῷ πάντες υἱοὶ θεοῦ *and let all sons of God worship him.* The difference is that if we retrovert the reading of the OG back into Hebrew we would get והשתחוו לו כל בני אלהים; that is, the OG has υἱοὶ *sons,* which reflects the fact that OG reads the typical Semitic idiom בני אלהים *sons of God* in its *Vorlage.* Third, the inclusion of עמו *his people* in our line 1 of 4QDeut^q reflects the second invocation to praise in the OG where it is the nations who are to offer praise to God's people. Thus, the clause with its exhortation for the angels to strengthen him in the OG is not otherwise represented in the Qumran fragment. So, while 4QDeut^q is similar to OG because it has *and worship him, every god* (or *all gods/divine beings*), the occurrence of עמו *his people* is found in both the OG and the MT, but in different places. Fourth, the OG agrees with 4QDeut^q (בניו *his children*) in its reading of υἱῶν αὐτοῦ *his children* against *his servants* in the MT. Fifth, though we did not include the whole of Deut 32:43 in our translation of the OG and MT, the clause ולמשנאיו ישלם *and he will repay his enemies* (line 5 above) is another omission in the MT that is represented in the OG.

The portion of Deut 32:43 in 4QDeut^q, the OG, and the MT can be compared more easily by aligning the texts.

	4QDeut^q	MT	OG
1	הרנינו שמים עמו		εὐφράνθητε οὐρανοὶ ἅμα αὐτῷ
2	והשתחוו לו		καὶ προσκυνησάτωσαν αὐτῷ
3	כל אלהים		πάντες υἱοὶ θεοῦ

4		הַרְנִינוּ גוֹיִם עַמּוֹ	εὐφράνθητε ἔθνη μετὰ τοῦ λαοῦ αὐτοῦ
5			καὶ ἐνισχυσάτωσαν αὐτῷ πάντες ἄγγελοι θεοῦ
6	כי דם בניו יקום	כִּי דַם־עֲבָדָיו יִקּוֹם	ὅτι τὸ αἷμα τῶν υἱῶν αὐτοῦ ἐκδικᾶται

	4QDeut[q]	MT	OG
1	*Praise, O heavens, his* ***people,***		*Praise, O heavens, together with him,*
2	*and worship him,*		*and let worship him* (3rd person impv.)
3	*every god,*		*all sons of God.*
4		*Praise, O nations, his people,*	*Praise, O nations, with his* ***people,***
5			*and let all angels of God strengthen him!*
6	*for he vindicates the blood of his* ***children.***	*for he vindicates the blood of his* ***servants.***	*for he vindicates the blood of his* ***children.***

The comparison of these three textual witnesses in this tiny portion of Scripture in Deut 32:43 reveals that there is no clear way to characterize agreements between any two of the texts that excludes the third. Rather, both 4QDeut[q] and the MT exhibit an independent relationship to the OG. 4QDeut[q] agrees with OG in preserving the opening invocation, but the omissions of εὐφράνθητε ἔθνη *praise, O nations,* which is preserved in the MT, and καὶ ἐνισχυσάτωσαν αὐτῷ πάντες ἄγγελοι θεοῦ *and let all angels of God strengthen him,* means that the second invocation to praise in the OG, which is preserved in the MT, has most likely been omitted during the course of the transmission of 4QDeut[q] from a text that was originally longer like that preserved in the OG. This conclusion is confirmed by the presence of **עמו** *his people* in 4QDeut[q] in line 1, because it is preserved in the OG and MT as part of the second invocation in line 4. At the same time, the agreement between 4QDeut[q] and the OG in lines 1-3 confirms that this section was omitted from the MT during the course of its transmission. Therefore, both the MT and 4QDeut[q] witness to variant readings that have been shortened from an originally longer text of this verse, which is similar to the way it is witnessed to in the OG, but the changes that occurred during the stages when the texts were copied by scribes are independent from one another.

Given the analysis of the text of Deut 32:43 based on the textual witnesses that we have provided above, it is interesting to compare our results with some modern English translations.

NIV	NRSV	TEV
Rejoice, O nations, with his people	*Praise, O heavens, his people, worship him, all you gods!*	*Nations, you must praise the Lord's people —*
for he will avenge the blood of his servants	*For he will avenge the blood of his children*	*he punishes all who will kill them*

We can make two observations based on the English versions. First, all of them have only one invocation to praise God. The same result was found when several other translations were checked, and the tendency for all of them, excluding the NRSV, is to follow the MT. Second, the NRSV follows 4QDeut^q. In other words, none of the versions follows the reading of the OG in any significant way, though the Greek does get an honorable mention of sorts. For example, a footnote in the NIV informs the reader that the Septuagint adds *and let all the angels worship him.* The NRSV actually has several footnotes, though the reader would never be able to piece together the differences between the texts, and one note is misleading. The NRSV correctly notes that the MT lacks *worship him, all you gods!* and that a manuscript from Qumran (4QDeut^q) and the Greek (they do not specify what Greek text) have *children* rather than *servants* as in the MT. However, the NRSV also suggests that the manuscript from Qumran and the Greek read *heavens* against *nations* in the MT. This is misleading because the OG does not use *heavens* in collocation with the phrase *with his people.* These are parts of two separate clauses in the OG. This brief foray into the modern translations is the type of evidence that confirms our earlier suggestion that there is a bias against the OG because it is a translation, especially when our analysis has shown that the longer version in the OG preserves the most original text that we can reconstruct.

Other Explanations for the Citation in Hebrews 1:6

Thus far our analysis of the witnesses to Deuteronomy has demonstrated the pluriformity of the biblical text, at least as we have it in Deut 32:43. The shorter readings preserved in the MT and 4QDeut^q appear to be related to the longer text in the OG, but their shorter readings are independent from each other. At the same time, we note that the text of Heb 1:6, which was the starting point of our investigation, does not clearly support the longer OG text in Deut 32:43 either. In OG Deut 32:43 we read καὶ ἐνισχυσάτωσαν αὐτῷ πάντες ἄγγελοι θεοῦ *and let all angels of God strengthen him*, while Heb 1:6 has the verb προσκυνησάτωσαν *worship*, which appears in the first clause of OG Deut 32:43. How do we explain the use of the different verb on the part of the writer of Hebrews? The fact that Heb 1:6 has καὶ προσκυνησάτωσαν αὐτῷ πάντες ἄγγελοι θεοῦ *and let all angels of God worship him* rather than *and all let angels of God strengthen him* might mean that ἄγγελοι *angels* was present in some Greek manuscript of Deuteronomy that the writer of Hebrews used; or there was a Hebrew manuscript with the word מלאכים *angels;* or the author of Hebrews knew of a text of Deut 32:43 that was similar to the reading that is preserved in the OG and creatively combined parts of the separate clauses together to make his point; or the citation is a result of some other process.

Prior to the discovery of the Dead Sea Scrolls (DSS), a different line of approach was to suggest that the quotation actually represents a conflation of a couple of different passages. We have already seen that the combination of passages does happen in the NT writings elsewhere. It is possible that this happened in Heb 1:6 because the text of LXX Ps 96(97):7 reads προσκυνήσατε αὐτῷ πάντες οἱ ἄγγελοι αὐτοῦ *worship him, all his angels.* Therefore, it could be argued that the Scripture cited by the writer of Hebrews is a combination of Ps 96:7 and Deut 32:43 from the Greek. The attraction of this suggestion is that it does combine an imperative form of the verb *worship* (though in the third person rather than the second) with *angels.*

Though LXX Ps 96(97):7 may have played a role in shaping Heb 1:6, it seems unnecessary to posit its use when all of the elements for the quotation are present in OG Deut 32:43. Why should we presume the combination of two separate texts when we require only the use of one? Beginning in 1:4 the writer of Hebrews contrasts the Son, meaning Christ, and the angels, by emphasizing the superiority of the Son through a series of citations from Scripture. The quotation from Deut 32:43 underscores the subordinate position of the angels in comparison to the Son because the angels *worship* him. Given the theological purposes of the writer in the context it would be reasonable to conclude that the author was aware of a manuscript of Deut 32:43 similar or identical to the longer form of the OG and combined the two similar clauses to produce the one that we have in Heb 1:6. In fact, the parallelism of the two phrases *all gods* or *all sons of God* and *all angels of God* invites the substitution, particularly since there is support among the Greek translators for making an identification of *angels* with the *sons of God* (see MT Job 1:6; 2:1; Ps 8:6[5]).[21]

Finally, the other possible answer to the question of the source for the citation in Heb 1:6 is that it represents a direct quotation from a different *Vorlage* similar to OG Deut 32:43.

To this point the evidence that we have discussed would at best indicate that an alternative *Vorlage* is only another possible explanation for the citation. Nonetheless, it is important that we acknowledge the possibility as a matter of principle. The fact is that there is conclusive evidence that Heb 1:6 is, indeed, a citation of an alternative source, but there are other cases in the NT where we do not have such evidence. The principle to be learned is that the fact that a citation in the New Testament does not agree with one of our known witnesses to the text of the OT/HB does not necessarily mean that the biblical text did not exist. In other words, the NT citations should be evaluated as witnesses to alternative biblical texts where their readings differ from the known witnesses.[22] The evidence from the DSS confirms this methodological principle because of the instances where a citation in the NT can be shown to be based on a text like that preserved at Qumran.[23] For example, the citation in 1 Pet 1:24-25, which is shorter than the text found in the MT Isa

---

21. In each of these cases where MT reads *god(s)* (אלהים) the OG translators have employed ἀγγέλους *angels*.

22. I employ the word "evaluated" because the fact that a citation does not agree with a known witness does not necessarily mean that the NT writer is citing a text verbatim either. Differences may exist for a variety of reasons, of which one may be that the author is citing an (as yet) unknown witness to the biblical text. Other reasons for differences have to do with the methodology of citation by NT writers, which is discussed elsewhere in this volume in the essay by Dennis Stamps. See also ch. 1 in McLay, *Use of the Septuagint*; R. Longenecker, *Biblical Exegesis in the Apostolic Period* (rev. ed.; Grand Rapids: Eerdmans, 1999) 6-35; and C. Stanley, *Paul and the Language of Scripture: Citation Technique in the Pauline Epistles and Contemporary Literature* (Cambridge: Cambridge University Press, 1992).

23. See also the discussion by T. Lim, *Holy Scripture in the Qumran Commentaries and Pauline Letters* (Oxford: Clarendon, 1997) 141-45.

40:6-8, parallels the text of Isa 40:6-7 in the OG and 1QIsaᵃ.[24] Such examples are to be expected given the diversity of the biblical texts during the period of the early church. In the case of the citation in Heb 1:6, which has already proven to be an excellent illustration of the diversity within the biblical texts, there is additional evidence in Odes 2:43 that confirms the citation is based on a biblical text like OG Deut 32:43. The text of Odes 2:43 agrees almost verbatim with Heb 1:6: καὶ προσκυνησάτωσαν αὐτῷ πάντες (οἱ) ἄγγελοι θεοῦ *and let all (the) angels of God worship him.*

Odes 2:43	OG Deut 32:43
εὐφράνθητε οὐρανοὶ ἅμα αὐτῷ	εὐφράνθητε οὐρανοὶ ἅμα αὐτῷ
καὶ προσκυνησάτωσαν αὐτῷ	καὶ προσκυνησάτωσαν αὐτῷ
πάντες οἱ ἄγγελοι θεοῦ	πάντες υἱοὶ θεοῦ
εὐφράνθητε ἔθνη μετὰ τοῦ λαοῦ αὐτοῦ	εὐφράνθητε ἔθνη μετὰ τοῦ λαοῦ αὐτοῦ
καὶ ἐνισχυσάτωσαν αὐτῷ	καὶ ἐνισχυσάτωσαν αὐτῷ
πάντες υἱοὶ θεοῦ	πάντες ἄγγελοι θεοῦ
ὅτι τὸ αἷμα τῶν υἱῶν αὐτοῦ	ὅτι τὸ αἷμα τῶν υἱῶν αὐτοῦ
ἐκδικᾶται	ἐκδικᾶται

Odes 2:43	OG Deut 32:43
Praise, O heavens, together with him.	*Praise, O heavens, together with him.*
and let all the	*and let all*
angels of God worship him.	*sons of God worship him.*
Praise, O nations, with his people,	*Praise, O nations, with his people,*
and let all sons of God	*and let all angels of God*
strengthen him,	*strengthen him,*
for he vindicates the blood of his children.	*for he vindicates the blood of his children.*

The major difference between Odes 2:43 and OG Deut 32:43 is that the clauses in which *angels* ἄγγελοι (plus the definite article *the* οἱ) and *sons* υἱοὶ appear are reversed. However, there are two clauses invoking praise just like the OG. Moreover, in addition to the agreement with the OG of Deut 32:43, the change in the clauses where *angels* and *sons* appear means that Odes 2:43 has an almost exact parallel to Heb 1:6: *and worship him, all (the) angels of God* καὶ προσκυνησάτωσαν αὐτῷ πάντες ἄγγελοι θεοῦ. Though the Odes

24. See my discussion in *Use of the Septuagint*, 116-17.

are a later Christian work,[25] the parallel between Odes 2:43 and OG Deut 32:43 indicates that the Odes are dependent on a source similar to the OG version. At the same time, the distinctive agreement between Odes 2:43 and Heb 1:6 in that they both read *and let all (the) angels of God worship him* means that their readings are directly related. Either Heb 1:6 is dependent upon the same tradition of OG Deut 32:43 as the Odes — that is, they are independent witnesses to a slightly different text — or one of the writers of Heb 1:6 or Odes 2:43 borrowed from the other.

Based on the evidence that we have, it is impossible to determine the exact nature of the relationship between Heb 1:6 and Odes 2:43; however, their testimony to the biblical text and the Scriptures is vital to our discussion. In the first place, like the MT and 4QDeut^q, they both provide further evidence to confirm that there was an earlier longer text of Deut 32:43 with two clauses invoking praise to God, which should be reflected in a modern translation of Deuteronomy. This is not surprising given the fact that the majority of NT citations exhibit dependence on sources that are known in our Greek witnesses rather than in Hebrew. Second, regardless of which reading was earlier or more original, all of the texts were respected and read as sacred Scripture. The understanding of what was regarded as Scripture at that time was quite broad and was definitely not confined to a definite fixed form. Otherwise, the different texts would not have been copied and preserved. Third, NT citations should be evaluated for the evidence that they provide for the texts of the Scriptures. Fourth, if Heb 1:6 is not dependent upon Odes 2:43, then together they witness to a slightly different text of Deut 32:43 than we have in the OG. Fifth, the relationship between Heb 1:6 and Odes 2:43 has implications for what was understood to be Scripture. For example, if the author of Hebrews was citing from Odes, then the Odes were understood to be Scripture. This would be another type of evidence that indicates the broader notion of what books were regarded as Scripture in the early church. For example, the Greek codices Sinaiticus, Vaticanus, and Alexandrinus, which originate from the fourth and fifth centuries, include a number of books like Judith, Tobit, Wisdom of Solomon, and others that eventually were excluded from the Hebrew canon.

To conclude our discussion of this complex passage, the net result is that the passages in Odes 2:43 and Heb 1:6 are both related to the longer

25. Swete, *Introduction to the Old Testament in Greek*, 254.

reading preserved in the OG that is not in the MT or *4QDeut*q. Thus, if we were to presume that the OG is in some way the "original" text, or at least that it represents the earliest witness to the original text that we presently have, then we can observe that the OG, *4QDeut*q, MT, and Odes 2:43/Heb 1:6 represent four separate and distinct ways that the biblical text was transmitted and that they all were regarded as Scripture.

The Quest for the Biblical Text

Our examination of Heb 1:6 illustrates the point that an essential characteristic of the Scriptures of the early church was pluriformity. Not only did many books that were regarded as Scripture exist in two different languages, but the process of copying these Scriptures resulted in corruptions to the texts so that significant differences were introduced and developed within the textual tradition of a particular book. The corruption that we encountered in the texts of Deut 32:43 is an example of unintentional errors that happened under the primitive writing conditions of ancient times long before the printing press. However, similar levels of corruption also entered into the texts when well-intentioned scribes introduced slight changes (intentional errors) to fix what they believed to be an error in the text, whether it was grammatical or theological in nature.[26]

In order to make our discussion of the Scriptures and biblical texts in the early church more complete, we will briefly consider the two other major reasons why the texts exhibited significant differences when read by first-century Christians: multiple literary editions and revisions. According to E. Ulrich, multiple literary editions may be defined as "a literary unit . . . appearing in two or more parallel forms . . . which one author, major redactor, or major editor completed and which a subsequent redactor or editor intentionally changed to a sufficient extent that the resultant form should be called a revised edition of that text."[27] For example, most readers are

26. Standard textbooks on textual criticism offer examples of the various types of errors made by scribes when copying the texts. For an excellent discussion of the influence of theology on the transmission of the NT, see B. Ehrman, *The Orthodox Corruption of Scripture* (Oxford: Oxford University Press, 1993).

27. E. Ulrich, "The Canonical Process, Textual Criticism, and Latter Stages in the Composition of the Bible," in *Sha'arei Talmon: Studies in the Bible, Qumran, and the Ancient Near East* (ed. M. Fishbane and E. Tov with W. W. Fields; Winona Lake: Eisenbrauns, 1992) 278.

aware of the significant differences in content between the versions of books such as Jeremiah, Job, Exodus, Samuel, Joshua, Daniel, and Proverbs in the LXX as compared to the MT. There is good evidence that most of these differences in content in the Greek versions of these books is based in an alternative Hebrew *Vorlage* from which the book was translated, but in some cases we have definite textual evidence from the Dead Sea Scrolls.[28]

How did such variant literary editions of some of the Scriptures come to be created and circulate among the Jews and then the Christians? On the basis of the differences between the MT, the Samaritan Pentateuch, the LXX, and some of the findings from the Dead Sea Scrolls, Frank Cross proposed a theory of local texts, which suggested that the Scriptures developed independently among the communities in Jerusalem, Babylonia, and Egypt.[29] The value of this theory was that it recognized the major centers of Judaism and saw that the transmission of the Scriptures was an organic process within those communities. For example, the Samaritan Pentateuch reads that the Israelites are to set up the stones *on Mount Gerizim* in Deut 27:4 rather than *on Mount Ebal* as it reads in the MT, because this reflects their center of worship. However, multiple literary editions did not depend on separate development in those centers. The differences of content between the Hebrew (and Aramaic for Daniel) and Greek versions of books like Jeremiah and Daniel seem to be rooted in originally separate semitic literary editions of those books, and it just happens that one of those editions was preserved in the Greek. The shorter Greek version of Jeremiah[30] was based on an earlier *Vorlage* than that witnessed to by the MT, whereas it is possible that the OG and MT versions of Daniel both represent secondary redactions of an alternative text.[31]

---

28. For example, see J. G. Janzen, *Studies in the Text of Jeremiah* (HSM 6; Cambridge: Harvard University Press, 1973); E. Ulrich, *The Qumran Texts of Samuel and Josephus* (HSM 19; Missoula: Scholars Press, 1978).

29. F. M. Cross, "The Evolution of a Theory of Local Texts," in *Qumran and the History of the Biblical Text* (ed. F. M. Cross and S. Talmon; Cambridge: Harvard University Press, 1975) 306-15.

30. For Jeremiah, see various publications by Tov, such as "The Literary History of the Book of Jeremiah in the Light of Its Textual History," in *Empirical Models for Biblical Criticism* (ed. J. Tigay; Philadelphia: University of Pennsylvania Press, 1985) 213-37.

31. The evidence for the redactional processes at work in the Scriptures of Daniel is demonstrated by the fact that we really have three editions of the story preserved, because the so-called Theodotion translation in the Greek is very similar to the version that is witnessed to by the Dead Sea Scrolls and the MT, but it has the apocryphal/deuterocanonical

The organic development within the book of Daniel reflects the type of inner-scriptural exegesis that was part of the Jewish tradition.[32] For example, on a large scale Deuteronomy is a reinterpretation of the Law, and Chronicles represents a retelling of the history of Israel, but the changes in Daniel are more similar to what might be associated with the early origins and development of the Pentateuch. That is, there was an internal process of revision and reinterpretation that was inherent in the preservation and transmission of the Scriptures. Thus, in some ways it is difficult to distinguish between a variant literary edition and the process of revising texts that was a natural part of the reinterpretation and reapplication of the Scriptures within Judaism. Revision and reinterpretation tend to be more evident in the Greek translations of what were regarded as the Scriptures because by virtue of being translations they were later than the originals.[33] Although most of the recensional activity by Origen and the more shadowy figures known as Theodotion, Aquila, Symmachus, and Lucian[34] was later than the first century, their activity is not only a witness to the continuing organic development of the Scriptures but also contributed to it.

Adding the unintentional and intentional errors that inevitably occurred while copying the Scriptures to the multiple literary editions that were available for some books and the revision and reinterpretation that happened, sometimes in two languages, within the books — all of this resulted in a multiplicity of texts that were identified with a particular book of

---

additions that are also part of the OG text. In addition, there are other Danielic stories among the Dead Sea Scrolls. See most recently P. Flint, "The Daniel Tradition at Qumran," in *The Book of Daniel: Composition and Reception* (2 vols.; ed. J. Collins and P. Flint; Leiden: Brill, 2001) 2.329-67. The literature on Daniel is extensive, but for specific studies relating to the redaction of the book see F. Wills, *The Jew in the Court of the Foreign King* (Minneapolis: Fortress, 1990) 75-152; E. Haag, *Die Errettung Daniels aus der Löwengrube* (SBS 110; Stuttgart: Verlag Katholisches Bibelwerk, 1983).

32. The most important contribution in this field remains M. Fishbane, *Biblical Interpretation in Ancient Israel* (Oxford: Clarendon, 1985).

33. For an excellent investigation of reinterpretation or "actualization" of the Scriptures, see A. van der Kooij, *The Oracle of Tyre: The Septuagint of Isaiah 23 as Version and Vision* (Leiden: Brill, 1998). The Minor Prophets Scroll, which has been dated as early as 50 BCE, and the Theodotionic version of Daniel, which is cited in the NT, both provide evidence that the process of revision had begun before the common era. See McLay, *Use of the Septuagint,* esp. ch. 4.

34. See N. Fernández Marcos for a thorough discussion of what can be known of these individuals and their activity in *The Septuagint in Context* (Leiden: Brill, 2001).

Scripture. This pluriformity of the texts makes the task of textual criticism very different for the OT/HB than for the NT. With the exception of the western text of Acts, which may be described as a variant literary edition, NT textual criticism can use the available texts to reconstruct what is close to an original text or what we might call the biblical text. Presently, textual criticism can proceed in that manner for some books of the OT where the witnesses are closely related, but for others it is not possible to evaluate the witnesses on the basis that one can reconstruct the original text of those books. For books like Daniel, Jeremiah, and Samuel it may be possible to reconstruct two or more versions of the text that reflect something similar to their variant literary editions, but where their texts depart in their literary editions it is not possible to compare and evaluate variant readings against one another since they are not related to the same source text. In one sense, it is questionable whether one can even refer to an original text of these books. On what basis and what criteria can one define the original text?[35]

Conclusion

The corollary to the fact that there was no canon of Scripture for the NT writers was that there was no biblical text either. The citation of Scripture in Heb 1:6 provides an excellent illustration of the pluriformity of the Scriptures that were available to the NT writers and some of the differences that developed within the texts in the course of their transmission. Recognizing the types of variant readings that could occur in the normal activity of copying a text through unintentional or intentional errors introduced by scribes, coupled with the creative process of reinterpretation and revision that included the production of multiple literary editions, at least for some books, explains the pluriformity. In brief, we might say that the organic way in which the Scriptures were written, translated, reinterpreted, and copied within Judaism and its major centers meant that the texts of the Scriptures for the writers of the NT were characterized by pluriformity. This pluriformity presents challenges for textual criticism and the quest to establish the Biblical Text, and entails for us, like the early church, that we struggle with the ambiguity and tension of heeding and applying the Scriptures.

35. Tov reviews the options in "Status of the Masoretic Text," 246-51.

Scripture, History, Messiah:
Scriptural Fulfillment and the Fullness
of Time in Matthew's Gospel

MICHAEL P. KNOWLES

Introduction

At the still point of the turning world. Neither flesh nor fleshless;
Neither from nor towards; at the still point, there the dance is. . . .[1]

I begin, not with the ancient text of Matthew's Gospel, but with the much
more recent text, composed in 1935, of "Burnt Norton," the first of Nobel
Laureate T. S. Eliot's *Four Quartets*. Why this particular text? Because it
seems to me that Eliot has succeeded in capturing something that is also
central to Matthew. True, this excerpt appears in isolation from its literary
context. True also that Eliot and the evangelist lived and wrote in vastly
dissimilar socioeconomic and political circumstances. Yet for all their distance, the two texts share a common theme, a common vision. Matthew
wrote in the face of social upheaval, political revolution, and religious catastrophe the dimensions of which we can barely comprehend. In addition
to the customary panorama of ethnic rioting, periodic famine, and
foreign-born administrators who made up with military brutality what
they lacked in administrative competence (for details of which one need
only skim a few pages of Josephus), Matthew's day was marked by the
greatest disasters a Jew could possibly imagine. These included not only
the conquest of God's land by idolaters; not just the buying, selling, and

---

1. T. S. Eliot, "Burnt Norton," II.16-17, from *Collected Poems 1909-1962* (London: Faber
and Faber, 1963).

political manipulation of the sacred high priesthood; but above all the death of the Messiah, followed in relatively short order by yet another destruction of the temple and traditional dwelling place of God's holy "name." Yet it is against this terrifying backdrop that Matthew confidently declares God to be "with us" in the person of a controversial Galilean teacher, Jesus of Nazareth. For his own part, Eliot composes his verse (as he later explains) *"entre deux guerres"* ("East Coker" V.2), between one world war and the next, painfully conscious of the desolation and futility of a human existence that leads only to death. Yet in the midst of such darkness, he too glimpses a vision of the transcendent, a "still point" in the turning, decaying, dying world.

What, then, is this "still point" of which Eliot writes? Is it, in keeping with the poem's epigraph, a piece of pre-Copernican metaphysics borrowed from that ancient Ephesian, Heraclitus? An echo of Aristotle and Saint John of the Cross? Or an allusion to Buddhist longings for the stillness of Nirvana? The complexity of Eliot's thought embraces each of these.[2] Yet at the same time, there are unmistakable echoes of orthodox Christology: Eliot envisages the divine dance or "perichoresis" — the interior motion of the Holy Trinity — distilling into fixity in the person of Jesus of Nazareth. Jesus is (to borrow the language of Eliot's 1930 poem, "Ash Wednesday") "The Word without a word" that takes flesh and falls silent at Bethlehem and again at Calvary, *"Erhebung* without motion,"

> the enchainment of past and future
> Woven in the weakness of the changing body,
> Protects mankind from heaven and damnation.[3]

This is not unlike Matthew's own vision, the "still point" in *his* churning world. Matthew's narrative is a good deal less poetic and, despite the rivers of ink it has inspired, considerably less convoluted and obscure.

---

2. See, e.g., Grover Smith, *T. S. Eliot's Poetry and Plays: A Study in Sources and Meaning* (Chicago: University of Chicago Press, 1974) 254-55; Paul Foster, *The Buddhist Influence on T. S. Eliot's "Four Quartets"* (Frankfurt: Haag and Herchen, 1977) 68-75; Martin Warner, *A Philosophical Study of T. S. Eliot's "Four Quartets"* (Lewiston, NY: Edwin Mellen, 1999) 52-60.

3. "Burnt Norton," II.28, 33-35. The multifaceted German word *Erhebung,* meaning variously "exaltation," "elevation," "upheaval," and "investigation," can be taken both literally and metaphorically, alluding both to Jesus' "elevation" on the cross and to the disruptive glorification that the cross represents.

But for all that, it is no less artistic in its own way, nor by any means less profound. Matthew's Gospel is a work made coherent by a single vision that unifies, in Eliot's words, "time future," "time present," and "time past":[4] "Both a new world/And the old made explicit, understood." For Matthew, of course, the "old world" is one of godly hope, pious self-preparation, and fervent — if varied — messianic expectation. It is the world of Second Temple Judaism, brought together despite its multitudinous factions and disputes by the hope of redemption, concentrated in the minds of many to a single point of longing for a Redeemer and Messiah, however that figure or function is defined. The poetry of Eliot captures the essence of Matthew's task, which is to make this old world "explicit, understood," in light of the messianic new. He is thus in the words of Jesus, and no doubt like Matthew himself, a scribe who brings forth from his treasure store both "old" and "new" (Matt 13:52).

Examining the New Testament use of authoritative antecedents from Scripture and history involves a range of related issues, including the specific text forms employed, questions of original context and meaning, possible sources from which Matthew derived his *testimonia,* and their relevance for subsequent audiences.[5] While many or all of these may be implied at various points in our study, the approach taken here concentrates in the first instance on the function of scriptural references for Matthew as an interpreter of text and history.

Jesus' Use of Scripture in the Gospel of Matthew

Contemporary scholarship encourages a measure of skepticism on matters of historical veracity. Yet if his account is to be accepted at face value (if only for the sake of understanding the mind of the evangelist), Matthew's interpretative methodology appears to take its cue from Jesus' own use of Scripture. This having been said, many of their respective quotations can be differentiated by the use of distinctive citation formulae. Jesus declares, "It is written [γέγραπται]," or demands of his hearers, "Have you not/

4. These themes are announced in the opening lines of "Burnt Norton" and repeated throughout the poem.

5. For a survey of relevant issues and recent responses, see Graham N. Stanton, "Matthew's Use of the Old Testament," in *A Gospel for a New People: Studies in Matthew* (Louisville: Westminster/John Knox, 1993) 346-63.

never read? [οὐκ/οὐδέποτε ἀνέγνωτε;]," whereas Matthew's editorial observations typically employ the verb πληρῶσαι, "to fulfill." These patterns are further distinguished by the observation that, whereas eight of nine occurrences of γέγραπται and three of six such instances of ἀναγινώσκειν derive from his literary sources, all but one of sixteen occurrences of πληρῶσαι are unique to Matthew's Gospel.[6] Although the tendency among many scholars is to emphasize the latter over the former, we must not overlook the fact that the evangelist has incorporated all such references into a coherent whole. Still, the question remains: How does Jesus himself employ Scripture in this Gospel, and how does his methodology compare to that which the narrative assigns to the evangelist?

Γέγραπται ("It is written"): Agreed Scriptural Authority

The importance of such an inquiry is suggested by the fact that Jesus' first conflict and, but for a single line addressed to John the Baptist, his first extended utterance in the Gospel is essentially a debate with Satan (derived from Q) about the substance and meaning of Scripture. Although his own adoption of it may not commend the methodology, Satan apparently shares with the Messiah the latter's respect for scriptural authority, as the opponents quote by turn from Deut 8:3 (Matt 4:4//Luke 4:4), Ps 91:11-12 (Matt 4:6//Luke 4:10-11), Deut 6:16 (Matt 4:7//Luke 4:12), and Deut 6:13 (Matt 4:10//Luke 4:8), emphatically declaring each time, "It is written . . ." At stake in this exchange is the question of Jesus' power and messianic identity, and the manner of their manifestation. The argument, in other words, is about what might legitimately be expected of the "Son of God" on the basis of Scripture, even though none of these texts is subject to messianic interpretation elsewhere in Second Temple Judaism.[7]

Four subsequent instances of γέγραπται all derive from Mark. In Matt 11:10, Jesus employs a combined citation of Exod 23:20 and Mal 3:1 (//Mark

---

6. The exception, Matt 26:56//Mark 14:49, is discussed below. Incidences: Matt, 16; Mark, 2; Luke, 9; John, 15; cf. ἀναπληρῶσαι at Matt 13:14. Regarding the fulfillment formulae, see M. Knowles, *Jeremiah in Matthew's Gospel: The Rejected-Prophet Motif in Matthaean Redaction* (JSOTSup 68; Sheffield: Sheffield Academic Press, 1993) 29-33.

7. See W. D. Davies and Dale C. Allison, *The Gospel according to Saint Matthew* (ICC; Edinburgh: T&T Clark, 1988-97) 1.361-74; there is, however, a likelihood that both Mosaic and Adamic typologies are in play.

1:2) to identify John the Baptist as Elijah *redivivus,* the prophet whose appearance was widely thought to herald the messianic age.[8] Insofar as it also occurs in *Exod. Rab.* 32, the combination of Exod 23:20 with Mal 3:1 appears not to be "a Christian innovation."[9] In repeating this combined citation, Matthew indicates that he shares with other Jews the fundamental conviction that all of Scripture speaks with one voice, and that he shares with Jesus and the earliest Christians (Mark among them) the view that this particular "voice" refers to John. In similar fashion, Matt 21:13 (//Mark 11:17) fuses Isa 56:7 with Jer 7:11: "'It is written,'" declares Jesus, "'My house shall be called a house of prayer'; but you are making it 'a den of robbers.'" Here the thought is that the temple stands under Jesus' own prophetic judgment, an ominous portent of its imminent destruction that appeals to Scripture for authority.[10] Although he does not cite a specific text, Jesus affirms that his own fate is similarly foreordained ("The Son of Man goes as it is written of him," 26:24//Mark 14:21), even as the disciples' wholesale abandonment of him conforms to Zech 13:7, a text that the Qumran sectarians also interpreted eschatologically: "It is written, 'I will strike the shepherd, and the sheep . . . will be scattered'" (26:31//Mark 14:27).[11]

This last pair of examples points to the hermeneutical centrality of Matthew's Messiah, who demonstrates his ability to interpret both Scripture and contemporary events as they find their meaning in him. By declaring *in advance* the meaning of the text and its current historical context, Jesus not only fulfills the role of prophet but implicitly serves as the interpretative focus for our own reading of the text. Whatever the evangelist's particular contribution to the narrative, such a presentation makes Jesus, rather than Matthew, the one who imposes his interpretative methodology on us.[12]

---

8. Cf. Sir 48:10, 4 *Ezra* 6:26, and, further, J. Jeremias, "'Ηλ(ε)ίας," *TDNT,* 2.928-34.

9. Davies and Allison, *Matthew,* 2.250, citing Krister Stendahl, *The School of St. Matthew and Its Use of the Old Testament* (ASNU 20; Lund: CWK Gleerup, [1967]) 50 (and see 51-52).

10. Knowles, *Jeremiah in Matthew's Gospel,* 173-76.

11. CD 19:5-9; cf. R. N. Longenecker, *The Christology of Early Jewish Christianity* (London: SCM, 1970) 48-49; Craig S. Keener, *A Commentary on the Gospel of Matthew* (Grand Rapids: Eerdmans, 1999) 635-66.

12. The one remaining (and uniquely Matthean) use of this formula is placed in the mouth of "chief priests and scribes," who determine that the Messiah is to be born in Bethlehem; "for so it is written," they declare, in Mic 5:1-3 (Matt 2:5-6).

Οὐκ ἀνέγνωτε; ("Have you not/never read?"):
Hermeneutical Transparency

The same is true for Jesus' use of οὐκ/οὐδέποτε ἀνέγνωτε, which, as was the case in his debate with Satan, appeals for a hearing on the basis of texts whose authority the hearers also accept:

> He said to them, "*Have you not read* what David did when he and his companions were hungry? He entered the house of God and ate the bread of the Presence, which it was not lawful for him or his companions to eat, but only for the priests. Or *have you not read* in the law that on the Sabbath the priests in the temple break the Sabbath and yet are guiltless?" (Matt 12:3-5; cf. Mark 2:25-26)

Of this pair of citations, only the first derives from Mark: Matt 12:5 underscores Jesus' point — and his methodology — by adding a second example. But the real clue to Jesus' purpose comes at the conclusion of this discourse, in his citation of Hos 6:6: "If you had known what this means, 'I desire mercy, and not sacrifice,' you would not have condemned the guiltless" (Matt 12:7). Evidently they do *not* know, and have *not* read. More clearly in Greek than in English, the contrary-to-fact condition indicates that the true meaning of Scripture is revealed not by the act of reading alone, but by reading *and understanding* what, by implication, is plainly there to be understood. Jesus makes the same point even more bluntly in his other citation of this text, also unique to Matthew, in response to the accusation that he keeps unsavory company: "*Go and learn* what this means, 'I desire mercy, and not sacrifice'" (Matt 9:13). Even though the phrase "Go and learn" is a standard rhetorical device, it represents a clear challenge to his hearers to return to a common heritage of familiar texts in order to read and understand them anew.

Similarly with Jesus' reply to the Pharisees on the question of divorce in Matt 19:4-5: although the basic outline of the debate derives from Mark 10, the Matthean wording, "*Have you not read* that he who made them from the beginning . . ." represents a significant addition. This formula, which consistently appears in the context of controversy (so also Matt 22:31-32//Mark 12:26, citing Exod 3:6), implies that the texts in question are hermeneutically transparent: not only that they are available to be read, but that reading them will lead necessarily in the direction implied by Jesus' own interpretation of the text. Or to state the matter more subtly, the challenge, "Have you not read?" appears on the surface to adduce the authority of Scripture. This observation is amply confirmed by the descriptions contained in the formulae themselves: "Have you not read *in the law . . ."* (12:5); *". . . in the Scriptures"* (21:42); "Have you not read *what was said to you by God* [τὸ ῥηθὲν ὑμῖν ὑπὸ τοῦ θεοῦ]?" (22:31). In practice, however, the interpretation in question depends at least as much on the authority of the *interpreter,* who by means of this formula imposes a reading that is implied to be self-evident. Yet to take the same line of reasoning one step further, the challenge "Have *you* not read?" places ultimate responsibility for proper interpretation firmly upon the reader. The text may be inspired, and the interpreter rhetorically (or even theologically) imposing, but it is the respondent who must read and understand. Again, Jesus' approach to the text, as Matthew presents it, represents an implicit challenge even for subsequent recipients of the text.

From a certain perspective, each of these debates might represent little more than disagreement over the application of particular texts to a life of piety. But in two further instances, much more than this is at stake. Matthew 21 relates Jesus' provocative entry into the city and temple: when the authorities object that he is permitting the acclamations of Ps 118:26-27 to be applied to himself (Matt 21:9, 15), Jesus retorts:

> *"Have you never read,* 'Out of the mouths of infants and nursing babies you have prepared praise for yourself' [LXX Ps 8:3]?" (Matt 21:16)

As with previous controversies, Jesus here implies that a proper reading of Scripture will lead them to acknowledge the praise that is indeed due to him. While this is provocative enough (given the apparent Mosaic associations of the text he quotes),[13] Jesus' own citation of Ps 118:22-23 (Matt 21:42//Mark 12:10-11) is even more pointed:

> *"Have you never read* in the scriptures: 'The stone that the builders rejected has become the cornerstone; this was the Lord's doing, and it is amazing in our eyes'?"

Although rabbinic applications of this text to Abraham, David, and the Messiah are apparently of later provenance, and contemporary Jewish interpre-

---

13. Davies and Allison, *Matthew,* 3.142.

tations refer either to the literal temple (*T. Sol.* 22:7-8; 23:4) or to the community of the faithful (1QS 8:7), Jesus boldly applies the passage to himself. He himself is its fulfillment, implying that even the rejection that he has already begun to suffer is demonstrably part of God's purpose for him.

Non-formulaic References

In assessing Jesus' use of Scripture in Matthew, it is possible to overemphasize the importance of explicit formula citations, for numerous less obvious quotations and allusions are also woven into the fabric of his language, indicating further ways in which Jesus' ministry conforms to patterns of prophetic expectation. Here three examples will suffice.

First, Jesus' call for Simon and Andrew to become "fishers of people" (Matt 4:19//Mark 1:17) likely alludes to Jer 16:16, depicting the disciples as gathering in the peoples for eschatological judgment. References to fishing as a metaphor for eschatological judgment, likely based on Jeremiah, are also found in Qumran literature (especially 1QH 13:8: "You made my lodging with many fishermen,/those who spread the net upon the surface of the sea,/those who go hunting the sons of iniquity").[14]

Second, Ps 110:1 ("The Lord says to my lord, 'Sit at my right hand'") appears not only in Matt 22:44 (//Mark 12:36), where Jesus cites it as a clue to his own identity, but also less obviously (in association with Zech 12:10 and Dan 7:13) in Matt 26:64, where Jesus offers a defiant challenge to the high priest: "Hereafter you will see the Son of man seated at the right hand of Power, and coming on the clouds of heaven" (//Mark 14:62; cf. Matt 24:30//Mark 13:26). Employing Psalm 110 in the context of controversy seems to assume that Jewish hearers would recognize its messianic potential; evidence for such associations in the case of Daniel 7 comes to hand from *1 En.* 62:5, *4 Ezra* 12–13, and rabbinic literature.[15] Not surprisingly, these latter texts and their adoption in New Testament literature have occasioned intense debate, with questions of historical accuracy to the fore.

---

14. See further, Knowles, *Jeremiah in Matthew's Gospel,* 194-97.

15. For a careful assessment of Psalm 110 in Jewish exegesis, see David Hay, *Glory at the Right Hand: Psalm 110 in Early Christianity* (SBLMS 18; Nashville: Abingdon, 1973) 19-33; for its association with Daniel 7, and Jewish messianic interpretations of the latter, see Donald Juel, *Messianic Exegesis: Christological Interpretation of the Old Testament in Early Christianity* (Philadelphia: Fortress, 1988) 162-70.

Yet the point remains that Matthew presents Jesus as one whose very language characterizes him as one who conforms to scriptural expectation, and in particular to texts that other contemporary Jews viewed as conveying messianic or eschatological overtones.

The third and most complex example comes from Matthew's "Sermon on the Mount." It is obvious on even a cursory reading that this extended discourse engages the question of scriptural interpretation both as a structural marker within the larger discourse (so 5:17//7:12) and as a key theme of Jesus' teaching (e.g. 5:21-45). Less evident, yet no less significant, is the way in which the Sermon's opening lines echo the language of passages such as Isaiah 61:[16]

Matthew 5	Isaiah 61 (LXX)
[3]Blessed are the poor [πτωχοί] in spirit, for theirs is the kingdom of heaven.	[1]The spirit of the Lord is upon me, because he has anointed me to proclaim good news to the poor [πτωχοῖς] . . .
[4]Blessed are those who mourn [πενθοῦντες], for they will be comforted [παρακληθήσονται].	[2]. . . to comfort all who mourn [παρακαλέσαι πάντας τοὺς πενθοῦντας]
[5]Blessed are the meek, for they will inherit the earth [κληρονομήσουσιν τὴν γῆν].	[7]. . . they shall inherit the earth [κληρονομήσουσιν τὴν γῆν]
[6]Blessed are those who hunger and thirst for righteousness [δικαιοσύνην], for they will be filled.	[3]. . . they shall be called generations of righteousness [δικαιοσύνης] . . .
[7]Blessed are the merciful, for they will receive mercy [ἐλεηθήσονται].	
[8]Blessed are the pure in heart, for they will see God. . . .	[1]. . . to heal the broken in heart
[12]Rejoice and be glad [ἀγαλλιᾶσθε], for your reward is great in heaven. . . .	[10]. . . let my soul be glad [ἀγαλλιάσθω] in the Lord. . . .

The parallels are striking in their own right, but all the more so in that (1) according to Luke 4:18-19, Jesus uses a combined citation of Isa 61:1-2 and 58:6 to announce the central themes of his ministry to the con-

---

16. Following Davies and Allison, *Matthew*, 1.436-39.

gregation of the Nazareth synagogue; (2) Luke's own version of the Beati-
tudes (Luke 6:20-23) contains similar language and themes, despite other
well-known differences of emphasis; and (3) in Matt 11:4-6 (//Luke 7:22-23)
Jesus declares:

> "Go and tell John what you hear and see: the blind receive their sight, the
> lame walk, the lepers are cleansed, the deaf hear, the dead are raised, and
> the poor have good news announced to them. And blessed is the one
> who takes no offense at me."

The significantly different settings of these various sayings suggests that,
notwithstanding the particular redactional influences that each of them
reveals, the echoes of Isaiah that are common to all of them do not derive
from the evangelists themselves. And given the fact that the same allusions
speak to the characteristic emphases of his ministry, there is nothing to
prevent us from attributing such a use of scriptural language to Jesus, who
fashions his ministry in accordance with prophetic expectation.

Even so, Isaiah 61 does not account for an essential feature of the "be-
atitudes" (including Matt 11:4-6//Luke 7:22-23), namely the language of
"blessedness" itself. For this we must look elsewhere, although a number of
likely sources quickly suggest themselves. The key term μακάριος (so also
LXX, for Hebrew אַשְׁרֵי), while not infrequent in biblical and extra-biblical
literature, occurs in several passages that closely echo the message of God's
gracious blessing on the poor and broken from Isaiah 61. Particularly reminiscent of the language of Isa 61:1-2 (and Jesus), for instance, is Ps 146:5, 7-9:

> *Blessed* the one whose help is the God of Jacob . . .
> who executes justice for the oppressed;
> who gives food to the hungry.
> The Lord sets the prisoners free;
> the Lord opens the eyes of the blind.
> The Lord lifts up those who are bowed down;
> the Lord loves the righteous.
> The Lord watches over the strangers;
> he upholds the orphan and the widow,
> but the way of sinners he brings to ruin.[17]

17. Elsewhere from Psalms compare also 34:8-9, 14-18; 40:4, 16-17; 41:1-2; 106:3; 119:1-2.

But while such themes are frequent in the Psalter, they also appear elsewhere in the Septuagintal text of Isaiah93, complete with the language of blessing:

> Therefore the Lord waits to be gracious to you;
> therefore he will rise up to show mercy [ἐλεῆσαι] to you.
> For the Lord is a God of justice;
> *blessed* [μακάριοι] are all those who wait for him. (Isa 30:18)

> Thus says the Lord:
> Maintain justice, and do what is right [δικαιοσύνην],
> for soon my salvation will come,
> and my deliverance be revealed.
> *Blessed* [μακάριος] the man who does these things,
> the one who holds it fast,
> who keeps the Sabbath, not profaning it,
> and refrains from doing any evil. (Isa 56:1-2)

As the parallels multiply, it becomes increasingly difficult to trace Jesus' words to a single text from the Scriptures of Israel. Rather, Jesus intentionally echoes language that is generally characteristic of God's oft-repeated promises of blessing, favor, and salvation for the weak and lowly. Even though Isa 61:1-2 remains a prominent source, the allusions are broadly thematic as much as text-specific.

From the evidence we have reviewed thus far, a number of basic principles governing the use of Scripture in Matthew's Gospel clearly emerge. The first is that, for Matthew, messianic exegesis — the interpretation of Scripture with reference *to* the Messiah — is ultimately based on interpretations of Scripture *by* the Messiah. Jesus, it would appear, is his own best exegete. Not least because of this specific focus, Scripture is for Matthew not only foundationally authoritative but also univocal in its prophetic testimony, with the result that otherwise divergent texts can legitimately be cited in relation to one another. Such testimony (whether explicit or merely allusive) addresses not only Jesus' own identity and life-circumstances (including the role of the disciples) but also the antecedents (such as John the Baptist) and even the later consequences of his ministry (e.g., the fate of the temple). To underscore the point once more, the most important observation to be adduced from such evidence is that, whatever use of Scripture

MICHAEL P. KNOWLES

Matthew himself will make as editor and expositor of Gospel traditions, it claims to be based in the first instance on the practice and authority of the Messiah himself, both as to method and as to substance.

Messianic Exegesis in Second Temple Judaism

Matthew, however, is not alone in this. All preachers and exegetes of sacred texts are familiar with the task of rendering the message of an ancient narrative into terms that subsequent audiences are likely to find relevant and meaningful. Even T. S. Eliot could be cited as an extreme example. We may characterize such a task in general terms as the "accommodation" of Scripture to new social and historical situations. Precisely so, pious exegetes of various communities within Second Temple Judaism were concerned to find in ancient Scripture and tradition the meaning of contemporary history, and to find in contemporary history patterns of providential design anticipated by the words of Scripture.[18] Such a project, impelled in principle by eschatological hope, became all the more acute in light of more specific messianic convictions. Since it was deemed self-evident that God's Messiah would conform to the expectations of prophecy, elucidating the various lines of continuity between these two sources of revelation emerged as a task of paramount importance. Indeed, although the use of such a term oversimplifies a considerably more complex phenomenon, we may appropriately designate this particular form of "actualizing" or "accommodational" interpretation as "messianic exegesis." Within this larger category, and in keeping with what we have seen already from Matthew's Gospel, we will continue to distinguish interpretation of Scripture with reference *to* a messianic figure or circumstances from scriptural interpretation *by* that individual.

Fortuitously, publication of the Qumran material has provided us with examples of just such a methodology against which to evaluate the

18. For a fuller account of this type of biblical interpretation within Second Temple Judaism, see Jacob Neusner, *What Is Midrash?* (Philadelphia: Fortress, 1987) and Richard N. Longenecker, *Biblical Exegesis in the Apostolic Period* (2nd ed.; Grand Rapids: Eerdmans, 1999) esp. 18-35; and in the early church, E. Earle Ellis, "Biblical Interpretation in the New Testament Church," in *Mikra: Text, Translation, Reading, and Interpretation of the Hebrew Bible in Ancient Judaism and Early Christianity* (ed. M. J. Mulder and Harry Sysling; CRINT 2.1; Assen: Van Gorcum; Philadelphia: Fortress, 1988) 691-725.

Christian evidence, as in the case of the following well-known passage from the community's commentary on Hab 2:2-3:

> And God told Habakkuk to write what was going to happen to the last generation, but he did not let him know the end of the age. And as for what he says: *"So that the one who reads it may run"* [Hab 2:2]. Its interpretation concerns the Teacher of Righteousness, to whom God has disclosed all the mysteries of the words of his servants, the prophets. *"For the vision has an appointed time, it will have an end and not fail"* [Hab 2:3a]. Its interpretation: the final age will be extended and go beyond all that the prophets say, because the mysteries of God are wonderful. *"Though it might delay, wait for it; it definitely has to come and will not delay"* [Hab 2:3b]. Its interpretation concerns the men of truth, those who observe the Law, whose hands will not desert the service of truth when the final age is extended beyond them, because all the ages of God will come at the right time, as he established for them in the mysteries of his prudence.[19]

Here we find affirmed, in turn, (1) God's initial inspiration of the prophet Habakkuk; (2) the fact that such inspiration is, nonetheless, incomplete; (3) the role of the community leader as, by contrast, the fully inspired interpreter of Scripture; (4) the conviction that Scripture itself authorizes the role of the leader within the present community; (5) the prospect of the eschatological age exceeding the bounds even of prophecy; and (6) the fulfillment of Scripture in the circumstances of the faithful community. With the possible exception of (5), these features are also characteristic of Jesus' treatment of Scripture, at least as Matthew presents it. Indeed, as we will now see, there is little discernible difference between the methodology attributed to Jesus and scriptural

---

19. 1QpHab VII.1-14, quoted from *The Dead Sea Scrolls Translated: The Qumran Texts in English* (trans. Florentino García Martínez; Leiden: Brill, 1994) 200. Subsequent citations of Qumran material are also from this translation. On biblical interpretation at Qumran, see Michael Fishbane, "Use, Authority, and Interpretation of Mikra at Qumran," in Mulder and Sysling, eds., *Mikra*, 339-437, esp. 360-66. The methodology of 1QpHab is more fully set out by Bruce Chilton, "Commenting on the Old Testament (With Particular Reference to the Pesharim, Philo, and the Mekilta)," in *It is Written: Scripture Citing Scripture: Essays in Honour of Barnabas Lindars* (ed. D. A. Carson and H. G. M. Williamson; Cambridge: Cambridge University Press, 1988) 122-27.

interpretations that evidently derive from the hand of Matthew or other early interpreters.

Matthew's Use of Fulfillment Citations: "Something Greater"

As noted earlier, the use of fulfillment citations based on the verb πληρῶσαι or a related compound is altogether characteristic of Matthew. Thus it is not possible to compare his use of such language with that of other Synoptists, apart from the single instance in which Jesus responds to his arrest by observing, somewhat more expansively than in the Markan parallel, "All this has taken place, that the scriptures of the prophets might be fulfilled [πληρωθῶσιν]" (26:56; cf. 26:54, and Mark 14:49, "But let the scriptures be fulfilled"). Yet this passage is especially significant for our purposes in that it provides grounds for the evangelist to claim a precedent for his use of fulfillment language in Jesus' own interpretative practices. "Do not think," declares Jesus, "that I have come to abolish the law or the prophets; I have come not to abolish but to fulfill [πληρῶσαι]" (Matt 5:17). What this statement establishes in principle, Matthew sets out to explore in detail, whether by means of explicit fulfillment formulae, through scriptural quotations and allusions, or via typology.

Matthew's fulfillment citations can tentatively be separated into two groups: those subject to apocalyptic or messianic interpretation in contemporary (non-Christian) Judaism, and those that appear unique to the early church. Granted, the division is somewhat arbitrary, since exact parallels to non-Christian messianic exegesis are difficult to establish, and there are likely to have been many contemporary lines of interpretation to which access has now been lost or obscured.

Nonetheless, it appears that, as was the case with his depiction of Jesus' interpretative method, Matthew too relies editorially on a common store of eschatologically significant texts from contemporary Judaism. The famously elliptical "citation" in 2:23 provides a case in point: "He made his home in a town called Nazareth, so that what had been spoken through the prophets might be fulfilled, 'He will be called a Nazorean [Ναζωραῖος].'" The debate continues as to what text Matthew had in mind, whether Gen 49:26 ("Joseph . . . prince [נְזִיר] among his brothers"), Judg 13:5 ("the boy [Samson] shall be a Nazirite [נְזִיר] to God from birth"), Jer 31:6 ("there will be a day when watchers [נֹצְרִים] cry out on the hills of Ephraim . . ."), or, as the most probable candidate, Isa 11:1 ("A shoot shall come out from the stump of Jesse, and a branch [נֵצֶר] shall grow out of his roots").[20] The issue may be clarified by the observation that Isa 11:1 in particular appears to have been widely interpreted as a messianic prophecy within Second Temple Judaism.[21] But however the matter is decided, the main point of Matthew's citation is not simply that Scripture points toward and finds its fulfillment in the events of contemporary history, but moreover that messianic history itself dictates what Scripture must mean. Granted, Jesus' deeds are said to be guided by prophetic expectation. But the inscrutability of the reference carries a lesson of its own, namely that what is most important here is neither the precise identity of the prophet nor the location of the scriptural passage, but rather a historical and geographical given that is external to both: that the Messiah had indeed resided in the otherwise all-but-unknown Nazareth.[22] If that is what happened, then that is what Scripture *must* mean: finding an exact text to match the facts was, it would appear, of secondary importance. This is not to imply that either Matthew or the tradition he drew upon in any way disparaged or denied the authority of the sacred text. Rather, given the foundational significance of Scripture, Matthew's method alerts us to the even greater authority of the Messiah himself.

Similarly tantalizing is Matthew's quotation of Isa 42:1-4, interpreted with reference to Jesus' ministry of healing and identifying him as God's chosen servant (Matt 12:18-21). On the basis of a cautious and thorough assessment, Richard Beaton concludes, "1QIsa[a], *1 Enoch*, *Psalms of Solomon*, and possibly the Targums indicated that the passage was read messianically prior to Matthew's composition," albeit with emphasis on themes of justice and judgment.[23] As another, more complex example, Zech 9:9 ("Behold, your king is coming to you, humble, and mounted on an ass"), which Matt 21:5 quotes in combination with Isa 62:11, is one of several instances in which the evangelist likens Jesus and his characteristic

---

20. See R. H. Gundry, *The Use of the Old Testament in St. Matthew's Gospel, with Special Reference to the Messianic Hope* (NovTSup 18; Leiden: Brill, 1967) 97-104.

21. Cf. *Tg. Isa.* 11:1; 4QpIsa[a] [4Q161] 8-10; *T. Jud.* 24:5-6; Juel, *Messianic Exegesis*, 52-53; Davies and Allison, *Matthew*, 1.277-78.

22. On the obscurity of Nazareth, see Davies and Allison, *Matthew*, 1.274.

23. Richard Beaton, *Isaiah's Christ in Matthew's Gospel* (SNTSMS 123; Cambridge: Cambridge University Press, 2002) 64-85, esp. 85.

humility to that of Moses, who was himself widely viewed as a messianic precursor.[24]

Although it concerns John the Baptist rather than Jesus himself, and appears already in Mark 1:3, Matthew's citation of Isa 40:3 is also relevant in this regard. "For this is he," explains the evangelist, "who was spoken of by the prophet Isaiah when he said, 'The voice of one crying in the wilderness: Prepare the way of the Lord'" (Matt 3:3). The community of Qumran, itself formed around the leadership of a messianic figure, saw in the same passage a validation of their own decision to withdraw into the wilderness:

> [The community] will be a tested rampart, the precious cornerstone . . . whose foundations do not shake. . . . And every matter hidden from Israel but which has been found out by the Interpreter, he should not keep hidden from them for fear of a spirit of desertion. And when these exist as a community in Israel in compliance with these arrangements, they are to be segregated from within the dwelling of the men of sin to walk to the desert in order to open there His path. As it is written: "In the desert, prepare the way of ****, straighten in the steppe a roadway for our God." (1QS 8:7-8, 11-14)

Here we may observe, as noted earlier, the application of Ps 118:22 to the community as a whole, a similar interpretation of Isa 40:3, and a clear distinction (evident throughout this chapter of the Community Rule) between those admitted to and those excluded from the special knowledge accorded their teacher. This is an important principle for which Matthew also finds scriptural support, in his case via the fulfillment of Isa 6:9-10 (attributed to Jesus; Matt 13:14-15) and of Ps 78:2 (Matt 13:35).[25]

No doubt, for Matthew, this explains why Jesus' messianic identity was not more widely acknowledged at the time: despite his conformity to scriptural patterns recognized elsewhere in Second Temple Judaism, only Jesus' closest disciples were party to the "secrets [τὰ μυστήρια]" of God's reign (Matt 13:11//Mark 4:11). Thus it fell to his followers to paint a fuller

---

24. On Mosaic typology and the motif of meekness, see Davies and Allison, *Matthew*, 2.272-73, 290 (on Matt 11:29, linked to 21:5 by the catchword association ζυγόν — ὑποζυγίου); 3.119-21.

25. Keener (*Matthew*, 378-81) cites extensive evidence for this characteristic in contemporary religious and philosophical teaching, within both Jewish and Hellenistic contexts.

picture of Jesus' scripturally informed life. It is almost certainly the case that Matthew and others in the early church not only examined the life of Jesus with an eye to sacred texts but also examined the sacred text with an eye to Jesus' life. This is particularly evident when it comes to matters of biographical geography. We have already seen how the historical necessity of affirming Jesus' residence in Nazareth takes precedence over literal or literalistic exegesis. Similarly, Mic 5:1, by which Matthew accounts for Jesus' origins in Bethlehem, is interpreted messianically in the Targums and conforms to broader expectations of a Davidic (that is, Judahite) Messiah.[26] But precisely because the Messiah has arisen from the locale to which it testifies, Matthew quotes the text in a sense opposite to that of any other known version: Bethlehem is no longer "insignificant" (MT צָעִיר; LXX ὀλιγοστός, "few in number"), but rather, "by no means least [οὐδαμῶς ἐλαχίστη]" (Matt 2:6).[27] Along the same lines, Jesus' move from Nazareth to Capernaum prompts the fulfillment quotation of Isa 8:23 and 9:1 ("Galilee of Gentiles — the people who sat in darkness have seen a great light," Matt 4:14-16) precisely because "the ministry of Jesus in Galilee ran counter to the dominant popular and learned expectation of Judaism that Jerusalem would be the centre for the advent of the age of the Messiah."[28]

Again, the difficulty of deriving Matthew's sense in 1:23, "Behold, a *virgin* shall conceive," from anything other than the Septuagintal text of Isa 7:14 is well known, yet the tradition of Jesus' birth had evidently made plain what the meaning of the text must be. And Gundry's observation on two further fulfillment citations in the opening chapters of Matthew is entirely apt: "The citations from Hos 11:1 and Jer 31:15 are so obscure that no one would have thought of them as bases for invention of the stories to which [Matthew] relates them."[29] Likewise the best explanation for Matt 27:9-10 citing a passage largely drawn from Zech 11:12-13 under the name of Jeremiah is that the evangelist thereby draws attention to an allusion that is sufficiently oblique — as scholarly efforts to explain the reference also attest — as to have otherwise been overlooked.[30]

26. Davies and Allison, *Matthew*, 1.242.

27. See Gundry, *Use of the OT*, 91-92.

28. W. D. Davies, *The Gospel and the Land: Early Christianity and Jewish Territorial Doctrine* (Berkeley: University of California Press, 1974) 235.

29. Gundry, *Use of the OT*, 195-96 (on Matt 2:15, 17-18), and similarly (200) on the allusion to 2 Sam 5:8 in Matt 21:14.

30. Cf. Knowles, *Jeremiah in Matthew's Gospel*, 52-81, esp. 76-77.

To push the matter even further, it is reasonable in the case of Jer 31:15 to ask what bearing the quoted text — "A voice was heard in *Ramah* . . . Rachel weeping for her children" (Matt 2:18) — has on the fate of Herod's actual or intended victims in the vicinity of *Bethlehem* (Matt 2:16), since that is the situation by which the prophetic text is said to be "fulfilled." As it happens, the location of Rachel's tomb was a matter of dispute. Differing traditions located it either near Ramah, "in the territory of Benjamin" north of Jerusalem (so 1 Sam 10:2), or, according to Gen 35:19 and 48:7, south of Jerusalem "on the way to Ephrathah" in the territory of Judah. Remarkably, Matthew acknowledges the one tradition by citing Jer 31:15, yet validates the other tradition against it by referring the text to Bethlehem.[31] Once again, the events of Jesus' life unlock for Matthew the intended meaning of Scripture — a meaning that would (presumably) never have emerged had the Messiah's advent not revealed it.

When artificially abstracted from the larger narrative, the various explicit references to Scripture, most including fulfillment formulae, produce a rough biographical and thematic outline of the Messiah's life and ministry (as indicated by the list in the following table).

Matthew	Text cited	Theme or event
1:22-23	Isa 7:14	Virgin birth, "Emmanuel"
2:5-6	Mic 5:1, 3	Birth in Bethlehem
2:15	Hos 11:1	Exile and return from Egypt
2:17-18	Jer 31:15	Opposition by Herod
2:23	(Isa 11:1?)	Upbringing in Nazareth
3:3 (//Mark 1:3; Luke 3:4)	Isa 40:3	Ministry of John the Baptist
4:4-10 (//Luke 4:4-10)	Deut 6:13, 16; 8:3; Ps 91:11-12	Debate with Satan over Jesus' identity
4:14-16	Isa 8:23; 9:1-2	Ministry in Galilee
5:17		Fulfillment of "the law and the prophets"
8:17	Isa 53:4	Ministry of healing
9:13	Hos 6:6	Ministry to outcasts
11:10 (//Mark 1:2)	Exod 23:20; Mal 3:1	Ministry of John the Baptist
12:3-5 (//Mark 2:25-26)	Num 28:9; 1 Sam 21:7	Controversy regarding Sabbath

31. See, more fully, Knowles, *Jeremiah in Matthew's Gospel*, 45-46.

Matthew	Text cited	Theme or event
12:17-21	Isa 42:1-4	"Chosen servant"
13:14-15 (cf. Mark 4:12)	Isa 6:9-10	Parabolic teaching
13:35	Ps 78:2	Parabolic teaching
15:7-9 (//Mark 7:6)	Isa 29:13	Controversy regarding parents
19:4-5 (//Mark 10:6-8)	Gen 1:27; 2:24	Controversy regarding marriage
21:4-5	Zech 9:9; Isa 62:11	Entry into Jerusalem
21:13 (//Mark 11:17)	Isa 56:7; Jer 7:11	Critique of temple misuse
21:16	Ps 8:2	Acclamation by children
21:42 (//Mark 12:10-11)	Ps 118:22-23	Rejection and vindication
22:31-32 (//Mark 12:26)	Exod 3:6	Controversy regarding resurrection
22:44//Mark 12:36	Ps 110:1	David's "Lord"
24:30//Mark 13:26	Dan 7:13-14	Exaltation to God's right hand
26:24 (//Mark 14:21)		"The Son of Man goes as it is written of him"
26:31 (//Mark 14:27)	Zech 13:7	Jesus as shepherd
26:54, 56 (cf. Mark 14:49)	"That the Scriptures of the prophets might be fulfilled"	Arrest
26:64//Mark 14:62	Zech 12:10; Dan 7:13; Ps 110:1	Exaltation and return
27:9-10	Zech 11:12-13; Jer 18; 19; 32	Fate of betrayer

The fact that such an outline can be delineated at all indicates the success of Matthew's interpretative method. Scriptural revelation and the revelatory event of the Messiah's advent thus not only conform but actually confirm one another. The testimony of each validates the testimony of the other, in keeping with the principle articulated in Matt 18:16.

Even so, the respective testimonies of text and Messiah are not altogether equivalent. We noted earlier how Jesus' use of the formula "Have you not read?" emphasizes the authority of the interpreter. Matthew's use of fulfillment formulae operates on a similar principle, although in this instance it is the Messiah's life that clarifies the meaning of Scripture, even to the point of implying that the true intent of key texts remains hidden apart from him. In both instances, and in a manner analogous to biblical interpretation at Qumran, fulfillment exegesis relativizes the authority of Scripture. Even as Jesus explicitly claims to represent "something greater" than the temple (Matt 12:6), Jonah, or Solomon (12:41-42//Luke 11:31-32), so this interpretative methodology implicitly lends him an authority even greater than that of Scripture itself.

Scripture as Context:
The Correlation of Hermeneutical Wholes

Notwithstanding his authority as onetime Archbishop of Canterbury, it is probably methodologically questionable to base one's analysis on the chapter divisions attributed to Stephen Langton (d. 1228). Nonetheless, chapter 21 of Matthew's Gospel, recounting Jesus' climactic entry into the city and temple of Jerusalem, offers a complete cross-section of the evangelist's many uses of Scripture and scriptural motifs. Approaching the Mount of Olives, Jesus sends a pair of disciples into the city in search of "an ass . . . and a colt with her" (Matt 21:2). "This took place to fulfill what was spoken by the prophet," explains the evangelist helpfully, meaning thereby Zechariah (and Isaiah with him: Matt 21:4-5). Three features may be noted here. First, whether Matthew found this detail in the tradition available to him, or inserted it himself, his account of two animals (against the single beast of the other three Gospels) conforms more closely to the text that he alone cites.[32] Second, as noted earlier, this textual reference implies a typological interest — in this instance with reference to Moses. In other words, Matthew sees in Jesus the fulfillment not just of specific texts but also of historical resonances of type to antitype. Not just the texts themselves but larger thematic and historical patterns suggested by them come to fruition and fulfillment in Jesus of Nazareth. Third, there is a further textual and typological allusion here: the fact that the she-ass is said to be "tied [δεδεμένην]" likely recalls Gen 49:11, a prophecy regarding Judah's future reign that was interpreted messianically in contemporary Judaism.[33]

Upon Jesus' entry into the city, the crowds acclaim him with words

---

32. Cf. Keener, *Matthew*, 491-92.

33. William L. Lane, *The Gospel according to Mark: The English Text with Introduction, Exposition, and Notes* (NICNT; Grand Rapids: Eerdmans, 1979) 395-96.

derived from Psalm 118 and, for Matthew, from Mark 11 (Matt 21:9). Immediately entering the temple, Jesus rebukes the resident entrepreneurs by citing from Isaiah and Jeremiah (Matt 21:13). "It is written," he declares, implying that whereas one prophet announces the true purpose of the temple ("My house shall be called a house of prayer," Isa 56:7), the presence of merchants and money-changers earns and fulfills the rebuke of the other ("You make it a den of thieves," Jer 7:11). Thereupon, we learn, "the blind and the lame came to him in the temple, and he healed them" (Matt 21:14). This allusion to the proverb recorded in 2 Sam 5:8, "The blind and the lame shall not come into the house," serves to define Jesus as "Son of David" (Matt 21:9, 15) in ways that differ significantly from the historical figure from whom this name derives.[34] When the authorities take offense at such acclamations, Jesus replies, "Have you never read . . ." and cites Ps 8:2.

So ends Jesus' first day in the city. The following morning brings the encounter with the fruitless fig tree (Matt 21:18-21//Mark 11:12-14, 20-21), an episode that draws not only on the role of the fig tree as a general symbol of fruitfulness and of the fruitful nation in particular, but also on specific prophetic texts (e.g., Judg 9:7-15; Isa 28:4; Jer 24; 29:17; Mic 7:1; Hos 9:10, 16) that deal with the judgment of Israel.[35] There follow a series of controversies and parables, among them the parable of the vineyard and tenants (Matt 21:33-41//Mark 12:1-9), which strongly recalls Isaiah's parable about recalcitrant Israel in Isa 5:1-2; this section concludes with Jesus once more demanding, "Have you never read in the Scriptures . . . ," citing Ps 118:22-23 (Matt 21:42//Mark 12:10-11). His ominous assessment, "The kingdom of God will be taken away from you and given to a people producing the fruits of it" (Matt 21:43), echoes the judgment of Samuel on a disobedient Saul: "The Lord has torn the kingdom of Israel from you this very day, and has given it to a neighbor of yours, who is better than you" (1 Sam 15:28).

From this miscellany of citations, allusions, and formulae in Matthew 21, the following observations suggest themselves. First and foundationally, Scripture forms the backdrop both of the Messiah's teaching and of the events of his life, without distinction. Word, deed, and text appear in

---

34. Cf. Gundry, *Use of the OT*, 140, 210. The passage is uniquely Matthean.

35. W. R. Telford, *The Barren Temple and the Withered Tree: A Redaction-Critical Analysis of the Cursing of the Fig-Tree Pericope in Mark's Gospel and Its Relation to the Cleansing of the Temple Tradition* (JSNTSup 1; Sheffield: JSOT, 1980) 134-63.

this respect entirely consonant. Second, Matthew does not prioritize one form of reference over another: textual and typological allusions, together with explicit formulae employing direct quotations of Scripture, whether cited by Jesus or by Matthew, whatever the literary source and regardless of their messianic potential elsewhere in Second Temple Judaism, are all juxtaposed without apparent preference. Matthew weaves together a variety of references from a range of sources to create, as far as possible, a seamless theological and narrative fabric. The purpose of this method — which appears in the aggregate rather than in particular details — is to demonstrate the correlation of Scripture as a whole with the revelatory reality that the Messiah represents. In other words, both Scripture and Messiah are viewed as hermeneutically entire and complete, both in themselves and in relation to the other (or at least this is the consequence of their correlation). Third, Matthew's method implies little or no apologetic intent (in contrast, for instance, to that of Luke or John). That is, insofar as both Messiah and Scripture are presented in relation to one another, they prove mutually illuminating, and, in tandem, self-sufficient and self-explanatory. Because his work thus assumes certain core theological values regarding the sources of divine truth, and because the evangelist makes no effort to account for these assumptions, Matthew's Gospel offers few if any concessions to those who approach it on the basis of other philosophical or creedal convictions.

"At the Still Point of the Turning World": Order amid Confusion

The reader of Matthew's Gospel might be forgiven for gathering the impression that the evangelist lived in and wrote about a comparatively simple world. To be sure, some had opposed Jesus, but a plain reading of relevant texts and an unprejudiced evaluation of his life would surely — according to Matthew's carefully crafted presentation — compel one to the conclusion that this was indeed the Messiah of Israel's long hope and expectation. But it is no derogation of Christian faith and conviction (my own included) to insist that nothing could be further from the truth. Even a cursory reading of Second Temple history and a rudimentary awareness of text-critical issues compel quite the opposite conclusion — namely, that faith, history, politics, social relations, and even the sacred text itself were all bedeviled by ambiguity and uncertainty, consistently obscuring the divine purpose from the eyes of pious observers.

On the social, political, and historical fronts, Pharisees, Sadducees, and separatists such as those at Qumran (to cite only the most familiar options) each competed for popular allegiance. Some, from high priests down to lowly tax gatherers (as illustrated by the example of Matthew himself: Matt 9:9; 10:3), chose collaboration with the Roman occupiers. Factions argued bitterly over whether the lunar or solar calendar was divinely sanctioned. Any number of candidates laid outright or implicit claim to the name of Messiah. The tragic fate of Jesus was, in fact, no different from that suffered by other contemporary candidates for the title, notwithstanding subsequent assertions by his followers of divine vindication in this particular case. To all this must be added the war with Rome and destruction of Jerusalem, which brought to a crushing end the brief period of relative political autonomy enjoyed by Palestinian Jews.

Recent studies have made it abundantly clear that matters were hardly less confusing where the sacred text was concerned. The Scriptures of Israel circulated not just in a predominantly Hebrew original, but also in Greek, as well as in periphrastic Aramaic. Not one but *all* of these traditions are now known to have existed in a variety of forms that were not fully standardized until after 70 CE.[36] Against this backdrop, the apparently simple challenge, "Have you not read?" begs a number of important questions, not least of which is which text or translation might be taken as authoritative in order for such a reading to occur.

The beauty of messianic revelation, by contrast, was its ability to bring compelling clarity to this situation. We may imagine, at an early stage of reflection both during and immediately after Jesus' earthly ministry, that disciples and prospective disciples alike (and doubtless opponents also!) would have carefully scrutinized his life and teaching in light of commonly accepted messianic prophecies. But once the conclusion had been reached that this was indeed the Messiah to whom Scripture pointed, the reverse process would have increasingly taken over: the life and teaching of Jesus became the key to illuminating all the mysteries of the biblical text, a living, more immediate "canon" against which to assess the meaning of the written text. Even here, however, the process would not have been a simple one: the examples of Jesus' Nazarene origins or his apparently rid-

---

36. Cf. discussion in Beaton, *Isaiah's Christ in Matthew's Gospel*, 49-55.

ing two animals into Jerusalem raise the question of how closely Scripture and messianic history needed to conform.

Matthew's Gospel, with its seemingly seamless coordination of text and history, represents the final outcome of this multi-directional hermeneutic. It is in this sense that we may speak of Jesus as a "still point" and interpretative touchstone in the confusing world of Second Temple and post-destruction Judaism. In this regard, and notwithstanding the evangelist's consistent emphasis on hermeneutical closure, the final chapter of his Gospel offers a brief and telling insight into the earlier situation. The first witnesses of the resurrection respond with contradictory "fear and great joy" (Matt 28:8). Despite their testimony, however, more prosaic explanations of Jesus' disappearance from the tomb gain widespread currency. The disciples are repeatedly directed to Galilee (26:32; 28:7, 10), signaling a shift away from Jerusalem as the locus of divine revelation. Most telling is the observation that, upon the disciples' arrival in Galilee, "they worshipped him, but some doubted" (28:17). Even so, this does not prevent Jesus from approaching them (which implies that they had hitherto remained at a certain distance), reiterating his authority, commissioning them to make further disciples, and promising his own abiding presence (28:18-20). In much the same manner as the scene depicted here, Matthew presents Jesus and his teaching as the final, authoritative revelation that stands over a complex, contradictory, and otherwise largely incomprehensible situation.

For Matthew, then, Jesus is the "still point" for which God's people have longed and toward which the Scriptures point, the fulfillment of Israel's history in the fullness of time: "both a new world/And the old made explicit, understood," "the enchainment of past and future/Woven in the weakness of the changing body" ("Burnt Norton" II.29-30, 33-34). That the words of an Anglo-American poet, penned nearly two millennia after the fact, should capture its meaning so succinctly bespeaks the enduring power of Matthew's vision and its ability to articulate the purpose, the significance, and the interpretative methodology of Jesus of Nazareth, "even to the end of the age" (Matt 28:20).

The Beginning of the Good News and the Fulfillment of Scripture in the Gospel of Mark

CRAIG A. EVANS

Introduction and Review of Recent Research

More than thirty years ago the late Samuel Sandmel, a much-loved Jewish scholar with expertise in New Testament studies, wisely commented that "Mark in many treatments is explained incorrectly because Matthew and Luke (and John) are read with him."[1] This problem manifests itself in studies devoted to Mark's use of the Old Testament. Nearly forty years ago Alexander Suhl concluded that the evangelist Mark had little interest in the theme of the fulfillment of Scripture.[2] Suhl thought the appearance of the Old Testament in Mark, if not incidental, was worked into the narrative to illustrate that the life, death, and resurrection of Jesus were, in general terms, "according to the Scriptures" (as in 1 Cor 15:3-4).[3] When Suhl's work is viewed in the light of Gospel research in the 1960s, it is not hard to see why he reached this conclusion. At that time redaction criticism in its classic understanding was all the rage.[4] It was understood that the Markan

---

1. S. Sandmel, "Prolegomena to a Commentary on Mark," in *New Testament Issues* (ed. R. Batey; London: SCM, 1970) 45-56.

2. A. Suhl, *Die Funktion der alttestamentlichen Zitate und Anspielungen im Markusevangelium* (Gütersloh: Mohn, 1965).

3. Suhl, *Die Funktion*, 37-44.

4. Suhl was in fact a pupil of Willi Marxsen, who pioneered redaction criticism of Mark in his *Der Evangelist Markus: Studien zur Redaktionsgeschichte des Evangeliums* (FRLANT 67; Göttingen: Vandenhoeck & Ruprecht, 1956; 2nd ed., 1959); ET: *Mark the Evangelist* (Nashville: Abingdon, 1956).

evangelist collected and edited inherited tradition, which already contained most of the Old Testament quotations and allusions that we find in his Gospel.

The conclusion that the Markan evangelist had minor interest in the Old Testament was encouraged by comparison of Mark's use of the Old Testament to its use in Matthew and Luke, because it was (and still is) widely believed that these Gospels made use of Mark. In Matthew the Old Testament is frequently and formally quoted, often introduced as "fulfilled." The fourth evangelist does the same thing, creatively developing a scriptural apologetic that transforms the shame of Jesus' crucifixion to his hour of glorification. The Lukan evangelist does not emphasize formal quotations of the Old Testament; instead, he weaves into the narrative fabric words and phrases from the Old Greek Bible, giving his Gospel a biblical flavor. In comparison to these deliberate, programmatic appropriations of the Old Testament, Mark does indeed appear to have little interest. But appearances can be deceiving.

How would we view Mark if Mark was the only Gospel we had? What if we had no Gospels of Matthew, Luke, and John with which to compare it? In this case would anyone read Mark and conclude that the evangelist had little interest in the Old Testament? To what extent and in what ways does the Old Testament appear in Mark?

In Mark we find both major divisions of Scripture — the Law and the Prophets (including the Psalms) — well represented.[5] We have at least seven quotations of or obvious allusions to the Law: Mark 1:2 (Exod 23:20); 6:34 (Num 27:17); 7:10 (Exod 20:12; Deut 5:16); 10:6-7 (Gen 1:27; 2:24); 10:19 (Exod 20:12-16; Deut 5:16-20); 12:26 (Exod 3:6); 12:29-31 (Deut 6:4-5; Lev 19:18). There is an eighth, if we take into account the reference by Jesus'

5. There is no compelling evidence that by the middle of the first century there was a clearly defined third division of Scripture (i.e., the Writings). The evidence of Luke 24 is sometimes misread. The risen Jesus says that what is written about him "in the law of Moses and the prophets and psalms" must be fulfilled (v. 44). Reference to "psalms" (which is not articular) is not a reference to a third division of Scripture but is an extension of "the prophets" (whose article applies to both "prophets" and "psalms"). This is consistent with the earlier statement in v. 27, where we are told of the risen Jesus, "beginning with Moses and all the prophets, he interpreted to them in all the scriptures." The words "all the scriptures" do not introduce a third division of Scripture; they refer to the just-mentioned "Moses" (i.e., the Law) and "all the prophets." As v. 44 makes clear, "all the scriptures" include "psalms." Two divisions of Scripture, with the psalms linked to the prophets, are attested at Qumran.

critics to Deuteronomy 24 (cf. Mark 10:4). We may also have an allusion to Deut 18:15 in the words spoken at the transfiguration (cf. Mark 9:7).

There are some twenty quotations of or obvious allusions to the Prophets and Psalms: Mark 1:2-3 (Mal 3:1; Isa 40:3); 1:11 (Ps 2:7); 4:11-12 (Isa 6:9-10); 4:29 (Joel 3:13); 7:6-7 (Isa 29:13); 8:18 (Jer 5:21); 9:48 (Isa 66:24); 11:9-10 (Ps 118:25-26); 11:17a (Isa 56:7); 11:17b (Jer 7:11); 12:1 (Isa 5:1-2); 12:10-11 (Ps 118:22-23); 12:36 (Ps 110:1); 13:14 (Dan 11:31; 12:11); 13:26 (Dan 7:13); 14:27 (Zech 13:7); 14:62 (Ps 110:1; Dan 7:13); 15:24 (Ps 22:18); 15:34 (Ps 22:1); and 15:36 (Ps 69:21). We may also have allusions to Mal 3:23 (cf. Mark 9:12); Ps 41:9 (cf. Mark 14:18); and Isa 53:12 (cf. Mark 14:24) and 50:6 (cf. Mark 14:65).[6]

We also find all three major text types represented in Mark's quotations of or allusions to the Old Testament: the Greek, the Hebrew (or proto-Masoretic Text), and the Aramaic (or proto-Targum). The Greek appears to be followed in Mark 1:3 (Isa 40:3); 9:7 (Deut 18:15); 9:12 (Mal 3:23); 12:10-11 (Ps 118:22-23); 12:36 (Ps 110:1); 14:18 (Ps 41:9); 14:62 (Ps 110:1); and 15:24 (Ps 22:18). We may have allusions to the Greek form of Isa 52:15 (cf. Mark 15:5); Ps 10:7-8 (cf. Mark 14:1); Pss 42:5, 11; 43:5 (cf. Mark 14:34); and Ps 37:32 (cf. Mark 14:55). The proto-Masoretic Hebrew appears to be followed in Mark 1:2 (Mal 3:1; Exod 23:20) and 14:62 (Dan 7:13). We may also have allusions to the Hebrew form of Isa 63:19 (cf. Mark 1:10). The Aramaic, or proto-Targum, seems to be followed in Mark 1:11 (Ps 2:7); 4:12 (Isa 6:9-10); 9:48 (Isa 66:24); 8:31 (Hos 6:2); 11:9-10 (Ps 118:25-26); 12:1 (Isa 5:1-2); and 15:34 (Ps 22:1).

Not only does the Markan evangelist make use of all parts of Scripture and all major text types; the evangelist also incorporates quotations of or allusions to Scripture at key points in his narrative. His Gospel commences with a quotation of Isa 40:3 (at Mark 1:3) and alludes to Scripture at Jesus' baptism, at his transfiguration, and in his passion. Jesus defends his teaching and activity by appeal to Scripture, as at Mark 2:23-28, where he appeals to the example of David in 1 Sam 21:1-6; or at 7:6-7, where he appeals to the prophetic word of the prophet Isaiah (Isa 29:13); or at 12:10-11, where he appeals to Ps 118:22-23 to clarify the identity of the rejected Son. Jesus explains to his disciples the mixed response to his proclamation of

---

6. I am influenced by the work of J. Marcus, *The Way of the Lord: Christological Exegesis of the Old Testament in the Gospel of Mark* (Louisville: Westminster John Knox, 1992) esp. 172-86, the treatment of the Psalms in Mark.

the kingdom of God by appeal to Isaiah's threatening prophecy in Mark 4:11-12 (cf. Isa 6:9-10), and he appeals to Scripture in the final days of his ministry, as seen in the words of institution at Mark 14:24 (Exod 24:8; Zech 9:11), the warning of the shepherd soon to be struck down at Mark 14:27 (Zech 13:7), the threatening reply to the high priest at Mark 14:62 (Dan 7:13; Ps 110:1), and in his cry from the cross at Mark 15:34 (Ps 22:1).

Happily, Suhl's negative conclusions have not had widespread or lasting influence. Several studies have appeared in which the importance of the Old Testament in Mark has been shown. Ulrich Mauser and Hans-Jörg Steichele trace significant Old Testament themes and motifs in Mark's usage of Scripture.[7] Joel Marcus, whose learned and creative study represents a major step forward, has focused on the evangelist's use of the Old Testament in developing Christology,[8] while Rikki Watts has shown how pervasive Isaianic themes are in Mark's story of Jesus.[9] Several other studies have appeared in subsequent years, emphasizing various aspects of the function of Scripture in the Gospel of Mark.[10]

The balance of the present essay will explore the possibility that the Markan evangelist may have presented Jesus as the fulfillment of prophecy as a conscious challenge to the rumors circulating in the Roman Empire that Jewish prophecy was fulfilled with the advent of Vespasian as the new emperor and, by virtue of his exalted office, the new "son of God." To be sure, the function of the Old Testament in the Markan Gospel reflects a Ju-

---

7. U. Mauser, *Christ in the Wilderness: The Wilderness Theme in the Second Gospel and Its Basis in the Biblical Tradition* (SBT 39; London: SCM; Naperville: Allenson, 1963); H.-J. Steichele, *Der leidende Sohn Gottes, Eine Untersuchung einiger alttestamentlicher Motive in der Christologie des Markusevangeliums: zugleich ein Beitrag zur Erhellung des überlieferungsgeschichtlichen Zusammenhangs zwischen Alten und Neuen Testament* (Regensburg: F. Pustet, 1980).

8. Marcus, *The Way of the Lord*. A strong point in Marcus's study is his treatment of the wider context of the passages quoted or alluded to in Mark.

9. R. E. Watts, *Isaiah's New Exodus in Mark* (WUNT 2/88; Tübingen: Mohr [Siebeck], 1997; repr. Biblical Studies Library; Grand Rapids: Baker Academic, 2000).

10. E. K. Broadhead, *Prophet, Son, Messiah: Narrative Form and Function in Mark 14–16* (JSNTSup 97; Sheffield: Sheffield Academic Press, 1994); R. Schneck, *Isaiah in the Gospel of Mark, I–VII* (Bibal Dissertation Series 1; Berkeley: BIBAL, 1994); T. Dwyer, *The Motif of Wonder in the Gospel of Mark* (JSNTSup 128; Sheffield: Sheffield Academic Press, 1996); E. K. Broadhead, *Naming Jesus: Titular Christology in the Gospel of Mark* (JSNTSup 175; Sheffield: Sheffield Academic Press, 1999); T. R. Hatina, *In Search of a Context: The Function of Scripture in Mark's Narrative* (JSNTSup 232; SSEJC 8; London and New York: Sheffield Academic Press, 2002).

daic setting. But the evangelist's bold assertion that the good news for the world begins in Jesus Christ, the son of God, is surely calculated to invite comparisons between the Roman son of God and the Jewish son of God.[11] That this was indeed the case is strengthened when it is recognized that in all probability Mark's Gospel was published shortly after Vespasian's accession to imperial power, at which time apologetic for the new emperor was at its height.[12] Thus, lying at the heart of the Markan Gospel is this question: Who really is the son of God and which one of these divine sons will occasion good news for a Roman world greatly troubled by recent war and political upheaval?

Christology and Prophecy in a Roman Context

Food shortages, debt problems, a surge in unemployment, and growing friction between many Jewish people and their Roman and Jewish overlords finally exploded in riot and rebellion in the year 66 CE. Whole garrisons of Roman troops and auxiliaries were annihilated. Unsure how to respond to the crisis, the hated and distrusted Nero, who was himself paranoid, sent General Vespasian to Israel to put down the rebellion. Nero

---

11. Several commentators suggest this: M.-J. Lagrange, *L'Évangile de Jésus-Christ: avec la synopsis évangélique* (2nd ed.; Paris: Gabalda, 1954) 2; C. E. B. Cranfield, *The Gospel according to Saint Mark* (CGTC; Cambridge: Cambridge University Press, 1959) 36; W. L. Lane, *The Gospel of Mark* (NICNT; Grand Rapids: Eerdmans, 1974) 43-44; C. Myers, *Binding the Strong Man: A Political Reading of Mark's Story of Jesus* (Maryknoll: Orbis, 1990) 122-24; R. H. Gundry, *Mark: A Commentary on His Apology for the Cross* (Grand Rapids: Eerdmans, 1993) 41.

12. I believe the most probable date of the publication of Mark is 69 CE or early 70, before the fall of Jerusalem. J. Marcus ("The Jewish War and the *Sitz im Leben* of Mark," *JBL* 111 [1992] 441-62) has argued for a date shortly after the war (probably 71 CE). However, in his recently published commentary (*Mark 1–8* [AB 27; New York: Doubleday, 2000] 38), Marcus seems open to a pre-70 date. This is a welcome shift. However, I am inclined, *pace* Marcus, to continue to view the Markan Gospel in the light of a Roman provenance. The strongest argument for a late-60s date for the Gospel is its emphasis (in chap. 13) of the dangers and trials of the war, yet its lack of knowledge of how the war actually turns out. Jesus' prophecy in 13:2 says nothing of the devastating fire, a point that is discussed in detail by Josephus (e.g., *Jewish War* 6.2.9 §§165-68, which is but one of many references to the fire). Moreover, Jesus' admonition to his disciples that they pray that the siege not take place in winter (13:18) is odd — if it is a *vaticinium ex eventu* — given that the siege takes place in the spring and summer.

chose Vespasian to serve as commander because he was from a relatively humble background. Nero had no reason to fear Vespasian and the fame that might well accrue to him should he prosecute the war well. But a year later, learning that the Senate had condemned him to death as a public enemy, Nero took his own life (Suetonius, *Nero* 49.2-4).

Galba succeeded Nero, but after reigning only seven months he was murdered. His successor was Otho, who after ninety-five days of rule committed suicide. The next short-lived emperor was Vitellius, who after the grossest abuses of power was seized by soldiers, dragged to the Forum, and stabbed to death. It was then, in 69 CE, that General Vespasian, commander of Roman forces in Galilee, was proclaimed emperor of the Roman Empire. His accession to the throne did not come a day too soon. The empire was in turmoil, following the death of the hated Nero, the last of the Julian emperors, and the failure of three would-be successors, Galba, Otho, and Vitellius: four dead emperors in a little less than two years. "The empire, which had long been unsettled and, as it were, drifting, through the usurpation and violent death of three emperors, was at last taken in hand and given stability by the Flavian family" (Suetonius, *Vespasian* 1.1). These are the words of Suetonius, who was born in the first year of Vespasian's reign and whose father had been an officer in the Roman army during this turbulent and uncertain period.

The accession of Vespasian came as a great relief and — at least according to some — as no surprise. For prophecies and omens had foretold the accession of the new emperor. These omens are mentioned briefly by Tacitus (cf. *Roman Histories* 1.10.3: "the secrets of Fate, and the signs and oracles which predestined Vespasian and his sons for power"; 2.1; 5.13) and Cassius Dio (*Roman History* 66.1.2: "Now portents and dreams had come to Vespasian pointing to the sovereignty long beforehand"). Suetonius describes them more fully: an old oak tree suddenly put forth a branch; while Vespasian was eating breakfast a stray dog approached and dropped a human hand under the table; a runaway ox, having slipped its yoke, burst into the dining room and fell at the feet of Vespasian; and he had a dream, which came to pass, that Nero would have a tooth extracted (Suetonius, *Vespasian* 5.2, 4-5).

Perhaps more interesting is the story of the prophecy of the priest of the "god of Carmel," whom Vespasian encountered during the war in Israel. According to Tacitus, "When Vespasian was sacrificing there and thinking over his secret hopes in his heart, the priest Basilides, after repeated inspection of the victim's vitals, said to him: 'Whatever you are planning, Vespasian, whether to build a house, or to enlarge your holdings, or to increase the number of your slaves, the god grants you a mighty home, limitless bounds, and a multitude of men.' Rumor caught up this obscure oracle and now was trying to interpret it" (Tacitus, *Roman Histories* 2.78.3-4; cf. Suetonius, *Vespasian* 5.6).

We are told of another Palestinian who foretold Vespasian's coming good fortune. This person was Rabban Yohanan ben Zakkai, who, according to the rabbis, escaped from besieged Jerusalem. When he saw General Vespasian, who granted him Yavneh, where the rabbis were allowed to gather after the war, he said: "Behold, you are about to be appointed king." Vespasian asked how he knew this, and ben Zakkai explained that it "has been handed down to us, that the temple will not be surrendered to a commoner, but to a king; as it is said, 'He will cut down the thickets of the forest with an axe, and Lebanon with its majestic trees will fall'" (Isa 10:34). The story goes on to say that, a few days later, word reached Vespasian that the emperor was dead and that he, Vespasian, had been proclaimed king (*Abot de Rabbi Nathan* A 4:5).

This story is a fiction, of course. Vespasian himself did not besiege Jerusalem; his son Titus did. And in any case, it is not too probable that ben Zakkai had conversations with the future emperor. However, the story does draw upon elements from the first century. For example, we know from the Dead Sea Scrolls that Isa 10:34 was understood as prophecy of battle with the Romans, when the wicked of Jerusalem and their Roman allies, including the emperor himself, would be slain (cf. 4Q161; 4Q285). In my view the rabbinic story is really a retelling of the experience of Josephus, a prominent Jew — a priest, not a rabbi — who did converse with Vespasian and did foretell his accession to the throne.[13]

Certainly the most dramatic prophecy of Vespasian's glory was that uttered by Josephus, or Joseph bar Matthias, as he was known then. Joseph, who had been given command of Galilee not long after the Jewish rebellion had begun in 66 CE, had been defeated and captured. About to be sent to Rome to face the wrath of Nero, Joseph requested an audience with

---

13. The rabbinic story at other points preserves reworked older tradition. When the temple is destroyed the ruling priests throw the keys of the sanctuary up into the sky and confess that they are no longer worthy to be custodians of God's house. This tradition reaches back to the end of the first century (cf. *2 Bar.* 10:18).

Vespasian and his son Titus. The proud, aristocratic priest, a descendant of the Hasmoneans, said to the Roman commanders: "You imagine, Vespasian, that in the person of Joseph you have taken a mere captive; but I come to you as a messenger of greater destinies. . . . You will be Caesar, Vespasian, you will be emperor, you and your son here. Bind me then yet more securely in chains and keep me for yourself; for you, Caesar, are master not of me only, but of land and sea and the whole human race" (*Jewish War* 3.8.9 §§401-2). Initially, Vespasian suspected Joseph ben Mathias of trickery, of playing for time, and of trying to avoid punishment. But various signs and omens led him to think that there might be something to Joseph's prophecy.

The story of Josephus's prophecy was known in the Roman world. It is related by Suetonius: "One of his [Vespasian's] high-born prisoners, Josephus by name, as he was being put in chains, declared most confidently that he would soon be released by the same man, who would then, however, be emperor" (Suetonius, *Vespasian* 5.6). Even the very omens that Josephus describes, omens of Jerusalem's defeat and the temple's destruction, were known to the Roman public (compare Tacitus, *Roman Histories* 5.13.1-2, with Josephus, *Jewish War* 6.5.3-4 §§288-315).

With his prophecy fulfilled, Josephus gained eventual release. When Vespasian was declared emperor, he was "led to think that divine providence had assisted him to grasp the empire and that some just destiny had placed the sovereignty of the world within his hands. Among many other omens, which had everywhere foreshadowed his imperial honors, he recalled the words of Josephus, who had ventured, even in Nero's lifetime, to address him as emperor. He was shocked to think that the man was still a prisoner. . . . 'It is disgraceful,' he said, 'that one who foretold my elevation to power and was a minister of the voice of God should still rank as a captive and endure a prisoner's fate'; and calling for Josephus, he ordered him to be liberated" (*Jewish War* 4.10.7 §§622-26).

Josephus was able to predict Vespasian's elevation because of his understanding of a prophecy in the Jewish scriptures. This too was known in Roman circles. According to Suetonius: "There had spread all over the east an old and established belief, that it was fated at that time for men coming from Judea to rule the world. This prediction, referring to the emperor of Rome, as afterwards appeared from the event, the people of Judea took to themselves; accordingly they revolted" (Suetonius, *Vespasian* 4.5). Suetonius may well have been influenced directly by Josephus.

In any event, it is Josephus who sheds the most light on the prophecy. He refers to it in two places. In the first passage he says: "Thus it was that the wretched people were deluded at that time by charlatans and pretended messengers of God; while they neither heeded nor believed in the manifest portents that foretold the coming desolation, but, as if thunderstruck and bereft of eyes and mind, disregarded the plain warnings of God. So it was when a star, resembling a sword, stood over the city, and a comet which continued for a year" (*Jewish War* 6.5.3 §§288-89). And in the second passage he adds: "But what more than all else incited them to the war was an ambiguous oracle, likewise found in their sacred scriptures, to the effect that at that time one from their country would become ruler of the world. This they understood to mean someone of their own race, and many of their wise went astray in their interpretation of it. The oracle, however, in reality signified the sovereignty of Vespasian, who was proclaimed emperor on Jewish soil" (*Jewish War* 6.5.4 §§312-14).

In my view it is almost certain that Josephus here has referred to Num 24:17, which foretells: "A star shall come forth out of Jacob, and a scepter shall rise out of Israel; it shall crush the forehead of Moab, and break down all the sons of Sheth." Josephus's description of the star, resembling a sword, and his reference to Vespasian, "proclaimed on Jewish soil," alludes to the star of the Numbers passage and to the prediction that it will "come forth out of Jacob" and "rise out of Israel." That this passage was understood messianically in the first century is quite probable, as seen in the War Scroll of Qumran:

> Neither our power nor the strength of our hand has done valiantly, but by Your power and the strength of Your great valor. Jus[t a]s You told us in time past, saying: "There shall come forth a star from out of Jacob, a scepter shall rise out of Israel, and shall crush the forehead of Moab and tear down all sons of Sheth, and he shall descend from Jacob and shall destroy the remnant from the city, and the enemy shall be a possession, and Israel shall do valiantly" [Num 24:17, 19, 18b]. By the hand of Your anointed ones, seers of things appointed, You have told us about the ti[mes] of the wars of Your hands in order that You may glorify Yourself among our enemies, to bring down the hordes of Belial, the seven vainglorious nations, at the hand of the oppressed whom You have redeemed [with powe]r and retribution; a wondrous strength. A heart that melts shall be as a door of hope. You will do to

them as You did to Pharaoh and the officers of his chariots in the Red Sea. (1QM 11:5-10)[14]

We may have a messianic allusion to the Numbers passage in the *Testament of the Twelve Patriarchs,* if the passage is in fact not a later Christian interpolation. The patriarch Judah says:

> And after this there shall arise for you a Star from Jacob in peace: And a man shall arise from my posterity like the Sun of righteousness. . . . This is the Shoot of God Most High . . . then he will illumine the scepter of my kingdom, and from your root will arise the Shoot. (*T. Jud.* 24:1-6)

Matthew's infancy narrative alludes to this passage, when the evangelist tells us of the Magi's quest for the "child who has been born king of the Jews," whose "star" has been observed (Matt 2:2). Other early allusions include 4Q175 1:11-13; Philo, *De vita Mosis* 1.52 §290; *De praem. et poen.* 16 §95.

Later Jewish tradition consistently views Num 24:17 as messianic. The passage is paraphrased as an explicit messianic prophecy in the Pentateuch Targums: "A *king* shall arise out of Jacob and *be anointed the Messiah* out of Israel. He shall *slay the princes* of Moab and *reign over all humankind*" (*Tg. Onq.* Num 24:17). Rabbi Aqiba's famous messianic identification of Simon ben Kosiba, whom he dubbed "bar Kokhba," was based on a word play that alluded to this passage:

> Rabbi Simeon ben Yohai taught: "Aqiba, my master, used to interpret 'a star [*kokab*] goes forth from Jacob' [Num 24:17] — 'Kozeba goes forth from Jacob.' Rabbi Aqiba, when he saw Bar Kozeba, said: 'This is the King Messiah.'" (*y. Ta'an.* 4:5)

A Proposal

Given the widespread rumor, promoted by Josephus himself and certainly encouraged by Vespasian and his supporters, that Jewish Scripture foretold

---

14. In most cases English translations of passages taken from the Dead Sea Scrolls are based on M. O. Wise, M. G. Abegg Jr., and E. M. Cook, *The Dead Sea Scrolls: A New Translation* (San Francisco: HarperCollins, 1996).

Vespasian's elevation to the emperorship, we should not be surprised if Christians, such as the evangelist Mark, should find it necessary to mount a challenge. In my view this is what the evangelist has done. His focus is not on Num 24:17, the probable passage to which Josephus alluded, but is directed in more general terms against the idea that the newly installed Emperor Vespasian is the fulfillment of prophecy and the world's savior. In other words, the Markan evangelist has challenged the imperial cult of the divine emperor.

For our purposes the most important statement of the cult is expressed in the Priene calendar inscription (*OGIS* no. 458), which dates to 9 BCE and is in honor of Augustus. It reads in part:

> It seemed good to the Greeks of Asia, in the opinion of the high priest Apollonius of Menophilus Azanitus [to declare:] "since Providence, which has ordered all things and is deeply interested in our life, has set in most perfect order by giving us Augustus, whom she filled with virtue that he might benefit humankind, sending him as a savior [σωτήρ], both for us and for our descendants, that he might end war and arrange all things, and since he, Caesar, by his appearance [ἐπιφανεῖν] [excelled even our anticipations], surpassing all previous benefactors, and not even leaving to posterity any hope of surpassing what he has done, and since the birthday of the god Augustus was the beginning of the good news for the world that came by reason of him [ἦρξεν δὲ τῶι κόσμωι τῶν δι' αὐτὸν εὐαγγελίων ἡ γενέθλιος τοῦ θεοῦ]," which Asia resolved in Smyrna. (lines 31-42)[15]

Augustus is regarded as divine, as savior, and as the beginning of the *good news* for the world.[16] In many other inscriptions and papyri Augustus is referred to as "son of God" (*IGR* 1.901; 4.309, 315; *ILS* 107, 113; PRyl 601;

---

15. For text, see *Orientis Graeci Inscriptiones Selectae: Supplementum Sylloges Inscriptionum Graecarum* (2 vols.; ed. W. Dittenberger; Leipzig: S. Hirzel, 1903-1905; repr. Hildesheim: Olms, 1986) 2:48-60; V. Ehrenberg and A. H. M. Jones, *Documents Illustrating the Reigns of Augustus and Tiberius* (2nd ed.; Oxford: Clarendon, 1955) 81-84.

16. The key terminology is εὐαγγέλιον ("good news" or "gospel," in the singular or plural) and its verbal cognate εὐαγγελίζεσθαι ("to announce good news" or "evangelize"). On the development of this concept in late antiquity, see J. Schniewind, *Euangelion: Ursprung und erste Gestalt des Begriffs Evangelium Untersuchungen* (2 vols.; BFCT 2.25; Gütersloh: Bertelsmann, 1927-31).

POslo 26 et al.). The official doctrine is continued by his successors, as we see in a papyrus that refers to Nero, who by all accounts was hardly a worthy successor of the great Augustus. Nero is described as the "good god of the inhabited world, the beginning [ἀρχή] of all good things" (POxy 1021).[17]

The language is applied to Vespasian when he was acclaimed emperor. According to Josephus, "every city celebrated the good news [εὐαγγέλια] and offered sacrifices on his behalf" (*Jewish War* 4.10.6 §618). Josephus later relates: "On reaching Alexandria Vespasian was greeted by the good news [εὐαγγέλια] from Rome and by embassies of congratulation from every quarter of the world, now his own. . . . The whole empire being now secured and the Roman state saved [σώζειν] beyond expectation, Vespasian turned his thoughts to what remained in Judea" (*Jewish War* 4.11.5 §§656-57).[18] The salvation of the empire "beyond expectation" is reminiscent of the hyperbolic language of the Priene inscription. In view of this evidence, Helmut Koester justly remarks that "it is most likely that the early Christian missionaries were influenced by the imperial propaganda in their employment of the word" εὐαγγέλιον.[19] Such influence is seen in Mark.

The opening verse, or incipit, of Mark directly challenges this Roman doctrine: "The beginning of the good news of Jesus Christ, Son of God" (Mark 1:1).[20] The Markan evangelist puts forward Jesus as the true Son of

17. See D. Fishwick, *The Imperial Cult in the Latin West: Studies in the Ruler Cult of the Western Provinces of the Roman Empire* (5 vols.; Études préliminaires aux religions orientales dans l'Empire romain 108; Religions in the Graeco-Roman World 145-46; Leiden: Brill, 1987-2002). Fishwick traces the origins of the emperor cult to the east, specifically to Asia and Bithynia during the time of Augustus, and studies its subsequent influence in the west, noting its revision and expansion with the accession of Vespasian.

18. For additional examples of texts that speak of imperial "good news," see Schniewind, *Euangelion*, 131-32; *TDNT* 2:710-12 (though most examples are from Greek history and literature). See also *OGIS* nos. 4 (line 42) and 6 (lines 31-32). Writing before Caesar's dictatorship, Lucretius (94-55 BCE) applies similar language to his beloved teacher: "he was a god, a god indeed who first discovered that rule of life that is now called philosophy . . . whose gospel [εὐαγγέλιον], broadcast through the length and breadth of empires, is even now bringing soothing solace to the minds of men."

19. H. Koester, *Ancient Christian Gospels: Their History and Development* (Philadelphia: Trinity Press International, 1990) 4.

20. In Jewish ears accustomed to reading or hearing Scripture, Mark's incipit would have had a biblical and prophetic ring to it: ἀρχὴ λόγου κυρίου πρὸς Ὡσῆε "The beginning of the word of the Lord to Hosea" (LXX Hos 1:2a). However, this verse is not the incipit of Hosea's prophecy. In the case of Mark, it is the collocation of "beginning," "good news," and "son of God" that gives the Markan incipit its distinctive imperial flavor.

God,[21] in whom the good news for the world really begins. But the very next word in the Markan text is καθώς, which links the incipit, with its imperial language, to the quotation of Scripture: "just as it is written in Isaiah the prophet" (Mark 1:2). Thus, Mark's Gospel opens with a challenge to the view circulating the very year that Vespasian was proclaimed emperor, that is, that Vespasian's accession and divinity were in fulfillment of Jewish prophecy. In all probability the Gospel of Mark was published the same year as Vespasian's accession and may also have been published in Rome itself.

The parallels go further. As soon as Vespasian is declared to be emperor, he is encouraged to demonstrate his divinity through healing. According to Suetonius:

> Vespasian as yet lacked prestige and a certain divinity, so to speak, since he was an unexpected and still new-made emperor; but these also were given him. A man of the people who was blind, and another who was lame, came to him together as he sat on the tribunal, begging for the help for their disorders which Serapis had promised in a dream; for the god declared that Vespasian would restore the eyes, if he would spit upon them, and give strength to the leg, if he would deign to touch it with his heel. Though he had hardly any faith that this could possibly succeed, and therefore shrank even from making the attempt, he was at last prevailed upon by his friends and tried both things in public before a large crowd; and with success. (*Vespasian* 7.2-3)

21. The textual authorities are divided, with old and important texts reading "Jesus Christ, Son of God" (A B D K L W 33 et al.) and a few other old and important texts omitting υἱοῦ θεοῦ "Son of God" (ℵ θ 28 et al.). Bruce Metzger comments that the omission of "Son of God" in some manuscripts "may be due to an oversight in copying, occasioned by the similarity of the endings of the *nomina sacra*. On the other hand, however, there was always the temptation . . . to expand titles and quasi-titles of books" (*A Textual Commentary on the Greek New Testament* [London and New York: United Bible Societies, 1971] 73). I accept the words as original, omitted accidentally as Metzger explains. They are original because they anticipate the divine recognition of Jesus throughout the Gospel, ending climactically with the centurion's confession in 15:39: "Truly this man was son of God [υἱὸς θεοῦ]!" The forward placement of the demonstrative pronouns implies that it is *this* man, as opposed to another, who is truly "son of God." Moreover, one would expect that if "son of God" were a later gloss, it would have been articular, i.e., τοῦ υἱοῦ τοῦ θεοῦ. On this point, see R. Schnackenburg, "'Das Evangelium' im Verständnis des ältesten Evangelisten," in *Orientierung an Jesus: Zur Theologie der Synoptiker* (J. Schmid Festschrift; ed. P. Hoffmann et al.; Freiburg: Herder, 1973) 309-24, esp. 321-23.

We have stories in Mark where Jesus effects healing with the use of spittle (cf. Mark 7:33: "taking him aside from the multitude privately, he put his fingers into his ears, and he spat and touched his tongue") and touching (cf. Mark 1:41; 6:56; 7:33). Of course, Jesus is not without faith; on the contrary, he urges all to have faith (cf. Mark 2:5; 5:34; 10:52, where a blind man is healed).

Jesus is also accused of threatening to destroy the Herodian temple and to build a new one, not made by human hands (Mark 14:58), an accusation that probably reflects something Jesus actually said (cf. John 2:19; Mark 13:2). We may again have correspondence with the Roman emperor, for, following the triumphal ceremonies celebrating the capture of Jerusalem and the stabilization of the empire, "Vespasian decided to erect a temple of peace" (Josephus, *Jewish War* 7.5.7 §158; cf. Dio Cassius, *Roman History* 66.15), which was completed in 75 CE.

When Jesus is arrested and delivered into the hands of the Romans, he is mocked and cruelly treated. The mockery is presented as mock recognition of a Roman emperor (and such mockery was suffered by Galba, Otho, and Vitellius not long before Mark's Gospel was published). Jesus is dressed in a purple (or red) cloak; a crown of thorns (which resembles the laurel wreath) is placed on his head; the soldiers kneel before Jesus, saluting him, "Hail, King of the Jews"; and then they hit his head with a reed (which probably plays the part of the scepter) and spit upon him (Mark 15:17-19). All of these details have their counterparts in triumphs and ceremonies in honor of the emperor (cf. Livy, *Epitomes* 10.7.9; 30.15.11; Dio Cassius, *Roman History* 62.4.3–6.2; 62.20.2-6; Suetonius, *Tiberius* 17.2: "clad in purple-bordered toga and crowned with laurel"; *Nero* 25.1: "he wore a purple robe . . . bearing on his head the Olympic crown and in his right hand the Pythian"; Josephus, *Jewish War* 7.5.4 §§123-31: "Vespasian and Titus issued forth, crowned with laurel and clad in the traditional purple robes . . . instantly acclamations arose from the troops"). It has accordingly been suggested that the mockery and crucifixion of Jesus have been modeled after imperial triumph traditions.[22]

When Jesus dies, preternatural signs take place, again paralleling the signs and omens that were said to have foreshadowed the deaths of the emperors. During the sixth hour (i.e., noon) there was a mysterious darkness

---

22. See T. E. Schmidt, "Mark 15.16-32: The Crucifixion Narrative and the Roman Triumphal Procession," *NTS* 41 (1995) 1-18.

over the land (Mark 15:33), and when Jesus dies the veil of the temple is torn in two (15:38). The Roman centurion, no doubt interpreting the significance of these omens and impressed by the manner of Jesus' death, exclaims, "Truly this man was son of God!" (15:39). Recognition as "son of God," of course, was reserved for the Roman emperor (as seen in many public inscriptions, e.g., *SIG* no. 760 [Julius Caesar]; *BGU* no. 628 [Augustus]; *SB* no. 8317 [Tiberius]; *IM* no. 157b [Nero]; *CPL* no. 104 [Vespasian]), not for a Jewish would-be Messiah. The final omen, of course, is the discovery of the empty tomb and the announcement of the young man that Jesus is "not here," but has gone before his disciples (16:6-7). Postmortem omens and apparitions were also part of the imperial lore (e.g., Suetonius, *Caligula* 59, where tales are told of ghostly apparitions in the vicinity of Caligula's tomb; Virgil, *Georgics* 1.461-69, where darkness follows the death of Julius Caesar: "the sun will give you signs . . . after Caesar sank from sight, [the sun] veiled its shining face in dusky gloom, and a godless age feared everlasting night"; Plutarch, *Caesar* 69: "There was also the dimming of the sun's light"; this is a legend known to the Jewish people, as attested in Josephus, *Antiquities* 14.12.3 §309: "we believe the very sun turned away, as if it too were loath to look upon the foul deed against Caesar"; cf. Hyginus, *Fabulae* 88).

One more interesting detail might be mentioned. When Jesus finds no fruit on the fig tree, he curses it and it dies, withering "to its roots" (Mark 11:12-14, 20). The death of the tree adumbrates the fate of the fruitless temple establishment. Here we may have yet another deliberate parallel with the stories and rumors of the Roman emperors in the turbulent 60s. Just before each Julian emperor died, so the story goes, the laurel that he had planted would die. And finally, in 68 CE, just before Nero died — the last of the Julian emperors — the whole grove of laurels (originally planted by Augustus) "died from the root up" (Suetonius, *Galba* 1.1), signifying the end of the Julian line.

In his incipit, the Markan evangelist has deftly welded together the overlapping Jewish and Roman conceptions of "good news." He has, in effect, brought together disparate, but at points parallel, eschatologies.[23] But

---

23. In another study I have argued this point, particularly in reference to the Priene calendar inscription; cf. C. A. Evans, "Mark's Incipit and the Priene Calendar Inscription: From Jewish Gospel to Greco-Roman Gospel," *Journal of Greco-Roman Christianity and Judaism* 1 (2000) 67-81. See also S. Samuel, "The Beginning of Mark: A Colonial/Postcolonial

Mark also links his incipit, his declaration that Jesus is Son of God, to Isa 40:3 (and of course it is qualified by its conflation with Mal 3:1). By doing this, the evangelist places the whole of Jesus' life and ministry into the context of a famous passage, a passage that foretold the restoration of Israel.[24] The eschatological interpretation of Isaiah 40 is attested in several Jewish sources from late antiquity. Baruch's vision of Israel restored and renewed is full of echoes of the Isaianic passage:

> [5]Arise, O Jerusalem, stand upon the height and look toward the east, and see your children gathered from west and east, at the word of the Holy One, rejoicing that God has remembered them. [6]For they went forth from you on foot, led away by their enemies; but God will bring them back to you, carried in glory, as on a royal throne. [7]For God has ordered that every high mountain and the everlasting hills be made low and the valleys filled up, to make level ground, so that Israel may walk safely in the glory of God. [8]The woods and every fragrant tree have shaded Israel at God's command. [9]For God will lead Israel with joy, in the light of his glory, with the mercy and righteousness that come from him. (Bar 5:5-9)

Writing at about the same time, the sage Jesus ben Sira said of Isaiah: "By the spirit of might he saw the last things, and comforted those who mourned in Zion. He revealed what was to occur to the end of time, and the hidden things before they came to pass" (Sir 48:24-25). The reference

---

Conundrum," *Biblical Interpretation* 10 (2002) 405-19. Samuel rightly recognizes the two cultures or "codes" (i.e., Jewish and Roman) presupposed by the Markan evangelist, especially as seen in the incipit. For a review of the debate between Christians and non-Christian Romans over the lordship and divinity of Caesar, on the one hand, and Christ, on the other, see L. Koep, "Antikes Kaisertum und Christusbekenntnis im Widerspruch," in *Das frühe Christentum im römischen Staat* (ed. R. Klein; Wege der Forschung 267; Darmstadt: Wissenschaftliche Buchgesellschaft, 1971) 315-17.

24. P. Katz, "Wie einer der Propheten? Das biblische Markusevangelium als Darbietung eines 'Vorevangeliums,'" *TZ* 58 (2002) 46-60. Contrary to most interpreters, who think the quotation of Isa 40:3 has only John the Baptist in mind, Katz thinks the quotation refers to Jesus. In support of Katz is the fact that the quotation of Isa 40:3 clarifies the "good news of *Jesus Christ*" (not of John the Baptist). In my view, the appeal to Isa 40:3 is part of a broader, more encompassing theology that sees Isaiah 40 as foretelling the ministries of both John and Jesus, the former who cries out in the wilderness in a preparatory function and the latter who proclaims the "good news." John's wilderness summons corresponds with Isa 40:3, while Jesus' proclamation of the gospel corresponds with Isa 40:9.

to comforting those who mourned in Zion alludes to Isa 40:1, which is understood to be part of a vision of things that will occur "to the end of time."

In the book of *1 Enoch,* Isa 40:4 ("every mountain and hill be made low") provides the imagery for an eschatological vision of things to come:

> [5]And all shall be smitten with fear, and the Watchers shall quake, and great fear and trembling shall seize them unto the ends of the earth. [6]And the high mountains shall be shaken, and the high hills shall be made low, and shall melt like wax before the flame, [7]and the earth shall be wholly rent in sunder, and all that is upon the earth shall perish, and there shall be a judgement upon all. [8]But with the righteous He will make peace. And He will protect the elect, and mercy shall be upon them. And they shall all belong to God, and they shall be prospered, and they shall all be blessed. And He will help them all, and light shall appear unto them, and He will make peace with them. [9]And behold! He comes with ten thousands of His holy ones to execute judgement upon all, and to destroy all the ungodly: And to convict all flesh of all the works of their ungodliness which they have ungodly committed, and of all the hard things which ungodly sinners have spoken against Him. (*1 En.* 1:5-9)

The same passage from Isaiah contributes to the vision of the *Testament of Moses,* in which time God's kingdom will appear and Satan will finally be defeated:

> 1 And then His kingdom shall appear throughout all His creation,
>   And then Satan shall be no more,
>   And sorrow shall depart with him.
> 2 Then the hands of the angel shall be filled
>   Who has been appointed chief,
>   And he shall forthwith avenge them of their enemies.
> 3 For the Heavenly One will arise from His royal throne,
>   And He will go forth from His holy habitation
>   With indignation and wrath on account of His sons,
> 4 And the earth shall tremble: to its confines shall it be shaken:
>   And the high mountains shall be made low
>   And the hills shall be shaken and fall. (*T. Moses* 10:1-4)

All of this literature predates the publication of the Gospel of Mark. The eschatological interpretation of Isaiah 40 continues in the later rabbinic writings. In the present world, the glory of God is seen only by a select few, but "in the time to come" all will see it, as it says in Isa 40:5: "The glory of the Lord shall be revealed, and all flesh shall see it together" (cf. *Lev. Rab.* 1:14 [on Lev 1:1]). In another midrash (cf. *Deut. Rab.* 4:11 [on Deut 12:20]), the promise that Israel's borders will be enlarged will be fulfilled when God lifts up the valleys and levels the mountains (and Isa 40:4 is quoted). The midrash is further developed to include reference to Mal 3:23 ("Behold, I will send you Elijah the prophet") and 3:1 ("Behold, I send my messenger and he shall clear the way before Me"), as well as passages from Zechariah, including 9:9 ("Rejoice greatly, O daughter of Zion . . . behold, your king comes to you"). And finally, the eschatological orientation of Isaiah 40 is intensified in the Aramaic paraphrase (e.g., v. 1: "Prophets, prophesy . . ."). Moreover, the good news of Isa 40:9 becomes, in the Aramaic paraphrase, the joyous proclamation: "The kingdom of your God is revealed!" (cf. the Hebrew, which simply says, "Behold your God!").

Perhaps the most pertinent use of Isaiah 40 is found in the Dead Sea Scrolls, especially in the *Rule of the Community,* which speaks of the righteous, the founders of the community: "When such men as these come to be in Israel, conforming to these doctrines, they shall separate from the session of perverse men to go to the wilderness, there to prepare the way of truth, as it is written, 'In the wilderness prepare the way of the Lord, make straight in the desert a highway for our God' [Isa 40:3]" (1QS 8:12-14). The leader of the community, the Teacher of Righteousness, "shall save reproof — itself founded on true knowledge and righteous judgment — for those who have chosen the Way, treating each as his spiritual qualities and the precepts of the era require. He shall ground them in knowledge, thereby instructing them in truly wondrous mysteries; if then the secret Way is perfected among the men of the community, each will walk blamelessly with his fellow, guided by what has been revealed to them. That will be the time of 'preparing the way in the wilderness'" (1QS 9:17-20).[25]

25. On Isa 40:3 in 1QS, see J. A. Fitzmyer, "The Use of Explicit Old Testament Quotations in Qumran Literature and in the New Testament," *NTS* 7 (1960-61) 297-333, esp. 317-18; repr. in Fitzmyer, *Essays on the Semitic Background of the New Testament* (London: Geoffrey Chapman, 1971; repr. SBLSBS 5; Missoula: Scholars Press, 1974) 3-58, esp. 34-36; S. Talmon, "The 'Desert Motif' in the Bible and in Qumran Literature," in *Biblical Motifs* (ed. A. Altmann; Texts and Studies 3; Cambridge, MA: Harvard University Press, 1966) 31-63;

Isaiah 40:3 is alluded to in the opening lines of the War Scroll, which speak of "the exiles of the sons of light" who are "exiled to the wilderness" and who "camp in the wilderness" in preparation for the final battle against the "sons of darkness" (1QM 1:1-7, esp. lines 2-3). In the pesher on Psalm 37, the members of the community refer to themselves as the "penitents of the wilderness, who will live a thousand generations in virtue" (4Q171 1-3 iii 1). Finally, other portions of Isaiah 40 also play a part in Qumran's anticipated future scenario. Words and phrases from vv. 6-8 are woven into the fabric of a vision of judgment in 4Q185 1-2 i 4-13, while in 4Q165 (frags. 1-2), the fifth pesher on Isaiah, v. 11 is linked to the Teacher of Righteousness himself, who shepherds God's flock. It seems clear that the Qumran community took Isaiah's "in the wilderness" quite literally. Other groups and individuals did, too.

Indeed, the evocative power of Isaiah 40 may well have contributed to the actions taken by such men as Theudas (Josephus, *Antiquities* 20.5.1 §§97-98; cf. Acts 5:36) and others who summoned the hopeful into the wilderness for signs of deliverance. Josephus tells us that "impostors and deceitful men persuaded the crowd to follow them into the wilderness [ἐρημία]. For they said that they would show them unmistakable wonders and signs according to God's foreknowledge" (*Antiquities* 20.8.6 §168; *Jewish War* 2.13.4 §259). Although the public ministry of the unnamed Jewish man from Egypt came to an end at the Mount of Olives, after he promised his following that at his command the walls of Jerusalem would collapse, his movement seems to have had its beginning in the wilderness: "A charlatan, who had gained for himself the reputation of a prophet, appeared in the country, collected a following of about thirty thousand dupes, and led them by a circuitous route from the desert [ἐρημία] to the mount called of Olives" (*Jewish War* 2.13.5 §261). The Egyptian Jew's reputation as a prophet was probably due to the wilderness summons, which in turn was probably part of the fulfillment of the prophecy of Isaiah 40. The "highway" of God led from the wilderness to Jerusalem, with the expectation of entering the holy city. Although this man, as well as others like Theudas,

---

G. J. Brooke, "Isaiah 40:3 and the Wilderness Community," in *New Qumran Texts and Studies: Proceedings of the First Meeting of the International Organization for Qumran Studies, Paris 1992* (ed. G. J. Brooke and F. García Martínez; STDJ 15; Leiden: Brill, 1994) 117-32; J. H. Charlesworth, "Intertextuality: Isaiah 40:3 and the Serek ha-Yahad," in *The Quest for Context and Meaning: Studies in Biblical Intertextuality in Honor of James A. Sanders* (ed. C. A. Evans and S. Talmon; BIS 28; Leiden: Brill, 1997) 197-224.

was guided by exodus and Joshua typologies, it is probable that the great vision of Isaiah 40, itself influenced by exodus and wilderness imagery, made an important contribution.[26]

We have therefore evidence of two — not one — influential Old Testament prophecies that apparently motivated Jewish prophets and reformers of late antiquity to take action. One was Num 24:17, the passage to which Josephus in all probability alluded. This passage, which speaks of a "star" and "scepter," readily accommodates application to a royal personage, such as the enthroned Vespasian. The other passage was Isa 40:3 (and context), which provided the broader eschatological framework, in the light of which hopes of restoration and renewal could be worked out. Just as leaders of Qumran retreated to the wilderness, awaiting the arrival of the Messiah (cf. 1QS 9:11), whose appearance would fulfill Num 24:17 (cf. CD 7:19-21; 1QSb 5:27-29; 1QM 11:6-7), so other groups and individuals summoned the faithful to the wilderness, promising signs of salvation and, in some cases, offering themselves as fulfillments of messianic prophecies.

The Markan evangelist's citation of Isa 40:3, itself introduced by the quotation of Mal 3:1,[27] taps into a rich vein of scriptural and eschatological tradition. Mark's announcement of "good news" and, a few verses later, Jesus' proclamation of the "good news" as "the kingdom of God has come"

26. This argument has been convincingly made by D. R. Schwartz, *Studies in the Jewish Background of Christianity* (WUNT 60; Tübingen: Mohr [Siebeck], 1992) 29-43, esp. 37-38, aspects of which were anticipated in R. W. Funk, "The Wilderness," *JBL* 78 (1959) 205-14, esp. 210-11; M. Hengel, *The Zealots: Investigations into the Jewish Freedom Movement in the Period from Herod I until 70 A.D.* (Edinburgh: T&T Clark, 1989) 249-55.

27. The conflation of Mal 3:1 (Mark 1:2) and Isa 40:3 (Mark 1:3) testifies to the interpretive richness of the wilderness tradition (e.g., Mauser, *Christ in the Wilderness*, 80-82). Detailed study shows that, although the Old Greek has influenced part of the quotation, the conflation itself was facilitated by the common Hebrew phrase פנה דרך ("prepare the way"). We have here an instance of *gezera shawa*, by which two or more passages of Scripture are drawn together because of common vocabulary. The conflated quotation, which as a whole is attributed to Isaiah the prophet, derives from pre-Markan tradition (so R. A. Guelich, *Mark 1–8:26* [WBC 34A; Dallas: Word, 1989] 8). For discussion of the textual details, see I. Abrahams, "Rabbinic Aids to Exegesis," in *Essays on Some Biblical Questions of the Day* (ed. H. B. Swete; London: Macmillan, 1909) 163-92, here 178-79; K. Stendahl, *The School of St. Matthew and Its Use of the Old Testament* (ASNU 20; Lund: Gleerup; Copenhagen: Munksgaard; rev. ed., Philadelphia: Fortress, 1968) 47-54; Steichele, *Der leidende Sohn Gottes*, 52-77; Guelich, *Mark 1–8:26*, 7-8; and Watts, *Isaiah's New Exodus in Mark*, 61-71. The evangelist's ingenious contribution lies in linking it directly to the incipit and its allusion to the imperial cult.

(Mark 1:14-15) surely hark back to Isa 40:9, especially in the Aramaic paraphrase, which defines the "good news" as "the kingdom of your God has been revealed." The multivalent "good news" resonates with great significance in the ears of both Jews and Romans. For Jews it recalls the promises of Isaiah 40; for Romans it recalls the mythic traditions of the success of the ruler.

However, the Markan evangelist has explicitly declared that the good news begins with Jesus — not Vespasian — and that Jesus is the fulfillment of Jewish Scripture. Mark's Gospel thus begins with a bold challenge to the Roman cult of the emperor, including the widespread opinion that the newly enthroned Vespasian fulfilled Jewish Scripture.

Conclusion

The Gospel of Mark was written and circulated during an uncertain and fearful time. Christians had recently endured cruel persecution at the hands of Nero, at whose death the empire plunged into chaos during a time of war. After three failed emperors, Vespasian ascended to the throne, hailed as the new "son of God," divinely empowered, able to heal. Omens hinted at his coming; Jewish prophecy foretold it. Surely in this man the Roman world would once again stabilize and benefit from the "good news," which has now begun.

Not so, says the evangelist Mark. The good news begins with Jesus Christ, the true Son of God — the Son recognized by God himself at the baptism and later at the transfiguration, the divine Son who is fearfully recognized by the spirits, the Son who can heal great numbers of sufferers with a word or a touch.

The Markan Gospel spoke well to a particularly difficult and dangerous time, so well that it became the principal source for the evangelists Matthew and Luke, who in their respective ways broadened Mark's scriptural apologetic to speak to new difficulties and challenges.

Scripture Justifies Mission:
The Use of the Old Testament in Luke-Acts

STANLEY E. PORTER

Introduction

Explicit quotations of the Old Testament in Luke and Acts are plentiful, although not as numerous or frequent as quotations in Matthew or Mark. The UBS[3] counts twenty-seven explicit quotations of the Old Testament in Luke's Gospel and forty-five in the book of Acts.[1] The most frequent text used by the author (though see the discussion below) is that of the Septuagint, the Greek version of the Old Testament.[2] This usage of the Old Testament in Luke-Acts has generated a significant amount of scholarly writing, although not nearly as much, it would appear, as has been generated in discussion of usage in Matthew's or John's Gospels. In this discussion, two major questions are often raised regarding the use of the Old Testament in Luke and Acts, whether they are treated together or separately. The first question is, How is the Old Testament used? And the second is, Does this use reflect the perspective of the author or of another? Concerning Luke's Gospel, there is the added dimension of whether the usage may in some instances reflect usage by Jesus. In this paper, I wish first to discuss briefly several of the recent proposals regarding how the Old Testament is

---

1. UBS[3], p. 901. On questions of method in determining quotations — a topic too complex to explore in this paper — see S. E. Porter, "The Use of the Old Testament in the New Testament: A Brief Comment on Method and Terminology," in *Early Christian Interpretation of the Scriptures of Israel: Investigations and Proposals* (ed. C. A. Evans and J. A. Sanders; JSNTSup 148; SSEJC 5; Sheffield: Sheffield Academic Press, 1997) 79-96.

2. See C. A. Evans, *Luke* (Peabody, MA: Hendrickson, 1990) 5.

thought to be used, and by whom, before introducing my own proposal and treating two major quotations of Old Testament texts, one each in Luke and in Acts.

Recent Proposals Regarding the Use of the Old Testament in Luke and/or Acts

Since there are two major questions that are often discussed under this category — how the Old Testament is used and whether this reflects the perspective of the author or another — I will take them in turn.

The first question concerns how scholars have seen the Old Testament being used in Luke and Acts in previous research.[3] Henry Cadbury began contemporary discussion by seeing in Luke a prediction and fulfillment motif in which apologetic motives are served by a sense of divine necessity.[4] In many ways, this notion was continued in the work of, among others, Hans Conzelmann, who contended that Scripture provides evidence of promise and fulfillment according to the plan of God;[5] Paul Schubert, who is most closely associated with the "proof from prophecy" motif;[6] Jacque Dupont, who argues for the apologetic use of the Old Testament in Acts;[7] Nils Dahl, who focuses upon the figure of Abraham;[8] I. Howard Marshall, who relates the "proof from prophecy" motif to ques-

3. Like others who have used it, I am grateful to the survey offered by D. L. Bock, *Proclamation from Prophecy and Pattern: Lucan Old Testament Christology* (JSNTSup 12; Sheffield: JSOT Press, 1987) 27-37; and Bock, "Proclamation from Prophecy and Pattern: Luke's Use of the Old Testament for Christology and Mission," in *The Gospels and the Scriptures of Israel* (ed. C. A. Evans and W. R. Stegner; JSNTSup 104; SSEJC 3; Sheffield: Sheffield Academic Press, 1994) 280-307, where the discussion is brought up to date. I use his survey as the basis for my own.

4. H. J. Cadbury, *The Making of Luke-Acts* (New York: Macmillan, 1927; repr. London: SPCK, 1958) 303-5.

5. H. Conzelmann, *The Theology of St. Luke* (trans. G. Buswell; London: Faber & Faber, 1960) 149-62.

6. P. Schubert, "The Structure and Significance of Luke 24," in *Neutestamentliche Studien für Rudolf Bultmann* (ed. W. Eltester; BZNW 21; Berlin: Töpelmann, 1954) 165-86.

7. J. Dupont, "L'utilisation apologétique de l'Ancient Testament dans les discours des Actes," *ETL* 29 (1953) 289-327; repr. in Dupont, *Études sur les Actes des Apôtres* (LD 45; Paris: Cerf, 1967) 245-82.

8. N. Dahl, "The Story of Abraham in Luke-Acts," in *Studies in Luke-Acts* (ed. L. E. Keck and J. L. Martyn; Philadelphia: Fortress, 1966) 139-58.

tions regarding the historical Jesus;[9] Jacob Jervell, who sees Scripture used by Luke in a prophetic way;[10] Jack Sanders, who focuses upon Luke's view of the Jews;[11] Darrell Bock, who expands the notion of prophecy to include typology;[12] Craig Evans, who emphasizes messianic motifs and their fulfillment;[13] Charles Kimball, who focuses upon Jesus' exposition of the Old Testament;[14] and Mark Strauss, who develops Bock's reformulation.[15] This motif has been a controlling one in much discussion of the use of the Old Testament in Luke-Acts, so much so that it has been referred to as a consensus, and continues to be so, at least in English-language Luke-Acts scholarship.

A growing number of scholars in recent times, however, have reacted against this notion of the use of the Old Testament in Luke-Acts being focused on prophetic proof. Arnold Ehrhardt believes that the "proof from prophecy" motif was not a Lukan idea but belonged to pre-Lukan thought,[16] while H. H. Oliver questions that the motif was even present in Luke.[17] Martin Rese rejects the notion of the movement from prophecy to fulfillment,[18] Eric Franklin believes that eschatology has been replaced by

9. I. H. Marshall, *Luke: Historian and Theologian* (Grand Rapids: Zondervan, 1970) 121-22.

10. J. Jervell, "The Center of Scripture in Luke," in Jervell, *The Unknown Paul: Essays on Luke-Acts and Early Christian History* (Minneapolis: Augsburg, 1984) 122-37; Jervell, *The Theology of the Acts of the Apostles* (New Testament Theology; Cambridge: Cambridge University Press, 1996) 61-75.

11. J. T. Sanders, "The Prophetic Use of the Scriptures in Luke-Acts," in *Early Jewish and Christian Exegesis: Studies in Memory of William Hugh Brownlee* (ed. C. A. Evans and W. F. Stinespring; Atlanta: Scholars Press, 1987) 191-98.

12. Bock, *Proclamation,* 261-79.

13. C. A. Evans, "Prophecy and Polemic: Jews in Luke's Scriptural Apologetic," and "The Prophetic Setting of the Pentecost Sermon," both in C. A. Evans and J. A. Sanders, *Luke and Scripture: The Function of Sacred Tradition in Luke-Acts* (Minneapolis: Fortress, 1993) 171-211, 212-24.

14. C. A. Kimball, *Jesus' Exposition of the Old Testament in Luke's Gospel* (JSNTSup 94; Sheffield: Sheffield Academic Press, 1994) 200-201.

15. M. L. Strauss, *The Davidic Messiah in Luke-Acts: The Promise and Its Fulfillment in Lukan Christology* (JSNTSup 110; Sheffield: Sheffield Academic Press, 1995) 4-15.

16. A. Ehrhardt, "The Disciples of Emmaus," *NTS* 10 (1963-64) 182-201.

17. H. H. Oliver, "The Lucan Birth Stories," *NTS* 10 (1963-64) 206-26.

18. M. Rese, *Alttestamentliche Motive in der Christologie des Lukas* (SNT 1; Gütersloh: Gerd Mohn/Gütersloher Verlagshaus, 1969); Rese, "Die Funktion der alttestamentlichen Zitate und Anspielungen in den Reden der Apostelgeschichte," in *Les Actes des Apôtres: Tra-*

salvation history in Luke's writings,[19] and Charles Talbert attempts to go beyond the notion of prophecy from the Old Testament.[20] Nevertheless, these voices have not carried the day in Lukan studies, and, especially in recent work, the consensus has reasserted itself in Lukan studies, so that it is fair to say, I believe, that the idea of prophetic fulfillment of the Old Testament passages in Luke and Acts is a useful hypothesis to utilize in Lukan studies. Nevertheless, I wish to go further by arguing that two passages in particular are especially significant to this theme, in that they go to the heart of the purpose of each of their respective books.

The second question concerns whether this usage reflects the usage of the author of Luke or Acts, or of someone else. Most of the work that has been done has focused upon the author of the two-volume work and his apologetic agenda. Some have disputed that the author is the originator of this approach, such as is found in the study of Ehrhardt. It is only recently that scholars have concentrated — in particular in the study of Luke's Gospel — upon determining Jesus' own approach to the Old Testament, an approach found in the monograph by Kimball. There is no doubt that all of the usage is Lukan in the sense that it is part of what the author has chosen to include in his narrative, even if he is not the originator of the way in which it is used. The question really is whether the usage in Luke, especially that which occurs on the lips of such figures as Jesus, is also to be attributed to that speaker. I will attempt to answer that question when I treat the individual instances below.

The Use of Scripture as Supporting and
Promoting the Mission of Luke and Acts

As a result of this overall viewpoint, a number of passages have repeatedly come to the fore in previous studies of the use of the Old Testament in Luke-Acts. Apart from treatments that have been primarily concerned

---

ditions, rédaction, théologie (ed. J. Kremer; BETL 68; Gembloux: Leuven University Press, 1979) 61-79.

19. E. Franklin, *Christ the Lord: A Study in the Purpose and Theology of Luke-Acts* (London: SPCK, 1975).

20. C. H. Talbert, "Promise and Fulfillment in Lucan Theology," in *Luke-Acts: New Perspectives from the Society of Biblical Literature* (ed. C. H. Talbert; New York: Crossroad, 1984) 91-103.

with other topics — such as Lukan Christology or pneumatology, or even determining the text used by Luke — significant studies have focused upon Luke 9:51–18:14; Luke 22–23; Luke 24, especially v. 44; Acts 2; Acts 13; and Acts 15; among other passages. A study such as this one could approach the use of the Old Testament in Luke-Acts from one of several ways. At this point, not being concerned specifically with the textual type, I could concentrate upon all of the uses of the Old Testament in each book, offering some kind of brief running commentary that ties each of them together with what I perceive as the purpose of the work. There have been a few studies such as this.[21] Many of them discuss these passages not only in terms of philological questions but also in terms of the redactional tendencies of the book and the technique of the authors in their citations. Another approach would be to concentrate upon a few select passages. This is the tendency of many scholarly studies, with attention often being given to Luke 24:44.[22] What I wish to do in this study is to shift the critical focus slightly in concentrating upon two instances of usage of the Old Testament that appear near the beginnings of Luke and Acts and that, I believe, are fundamental for establishing the overall purpose of these entire respective works.

There has been some recent dispute over the unity of Luke and Acts.[23] Even though there is a possible generic shift from the biographical stance of Luke's Gospel to the historiographic purpose of Acts, these two genres are sufficiently closely related — and the other evidence for unity is so overwhelming, including the introductions[24] — that I will proceed from the standpoint that each is a volume of a two-volume work by the person we call Luke.[25] What is important about this discussion of unity is that I believe that the author utilizes the same pattern in both works to es-

21. E.g., Evans, "Prophecy and Polemic," 171-211.

22. Attention is also often given to Acts 1:8 as determinative for the book of Acts, but it does not cite the Old Testament either.

23. See the discussion in I. H. Marshall, "Acts and the 'Former Treatise,'" in *The Book of Acts in Its Ancient Literary Setting* (ed. B. W. Winter and A. D. Clarke; BAIFCS 1; Grand Rapids: Eerdmans, 1993) 163-82.

24. See L. C. A. Alexander, *The Preface to Luke's Gospel: Literary Convention and Social Context in Luke 1.1-4 and Acts 1.1* (SNTMS 78; Cambridge: Cambridge University Press, 1993).

25. There is no need here to discuss the identity of this figure, although I am convinced that the traditional ascription is correct.

tablish the purpose of the work and to establish the mission of Jesus and the church. In each instance, the author introduces early on in the book a key event, in which Scripture is central, as formative for the life and mission of the individuals involved. Central to these particular episodes are several factors. One is the focus upon individuals who are called upon to proclaim their mission and who, by doing so, establish the purpose of the book. Another is the central place that Scripture plays in such a scenario. An extended scriptural passage or composite scriptural passage is invoked that proves to be programmatic for the entire book. The themes and ideas that are adumbrated in the use of the Old Testament passage then turn out to be important concepts found throughout the rest of the work.

The Use of Isaiah 61:1-2 in Luke 4:18-19 and Its Implications

The first instance is Jesus' citing of Isa 61:1-2 in Luke 4:18-19 in the Nazareth synagogue. Several uses of Old Testament citations occur in Luke's Gospel before this event.[26] These include two incidental quotations in support of Jesus' presentation in the temple in Luke 2:23-24 (citing Exod 13:2, 12, 15; Lev 12:8), an extended quotation by John the Baptist in Luke 3:4-6 (citing Isa 40:3-5), and Jesus' brief responses to the devil during his temptation in Luke 4:4, 8, 10-11, 12 (citing Deut 8:3; 6:13; Ps 91:11-12; Deut 6:16). However, the usage in Luke 4:18-19 is significant for several reasons.[27] This is the first extended use of the Old Testament specifically by Jesus after the beginning of his public ministry. To this point in the narrative, the Old Testament has been cited either by the author, by John the Baptist, or by Jesus in staccato dialogue with the devil. Furthermore, this is the first sermon of Jesus in this Gospel. As a result, it has the character of an inaugural address. Along with this, there are both statements by Jesus that interpret the Old Testament quotation, and then the chronicled response by those who hear this address. All of these factors point to the significance of this initial sermon of Jesus, which is an exposition of an Old Testament passage.

26. See A. J. Köstenberger and P. T. O'Brien, *Salvation to the Ends of the Earth: A Biblical Theology of Mission* (NSBT; Leicester: Apollos/Downers Grove: InterVarsity, 2001) 111-15, within their discussion of Luke-Acts (pp. 111-59). I am grateful to Dr. Köstenberger for bringing his work to my attention.

27. On the context of usage here in the light of themes presented, see Strauss, *Davidic Messiah*, 219-24.

This episode, which gives us some idea of what a first-century syna-gogue service was like,[28] occurs in the Galilean town of Nazareth, where Je-sus was reared. The passage is generally thought to reflect the episode re-lated in Mark 6:1-6, although the Markan passage does not have the Old Testament quotation, and Luke places the event at the outset of Jesus' min-istry.[29] In the Lukan account, Jesus went to the synagogue on the Sabbath, as was customary, and, apparently after a reading from the Torah, Jesus stood (as was customary) to read a passage from the prophets. We do not know how fixed lectionary material in the prophets was at this stage,[30] but it appears that Jesus selected the passage he wished to read. It was from Isa 61:1-2, with a line from 58:6:[31]

> The Spirit of the Lord is upon me, because of which
> > he has anointed me to preach good news to the poor,
> > he has sent me to preach forgiveness to the captives and sight to
> the blind,
> > > to send out the oppressed in forgiveness [Isa 58:6],
> > > to proclaim the acceptable year of the Lord.
> > > > > > (Luke 4:18-19; my translation)

When everyone was watching Jesus, he then began his sermon — the prac-tice appears to have been to have a reading of Scripture and then an interpre-tation of it — with the declaration that "Today this Scripture is fulfilled in your ears."[32] So far so good, since the people thought that to this point he had done well, especially considering that he was Joseph's son, a local boy who had made good. Jesus went on, however, to point these words, which he has just declared to be fulfilled, away from Israel to those outside of Israel. At this point, the people in the synagogue became angry with him and wanted to kill him, and he walked through the crowd and went on his own way.

---

28. Evans, *Luke*, 73.

29. See, e.g., R. C. Tannehill, "The Mission of Jesus according to Luke," in *Jesus in Nazareth* (ed. W. Eltester; BZNW 40; Berlin: de Gruyter, 1972) 51-75, esp. p. 52. Issues raised by the fact that Luke cites Jesus speaking, but Mark does not, are discussed below.

30. See Kimball, *Jesus' Exposition*, 102, for discussion.

31. See Evans, *Luke*, 73. Evans notes that the passage is Isa 61:1a, b, d; 58:6d; 61:2a. Omitted are Isa 61:1c and 2b, c.

32. Many think that this is a summary of Jesus' interpretive sermon. See Kimball, *Je-sus' Exposition*, 133. But see below.

This episode, and especially the use of the Old Testament passage, has raised a number of critical questions. Initially, it seems as if his hearers react, not to the use of the Old Testament passage, but to Jesus' interpretation and application of it to those outside of Israel.[33] I believe that by examining a number of the issues connected with this passage we can understand the significance of the passage and the nature of the reaction that it generates, and how this passage sets the agenda for the entire Gospel of Luke.

The Form and Meaning of Isaiah 61:1-2 in Luke 4:18-19

There are two important questions regarding the quotation of Isa 61:1-2 in Luke 4:18-19. The first regards the form of the text, and the second regards the meaning of it.

A number of scholars have discussed the quotation and history of transmission of Isaiah 61 in Jewish thought and literature.[34] The quotation appears to reflect the Septuagint in most respects, although there are several noteworthy variances.

(1) Not all of Isa 61:1-2 is quoted, but only up to the first clause of v. 2. This is not so much a matter of noting variance as it is of noting (as some scholars do) that the words of judgment that follow are omitted.[35] This passage — whether it is by Luke or Jesus (see the discussion below) — appears to be either a summary of what Jesus said at greater length on the occasion, or an allusive passage that invokes many other motifs (also see below for further discussion). Because of this, it may well be that the theme of judgment is also included in what is being alluded to here, even if the wording is not cited explicitly, since Jesus includes it elsewhere in the Gospel (e.g., Luke 7:22-23; 18:7).[36] Certainly 11QMelch 2 (treated below), which alludes to Isaiah 61, makes mention of vengeance (2.13), and there appears

---

33. Many scholars have noted apparent differences in the response recorded in Mark. This will be considered below.

34. See J. A. Sanders, "From Isaiah 61 to Luke 4," in Evans and Sanders, *Luke and Scripture*, 46-69; Bock, *Proclamation*, 105-11.

35. E.g., Strauss, *Davidic Messiah*, 220.

36. Cf. J. Jeremias, *Jesus' Promise to the Nations* (SBT 24; London: SCM, 1958) 45-46, who argues that the reason the crowd reacts so strongly to Jesus is that he had left out the message of judgment.

to have been a view by the Qumran community, and hence within at least certain streams of Judaism, that vengeance and comfort went hand in hand with the coming of the Messiah.[37]

(2) In v. 18, the phrase in Isa 61:1 referring to healing those who are brokenhearted is omitted. There is some textual evidence for inclusion of the phrase, but the far stronger evidence is for its exclusion. This variant appears to have arisen as an attempt to fix a problem with the text. If this sermon itself is a summary, some of the text may have been omitted in this shortened form, including this phrase.

(3) The line from Isa 58:6 is added, but with the verb form altered from an imperative to an infinitive to fit the syntax. Kimball offers eight possible positions on why this phrase from Isa 58:6 was quoted here.[38] Several scholars have noted that the Isa 58:6 passage is conceptually linked to the Isa 61:1 passage around the word "forgiveness."[39] In the light of this, it is likely that there is some kind of midrashic uniting principle at work here. Some scholars think that this is a Semitically based midrash, but the linkage works only in Greek, not in Hebrew (where the words behind "forgiveness" are different).[40] This does not necessarily mean that the formulation is pre-Lukan or even Lukan. As James Sanders recognized in his treatment of this verse a number of years ago, Jesus himself may well have been the one who created the wordplay in Greek.[41]

(4) Finally, the verb is changed in v. 19 from "call" to "proclaim." Some have thought that the verb "proclaim" is a typically Lukan word, but it is not any more Lukan than it is Matthean or Markan.[42] Bock thinks that the use of the verb "proclaim" is traditional, but Evans thinks that it reflects a more poignant way of emphasizing the eschatological thrust of the passage.[43]

More important than these textual variants — as valuable as they

---

37. Evans, *Luke*, 74.

38. Kimball, *Jesus' Exposition*, 105.

39. Evans, *Luke*, 73-74. There is also linkage between Isa 58:5 and Isa 61:2 around "acceptable."

40. Bock, *Proclamation*, 106.

41. See Sanders, "From Isaiah 61," 66 n. 66; followed by Kimball, *Jesus' Exposition*, 107. A further factor to consider in support of the initial words being uttered in Greek — besides general linguistic competence of those of the Hellenistic world — is the thorough Hellenization of the Galilee, its higher rates of Greek literacy than other places in Palestine, and the fact that this episode is set in Galilee.

42. Bock, *Proclamation*, 316-17 n. 55.

43. Bock, *Proclamation*, 106; Evans, *Luke*, 74.

may be in establishing the final form — is the question of the nature of the kind of figure reflected in this passage who could be depicted with these characteristics. Kimball proposes that the passage supports a combined figure who is final eschatological prophet, messiah, and servant, to which, with Strauss, may be added a fourth, that of royal figure. The support for each of these is strong, and can be summarized briefly.[44]

(1) *Final eschatological prophet.* The reasons for seeing this passage as referring to the final eschatological prophet are several. (a) Isaiah 61 was connected with the year of Jubilee on the basis of the phrase in v. 1 regarding the proclaiming of release (see Lev 25:10; Jer 34:8, 15, 17).[45] This interpretation is confirmed by Isaiah 61 being linked to the year of Jubilee in 11QMelch 13.[46] 4Q521 1 ii 8 and 12 also allude to Isaiah 61, including their references to the release of prisoners.[47] Strauss believes that inclusion of Isa 58:6, a text also with Jubilee associations, further reinforces the strength of the reference to Jubilee in the passage quoted from Isa 61:1-2 in Luke 4.[48] In both 11QMelch 13 and Luke 4:18-19, Isa 61:1-2 is interpreted as being eschatological. (b) The anointing language seems to represent at the least the anointing of the prophet, and by transference Jesus. (Luke is the only writer apart from the author of Heb 1:9 who refers to Jesus' anointing, doing so also in Acts 4:27; 10:38.)[49] Reference to a prophet not being accepted in his hometown is explicit in Luke 4:24, and Elijah and Elisha are invoked as well in vv. 25-27.[50] (c) Finally, in numerous places elsewhere in Luke's Gospel Jesus is seen as a prophet (Luke 7:16, 39; 13:33-34; 24:19).

---

44. These, and arguments for each of them, are gleaned from Kimball, *Jesus' Exposition,* 111-12; and Strauss, *Davidic Messiah,* 226-33.

45. See Strauss, *Davidic Messiah,* 220 esp. n. 2. A. Strobel ("Die Ausrufung des Jobeljahres in der Nazarethpredigt Jesu; zur apokalyptischen Tradition Lc 4.16-30," in Eltester, ed., *Jesus in Nazareth,* 38-50, esp. p. 50) goes so far as to use the reference to Jubilee to date the passage.

46. This was shown by M. P. Miller, "The Function of Isa 61.1-2 in 11Q Melchizedek," *JBL* 88 (1969) 467-69. For recent treatment of the text, see C. A. Evans, *Jesus and His Contemporaries: Comparative Studies* (Leiden: Brill, 1996) 118-22; cf. Sanders, "From Isaiah 61," 56-57; Strauss, *Davidic Messiah,* 220-21.

47. See Evans, *Jesus and His Contemporaries,* 127, 128. Cf. F. García Martínez and E. J. C. Tigchelaar, *The Dead Sea Scrolls Study Edition* (2 vols.; Grand Rapids: Eerdmans, 1997, 1998) 1044, 1045.

48. Strauss, *Davidic Messiah,* 220 and n. 4.

49. Kimball, *Jesus' Exposition,* 102.

50. See Köstenberger and O'Brien, *Salvation to the Ends of the Earth,* 118.

(2) *Messiah.* (a) The suffering servant (see below) was seen to be messianic. (b) Reference in Luke 4:18 to anointing clearly has messianic implications in the light of what it is that the anointed one is called upon to proclaim. This is reinforced by the inclusion of the line from Isa 58:6. (c) According to 11QMelch, one of the duties of the Messiah was to proclaim the year of Jubilee.[51]

(3) *Servant.* (a) In 11QMelch 2, there is a linkage of Isa 61:1-2 with Isa 52:7. According to Evans, Isa 52:7 appears to be the beginning of the Suffering Servant Song (from 52:7 to 53:12), according to the ancient paragraph markers.[52] (b) Kimball has argued that Isa 61:1-3 is either a Suffering Servant Song or a midrash upon one.[53]

(4) *Royalty.* A number of arguments endorse this attribution as well. (a) Although the anointing language here is clearly prophetic, the references to anointing and the Spirit in the Old Testament occur only with reference to anointing a king (1 Sam 16:12-13; 2 Sam 23:1-2).[54] (b) Some scholars have noted that the content of Luke 4:18-19 matches ancient Near Eastern royal speeches. More than that, however, is the fact that the figure involved is seen to do more than simply proclaim but also to accomplish these actions. This royal action is especially pertinent to the release of captives. (c) The Jubilee references are linked to the king proclaiming the year of Jubilee. (d) Finally, the Melchizedek of 11QMelch 2 was seen to be a royal priestly personage.

It is difficult to decide among these four options as to who the figure depicted might be. Such a choice may be unnecessary, since the portrait that emerges implicates more than just these four individual characterizations of the personage involved. I think that it is worth considering whether there is a veiled reference to Jesus' divinity being made by this quotation as well, whether on the part of the Gospel writer or even, possibly, by Jesus himself in his use of it. The combination of the figures above could be seen to be pushing in this direction, since the figure depicted takes on the characteristics of more than simply a single figure; rather, he is a complex figure that encompasses messianic, eschatological, and royal enthronement elements. Some extra-biblical evidence also points in this direction. In 4Q521 1 ii 1-13, a passage noted above for its allusions to Isaiah

51. Evans, *Luke,* 75.

52. Evans, *Luke,* 74.

53. Kimball, *Jesus' Exposition,* 112, referring to E. E. Ellis (*The Gospel of Luke* [NCB; Grand Rapids: Eerdmans, 1974] 97) and Sanders ("From Isaiah 61," 49).

54. Cf. Strauss, *Davidic Messiah,* 230, 227-28.

61, the figure who is speaking and appropriating for itself the actions of Isaiah 61 appears to be God. The Messiah is mentioned specifically in line 1, with reference to the heavens and earth obeying him. Then, in line 5, the Lord is said to visit the pious. It is the Lord who will "glorify the pious ones on the throne of the eternal kingdom" and who will "release the captives, make the blind see, raise up the downtrodden," and (though this is not certain due to a lacuna in the manuscript) "heal the slain, resurrect the dead, and announce glad tidings to the poor."[55] In other words, there was a tradition in the Judaism of the time in which God himself was the one who was appropriating the proclamation and accomplishment of the actions of Isaiah 61. If the Scroll switches subjects in the lacuna — and this is not certain — then at the least the Messiah is depicted as performing the same kinds of actions that God himself also performs.

The crowd does not react immediately at this statement by Jesus, even when he says that this is fulfilled in their hearing, though they do get furious with him later. This delayed response has raised questions for scholars, many of whom see a contradiction and posit various source hypotheses.[56] I believe that there is a simpler way to explain the action of the narrative. The reason for the delayed reaction of the crowd is that to this point there is not a personal application of the passage by Jesus to himself. At the outset, he simply affirms that the passage stands fulfilled in their hearing.[57] When Jesus goes on to make clear that, by being the anointed one, he is the physician who is called upon to act in his hometown, and that he sees himself as not accepted, though a prophet (and a prophet is one of the depictions in the Isaiah passage), and he applies the application to those outside of Israel, then the crowd reacts furiously and seeks to kill him. The crowd hears not just a messianic claim (in itself not offensive to

55. See Evans, *Jesus and His Contemporaries*, 128, for translation; cf. p. 129, where he discusses whether the last statement does not suggest that the Messiah is now the subject of the verbs.

56. See Tannehill, "Mission of Jesus," 62-63.

57. The use of the perfect tense form conveys a stative aspect, indicating that the events depicted stand in a completed state. There is no implication from the verb of its necessarily being completed now or in Jesus himself. This sense comes from the narrative itself (e.g., emphatic placement of "today"; see I. H. Marshall, *The Gospel of Luke* [NIGTC; Grand Rapids: Eerdmans, 1978] 185). The emphasis is upon this particular Scripture being fulfilled. On the stative aspect, see S. E. Porter, *Idioms of the Greek New Testament* (BLG 2; 2nd ed., Sheffield: Sheffield Academic Press, 1994) 39-40.

many of the time) or a suffering servant claim (the imagery was already long familiar) or an eschatological prophetic claim (Israel had had many prophets, even if it did not always treat them well) or even a claim to royalty (this was often linked to a messianic claim) but quite possibly a veiled claim to divinity by quoting an Isaianic passage that was also linked to divine prerogatives. In fact, one could well argue that the force of the reaction against Jesus warrants the kind of claim that Jesus appears to be making regarding his divinity — that he is the Lord who is depicted by some Jewish traditions as fulfilling the pronouncements of Isaiah 61.

Did Jesus Utter These Words?

One of the critical issues that remains with this passage is whether it is possible that Jesus could have possibly uttered these words, especially since they seem so bold. As noted above, Mark 6:1-6, the possible source of this episode in the Synoptic tradition, does not have the quotation from Isaiah, which has led a number of scholars legitimately to ask whether the inclusion of the Old Testament quotation is Luke's interpretation of Jesus' actions as depicted in Mark. Others have thought that Luke may well have had access to other traditions that had this account.[58] Even though the passage cited is a mix of Isaiah 61 and 58, the passage may be a summary of what was said, or even possibly reflective of what Jesus is recorded as doing elsewhere — quoting conflated passages.[59] As noted above, one of the arguments used to dispute the authenticity of the quotation of Isaiah by Luke is that it appears that the quotation and the words of fulfillment, which appear to be accepted, fit awkwardly with the hostile response that soon follows. However, I think that when the statement and its gradual appropriation by Jesus are taken into account, the initial positive response giving way to the murderous reaction makes good sense of the passage. There are also so many other differences between the Markan and Lukan accounts that would not have been necessary for Luke to change that it indicates to many scholars that Luke had an independent tradition.[60] Fur-

---

58. See Tannehill, "Mission of Jesus," 52.
59. Jeremias, *Jesus' Promise,* 45-56.
60. Strauss, *Davidic Messiah,* 224-25. Strauss lists such things as the lack of verbal agreement and the distinctly Lukan characteristics.

thermore, there is no other explicit usage of this Old Testament passage in the entire New Testament. This indicates that there was no early church tradition to show that this was how Jesus was to be thought of, which Luke could have appropriated (or which was appropriated by others). There is the further consideration that, if what we know about the author of the Gospel is correct — that is, that he was a non-Jew from outside of Palestine — the level of knowledge of Palestinian Jewish literary interpretation and tradition, especially the parallel use of Scripture at Qumran, reflected by the episode points not only to an earlier tradition but also quite possibly to a tradition that could only have found initial articulation by Jesus.

Implications for the Use of the Old Testament as Programmatic for Jesus' Mission and the Purpose of Luke's Gospel

Scholars have long been agreed that Luke 4:18-19 is crucial for understanding Luke's Gospel.[61] I wish to go further and contend that this passage is a clear instance of prophetic fulfillment of the Old Testament as seen both by Luke and by Jesus, and that the passage itself provides guidance to both the major themes of the Gospel and Jesus' ministry. In other words, this passage uses the Old Testament to outline Jesus' mission and, hence, to describe the purpose of the Gospel itself. Several significant themes can be articulated.[62]

1. Jesus comes as Messiah, anointed by God's Spirit, and proclaiming a message of salvation (cf. Luke 7:21-22).[63] The opening of the passage proclaims that the Spirit of the Lord is upon this figure anointed in order to

61. See, e.g., Tannehill, "Mission of Jesus," 1, who begins his essay with these words: "By the scene at Nazareth with which he introduces his narrative of the ministry of Jesus, Luke intends to reveal to the reader certain fundamental aspects of the meaning of that ministry as a whole." He makes similar statements throughout the first two paragraphs of this important essay.

62. Here I use W. L. Liefeld, *Luke*, in The Expositor's Bible Commentary (vol. 8; ed. F. E. Gaebelein; Grand Rapids: Zondervan, 1984) 867; and Marshall, *Luke: Historian and Theologian*, 88-102, 124-28, as starting points for theological concepts and their representatives.

63. E.g., Strauss, *Davidic Messiah*, 337-43. In Luke, as well as Acts, this message of salvation may include more than simply spiritual salvation. See B. Witherington III, "Salvation and Health in Christian Antiquity: The Soteriology of Luke-Acts in Its First Century Setting," in *Witness to the Gospel: The Theology of Acts* (ed. I. H. Marshall and D. Peterson; Grand Rapids: Eerdmans, 1998) 145-66.

proclaim good news. The actions of Jesus, and the Gospel as a whole, confirm Jesus' messianic claim and endorsement.

2. Jesus comes as the suffering servant, who identifies with his people in their plight of oppression. Whether this passage was actually one of the Suffering Servant Songs, it appears to have been linked by Jewish literary usage of the time with the Isaianic suffering servant motif. The list of proclamations is addressed to those who are poor, captive, blind, and oppressed — in other words, those who are in need of God's salvific power. Jesus' suffering culminates in the crucifixion.

3. Jesus comes as the final eschatological prophet and proclaims the year of the Lord's favor upon his people. Jesus' identification with the anointing and with the words of the prophet Isaiah casts his work in a prophetic mode.[64] The last phrase, with its changed verb from "call" to "proclaim," its link to the Jubilee language, and the way that this language is used elsewhere (e.g., Luke 21), sets the entire passage in an eschatological context.

4. Jesus comes as the royal figure who, by implication, brings a message of the coming of God's kingdom.[65] The anointing, while certainly prophetic, goes beyond this to denote a royal figure who has the power to effect the proclamations. Even though the language of kingdom is not used explicitly here, it is used in other passages of the time (e.g., 4Q521) that allude to Isaiah 61.[66] Nevertheless, one of the implications of kingship is a kingdom.

5. Jesus comes as in fact God himself, as the one who both proclaims and accomplishes his purposes. The fact that the language of Isaiah 61 is being declared by the Lord in 4Q521 indicates that some Jews of the time viewed this figure as divine in nature. Jesus' explicit appropriation of a passage that has such possible implications accounts for the hostility shown to him. This motif finds its final expression in the declaration of the centurion (Luke 23:47).

---

64. The classic study that emphasizes Jesus' prophetic dimension is still G. W. H. Lampe, "The Holy Spirit in the Writings of St. Luke," in *Studies in the Gospels: Essays in Memory of R. H. Lightfoot* (ed. D. E. Nineham; Oxford: Blackwell, 1957) 159-200.

65. E.g., see A. R. C. Leaney, *A Commentary on the Gospel according to St. Luke* (New York: Harper, 1958) 34-37, who emphasizes Jesus Christ as king; cf. Strauss, *Davidic Messiah,* 337-43.

66. Contra some scholars, such as Marshall (*Luke: Historian and Theologian,* 125), who downplay the importance of kingdom.

6. The purposes of God are the salvation of a people, with the implicit and veiled message that judgment follows for those who are not his people.[67] The salvation message is clear from the passage quoted. The message of judgment that follows in Isa 61:2 was probably also being alluded to, especially since there is a sense of possible exclusion when Jesus says that non-Israelites will be included.

7. These people include those who go beyond the nation of Israel. Jesus' interpretation of the words of Isa 61:1-2 includes a message in which those who are outside of Israel are offered the liberation that he declares. From the outset of Luke's Gospel, the message of salvation is extended universally.

The Uses of Joel 2:28-32, Psalm 16:8-11, and Psalm 110:1 in Acts 2:14-36 and Their Implications

The opening of the second of Luke's two volumes begins likewise with a programmatic statement for the book. This occurs when Peter stands up and addresses the crowd in order to explain the behavior of his fellow disciples, and he explicitly cites Joel 2:28-32 (LXX 3:1-5) in Acts 2:17-21; Ps 16:8-11 in Acts 2:25-28; and Ps 110:1 in Acts 2:34-35.[68] As in Luke's Gospel, these extended quotations are not the first use of the Old Testament in the book.[69] In Acts 1:20, Peter uses two short quotations from the Old Testament in his instructions regarding the new disciple to replace Judas (Ps 69:25; 109:8). Though not the first quotation of the Old Testament, the quotations in Acts 2 are the first *sustained* quotations from the Old Testament. They appear in what Strauss calls the "first missionary proclamation of the apostles."[70]

In the narrative of the book of Acts, Jesus is taken up into heaven, leaving the disciples with word that the power of the Holy Spirit will come upon them, so that they will be witnesses in Jerusalem, Judea, Samaria, and

---

67. See Marshall, *Luke: Historian and Theologian*, 94-102; J. Nolland, "Salvation-History and Eschatology," in Marshall and Peterson, eds., *Witness to the Gospel*, 63-81, esp. p. 77.

68. There is also the allusive use of Old Testament language in Acts 2:30 and 31, the latter paraphrasing Psalm 16:10.

69. See Köstenberger and O'Brien, *Salvation to the Ends of the Earth*, 130-31.

70. Strauss, *Davidic Messiah*, 131.

to the ends of the earth (Acts 1:8). Then, after a successor to Judas is selected, on the day of Pentecost, the Holy Spirit fills those gathered together. Because of the events of the festival, there were many Jews in Jerusalem, and when they heard the Spirit-filled apostles speaking in tongues they at first suspected that they were drunk. In response, Peter addresses the crowd by saying that they are not drunk but that the prophet Joel speaks to their situation. The quotation from Joel includes a number of elements: the mention of pouring out of God's Spirit on all people, the appearance of various eschatological signs, and the extension of salvation to any who call on the name of the Lord. Peter then describes how the people of Israel treated Jesus of Nazareth, including his being handed over and put to death, but also his being resurrected. He then cites the second passage, from Ps 16:8-11. This passage depicts a figure who is not abandoned to the grave, as the speaker fears for himself, but one who is bodily resurrected. Peter goes on to relate this notion to David speaking of the resurrection of Christ, and to God exalting him to his right hand. Then Peter cites Ps 110:1, noting that David was not the one who ascended when he affirmed that the Lord said to his Lord to sit at his right hand — in other words, that God had made Jesus both Lord and Messiah. Traditionally, the speech is linked with the events of Pentecost in terms of the coming of the Holy Spirit and the speaking in tongues. There is no doubt that this is an important part of the context in which these words were uttered by Peter. However, clearly this is only one of the parts of the entire episode. When taken in combination, this set of three quotations of the Old Testament sets the agenda for the entire book of Acts.

There are two sets of issues to be addressed with regard to these passages, text-critical and theological, and they have relations that can be discussed together.

Textual Problems with Theological Significance

1. Joel 2:28-32 in Acts 2:17-21

Peter's initial use of the Old Testament reads as follows:

> And it will be in the last days, God says,
> I will pour out from my spirit upon all flesh,

> and your sons and your daughters will prophesy,
> and your youth will see visions,
> and your elders will dream dreams.
> And indeed upon my male slaves and upon my female slaves
> in the last days I will pour out from my spirit,
> and they will prophesy.
> And I will give omens in heaven above and signs upon the earth
> below,
> blood and fire and vapor of smoke.
> The sun will be changed into darkness
> and the moon into blood,
> before the great and glorious day of the Lord comes.
> And it will be that everyone who calls upon the name of the Lord
> will be saved.   (my translation)

Bock has surveyed the numerous text-critical problems connected with Joel 2:28-32. On the basis of several changes from the Septuagint text, some of which appear to be theologically motivated while others do not, he concludes that the passage reflects an earlier tradition.[71] This may be correct, although it may also be that Peter is interpreting a Septuagint passage for his audience in context. For my purposes, two textual variants are of special significance, and they both occur in the first line of the passage.

First, in Acts 2:17, the text of Acts according to Sinaiticus, Alexandrinus, and Bezae — a spread of texts over Alexandrian and Western witnesses — reads, "and it will be in the last days. . . ." The Masoretic Text and the Septuagint, followed by Vaticanus and 076 (fifth/sixth century), read, "and it will be after these things. . . ." Some scholars have defended the reading in Vaticanus and the Masoretic Text and Septuagint on the grounds that the later scribe would have changed the text to make it conform to the theological thrust of the passage.[72] Most scholars have not accepted this explanation, however, arguing that the Alexandrian corrector has tried to conform the text to the Masoretic Text and Septuagint.[73]

71. Bock, *Proclamation*, 163.

72. E.g., G. D. Kilpatrick, "Some Quotations in Acts," in Kremer, ed., *Les Actes des Apôtres*, 81-97, here p. 82; E. Haenchen, *The Acts of the Apostles: A Commentary* (Philadelphia: Westminster, 1971) 179.

73. E.g., B. M. Metzger, *A Textual Commentary on the Greek New Testament* (London: UBS, 1971) 293.

Therefore, the reading "in the last days" is probably correct — it certainly has far wider and generally earlier textual support. This reading clearly introduces an eschatological dimension to the passage at the outset, since it takes the Joel passage and relates it to the last days. More than that, this reading and its use in this context imply from the standpoint of Luke — and Peter, if he indeed did utter this statement (there is no good reason in my mind to doubt that he did) — that "the last days are upon us"; in other words, that the time of fulfillment of the Scriptures in the present context implies entering the period that culminates in the coming of the Day of the Lord.[74]

The second variant, also in Acts 2:17, is the addition of the words "God says." Neither the Masoretic Text nor the Septuagint ascribes the passage to a direct speaker, but some speaker is designated in the New Testament manuscripts. Bezae and Ephraim have "Lord," while Sinaiticus, Alexandrinus, and Vaticanus, as well as most other manuscripts, have "God." Clearly "God" is the better reading.[75] The Western tradition has probably changed the text to "Lord" to conform to Old Testament reference to God. However, the effect of either reading is really the same. The clear implication of this textual addition is the ascription of the passage not only to the prophet — that is a given in the light of the acknowledgment that this was what was spoken by Joel the prophet (Acts 2:16) — but to God himself (or the Lord, who is God) as the speaker of it. This is a direct word from God.[76]

2. Psalm 16:8-11 (LXX 15:8-11) in Acts 2:25-28

This passage reads as follows:

> I have seen the Lord before me always,
>> because he is at my right so that I might not be shaken.
> On account of this my heart has been made to rejoice and my
>> tongue is glad,
>> but still my flesh indeed will dwell in hope.
> Because you will not abandon my spirit into hades,

---

74. Bock, *Proclamation*, 161; R. P. Menzies, *The Development of Early Christian Pneumatology with Special Reference to Luke-Acts* (JSNTSup 54; Sheffield: Sheffield Academic Press, 1991) 215.

75. So most commentators; contra Kilpatrick, "Some Quotations in Acts," 96.

76. See Menzies, *Development of Early Christian Pneumatology*, 217.

> nor will you give your holy one to see decay.
> You have made known to me ways of life,
>> you will fill me with joy with your face.   (my translation)

There are no significant textual variants in Ps 16:8-11 that have bearing upon this paper.[77] The passage cited clearly conforms to the text of the Septuagint. What is important to note here is that the Septuagint text is followed, which raises the question in some scholars' minds of whether the passage being cited makes the same sense in the Hebrew as it does in Greek — especially since there are a number of places where the Septuagint is apparently different from the Hebrew text. As Bock notes, three of the changes do not carry theological significance here, but three of the changes are important: reference to living "in hope" rather than "in security" (v. 26), mention of "decay" rather than "the pit" (v. 27), and use of "ways of life" rather than "a well-pleasing life" (v. 28).[78] The first change adds an eschatological dimension, while the second indicates, if not a full "*bodily* resurrection," at least a "*bodily* preservation." The third introduces the idea of eternal life, since that is what the phrase "ways of life" means in the Septuagint.[79] Significant is the fact that the Septuagint translator also apparently found this reference to bodily resurrection — or at least understood it in this way — in the Masoretic Text, since he chose to translate the Hebrew in such a way to emphasize this potential dimension in his Greek rendering.[80] Not only is an eschatological dimension further encouraged by such changes, therefore, but, as Bock points out, there is now a clear reference in the text to a bodily resurrection.

3. *Psalm 110:1 in Acts 2:34-35*

This text reads as follows:

> The Lord said to my Lord,
> Sit at my right
>> until I might put your enemies under your feet.   (my translation)

77. See Bock, *Proclamation*, 171-72, on the one variant.
78. Bock, *Proclamation*, 172-77.
79. Bock, *Proclamation*, 176.
80. Bock, *Proclamation*, 177. I do not agree with Bock that the meanings suggested here are necessarily simply derived from the Hebrew text (p. 176); rather, they are indicated in the Greek text on the basis of this interpretation of the Hebrew text.

The issue with the citation of Ps 110:1 is whether Ps 68:19 stands in the background of citation of this passage,[81] and hence whether there is reference here to the giving of the law by Moses. Most scholars do not think so.[82] Hence, there is not a Moses typology being created here, but it is Jesus, the one who pours out the Spirit (v. 33; attributed to God in Acts 2:18),[83] who is seen to sit at God's right hand and who exercises divine power as the already enthroned Messiah.[84] This is what is meant by Peter's stating further that God made Jesus both Lord and Christ.[85]

Implications for the Use of the Old Testament as Programmatic for the Purpose of Acts

A number of themes are introduced by quotation of these Old Testament passages that provide a programmatic introduction to the major themes of Acts and define the mission and purpose of the book.[86] These include the following.

1. God is clearly at work through Jesus Christ, who is bringing the Holy Spirit. God is the one speaking through Joel and the authors of the other passages to declare what he is doing in the world. This action involves Jesus Christ in particular, but also the Holy Spirit. The interplay of the work of Jesus Christ and the Holy Spirit is one of the most important — and widely written about — themes in the entire book of Acts.

81. According to one of the most recent advocates, the most thorough defense is offered by J. Dupont, "Ascension du Christ et don de l'Esprit d'après Actes 2.33," in *Christ and Spirit in the New Testament* (ed. B. Lindars and S. S. Smalley; Cambridge: Cambridge University Press, 1973) 219-27, esp. pp. 226-27. The recent advocate is M. Turner, *Power from on High: The Spirit in Israel's Restoration and Witness in Luke-Acts* (JPTSS 9; Sheffield: Sheffield Academic Press, 1996) 287-88.

82. See Strauss, *Davidic Messiah*, 145-46. This includes those identified with the Pentecostal movement, such as Menzies, *Development of Early Christian Pneumatology*, 229-44.

83. See H. D. Buckwalter, "The Divine Saviour," in Marshall and Peterson, eds., *Witness to the Gospel*, 107-23, esp. p. 115.

84. See I. H. Marshall, *The Acts of the Apostles* (TNTC; Grand Rapids: Eerdmans, 1980) 80.

85. Cf. Bock, *Proclamation*, 184-85; Strauss, *Davidic Messiah*, 144-45.

86. See J. D. G. Dunn, *Jesus and the Spirit: A Study of the Religious and Charismatic Experience of Jesus and the First Christians as Reflected in the New Testament* (Grand Rapids: Eerdmans, 1997 [1975]) 153.

2. Jesus Christ, who did not see the bodily decay of the grave, but was resurrected to life, is seen further as the Messiah who is exalted to the side of God himself, when he is enthroned at God's right hand, so much so that he is himself addressed as Lord, that is, God.[87]

3. The coming of the Holy Spirit is seen as marking the entering of the "last days." With the coming of the Holy Spirit come such things as the speaking in tongues and various other signs and wonders to mark this eschatological period that will culminate in the Day of the Lord.

4. This message of the coming of the Holy Spirit is one of salvation for all people who call upon the name of the Lord.[88] Salvation language has long been noticed as a distinctive element of Luke-Acts, and for Acts it is established early on in Peter's quotation of Joel, and then continued throughout the book.[89] What is meant by all people seems to encompass those of every nation, of both genders, of any age, and of no particular social or society class. The Spirit is poured out on all equally.

Conclusion

In this conclusion, I run the risk of introducing new ideas, when I suggest that these two sets of themes from Luke and Acts can be brought together to show a continuity between Luke and Acts around their common theology.[90] A mere listing of some of the common themes will have to suffice. These include — but are not limited to — the divine enthronement of Jesus, God's appointed Messiah and prophet, the work of the Holy Spirit as in some way empowering and extending the mission and message of Jesus,[91] and the proclamation of a message of universal salvation. More important

87. He also pours out the Holy Spirit (see Acts 2:33).

88. See Evans, "Prophetic Setting," 212. Cf. J. H. E. Hull, *The Holy Spirit in the Acts of the Apostles* (London: Lutterworth, 1967) 73, who rightly notes that in the original context those referred to by Joel would probably have been those of Israel.

89. See J. B. Green, "'Salvation to the End of the Earth' (Acts 13:47): God as Saviour in the Acts of the Apostles," in Marshall and Peterson, eds., *Witness to the Gospel*, 83-106, esp. p. 86.

90. See, e.g., Turner, *Power from on High*, 290-303; and Green, "'Salvation to the End,'" esp. 93.

91. To the point that some wish to see the Holy Spirit as a character in its own right. See W. H. Shepherd Jr., *The Narrative Function of the Holy Spirit as a Character in Luke-Acts* (SBLDS 147; Atlanta: Scholars Press, 1994).

for this paper, however, is the realization that these major themes, which it is agreed are found in the citation of Isa 61:1-2 in Luke 4:18-19 and the citation of the complex of Old Testament passages in Acts 2:14-36, are introduced, explicated, and/or developed within Luke and Acts through Scripture. Luke is not unique in relying upon Old Testament texts to formulate his theology, but "Scripture is used to give shape to the narrative."[92] In that sense, we see that the notion of fulfillment of scriptural texts seen as prophetically uttered is a fundamental hermeneutical principle in Luke-Acts.

92. Evans, "Prophetic Setting," 223.

"They Saw His Glory and Spoke of Him": The Gospel of John and the Old Testament

PAUL MILLER

Early Christian Exegesis

Between the resurrection of Jesus and the writing of the Gospels, the early Christians busied themselves with a complex process of interpreting, assimilating, and adapting the primitive traditions of Jesus that had been passed on to them. Through preaching, teaching, and prophesying, through liturgy and catechesis, the church both encountered the living Christ and answered the question "Who is Jesus?" at deepening levels of comprehension.

Exegesis of Scripture was an indispensable tool in this "Christology in the making." Biblical study and christological reflection were dynamically related and mutually enriching. Faith in the risen Christ guided their approach to the Scriptures, and their interpretations of Scripture informed their understanding of Jesus. I want to explore this interrelationship between Scripture and Christology as it pertains to the Gospel of John. I am a historian and theologian by training and a pastor and preacher by trade, and I will approach the task at hand as such. This is appropriate, however, because the Fourth Gospel, like most of the New Testament, does not differentiate sharply among exegesis, theology, and pastoral concerns. John interpreted Scripture (exegesis) so he could better proclaim Jesus the Way, the Truth, and the Life (theology); but he did so with a pastoral burden for a community struggling to affirm Christ's lordship in the face of determined opposition and competing truth claims. Is it any different today? Christians must wrestle practically with what it means to follow the one who was God's Word made flesh in a radically pluralistic environment. This raises vexing issues, and yet it is a claim that Christians cannot evade. I will be arguing that Christ was John's primary hermeneutical principle in whose light the Scriptures of Israel were to be properly construed. Because this approach raises such problems, I will follow an exploration of John's treatment of Scripture with some reflections on what it all means today.

Christological Function Determines Form

John's use of Scripture was guided by his Christology. We can see this when we examine seemingly technical, non-theological matters such as his selection of biblical texts. Whether drawing on passages common to the New Testament tradition, like Isa 6:9-10 (John 12:40) or Ps 22 (19:24), or highly unusual texts like Zech 12:10 (19:37), Christology was the determining factor. The apparently straightforward question of how John made use of Scripture in his presentation of Jesus the Messiah conceals a world of complexities. Issues of translation, tradition, and intertextuality lead directly to deeper christological and theological concerns.

For example, we might start with the seventeen or so instances in which John quotes Scripture explicitly and ask, When John quotes the Bible, which "Bible" does he quote? John uses those texts and versions that serve his christological purposes. He quotes often from the Greek, but at least once from the Hebrew against the Greek (19:37), indicating his familiarity with the Hebrew text and his facility in its use.[1] There is evidence that John knew the Aramaic Targums.[2] However, in several cases his quo-

---

1. John 19:37 quoting Zech 12:10. See C. K. Barrett, *The Gospel according to St. John: An Introduction with Commentary and Notes on the Greek Text* (2nd ed.; Philadelphia: Westminster, 1978) 28.

2. For example, Raymond Brown notes that the MT of Deut 18:19 says that God will take vengeance on the one who does not listen to the prophet, while Targums *Neofiti I* and *Pseudo-Jonathan* say that the word *(memra)* itself will take vengeance. This is reflected in John 12:48: "that very word which I spoke will condemn him in the last day" (*The Gospel according to John* [2 vols.; AB 29, 29A; Garden City, NY: Doubleday, 1970] 1:492). See also Barrett, *John*, 29; Craig A. Evans, *Word and Glory: On the Exegetical and Theological Background of John's Prologue* (Sheffield: Sheffield Academic Press, 1993) 158; Martin McNamara, *Targum and Testament: Paraphrases of the Hebrew Bible: A Light on the New Testament* (Shannon, Ireland: Irish University Press, 1972) 142-59.

tations depart from all known versions; and in at least two instances (7:38 and 17:12) he cited a reference so obscure that generations of scholars have been kept busy trying to figure out exactly what he is quoting. As with other New Testament exegetes, function determines form in John's use of Scripture. The text was a tool for illuminating some aspect of Christology, and John picked the version that best supported his purpose. Frequently, he altered or adapted the wording if it would bring out his point more clearly.[3]

This phenomenon of textual variance is characteristic of Jewish exegetical practice, with which John was certainly familiar. It is now a commonplace that the early Christian exegetes inherited and adapted forms of Jewish Scripture study. Early rabbinic scholarship attempted to "contemporize" the Scriptures to make them relevant to the concerns of the first century.[4] The rabbis did this in often ingenious ways. The early church adopted Jewish approaches, especially the method broadly referred to as *midrash,* which refers to the practice of commenting on Scripture in order to bring out meanings latent within the text. Close study of the New Testament shows many places where authors quote an Old Testament text and then follow it with an exposition according to a pattern found in rabbinic exegesis.[5] For example, John 6 has been read as an extended midrash on Ps 78:24, "He gave them bread from heaven to eat." But while Christians and Jews shared a general desire to make Scripture meaningful to a new situation, they had fundamentally different aims. The rabbis wanted to use both the narrative (haggadic) and legal (halakic) traditions of the Torah to shape Jewish identity and practice in a rapidly changing context. Christians wanted to show that Scripture anticipated Jesus, and they used biblical interpretation in their controversy with the synagogue to demonstrate that their claims on behalf of Jesus were supported by the very Word of God.

---

3. E. Earle Ellis, *Prophecy and Hermeneutic in Early Christianity: New Testament Essays* (Tübingen: J. C. B. Mohr, 1978) 148; Bruce G. Schuchard, *Scripture within Scripture: The Interrelationship of Form and Function in the Explicit Old Testament Citations in the Gospel of John* (Atlanta: Scholars Press, 1992) xvi.

4. Ellis, *Prophecy and Hermeneutic,* 151, referring to the seminal article on "Midrash" by Renée Bloch in *Supplément au dictionnaire de la Bible* (ed. by L. Pirot, A. Robert, and Henri Cazelles; Paris: Librairie Letouzey et Ané, 1957); Jacob Neusner, *Invitation to Midrash* (San Francisco: Harper & Row, 1989) vii, 141-42.

5. Ellis, *Prophecy and Hermeneutic,* 155-59.

The Dead Sea Scrolls show the prevalence in the first century of that peculiar form of midrash known as *pesher,* which "receives its name from the Hebrew word used in the explanatory formula, 'the interpretation *(pesher)* is.'"[6] *Pesher* exegesis is first and foremost eschatological because it assumes that the text contains a hidden meaning that is uncovered only in events occurring in the time of the interpreter, indicating that the interpreter is living at the climax of history.[7] The purpose of *pesher* exegesis is to find concealed eschatological mysteries beneath the surface of the biblical word. Throughout the New Testament we find evidence of *pesher* type exegesis as the early church sought to demonstrate that the prophetic meaning of Scripture was fulfilled in the life, death, and resurrection of Jesus.[8] Christ was a mystery hidden for long ages but in the fullness of time made known to the world.[9] John does not tend to follow the *pesher* technique formally by explicitly spelling out that the proper interpretation of a given text is such-and-such, but he certainly moves within the same conceptual orbit of promise and fulfillment as the practitioners of *pesher* exegesis.[10] The quotations in the latter part of the Gospel, 19:28-29, for example, are intended to show that Christ's Passion was not the failure of God's Word, as it seemed, but its fulfillment.

Another feature of Johannine exegesis is his distinctive use of formulae to introduce his Scripture quotations. Introductory formulae did not originate with John but were widespread in the Old Testament, Qumran, Philo, and among the rabbis.[11] Matthew and John, alone among the four Gospels, use standardized formulae to introduce scriptural quotations. However, even this technique, whose repetitiveness might suggest a lack of imagination, is a subtle theological tool in John's hand. We can illustrate this by noting that John's introductory formulae change at a certain point in his narrative. Structurally, the Gospel of John falls into two main sections — chapters 2 to 12, and chapters 13 to 20 — with a Prologue (chapter

---

6. Ellis, *Prophecy and Hermeneutic,* 160.

7. Richard N. Longenecker, *Biblical Exegesis in the Apostolic Period* (2nd ed.; Grand Rapids: Eerdmans, 1999) 139.

8. Ellis, *Prophecy and Hermeneutic,* 160.

9. This understanding of Scripture is stated clearly in Rom 16:25-26.

10. John Painter, "The Quotation of Scripture and Unbelief in John 12:36b-43," in *The Gospels and the Scriptures of Israel* (ed. Craig A. Evans and W. Richard Stegner; Sheffield: Sheffield Academic Press, 1994) 430.

11. Ellis, *Prophecy and Hermeneutic,* 148.

1) and epilogue (chapter 21) added.[12] The first section (2–12) deals with Je-sus' public ministry when the Word made flesh appeared in Galilee and Judea. During this time, Jesus performed signs that pointed to his true identity as the revealer of God, the light come into the darkness, and, more important, that confronted the world with a choice whether to receive that light or to reject it. In these chapters, biblical quotations are introduced with the words "It is written," "as the Scripture says," or something simi-lar.[13] According to E. E. Ellis, this particular formula was employed to "in-troduce an eschatological . . . summation or elaboration of the Old Testa-ment," or to imply "that the revelational 'Word of God' character of Scrip-ture is present within the current interpretation."[14] During the period of Jesus' ministry in which his claim to be the light of the world was being ad-vanced and tested, Scripture itself functions as a kind of sign pointing ahead to the appearance of the Word.[15] It is a proleptic announcement of what is to come that carries the stamp of divine authority. After chapter 12, however, when Jesus has been completely abandoned by the world and is preparing to go to the cross, the formula changes to "in order to fulfill."[16] In chapters 13–20, Jesus glorifies the Father, and the Father glorifies Jesus as he embraces fully his mission of love and is lifted up on the cross. John is telling us that, once the chain of events leading to the crucifixion is set in motion, the role of Scripture changes. Scripture does not only point to Je-sus but is fulfilled in two senses: first, its meaning is fully disclosed in Christ; and secondly, it is completed, superseded, and even replaced by the living words of Jesus.[17] The true meaning of Scripture cannot be found within the text itself, but only in its fulfillment in Jesus and in the sending of the Spirit. Through the rather workaday editorial device of the intro-ductory formula, then, John deepens and expands his christological vision.

12. C. H. Dodd calls the two principal sections "The Book of Signs" and "The Book of the Passion" (*Interpretation of the Fourth Gospel* [Cambridge: Cambridge University Press, 1963]). Raymond Brown calls them "The Book of Signs" and "The Book of Glory" (*The Gos-pel according to John*).

13. 1:23; 2:17; 6:31; 6:45; 7:38; 7:42; 10:34; 12:14-15.

14. Ellis, *Prophecy and Hermeneutic*, 148.

15. The relation of Scripture to signs in the Fourth Gospel will be taken up in more detail below.

16. 12:38; 13:18; 15:25; 17:12; 19:24; 19:28; 19:36.

17. Judith Lieu, "Narrative Analysis and Scripture in John," in *The Old Testament in the New Testament: Essays in Honour of J. L. North* (ed. Steve Moyise; Sheffield: Sheffield Ac-ademic Press, 2000) 158.

Barnabas Lindars has compared Matthew's and John's use of formal quotations. He argues that Matthew took stock texts from the tradition and applied them in a merely "pictorial" manner without exploiting their full theological potential. Matthew, he says, might quote a text simply on the basis of a common catchword, for example, or a merely semantic resonance. For example, he uses Isa 7:14 ("Behold, a virgin shall conceive and bear a son," Matt 1:23) mainly because the word "virgin" illustrates his account of Jesus' conception and birth without adding anything of true christological substance.[18] John, Lindars argues, deals with Scripture on a more sophisticated level. For instance, in 19:33-36, John tells us that the soldiers came to break Jesus' legs to hasten his demise but found him already dead. This was in order to fulfill Exod 12:46: "Not one of his bones shall be broken." This is not an arbitrary proof text, but a significant contribution to John's Christology. The original verse from Exodus refers to the Passover lamb. When John brings the verse into proximity with his Passion narrative, it exerts a powerful centrifugal pull, drawing a whole constellation of biblical imagery to itself, declaring that Christ is the true Passover lamb without blemish, with all that that association implies. Whether Lindars is being entirely fair to Matthew or not, he is certainly right about John. As this example demonstrates, each of the relatively small number of explicit quotations in the Fourth Gospel is a tiny window opening onto the vast panorama of the biblical story. John is such a skilled exegete that he can use a mere fragment of biblical texts as a kind of exegetical magnet, attracting whole clusters of other texts and themes to it.

However, John's use of Scripture goes well beyond explicit quotations. Compared to Matthew, for instance, John quotes Scripture relatively infrequently. However, none of the other evangelists has assimilated the overall sweep of the biblical story as completely as John. C. K. Barrett noted this over fifty years ago. No other New Testament book, Barrett argues, exceeds John in its thorough incorporation of the Bible from start to finish:

> the evangelist had a wide knowledge of the Old Testament but . . . he used it, not in the primitive Christian manner of citing proof texts but as a whole. . . . For him, the OT was itself a comprehensive unity, not a mere quarry from which isolated fragments might be hewn. . . . The

18. Barnabas Lindars, *New Testament Apologetic* (London: SCM, 1961) 259-65.

whole body of the OT formed a background, a framework, upon which the new revelation rested.[19]

John's Gospel is permeated by the great themes of salvation history narrated in the Scriptures, a fact that we could miss if we confine our attention to the relatively small number of explicit quotations. Jesus, according to John, discloses the true and full meaning of such biblical motifs as creation, the Exodus, the Jewish feasts, the Jacob tradition, the motif of the shepherd, and divine wisdom.[20]

John's Hermeneutics

These observations outline the basic contours of John's use of Scripture. However, we can pursue the matter even deeper by inquiring into John's underlying hermeneutical presuppositions. Technical questions of method lead us to John's understanding of the nature of Scripture itself. Like all New Testament writers, John believed that Scripture had divine authority. However, I would argue that the manner in which John spelled out his particular understanding of the relation of Scripture to Christ is distinctive.

19. C. K. Barrett, "The Old Testament in the Fourth Gospel," *JTS* 38 (1947) 168.

20. On creation, see E. C. Hoskyns, "Genesis i–iii and St. John's Gospel," *JTS* 21 (1920) 210-18; Calum M. Carmichael, *The Story of Creation: Its Origin and Its Interpretation in Philo and The Fourth Gospel* (Ithaca, NY: Cornell University Press, 1996). On the Exodus, see Wayne A. Meeks, *The Prophet-King: Moses Traditions and Johannine Christology* (Leiden: Brill, 1967); Peder Borgen, *Bread from Heaven* (Leiden: Brill, 1965); T. F. Glasson, *Moses in the Fourth Gospel* (London: SCM, 1963); Jacob J. Enz, "The Book of Exodus as a Literary Type for the Gospel of John," *JBL* 76 (1957) 208-15. On the Jewish feasts, see Gale A. Yee, *Jewish Feasts and the Gospel of John* (Wilmington, Del.: Michael Glazier, 1989). On the Jacob tradition, see Ellen B. Aitken, "At the Well of Living Water: Jacob Traditions in John 4," in *The Interpretation of Scripture in Early Judaism and Christianity* (ed. Craig A. Evans; Sheffield: Sheffield Academic Press, 2000) 342-52. On the shepherd motif, see Johannes Beutler and Robert T. Fortna, eds., *The Shepherd Discourse of John 10* (Cambridge: Cambridge University Press, 1991). On divine wisdom, see Sharon H. Ringe, *Wisdom's Friends: Community and Christology in the Fourth Gospel* (Louisville, KY: Westminster/John Knox, 1999). When looked at from the perspective of broad themes, John's use of Scripture resembles not so much that of Matthew but of the Apostle Paul (see E. Earle Ellis, *Paul's Use of the Old Testament* [Edinburgh: Oliver and Boyd, 1957] 11).

I want to start with three fascinating and unusual verses that give us an initial clue to John's understanding of Scripture:

5:46: "If you believed Moses, you would believe me, *for he wrote about me.*"

8:56: "Your father Abraham *rejoiced to see my day; he saw it and was glad.*"

12:41: "Isaiah said this because *he saw his [Jesus'] glory and spoke of him.*"

We will deal with these texts in detail below, but note the prevalence of verbs of seeing and of making known ("speaking" or "writing"). This suggests a dynamic interaction of seeing and testifying, of vision and witness. "John affirms that the Word, through whom creation had its being, was revealed to Moses and the Prophets."[21] But that Word is rightly understood only by those who see that it refers to the Logos who was manifested most completely in Jesus. In fact, Scripture is not really the direct self-disclosure of the Father, but testimony to the Son whom the Father has made known. The witness of Scripture, though true, cannot be anything but partial and provisional; and those who read it truthfully must realize that "Moses and the prophets bear witness to Jesus."[22] John shares with the other New Testament writers this basic understanding of "the christologically founded *unity* of the Scriptures";[23] but he is unique in the way he makes this hermeneutic explicit. John's hermeneutic could be stated briefly like this: *Scripture is the enduring record of those who saw the activity of the divine Logos prior to its appearance in Jesus and then testified to what they had seen.* What John says of the prophet Isaiah in 12:41 is true of all Old Testament witnesses: they saw Christ's glory and spoke of him.

"Seeing" in the Fourth Gospel

If the above definition of John's understanding of Scripture is valid, we need to consider how he uses vision as an epistemological and theological

21. John Painter, *The Quest for the Messiah* (Nashville: Abingdon, 1993) 32.
22. Painter, *Quest for the Messiah*, 32.
23. Martin Hengel, "The Old Testament and the Fourth Gospel," in Evans and Stegner, eds., *The Gospels and the Scriptures of Israel*, 389.

category. It has been noted that "seeing" is the predominant metaphor in John for the knowledge of Jesus that comes by faith.[24] There is no question that verbs of seeing dominate the Fourth Gospel. What is open to debate is the relationship between seeing and believing. Some have argued that John opposes faith and vision, exalting the latter and denigrating the former, on the basis of passages like 20:29: "Because you have seen me you have believed; blessed are those who have not seen and yet have believed." This reading fails to appreciate the complexity of John's understanding of vision. G. L. Phillips has noted that vision and faith are not mutually exclusive but stand at different points on a continuum of modes of apprehension. Throughout the Gospel there is "the mounting significance of intensity of vision," culminating "in faith which is here conceived . . . as the consummation of an act of illumination which derives its quality from what it sees, rather than a decision which we make with reference to some external object."[25] Phillips analyzes a hierarchy of terms for various levels of "seeing." He begins with βλέπω, which is the most basic kind of seeing, mere oracular vision or garden-variety "eyesight." John uses this word fifteen times.[26] The main cluster of occurrences is found in chapter 9, in which Jesus heals the man born blind. However, βλέπω is not an inherently negative term. Everyone needs to see at this level all the time. But the mode of seeing must be appropriate to that which is to be seen; and if one insists on seeing superficially with the eyes what can only be perceived on a deeper level, one will be misled. Βλέπω is perfectly adequate for negotiating the everyday reality of life, but not for apprehending deep spiritual truth. It is useful, but not adequate in and of itself.

Next up the ladder, according to Phillips, is θεωρέω. It means "to look at with concentration" but without "a very high perception of the significance of what is contemplated."[27] It is used twenty-two times, often in reference to those who witness Jesus' signs but do not grasp the deeper meaning to which they point.[28] Closely related is θεάομαι, which carries

24. Craig A. Evans, *To See and Not Perceive: Isaiah 6:9-10 in Early Jewish and Christian Interpretation* (Sheffield: Sheffield Academic Press, 1989) 129.

25. G. L. Phillips, "Faith and Vision in the Fourth Gospel," in *Studies in the Fourth Gospel* (ed. F. L. Cross; London: A. R. Mowbray, 1957) 83.

26. 1:29; 5:19; 9:7, 15, 19, 21, 25, 39, 41; 11:9; 13:22; 20:1, 5; 21:9, 20.

27. Phillips, "Faith and Vision," 83.

28. 2:23; 4:19; 6:2, 19, 40, 62; 7:3; 8:51; 9:8; 10:12; 12:19, 45; 14:17, 19; 16:10, 16, 17, 19; 17:24; 20:6, 12, 14.

the added nuance of looking at a spectacle, of "beholding" something sensational.[29]

Ὁράω is a critical, pivotal term in the Fourth Gospel. It suggests that "the intellectual content of what has been seen has come to dominate the physical act of seeing,"[30] and it is John's most frequently used "seeing" word.[31] Ὁράω often stands as the gateway to the most exalted type of vision, πιστεύω (belief), which means a full relational encounter with the one who is seen.

In general, Phillips's analysis stands up to scrutiny.[32] This is not to say that we can lock the Fourth Gospel into an unbending terminological straitjacket. John is too sophisticated for that. There is a fluidity to his use of seeing terms that resists a rigid one-to-one correspondence. However, what Phillips says is sound. In the Gospel of John there are different levels of seeing that result in different degrees of knowledge; but the pinnacle of that hierarchy is faith or belief. This is an important point because it goes against the idea that seeing and believing are contradictory modes of perception. John's hierarchy of vision accounts for the ironic blindness of those who see Jesus with their eyes but to whom the truth about him remains hidden on a deeper level. They "see," but improperly. The Johannine Jesus teaches that these blind can be deeply pious because they rely on the words of Scripture (5:39); but they are nonetheless blind because they refuse to see the true meaning of that for which they so diligently search. When Jesus says, "Blessed are those who have not seen (μὴ ἰδόντες) and have believed," he is not making a sharp distinction between two mutually contradictory phenomena but cautioning against those who would stop short of the full vision of faith. We might render John 20:29b (somewhat clumsily) like this: "Blessed are those who, though lacking the sensory evidence satisfying to lower levels of seeing, have entered into such a relationship of intimate communion with Christ that they see the truth in all its fullness, not with the eyes, but by faith."

This analysis is important for our purposes because Scripture origi-

---

29. 1:14, 32, 38; 4:35; 6:5; 11:45.

30. Phillips, "Faith and Vision," 83.

31. 1:18, 34, 39, 50, 51; 3:11, 32, 36; 4:45; 5:37; 6:36, 46; 8:38, 57; 9:37; 11:40; 14:7, 9; 15:24; 16:16, 17, 19, 22; 19:35, 37; 20:18, 25, 29.

32. However, John Painter, following Bultmann, rejects out of hand the notion that John's several verbs for seeing carry different nuances of meaning. They are interchangeable, according to Painter. See *John: Witness and Theologian* (London: SPCK, 1975) 71.

nates with those who have "seen" the Logos even though the evidence was only indirect and hidden.[33] Although he does not come right out and say it, John regards the Old Testament witnesses as those who saw the Logos by faith. Otherwise, in what sense could they have "seen" at all since the Logos was not yet fully visible? Scripture communicates the experience of those who preceded the λόγος ἔνσαρκος but were blessed with a vision of the truth that appeared in Christ.

John's method of employing Scripture could be described as typological in the sense that the correspondence with the past is rooted more in historical events than in the written text.[34] However, I would argue that John is not interested even in "events" in the sense of historical happenings per se, but in the recurrent "event" of "seeing" the Logos of God in diverse settings, manners, and contexts by those graced with prophetic vision. Scripture is essentially the preserved record of those who have seen the Logos and borne testimony to what they have seen.

Vision and Witness:
John the Baptist, Abraham, Isaiah, and Moses

It is time to return to the three texts cited above (5:46; 8:56; 12:41). In keeping with what I have just argued, however, I want to consider the figures behind these texts — Moses, Abraham, and Isaiah — and add to them a fourth, John the Baptist. I am following Martin Hengel, who has argued that John regards these four as the paradigmatic recipients of the Logos in Israel.[35] All four can be seen as "Old Testament" figures, though not in precisely the same sense. Moses and Isaiah are biblical authors. Abraham is a key actor in the biblical drama. John the Baptist stands between Scripture and the enfleshment of the Logos. All are relevant to our discussion because they demonstrate the role of seeing and testifying that preceded the coming of Jesus. By examining these four exemplary witnesses, we can un-

---

33. "[T]he Logos was both the visibility and audibility of God . . . and [John] regards all those occasions on which God is described in Scripture as having been either seen or heard as manifestations of the pre-existent Logos." A. T. Hanson, "John's Technique in Using Scripture," in *New Testament Interpretation of Scripture* (London: SPCK, 1980) 163.

34. James D. G. Dunn, *Unity and Diversity in the New Testament* (London: SCM, 1977) 86.

35. Hengel, "The Old Testament and the Fourth Gospel," 386.

derstand the theological framework out of which John worked and in terms of which he thought of Scripture.

John the Baptist, even though not strictly speaking an Old Testament figure, illustrates the relation between seeing and testifying most clearly. John is both "the quintessential witness to the Logos"[36] and a transitional figure between the old and new eras of salvation history. He is "the representative of believing Israel all through the ages, the last of the prophets who sums up in himself the message of the prophets."[37] Unlike the prophets of the Old Testament, however, John saw Jesus in the flesh, so his testimony bears a special weight. He "came to testify to the light, so that all might believe in him. He was not the light, but he came to testify to the light" (1:7-8). John's special status as the one who points to the light is made clear in the Gospel. John identified Jesus as "the Lamb of God" (1:29, 36), witnessed the descent of the Spirit on Jesus (1:33), and recognized the presence of the Son of God (1:34). However, he is not to be confused with the one to whom he testifies: "[John] himself was not the light; he came only as a witness to the light" (1:8). In so doing, the Baptist demonstrates both the importance and the limitation of the forerunners of Christ. Their testimony is valid as far as it goes, but it must give way to the infinitely fuller and more glorious revelation of the Father in Christ. John describes his own function in 3:30: "He [Jesus] must increase, but I must decrease." To heed John but fail to see that his light was purely derivative would be to remain in the darkness. Many were able to see in John a "burning and shining lamp" (5:35) but could not see beyond his reflected light to the one to whom he pointed.[38] John's role in relation to Jesus is essentially the same as that of the Old Testament witnesses who went before him.

The language and imagery of Isaiah, and particularly Deutero-Isaiah, furnish John with many of his main themes.[39] The text in which John explicitly states Isaiah's role in seeing and testifying to the Logos is 12:36b-41, a passage set at a critical juncture in the Gospel, drawing chapters 2 to 12 to a close and providing a transition to chapters 13 to 20. Francis Moloney calls chapter 12 "The Hour Has Come," underlining its climactic place in

36. Schuchard, *Scripture within Scripture*, 12.

37. Hanson, "John's Technique in Using Scripture," 164.

38. Francis J. Moloney, *Signs and Shadows: Reading John 5–12* (Minneapolis: Fortress, 1996) 22.

39. F. W. Young, "A Study of the Relation of Isaiah to the Fourth Gospel," *ZNW* 46 (1955) 215-33.

John's narrative. If the testimony of John the Baptist in chapters 1 to 3 provides an introduction to the Book of Signs, 12:37-50 forms an epilogue to this section, summarizing Jesus' public ministry as "a story of [human] refusal of divine light and life."[40] John the Baptist and Isaiah serve to frame the first main section of the Gospel.

> [36]"While you have the light, believe in the light, so that you may become children of the light." After Jesus had said this, he departed and hid from them. [37]Although he had performed so many signs in their presence, they did not believe in him. [38]This was to fulfill the word spoken by the prophet Isaiah: "Lord, who have believed our message, and to whom has the arm of the Lord been revealed?" [39]And so they could not believe, because Isaiah also said, [40]"He has blinded their eyes and hardened their heart, so that they might not look with their eyes, and understand with their heart, and turn — and I would heal them." [41]*Isaiah said this because he saw his glory and spoke about him.* (John 12:36-41)

John quotes Isa 53:1 and 6:9-10, two passages from the primitive tradition found also in the Synoptics, the Book of Acts, and Paul.[41] John uses these texts to ponder the puzzling failure of Jesus to win a greater following. John's narrative up to this point has, in a sense, been commentary on 1:11: "He came to his own and his own received him not."[42] Lesslie Newbigin says in regard to this passage that it concerns "the inescapable paradoxes of revelation. How can the truth be grasped by a world whose fundamental patterns of thought are shaped by the lie?"[43] Jesus has performed signs and wonders like Moses before him, but they are met with stubborn unbelief. However, from John's perspective, this is only to be expected because the entire story of Israel bears witness to the disinclination of God's people to accept God's word. The experience of Moses and the prophets foreshadows that of Jesus. Their words were also words of judgment on those who refused to hear.

The theme of rejection is explicated in John's editorial comment:

40. Dodd, *Interpretation of the Fourth Gospel,* 379.

41. Mark 4:11-12; 8:17-18; Matt 13:13-15; Luke 8:10; 19:42; Acts 28:26-27; Rom 10:16; 11:8, 10.

42. Dodd, *Interpretation of the Fourth Gospel,* 380.

43. Newbigin, *The Light Has Come: An Exposition of the Fourth Gospel* (Grand Rapids: Eerdmans, 1982) 162.

"Isaiah said this [that they will be blinded by unbelief] because he saw his [clearly, Jesus'] glory and spoke about him" (12:41). What the evangelist is trying to say is not immediately obvious, however. John maintains that Isaiah's words were fulfilled in the refusal of Jesus' own people to accept him. What does this have to do with his vision of Jesus' glory? Immediately we hear an echo of Isaiah 6 in which the prophet saw "the Lord, high and lifted up." *Targum Jonathan* says that the prophet saw the "glory" of the Lord in the temple.[44] But there is another "lifting up" in Isaiah. In 52:13 God says through Isaiah, "See, my servant will act wisely; he will be raised and lifted up and highly exalted." According to Craig Evans, the Isaiah texts help to explain the rejection of Jesus by identifying Jesus as the servant of the Lord about whom Isaiah spoke.[45] John's use of Isaiah in chapter 12 evokes an implicit but unmistakable reference to Isaiah 52 and 53, Evans argues. This allusion is especially meaningful coming as it does at the point of transition to the Passion narrative. Isaiah saw the truth that the Logos would glorify God and be glorified by God as he was lifted up on the cross. By means of the key word "lifted up," John links the temple vision of Isaiah 6 with the theme of the suffering servant in Deutero-Isaiah. The Servant Songs are the key scriptural background to this passage, according to Evans; otherwise it is difficult to make any sense out of verse 41.[46] This is consistent with John's overall employment of Scripture: "Isaiah passages are not quoted and specifically related to their fulfillment in the light of Christ. Instead, the metaphors and figures of Isaiah are interpreted symbolically and spiritually and become the media for the expression of the meaning of Jesus Christ and his words."[47] The reason the texts are able to function like this is that their author saw Christ in the temple and spoke of his destiny of righteous suffering. In 12:36b-41, then, John presents Scripture as preserving Isaiah's vision of the Lord/Logos to whom the prophet bore witness.

John the Baptist and Isaiah illustrate the vision-witness schema and form a kind of frame around the Book of Signs. Abraham and Moses do

---

44. McNamara, *Targum and Testament*, 49.

45. Craig A. Evans, "Obduracy and the Lord's Servant: Some Observations on the Use of the Old Testament in the Fourth Gospel," in *Early Jewish and Christian Exegesis: Studies in Memory of William Hugh Brownlee* (ed. Craig A. Evans and William F. Stinespring; Atlanta: Scholars Press, 1987) 221-36.

46. Evans, "Obduracy and the Lord's Servant," 236. Also, Young, "Study," 235ff.

47. Young, "Study," 235.

not fit the pattern quite so neatly because, while John says that Abraham saw the Logos, he does not mention Abraham's testimony; and while Moses testified (wrote) about Jesus, he did not, strictly speaking, see him. However, each of these objections may be dealt with in due course.

Turning to the treatment of Abraham in the Fourth Gospel, we note that John is unique among the evangelists in the emphasis he places on Abraham, a tradition that is not central to the Synoptics.[48] John's purpose in using the Abraham tradition is twofold: to prove that true descent from Abraham comes from faith and obedience, not birth; and to show that Abraham saw the future salvation in Christ. The key text for our purposes is 8:51-59:

> [51]"Very truly I tell you, whoever keeps my word will never see death." [52]The Jews said to him, "Now we know that you have a demon. Abraham died, and so did the prophets, yet you say, 'Whoever keeps my word will never taste death.' [53]Are you greater than our father Abraham, who died? The prophets also died. Who do you claim to be?" [54]Jesus answered, "If I glorify myself, my glory is nothing. It is my Father who glorifies me, he of whom you say, 'He is our God,' [55]though you do not know him. But I know him; if I would say that I do not know him, I would be a liar like you. But I do know him and I keep his word. [56]*Your ancestor Abraham rejoiced that he would see my day; he saw it and was glad.*" [57]Then the Jews said to him, "You are not yet fifty years old, and have you seen Abraham?" [58]Jesus said to them, "Very truly, I tell you, before Abraham was, I am." [59]So they picked up stones to throw at him, but Jesus hid himself and went out of the temple.

This passage is set in a longer section (chapters 7 and 8) that takes place at the Feast of Tabernacles, and John builds the narrative around allusions to two Jewish rituals: the carrying of water from the Siloam pool up the steps of the temple and the lighting of lights. By the first century, the Feast of Tabernacles "had become filled with a strong element of eschatological expectation,"[49] and John skillfully uses his narrative to argue that Jesus is the

48. A significant exception is the Q passage Matt 3:9//Luke 3:8: "I tell you, God is able from these stones to raise up children to Abraham," an interpretation similar to that found in John. Paul uses Abraham extensively as the paradigm of faith, but, like John, Paul also ascribes to Abraham foreknowledge of Christ (Gal 3:8).

49. Newbigin, *The Light Has Come,* 91.

fulfillment of those expectations. In chapter 7, Jesus says that he is the one out of whom "streams of living water" flow (7:38). In chapter 8, he identifies himself as the "light of the world" (8:12), a claim that triggers conflict with the unbelieving "Jews" who "see" but do not really see. Jesus is talking to the chief priests and Pharisees, the religious leadership of Israel, who ought to recognize the light but instead are willfully blind.

The controversy centers on their insistence that they are descendants of Abraham. Their freedom and dignity come from their relationship to Abraham, but John makes clear that they are only descendants (σπέρμα) after the flesh, not children (τέκνα) after the Spirit. They may very well be biological descendants of Abraham; but, Jesus says, "if you were Abraham's children, you would be doing what Abraham did" (8:39). Jesus has brought the truth to light. They refuse to see the truth, thereby showing that their father is not Abraham — or God — but the devil.

Telling the professionally religious that they are children of the devil is one sure way to get a reaction. In verse 52, Jesus' interlocutors say, "Now we know that you have a demon. Abraham died and so did the prophets. . . . Are you greater than our father Abraham?" Even though they "see" only at a lower level, they bear inadvertent witness to the truth. Indeed, "I *am* greater than Abraham," Jesus says, "because Abraham rejoiced that he would see my day; he saw it and was glad" (8:56).

In Jewish tradition, Abraham was granted a vision of the future fulfillment of God's promises.[50] Early Christianity revered Abraham as a man of faith because of "his openness to the word of God."[51] He lived in faithful anticipation of the promises of God, and his only security was in radical dependence on God. In John's view, the texture of Abraham's own life anticipated fulfillment in Jesus. By faith, Abraham saw that dependence on God would be established as the ultimate truth of the cosmos. Abraham foresaw that Jesus' mode of glorifying the Father through perfect obedience would be the ultimate glorification. However, "Abraham, for all his greatness belongs to the sequence of events that mark time. . . . His story is finished; he has come and gone." Jesus, because he is the Logos, "reaches back behind the days of Abraham, behind any time,

---

50. Brown, *The Gospel according to John*, 1:359; Moloney, *Signs and Shadows*, 112. See, e.g., Tg. Onq. on Gen 17:16-17; *Gen. Rab.* 44:22, 28; *4 Ezra* 3:14; *T. Levi* 18:14; *2 Baruch* 4:4; *Apocalypse of Abraham* 31:1-3.

51. Moloney, *Signs and Shadows*, 107.

to proclaim that before the time of Abraham, he was already in existence."[52] Abraham's worthiness derived from his insight into the ways of the Logos.

The most prominent Old Testament figure in the Gospel of John by far is Moses. Of all the evangelists, John most clearly interprets Jesus against a Mosaic background. John draws many of his key christological titles and motifs from the Moses traditions. It is perhaps not necessary to find references to Moses behind every turn of phrase (as T. F. Glasson does)[53] to recognize the extent to which Moses permeates the entire Johannine portrait of Jesus. However, John's Jesus is not a "second Moses" in the sense of merely recapitulating or building on the mission of his predecessor. John states quite clearly that Jesus supersedes and replaces Moses as the decisive bearer of revelation. This is an obviously polemical point, made against a Judaism that continued to turn to the Mosaic Torah for inspiration. The relation of Moses to Jesus is that of forerunner to fulfiller. Jesus is the full flowering of the truth to which Moses, for all his greatness, merely hinted. "The Law was given through Moses," the Prologue to the Gospel declares; "grace and truth come through Jesus Christ" (1:17). Moses, like John the Baptist, recedes into the background with the coming of Christ.

John presents Jesus as the prophet foretold in Deut 18:15-19. After Jesus feeds the crowds with the loaves and fishes, the people begin to say, "Surely this is the prophet who is to come into the world" (6:14). But they misunderstand the significance of Jesus' role because they try to make him king by force. Jesus is much more than the Mosaic prophet.[54] The successor is so immeasurably greater than the predecessor that he establishes an entirely new paradigm of revelation. Moses' raising up of the serpent in the wilderness furnishes but a pale echo of the glory and splendor that were made known when Christ was raised up on the cross. The manna that Moses gave the children of Israel in the wilderness was nothing more than a

---

52. Moloney, *Signs and Shadows*, 113.

53. Glasson, *Moses in the Fourth Gospel*.

54. John is adapting a standard technique used in rabbinic exegesis known as *qal wahomer*, in which what is true of a less important case is taken to be true of a more important case. The rabbis used it in both halakic and haggadic exegesis, and it made an easy transition into Christian circles. This argument is used extensively by Matthew, Paul, and the author of Hebrews ("If such and such is true of the old covenant . . . *how much more* is it true of the new?"). Longenecker, *Biblical Exegesis*, 20.

poor foreshadowing of Christ the Bread of Life.[55] The water that Moses brought forth from the rock in the wilderness was but a hint of Jesus, the living water. Jesus is the Light of the world, the eschatological fulfillment of the divine reality only dimly prefigured in the Torah of Moses.[56] Moses, although preeminent among Old Testament visionaries and witnesses, must be seen within the same schema of preliminary seeing and testifying as the other figures we have considered.

Several texts could demonstrate this, but for our purposes 5:39-47 is most instructive:

> [39]"You search the Scriptures because you think that in them you have eternal life; and it is they that testify on my behalf. [40]Yet you refuse to come to me to have life. [41]I do not accept glory from human beings. [42]But I know that you do not have the love of God in you. [43]I have come in my Father's name, and you do not accept me; if another comes in his own name, you will accept him. [44]How can you believe when you accept glory from another and do not seek the glory that comes from the one who alone is God? [45]Do not think that I will accuse you before the Father; your accuser is Moses, on whom you have set your hope. [46]*If you believed Moses, you would believe me, for he wrote about me.* [47]But if you do not believe what he wrote, how will you believe what I say?"

This passage is set in a longer section (5:1-47) in which Jesus heals a paralyzed man on the Sabbath and then is persecuted by "the Jews" for violating the Sabbath and for blasphemy by "calling God his own Father, thereby making himself equal to God" (5:18). The dominant theme in this chapter is μαρτυρία — testimony. Jesus' words and actions are validated by the testimony of God himself (5:32). Messengers like John the Baptist ("a burning and shining lamp") have pointed the way to Jesus, but their testimony is derivative and their light merely reflective. It is the Father's own testimony that establishes the truth of Jesus and his work (5:31-38).

To "the Jews," Jesus says, "you have never heard [God's] voice or seen his form; and you do not have his word [λόγον] abiding in you, because

---

55. Peder Borgen, *Bread from Heaven*; also Borgen, "John 6: Tradition, Interpretation, Composition," in *From Jesus to John: Essays on Jesus and New Testament Christology in Honor of Marinus de Jonge* (ed. Martinus C. De Boer; Sheffield: Sheffield Academic Press, 1993) 268-91.

56. Stephen J. Castelli, "Jesus as Eschatological Torah," *TrinJ* (n.s.) 18 (1997) 15-41.

you do not believe in him whom he has sent" (5:37-38). In other words, seeing God is tied to the apprehension of the Logos of God who has appeared visibly in Jesus. "The Jews" search the Scriptures; but their efforts are ultimately futile and deeply ironic because, while the Scriptures testify to Jesus, they do not see it. "It is they [the Scriptures] that testify on my behalf," Jesus says (5:39). Yet, on allegedly scriptural grounds, "the Jews" seek to kill Jesus, the very one to whom the Scriptures testify. They are seeking glory from merely human sources and failing to trace those sources upward to the true glory to which they point (5:44). Moses, Jesus says, is not their justifier but their accuser because Moses "wrote about me." Earlier Philip says, "We have found the one Moses wrote about in the Law and about whom the prophets also wrote — Jesus of Nazareth, the son of Joseph" (1:45). This is an encapsulated description of the role of Moses. Moses "saw God." Moses apprehended the glory of the Logos and witnessed to him. The Scriptures that bear the name of Moses preserve this witness until it is fulfilled in Jesus. "The witness of Moses is the witness of the Scriptures. To believe Moses implies believing Jesus."[57]

It is in his use of the Moses tradition that the boldness of John's approach becomes evident. He does not depict Jesus as a "new Moses" in the same way as does Matthew, for whom the relationship between Moses and Jesus is that of type to antitype. John's Logos Christology leads to this startling exegetical phenomenon: Moses is not the pattern for Jesus; rather, Jesus is the pattern for Moses. Moses said and wrote what he did because he saw the Logos who appeared later in Jesus.

As noted above, it may seem that Abraham and Moses do not really fit the "vision and witness" schema that I have posited because John says that Abraham saw Jesus but not that he witnessed to him, while Moses witnessed to Jesus (wrote about him) but did not see him. However, what John does not state explicitly is often implied. For example, John does not say that the healing of man at the pool of Bethesda in chapter 5 is one of Jesus' signs, but quite clearly he intends this episode to be included among the signs.[58] Abraham does not bear self-conscious witness to posterity of his vision of the Logos, but through the work of Moses his life is available

57. Painter, *Quest for the Messiah*, 243.
58. Andreas Köstenberger has argued that it is quite likely John intended there to be seven signs because of the symbolic importance of the number seven in the Gospel, even though he identifies only six. "The Seventh Johannine Sign: A Study in John's Christology," in *Studies on John and Gender: A Decade of Scholarship* (SBL 38; New York: Peter Lang, 2001).

as a testimony. And while John does not explicitly attribute a vision of the Logos to Moses, I think that was his intention. While it is true that the essential contrast between Jesus and Moses is that Moses, like other mere mortals, had "never seen God" (1:18), Moses was granted privileged insight into the nature of the divine glory. Exod 33:11 says that "the Lord used to speak to Moses face to face as friend with friend." Moses' request to see God's glory was not granted, but he was shown God's "back" (Exod 33:18-28). Moses was witness to the signs and wonders that pointed to God's power. "Before all your people," the Lord says, "I will perform marvels, such as have not been performed in all the earth or in any nation; and all the people among whom you live shall see the work of the Lord (LXX τὰ ἔργα τοῦ κυρίου)" (Exod 34:10). Moses saw the prefigurations of tabernacle, signs and wonders, manna and water, whose full meaning was made known in Jesus.[59] The fact that Moses did not see the face of God does not contradict the point because prior to the incarnation no one saw God fully; and yet, John explicitly states that Isaiah and Abraham *saw* Christ, and the same can be inferred of Moses. In the partial and imperfect manner of all Old Testament witnesses, Moses did see the glory of God in the Logos and bore witness to the same.

59. There is a Jewish tradition of Moses being granted divinely inspired vision. This was tied to the tradition of the ascension of Moses into the heavens where he saw the Kingdom. See Meeks, *The Prophet-King*, 296-301. Moses was regarded as a prophet, which, in certain circles, entailed the gift of vision. E.g., 2 Esdras 14:3-5: "I revealed myself in a bush and spoke to Moses when my people were in bondage in Egypt; and I sent him and led my people out of Egypt; and I led him up on Mount Sinai, where I kept him with me many days. I told him many wondrous things and *showed him the secrets of the times* and declared to him the end of the times. I commanded him, saying, 'These words you shall publish openly, and these you shall keep secret.'" Later, *Lev. Rab.* 1:3 says that Moses is "the father of the prophets who see by the Holy Spirit." More work would be required to establish any kind of connection between these traditions and John, and I am doing no more than making a possible suggestion. However, it would certainly not be farfetched to think that John regarded Moses as seeing the Logos, especially since the line between hearing and seeing is a somewhat fuzzy one in the Fourth Gospel.

The Uniqueness of John's Use
of the Old Testament Witnesses

I have tried to argue that, while John shares much in common with the other New Testament authors in his use of the Old Testament, his approach is unique in several respects. I have tried to illustrate this with the examples of John the Baptist, Isaiah, Abraham, and Moses, who saw the Logos and testified to him. These biblical exemplars function differently in John than they do in the rest of the New Testament because of the Johannine emphasis on seeing and witnessing rather than text per se.

Moses is certainly a key figure throughout the New Testament. But the Synoptic Gospels tend to refer to Moses mostly in the context of halakic disputes between Jesus and his adversaries. Jesus offers the proper interpretation of the Torah of Moses.[60] Several passages in Luke-Acts contain the introductory formula "Moses writes" or "Moses says," but these are simply conventional vehicles for delivering the kergyma of Jesus' suffering and death.[61] Paul refers to Moses frequently in Romans 9–11 as the source of *testimonia* texts confirming the election of Israel, and 2 Cor 3:12-18 is a midrash on Exod 34:29-35. But one would have to say that none of these passages makes the precise point that Moses wrote about Christ.

Isaiah, when mentioned by name, is almost always incorporated into a standard introductory formula, either in the passive voice ("what was spoken of by the prophet Isaiah")[62] or the active voice ("Isaiah said/prophesied").[63] Again, there is nothing that parallels John's statement that "Isaiah saw [Christ's] glory and spoke of him."

Abraham plays a prominent role in the New Testament as well. He is the prototype of those who are justified by faith,[64] or he is the recipient of the divine promise.[65] But nowhere else in the New Testament is Abraham described as "seeing" Christ.

Interestingly, the one figure who is treated in somewhat the same manner as John treats Moses, Abraham, and Isaiah is King David, who is not mentioned in an exegetically significant way in the Fourth Gospel at all. The

---

60. Matt 19:7//Mark 10:3; Matt 22:24//Mark 12:26//Luke 20:28; Mark 1:44; 7:10.
61. Luke 24:27; Acts 3:22; 26:22.
62. Matt 3:3; 4:14; 8:17; 12:17; Acts 28:25.
63. Matt 15:7//Mark 7:6; Rom 9:27, 29; 10:16, 20; 15:12.
64. Rom 4:3; Gal 3:6; James 2:23.
65. Luke 1:55, 73; Acts 3:25; 7:21ff.; Rom 4:13; Gal 3:18; Heb 6:13.

Synoptic tradition relates a midrashic interpretation of Ps 110:1, in which Jesus asks, "How is it that David calls [Christ] 'Lord'?" (Matt 22:43//Mark 12:36//Luke 20:44); and the book of Acts says that the Holy Spirit spoke through David concerning Christ (Acts 1:16; 2:25; 4:25). There is a certain affinity between David's prophetic experience of Christ in the Synoptic tradition and the vision and witness of Abraham, Moses, and Isaiah in John; but why John does not make the obvious connection between seeing and testifying to the Logos and David is a topic we can only leave for further study.

Is Scripture a "Sign"?

One final aspect of John's understanding of Scripture is its relation to his doctrine of signs. Johannine signs "point to God's glory displayed in Jesus, thus revealing Jesus as God's authentic representative."[66] Signs (σημεῖα) are analogous to the Synoptic tradition's works of power (δυνάμεις.)[67] Signs in the Fourth Gospel, however, are distinguished by their profound ambiguity, because they derive their significance solely from that to which they point and their efficacy is therefore dependent on the willingness of the perceiver to see correctly. For this reason, signs sometimes evoke belief (2:11; 20:30-31), but sometimes they reinforce unbelief because they are not interpreted according to faith (12:36-37; 2:23-25; 4:48; 20:25).

Properly speaking, Johannine signs occur only during the period of time when Jesus appeared on earth. They are public acts performed by Jesus himself. In this sense, Scripture is not a sign. However, Scripture has a "sign-like" quality in that it conveys the pre-incarnation vision of Old Testament witnesses and it confronts the recipient with a choice between faith, which gives true vision, and unbelief, which is both caused by and leads to blindness. Like the signs of Jesus' ministry, Scripture is valuable because it evokes a response to Christ; but it is insufficient in itself to give a full knowledge of God. Only when seen with the light of Christ do the signs and Scripture serve a positive purpose. Apart from that light, they mislead and distort the truth. We might say that functionally, if not formally, Scripture is related to the signs in its preparatory role.

66. Köstenberger, "The Seventh Johannine Sign," 106.
67. Marianne Meye Thompson, *The Humanity of Jesus in the Fourth Gospel* (Philadelphia: Fortress, 1988) 53.

John and the Old Testament Today

I have been making the case that the key to John's understanding of the Old Testament is his unique Christology. Scripture witnesses to Christ through the agency of those who had a pre-incarnation vision of the Logos. The vision that gave rise to the text has priority over the text itself, and the interpretation of Scripture is thoroughly controlled by Christology. John wrestled with the problem, at the end of the first century, of how to find the true meaning of the Scriptures of Israel. Today, our challenge is somewhat different: How to find meaning in John's christocentric interpretation of Scripture in the midst of a pluralistic context. John interpreted Scripture. But for Christians John *is* Scripture. The Gospel has an authority for us analogous to that which the Old Testament had for John. And yet, our world is much different from his. The context in which contemporary Christians read the Fourth Gospel is highly pluralistic, with numerous competing voices claiming to represent the truth.

I think it is safe to say that the Fourth Gospel presents special problems for contemporary Christians because its claim to Jesus as the exclusive source of divine revelation is presented with such force. Some have seen John as the most anti-Semitic of the Gospels, expressing Christian hatred of the Jews at its most pathological. According to Rosemary Radford Ruether, the New Testament in general, but the Gospel of John in particular, is the spring from which Western anti-Semitism has flowed. John's exclusivist Christology makes any version of the truth other than his own wrong in principle, a claim that can no longer be sustained in a pluralistic culture.[68] In her latest book, Elaine Pagels offers a negative comparison of the Gospel of John, which demands exclusive belief in Jesus, to the *Gospel of Thomas,* which teaches "that God's light shines not only in Jesus but, potentially at least, in everyone."[69] Those who proclaim Jesus as the Way, the Truth, and the Life contend these days with those who "seek to know God through one's own, divinely given capacity, since all are created in the image of God."[70]

In this climate, however, John's presentation of Jesus not as a religious option but as the self-revelation of God becomes not only more

68. Rosemary Radford Ruether, *Faith and Fratricide: The Theological Roots of Anti-Semitism* (New York: Seabury, 1979) 111-16.

69. Elaine Pagels, *Beyond Belief: The Secret of the Gospel of Thomas* (New York: Random House, 2003) 34.

70. Pagels, *Beyond Belief,* 34.

scandalous but in a sense more necessary. Christianity is founded on the claim that in Jesus we have seen the light, and Christian faith will stand or fall on that claim. According to our gospel, we do not find the truth within ourselves but only in the one who has come from beyond, bearing the truth. We do not remember what we have always known in a platonic act of recollection; rather, we are seized by revelation. The choice that confronted those who first read the Gospel of John still confronts Christians today: Will you see the light of Jesus or will you not?

John did not deny the truth of the Scriptures of Israel. These Scriptures, he wrote, testified not to a new religion but to God's self-manifestation. This is an essential point in this time when all religion is reduced to an expression of time-bound human culture. John challenges us to distinguish between our religious beliefs and practices and the ultimate source from which they arise. And here is where John's witness becomes all the more essential for our time. The truth of God confronts us from beyond ourselves in Jesus Christ, and that truth is the ultimate and uncompromised claim of divine love. So often, Christianity is portrayed as a bullying religion that brooks no dissent; and, unfortunately, the behavior of Christians has done much to contribute to that perception. But Christianity is founded on him who walked the way of the cross. John's essential insights are those of Paul and the other evangelists: in Jesus we witness nothing other than the incredible self-offering of God out of love for the world. The revelation of divine love is at the same time fraught with divine risk. Jesus is the one who gave his all out of obedience to the Father and love for the Father's world, even though he was greeted with far more rejection than acceptance. "It is because Jesus seeks nothing for himself," Richard John Neuhaus writes, "that he is the complete manifestation of the glory of God. . . . We know no Christ other than the crucified Lord, who is Lord precisely in submitting himself to all that defies his lordship."[71] John presents Jesus as the one who said, "Unless a grain of wheat falls to the earth and dies it remains alone; but if it dies it bears much fruit" (12:24). Jesus incarnated this principle in his life and extended it to his followers. I suggest that the main scandal of the gospel in the culture of narcissism is not so much Jesus' claim to be *the* truth but his awful demand of self-giving love and the maddening paradox that we find life only if we are

71. Richard John Neuhaus, *Death on a Friday Afternoon: Meditations on the Last Words of Jesus from the Cross* (New York: Basic Books, 2000) 71, 169.

willing to lose it. John went to the Scriptures of Israel for assistance in proclaiming this Jesus. He drew on the messianic texts that focused on the self-giving of Christ. He presented Christ, not as one truth among many, *a* truth standing as an equal alongside the truth of Israel's Torah or of Platonic or Stoic cosmology, but as *the* truth by which all other truth claims are judged and to which they must conform insofar as they are true. Jesus establishes the true meaning of Scripture, not vice versa.

We must interpret John, including his use of Scripture, with an eye to our distance from him as well as our proximity to him. John's situation was one marked by the initial cleavage between church and synagogue. In that context, he mounted an aggressive apologetic defense against those who denied the claim of Christ. In all likelihood, he did so in a situation of isolation from, rather than dialogue with, the living reality of Judaism. We cannot simply mimic this attitude and orientation as if two thousand years of history had not intervened. We have discovered that we must find a way to coexist with those different from us in a shrinking global village. At stake may be nothing less than the survival of the world. We cannot, must not, continue to speak of "the Jews," for example, as the embodiment of ignorance and God-rejection, especially not since the Holocaust. And our relations with the Jews provide an analogy for our relations with other faiths.

However — and here we return to John — when we relate to persons of other faiths we do so with integrity *as Christians.* We are those who have seen the Lord by faith, and what we have seen we cannot keep to ourselves. Christians today, as in John's day, have an obligation to announce that the standard of truth is found in Jesus Christ. What we can take from John's treatment of the Scriptures of Israel is his foundational claim that the self-emptying way of Jesus Christ is the measure of all truth. Christians cannot present this claim as merely what is true "for us" or as "one way to the truth." Surely not. It is the truth. Whatever truth there may be in other belief systems or religions is true insofar as it participates in the fundamental truth revealed in Jesus, the Word made flesh. That is the glory which the prophets foresaw and of which we are heirs and custodians. I would suggest that John's treatment of the Scriptures of Israel leads us to subordinate all cultural and religious expressions to the primary truth of God's self-giving love, revealed in Jesus, even as we recognize that Jesus can be spoken of only in the linguistic forms that our culture gives us. In the maelstrom of postmodernity, the Fourth Gospel calls us to live as those who have also seen the glory of self-giving love and who desire to speak of him.

Written Also for Our Sake:
Paul's Use of Scripture in the Four Major Epistles, with a Study of 1 Corinthians 10

JAMES W. AAGESON

Introduction

A review of scholarship on the use of Scripture in the major Pauline epistles during the past one hundred years suggests that there are at least five important areas of investigation:

1. the textual traditions reflected in Paul's explicit citations and his manipulation of the biblical texts;[1]
2. the comparison of Paul's usage with that of other Jewish interpreters of the period;[2]
3. the prospect that Paul used earlier Christian *testimonia* or *excerpta* and that these influenced his selection of texts;[3]

---

1. See, e.g., Dietrich-Alex Koch, *Die Schrift als Zeuge des Evangeliums: Untersuchungen zur Verwendung und zum Verständnis der Schrift bei Paulus* (Tübingen: J. C. B. Mohr [Paul Siebeck], 1986) 11-101; Timothy H. Lim, *Holy Scripture in the Qumran Commentaries and Pauline Letters* (Oxford: Clarendon, 1997) 3-181; Otto Michel, *Paulus und seine Bibel* (BFCT; Gütersloh: C. Bertelsmann Verlag, 1929) 55-68; and Christopher D. Stanley, *Paul and the Language of Scripture: Citation Technique in the Pauline Epistles and Contemporary Literature* (Cambridge: Cambridge University Press, 1992) 65-264.

2. See, e.g., Joseph Bonsirven, *Exégèse rabbinique et exégèse Paulinienne* (Paris: Beauchesne et ses Fils, 1939); E. Earle Ellis, *Paul's Use of the Old Testament* (Grand Rapids: Eerdmans, 1957); Lim, *Holy Scripture*; Michel, *Paulus und seine Bibel*.

3. See J. Rendel Harris, *Testimonies I-II* (Cambridge: Cambridge University Press, 1916, 1920); and Lim, *Holy Scripture*, 150-52.

4. the investigation of Paul's scriptural quotations and arguments and their relation to larger Old Testament contexts;[4]
5. the character of *intertextuality* and *inner biblical exegesis* in Paul's letters.[5]

These are rarely presented as unconnected issues, and rightly so, but they are dimensions of Paul's use of Scripture that have received and continue to receive considerable attention. Since each of these areas alone warrants its own investigation, I intend to focus on certain aspects of numbers 4 and 5. In particular, I will consider issues related to the Old Testament context of Paul's citations, the character of *intertextuality/inner biblical exegesis* in Paul's major epistles, and the problem of scriptural echoes as put forth by Richard Hays in his book *Echoes of Scripture in the Letters of Paul*. I will also address the hermeneutical distinction sometimes made between Christology and ecclesiology in Paul's use of Scripture. Then I will develop in detail issues of *intertextuality/inner biblical exegesis* and Christology/ecclesiology in one specific Pauline example, namely, 1 Cor 10:1-33. In this way, the more general insights can be developed in a detailed and focused way. Finally, I will reflect briefly on some of the contemporary hermeneutical and theological implications of Paul's use of Scripture.

Paul and the Use of Scripture

Intertextuality and Inner Biblical Exegesis

If we survey the approximately ninety explicit quotations of Scripture in Paul's four major epistles, we see that the majority of them cluster in Galatians 3-4, Romans 4, and Roman 9-11, with the last displaying the highest concentration of citations found anywhere in these letters. For example, Paul in Romans 6-8 displays little interest in quoting Scripture directly, only to turn to it in an unprecedented fashion in 9-11. These explicit

4. See C. H. Dodd, *According to the Scriptures: The Sub-Structure of New Testament Theology* (London: Nisbet, 1952); and Richard B. Hays, *Echoes of Scripture in the Letters of Paul* (New Haven and London: Yale University Press, 1989).

5. See, e.g., James W. Aageson, *Written Also for Our Sake: Paul and the Art of Biblical Interpretation* (Louisville: Westminster/John Knox, 1993); Hays, *Echoes of Scripture;* and Michael Fishbane, *Biblical Interpretation in Ancient Israel* (Oxford: Clarendon, 1985).

citations in no way exhaust Paul's use of Scripture, of course, but they do raise important questions. What is it about these discussions and arguments that prompts Paul to turn to Scripture in such an overt and dramatic way? Or to put it the other way around, what is it that connects these three Pauline texts? In short, these are all texts where issues of Jew-Gentile concern broadly conceived come to the fore: righteousness by faith, law and faith, the "unbelief" of Israel, and the faithfulness of God to the covenant. It may be that Paul's interlocutors have attempted to refute Paul by resorting to Scripture, and hence he simply appeals to Scripture in turn to refute them. But it seems there is more at stake than this. These issues are so contentious and conflicted, especially in Galatia and Rome, that Paul brings the full authority of Scripture to his discussion. Moreover, he seeks to establish among his readers the correct interpretation of Scripture concerning these matters and in some cases to refute incorrect readings. Of all the rhetorical and theological resources at Paul's disposal, it is Scripture that leaves a dramatic stamp on these arguments. Scripture is woven into the very fabric of these texts, and the rhetorical character of the texts presumes a kind of scriptural authority and reasoning.

But here we need to be more precise. If we look carefully at Paul's explicit quotations of Scripture in these three texts and elsewhere, a basic pattern emerges: (1) an opening theological statement or assertion, (2) an introductory formula indicating that a citation is to follow, and (3) a quotation or series of quotations (e.g., Rom 3:9-18; 9:24-29; 10:18-21; 11:7-10; 15:8-12) from Scripture. Frequently the discussion following the quotation continues without much direct explication of the biblical material, but often there is a verbal hint that Paul is actually explicating the text or at least is shaping his ensuing discussion in light of the scriptural reference. He introduces his interpretation or application of the text with a transition word or phrase such as "so too," "for whatever," "thus," "it was written for our sake," "now therefore." In other cases, Paul attaches an exhortation to the quotation (Rom 12:19-20; 1 Cor 3:19-21; 2 Cor 6:16–7:1).

At the end of the argument about Abraham and faith in Romans 4, Paul writes in 4:23-24: "Now the words, 'it was reckoned to him,' were written not for his sake alone, but for ours also." The words "it was reckoned to him" in Genesis are directed to Abraham, but in Romans they are applied to those who believe in the one who raised Jesus from the dead. And in Gal 4:21-31 Paul applies the Sarah/Hagar material to his own historical and theological context. He writes in Gal 4:29: "But just as at that time the child who was born according to the flesh persecuted the child who was born according to the Spirit, so it is now also." Paul then appends a quotation from Gen 21:10: "Drive out the slave and her child; for the child of the slave will not share the inheritance with the child of the free woman." To make his interpretation of the text explicit, Paul continues: "So then friends, we are children, not of the slave but of the free woman" (v. 31). And in 1 Cor 9:9-10 Paul writes: "For it is written in the Law of Moses, 'You shall not muzzle an ox while it is treading out the grain.' Is it for oxen that God is concerned? Or does he not speak entirely for our sake? It was indeed written for our sake."

Given Paul's most basic form of quoting Scripture — that is, an opening statement followed by an introductory formula and citation — some interpreters of Paul have tended to see his explicit exegesis largely in the category of proof text. Paul makes a theological claim that he seeks to support by reference to the authoritative words of Scripture. This, however, is a much too simplistic reading of Paul's use of the Old Testament and is probably an emphasis born of Protestant ideas of Scripture and its authority. For Paul, the Jew, Scripture is holy (Rom 1:2). It is a source of inspiration for life and a basis for interpretation and religious argumentation, as well as an expression of the will of God. It is dynamic and engaging, not simply a source of authority to which one turned for support. So when Paul cites Scripture, he does not merely view it as an authoritative record to prove his arguments. It is a source of edification, inspiration, and stimulation, both verbal and conceptual. It is a sacred realm where one comes to probe and to understand something about the nature of divine action and redemptive reality. When Paul hears the words in Scripture of Abraham's righteousness grounded in his faith, he claims to know something of the very structure of righteousness according to faith. It is this truth that he claims to know and that connects his circumstance in Christ as an apostle to the Gentiles with Scripture. What was true then is true now. For Paul, the truth of Scripture is opened to him in Christ and in the truth revealed to him through Christ. Scripture is more than a static source of authority to be mined at will. It is a well-spring of interpretation and life-giving nourishment. Hence, interpretation for Paul is more than a matter of discerning the meaning of a literary text but rather of discovering and indeed generating a sense of God's purpose for the world and its redemption.

In that sense, his hermeneutic is inherently theological and is governed by his experience on the Damascus road and its legacy. From a persecutor of the early church, Paul was transformed into a man with a mission to carry the name of Jesus to the Gentile world. The divine mystery that was revealed to Paul in Christ opens for him new ways of reading and listening to the ancient texts of the Jewish people. His belief in Christ is both an experience and a conviction that, in his eyes, allows him to comprehend the "true" meaning of the religion of his people and their sacred texts. Christ and Scripture are closely connected for Paul; and, I would argue, it is impossible to speak about his reading of Scripture apart from his Christology. Christ is the presupposition for his encounter with Scripture. It is the revelation of Christ that shapes his understanding of God's people and God's purposes. For Paul, as for many other interpreters of Scripture in his own day and beyond, the Scriptures yield their "true" meaning to those who are guided and transformed by the Spirit. Typical of sectarian hermeneutics, Paul's conception of scriptural interpretation implies a special knowledge of divine truth. And in this encounter between Christology and Scripture, he arrived at conclusions about the sacred traditions that must have dumbfounded many of his Jewish contemporaries. Although he used methods of interpretation familiar to these contemporaries, he drew conclusions that would have surprised them, if not shocked them.

The claim that Paul's use of Scripture is christological, however, requires further clarification. In Rom 1:1-2, Paul writes: "Paul, a servant of Jesus Christ, called to be an apostle, set apart for the gospel of God, which he promised beforehand through his prophets in the holy Scriptures." In Rom 3:21 he writes in a similar vein: "But now, apart from the law, the righteousness of God has been disclosed, and it is attested by the law and prophets." And in 1 Cor 15:3-4 Paul writes once again: "For I handed on to you . . . what I in turn received: that Christ died for our sins in accordance with the Scriptures, and that he was buried, and that he was raised on the third day in accordance with the Scriptures." In these three texts, Paul operates within a promise-fulfillment framework, but in none of these texts does he cite the scriptural references he has in mind. By itself this may not say much. But when we couple this with the observation that, by and large, Paul does not use direct scriptural quotations to establish his Christology, let alone to prove that Jesus is the Christ, we are reminded of the need to be precise about what we mean when we say that Paul uses Scripture christologically. Jew-Gentile issues prompt him to quote Scripture in abundance, but the issue of Jesus' Messiahship does not.

Here, too, we can contrast Luke's portrayal of Paul in Acts. In 17:2-3 Luke writes that Paul went into the synagogue "as was his custom, and on three Sabbath days argued with them from the scriptures, explaining and proving that it was necessary for the Messiah to suffer and to rise from the dead." Similarly, in 28:23 Luke portrays Paul imprisoned in Rome and reports that "from morning until evening he explained the matter to them, testifying to the kingdom of God and trying to convince them about Jesus both from the law of Moses and from the prophets." It is no surprise, but this is not how Paul uses Scripture in the major epistles. To be sure, Luke reinterprets Paul and his legacy to conform to his own situation and intention, but this particular discrepancy may simply be due to the different circumstances of the respective genres and the way Paul is portrayed (or portrays himself) in each of them. At the risk of oversimplification, we might say that Paul's hermeneutic in these letters is thoroughly christological, but his direct use of Scripture conforms more closely to his concern that Jews and Gentiles live together in the unity of the one church, the body of Christ.

Having said this, however, I judge that it is a distortion of Paul's use of biblical material to set ecclesiology over and against Christology (or vice versa for that matter), as some scholarship on the topic does. To separate these or to emphasize one at the expense of the other presents us with a false dichotomy. The not-so-subtle turn in much recent Pauline scholarship toward sociology and anthropology rightly focuses attention on the ecclesiological character of Paul's use of Scripture, but this must not be done at the expense of his theology and Christology. For Paul, these work together. The church is, after all, the body of Christ. And that frames how he thinks about Scripture and its application to issues of the Christian life.

It may go without saying after two thousand years of history and after the revolution of thought we call the Enlightenment, but we in the West cannot simply reproduce Paul's hermeneutic or exegesis of Scripture in our own day, whether in the church or in the academy. Even if it were possible, it would be a violation of our own responsibility to come to the texts of Scripture, Paul's letters included, as interpretive agents who take our contexts as seriously as Paul took his own. Thus, for me, one of the lessons to be learned from Paul's exegesis of Scripture is that scriptural interpretation ought not (perhaps cannot) be reduced to a mere task of trying to discover meaning in the texts of Scripture, as if Scripture were something to mine for nuggets of truth. Rather, it is a generative and creative task that is invariably open-ended and that speaks to our own circumstance in the contemporary world. At the risk of entering into a postmodern interpretive house of mirrors, let me argue that Paul's reading of Scripture added yet one more element to the rich tradition of post-biblical interpretation, and our readings of Scripture will do similarly as we seek to appropriate those Scriptures in our time. To seek to do otherwise may simply render the texts mechanical, archaic, and lifeless. This means that Paul's own experience and context were as important in the interpretive enterprise as were the texts of Scripture; and, I submit, this is true as well for those of us today who take these texts seriously.

For me, Romans 9–11 is the best exemplar of this generative and open-ended quality of Paul's use of Scripture and method of argumentation. In this discussion Paul struggles to come to terms with the brute reality that the vast majority of Jews have not come to believe in Christ. This fact and its implications strike close to the heart of Paul's theology, and he must address the issue as a matter of both theological necessity and pastoral responsibility. When I read the discussion in these chapters, I see a work in progress, not a polished theological treatise. I see a man struggling to make sense of a thorny issue that for him does not submit to easy resolution. Quoting Scripture in abundance, Paul embarks on a discussion that is marked by sharp turns, twisted logic, and unrelenting attempts to make sense of the issue at hand. Along the way, the discussion is punctuated by Pauline theological convictions (e.g., the children of the promise are Abraham's descendants, and God has not abandoned the people of Israel) that are strung together by arguments that give the reader a sense of what is important for the question and its contemplation. But it does not present the reader with anything resembling a systematic theology. When Paul gets to the end of the discussion in 11:33-36, he bursts forth into a doxology that provides a telling commentary on the entire discussion. "O the depth of the riches and wisdom and knowledge of God! How unsearchable are his judgments and how inscrutable his ways! 'For who has known the mind of the Lord? Or who has been his counselor?' 'Or who has given a gift to him, to receive a gift in return?' For from him and through him and to him are all things. To him be the glory forever. Amen." I can almost see Paul looking to heaven and throwing his hands into the air as he utters these words. As if to say, "I have given it my best, yet who knows the answer except you, O Lord?" Paul brings his discussion to a close.

If this characterization is correct, how might the church today approach this text and its use of Scripture? The goal of contemporary exegesis and theology cannot be merely to repeat what we think Paul is saying in these chapters as if that provides a satisfying answer to Christian understandings of Judaism and the relationship between the two communities. Rather, I argue, Paul invites each theological generation into the question anew, and he prods us to see again that the faithfulness of God is rooted in divine faithfulness to the covenant made with Israel. Christ's appearance does not somehow negate this faithfulness, despite layers of Christian theology that have implied so. The Pauline mandate, if there is one, is to engage the question and to acknowledge the theological boundaries he set, not to repristinate Paul's response to it, or his use of the Old Testament for that matter. Paul did not pronounce the final word on the subject of Israel, Christ, and the word of God in Romans 9–11. Rather, he prompted and contributed to the church's ongoing conversation on the subject. And implicitly he invited those of us who come after to enter into this conversation as well.

Beyond Quotations: Echoes and Allusions

But the role of Scripture certainly is not limited to explicit quotations and direct exegesis. Scholars have long tried to tease from Paul's letters echoes of Scripture as well as allusions to it. Yet it was not until the publication of Richard Hays's book *Echoes of Scripture in the Letters of Paul* in 1989 that literary theory was brought to the issue of Paul's use of Scripture in a sustained way. Drawing on the work of literary critics, as well as Michael Fishbane's insightful book *Biblical Interpretation in Ancient Israel,* Hays tries to give us a framework for recognizing echoes of Scripture in Paul's letters and for seeing them on a continuum between the extremes of explicit quotation and faint echo.[6] This places Paul's use of Scripture broadly in an *intertextual* frame of reference, to use literary-critical terminology, and in a framework of *inner biblical exegesis,* to use perhaps more traditional biblical language. From a Christian canonical point of view, Paul is an inner biblical exegete standing in a long line of inner biblical exegesis extending back to early stages of Israelite scriptural formation. This includes his overt use of Scripture as well as his more subtle and indirect use of the material. From a hermeneutical perspective, the most helpful part of

6. Hays, *Echoes of Scripture,* 14-24.

Hays's work is the way he identifies the possible *loci* of the interpretive event: Paul's mind, the original readers of the epistle, the text, the act of reading, or the interpretive community.[7] This is a helpful way of thinking about the issue and brings to mind the presumed interactions that go on among all of these as Paul turns to Scripture and as Scripture likewise imposes itself on him.

From my perspective, perhaps the most important observation is that intertextuality is less about genetic and causal relationships between traditions than it is about identifying the discursive space of a culture of interpretation. Hays writes:

> The vocabulary and cadences of Scripture — particularly of the LXX — are imprinted deeply on Paul's mind, and the great stories of Israel continue to serve for him as a fund of symbols and metaphors that condition his perception of the world, of God's promised deliverance of his people, and of his own identity and calling. His faith, in short, is one whose articulation is inevitably intertextual in character.[8]

This significantly expands our field of vision. Hence, Paul's interpretive space is not the text of Scripture alone but also the way Scripture came to be understood and the matrix of symbols that came to surround it over time. This, too, is part of the intertextual and inner biblical world of Paul's use of Scripture, and it may be as important as the actual text of Scripture itself. This also affects our perception of the scriptural context of Paul's references, for he may be conjuring up not only the wider textual context but even more broadly the wider interpretive context of the passage. This, it seems to me, is the case in Paul's use of Scripture in 1 Cor 10:1-33.

On other occasions, of course, Paul makes explicit that the biblical context of the material is critical to his argument. In Romans 4, when Paul asks if Abraham was reckoned righteous before or after he was circumcised, he replies to his own question with a direct reference to the fact that in Genesis 15 Abraham is declared righteous on the basis of faith and not until Genesis 17 is he circumcised. For Paul, the literary sequence indicates a historical sequence, which in turn represents a theological sequence: righteousness comes through faith, not the requirement of circumcision.

---

7. Hays, *Echoes of Scripture*, 26.
8. Hays, *Echoes of Scripture*, 16.

With these intertextual echoes and allusions reverberating through Paul's letters, we can perhaps only speculate about what any individual actually heard. Some in the audience, finely tuned to the Jewish Scriptures, undoubtedly heard more than did others who knew little or nothing of these biblical stories and traditions. It is no surprise to contemplate that Paul's letters had different intertextual effects on different members of the audience and that this opened the way for different levels of understanding. We can also surmise that this would have complicated Paul's task of trying to convince his audience of the finer points of his theology. The only suggestion I would make about this is that the people involved in the Jew-Gentile debates may also have been the people most apt to hear the scriptural echoes and respond to the allusions. They were the ones who knew Scripture best. They were the ones who contended over the manner of Gentile inclusion and the relationship between Jews and Gentiles in the church. They were the ones for whom this issue really mattered. And from the point of view of both sides, Scripture was a perfectly good arena within which to carry on this debate.

The Example of 1 Corinthians 10

Defining the Issues

In his provocative discussion of 1 Cor 10:1-22, Hays claims that Paul is reading the wilderness story filtered through the lens of Deuteronomy 32. In 10:22, Paul apparently echoes Deut 32:21 when he asks: "Shall we provoke the Lord to jealousy? Are we stronger than he?"[9] Hays writes:

> If indeed Paul is reading the wilderness story through the lens of Deuteronomy 32, one puzzling feature of his conceit turns out to be more explicable. Why does he identify the rock with Christ? The Hebrew text of Deuteronomy 32 repeatedly ascribes to God the title "the Rock" (vv. 4, 15, 18, 30, 31). Though the LXX — regrettably for Paul's purposes — eliminates the metaphor, translating each of these references with the

---

9. Hays, *Echoes of Scripture*, 93-94. Cf. 1 Cor 10:6. See also Andrew J. Bandstra, "Interpretation in 1 Corinthians 10:1-11," *CTR* 6 (1971) 14-21; and Wayne Meeks, "'And Rose Up to Play': Midrash and Paraenesis in 1 Corinthians 10:1-22," *JSNT* 16 (1982) 72.

generic *theos,* Paul surely knows the tradition. However, since he is writing to Greek readers who would not know the Hebrew text, he cannot quote Deuteronomy 32 to support his assertion. To explain to the Corinthians the difference between their Greek Bible and its Hebrew *Vorlage* would interrupt Paul's argument. In any case, the identification of the rock with Christ is a parenthetical remark, an embellishment of the Israel/church trope. Consequently, rather than digressing to explain the grounds for his imaginative leap, he just leaps.

The leap creates an extraordinarily interesting case of metalepsis: the trope of 1 Cor 10:4 is fully intelligible only as a transformed echo of a text cited later in the chapter.[10]

Given the direct quotation of Deut 32:21 in Rom 10:19 and the imagery from Deut 32:21 and 32:17, which is woven into the very fabric of 1 Cor 10:1-22, there is little doubt about the importance of this text for Paul. Concepts from Deut 32:10-14 may also be reflected in the pastoral comment in 10:13. However, there is little reason to assert that Paul's entrance point into the argument in 10:1-33 is the christocentric assertion that the "rock was Christ."[11] That seems highly improbable.

Is it likely that the identification between the rock and Christ came about under the symbolic influence of Deuteronomy 32 in general and 32:21 in particular?[12] To assert that Paul knew the Hebrew textual tradition behind the LXX of Deuteronomy 32 and had this in mind is certainly questionable and, in my view, less plausible than to claim that the christological structure of his argument was shaped by the rich interpretive tradition ensuing from the wilderness rock stories in Exodus and Numbers.[13] To be sure, Paul's ethical concern drives the discussion. Idolatry, immorality, testing the Lord, and grumbling are all at issue, though the problem of idolatry clearly predominates (1 Cor 10:14-22). But equally obvious is Paul's strategy of using baptismal and Eucharistic imagery to develop his argument (10:1-

10. Hays, *Echoes of Scripture,* 94.

11. Hays, *Echoes of Scripture,* 98.

12. Richard Horsley doubts that Paul was alluding to God as the rock of Israel's salvation from the Song of Moses in Deuteronomy 32. Richard A. Horsley, *1 Corinthians* (ANTC; Nashville: Abingdon, 1998) 137.

13. Allusions or echoes reflecting LXX language appear in 1 Cor 10:6, 9, and 10. Exod 32:6 LXX appears virtually verbatim in 10:7 and Ps 23:1 LXX in 10:26. Stanley, *Paul and the Language of Scripture,* 68, 197.

4, 16-17, 21). This suggests that several sets of metaphors are in view in Paul's construction of the images and the argument. Sacramentology as such is not the issue at stake, but baptismal and Eucharistic imagery (both in Scripture and in the present) merge metaphorically with the concerns arising out of the apostle's ethical and ecclesiological dilemma. Indeed, it is no distortion to say that Paul uses the symbolism associated with baptism and especially Eucharist to address the ethical problem of idolatry. Thus, in the literary world of Paul's text, Christology related to the images of spiritual food, spiritual drink, and water is closely connected to the larger ethical problem of idol worship and meat offered to idols.[14]

This suggests that to understand the rhetorical function of the christological identification in 10:4, we ought to focus carefully on the imagery associated with the rock and also on the power of the wilderness rock story to generate its own symbolic world. To put it baldly, do the images and ideas provoked by the wilderness rock tradition in the history of Jewish interpretation shed any light on Paul's christological identification in 10:4? Do they help us understand why Paul makes this connection? Do they help us understand the appropriateness of this identification for the symbolic world that Paul constructs in 10:1-4, 16-17, and 21? This approach is arguably more helpful in determining the symbolic strategy of Paul and his use of Scripture in rendering pastoral counsel than the claim that the connection between Christ and the rock is an echo of the Hebrew text of Deuteronomy 32, a text that stands behind the Greek versions of Deuteronomy. Moreover, this highlights the larger literary problem of scriptural echoes and their function within the Pauline text. Does the echo of Deuteronomy 32 figure substantively in the rhetoric of the text, or is it simply background noise? These are all related issues, and they affect how we understand Paul's use of Scripture and tradition in 1 Cor 10:1-33.

The Wider Tradition

For over a century, Pauline scholars have investigated the traditions surrounding the apostle's connection of Eucharistic imagery with the wilder-

---

14. Wendel Lee Willis, *Idol Meat in Corinth: The Pauline Argument in 1 Corinthians 8 and 10* (SBLDS 68; Chico: Scholars Press, 1985) 160-61.

JAMES W. AAGESON

ness experience of the Hebrews.[15] Some of this work, supplemented by new insights, needs to be rehearsed. In Exod 17:1-7 the wandering Hebrews are camped at Rephidim, but according to the biblical text there is no water for the people to drink and they begin to grumble against Moses. Moses cries out to the Lord and is instructed to take the rod with which he had struck the Nile and go: "I will be standing there in front of you on the rock at Horeb. Strike the rock, and water will come out of it, so that the people may drink."[16] Having done this, Moses names the place Massah and Meribah (see also Ps 78:12-31).

In Num 20:1-13 a related story is recounted. On this occasion the people are at Kadesh, and as in the Exodus story they are without water. Again the people contend with Moses, and he is instructed to take the rod, assemble the congregation, and tell the rock to yield its water. He strikes the rock with his rod,[17] and according to the text water comes forth abundantly. It is then announced that these are the waters of Meribah. That the waters at Rephidim and Kadesh are both called Meribah has apparently suggested by rabbinic times that water from the same rock is present in both places:[18] "And so the well which was with the Israelites in the wilder-

15. As long ago as 1889, S. R. Driver addressed the issue of the traditions related to 1 Cor 10:4: "Notes on Three Passages in St. Paul's Epistles," *The Expositor* series 3, 9 (1889) 15-23; E. Earle Ellis, "A Note on 1 Corinthians 10:4," *JBL* 76 (1957) 53-56 (reprinted in his collection of essays entitled *Prophecy and Hermeneutic in Early Christianity* [Tübingen: Mohr, 1978] 209-12); G. B. Caird, "The Descent of Christ in Ephesians 4,7-11," *Studia Evangelica* (vol. 2; ed. F. L. Cross; Berlin: Akademie-Verlag, 1964) 541-43; J. W. Doeve, *Jewish Hermeneutics in the Synoptic Gospels and Acts* (Assen: Van Gorcum, 1954) 110-13; Hans-Josef Klauck, *Herrenmahl und Hellenistischer Kult: Eine Religionsgeschichtliche Untersuchung zum ersten Korintherbrief* (NTAbh 15; Münster: Aschendorff, 1982) 252-56; H. J. Thackeray, *The Relation of St. Paul to Contemporary Jewish Thought* (London: Macmillan, 1900) 205-8; *Str-B*, 3:406-8; Willis, *Idol Meat*, 133-42.

16. The use of the name "Horeb" is ambiguous and cannot be associated directly with the law, but the term appears to represent the mountain of God where Moses encountered the burning bush and received the commandments. W. H. Propp, *Water in the Wilderness: A Biblical Motif and Its Mythological Background* (HMS 40; Atlanta: Scholars Press, 1987) 60-61; B. S. Childs, *Exodus: A Commentary* (OTL; London: SCM, 1974) 308. See also Philo, *De Vita Mosis* 1.210.

17. Moses was commanded to tell the rock but instead he struck the rock. See M. Noth, *Numbers: A Commentary* (OTL; London: SCM, 1968) 146; G. J. Wenham, *Numbers: An Introduction and Commentary* (Downers Grove, IL: InterVarsity, 1981) 149-50.

18. See Doeve, *Jewish Hermeneutics*, 111. See also Deut 8:15; 32:13; and 33:8-11 (also cited in 4QTestim).

ness was a rock. . . . Wherever the Israelites would encamp, it made camp with them" (*t. Sukkah* 3:11).[19]

In *t. Sukkah* 3:11 the identification between the image of the well and the rock is explicit, and this connection appears to stem from Num 21:16-18: "From there they continued to Beer; that is the well of which the Lord said to Moses, 'Gather the people together, and I will give them water.' Then Israel sang this song: 'Spring up, O well! — Sing to it! — the well that the leaders sank, that the nobles of the people dug, with the scepter, with the staff.'"[20] In *Midr. Num* on 1:1 the biblical imagery is developed still further:

> And the well was due to the merit of Miriam. For what does Scripture say? "And Miriam died there, and was buried there." And what is written after that? "And there was no water for the congregation." How was the well constructed? It was rock-shaped like a bee-hive, and wherever they journeyed it rolled along and came with them. When the standards (under which the tribes journeyed) halted and the tabernacle was set up, that same rock would come and settle down in the court of the Tent of Meeting and the princes would come and stand upon it and say, "Rise up, O well," and it would rise.[21]

The rock that Moses struck in the wilderness and from which water flowed is identified with the well recounted in Num 21:16-18. Moreover, this well/ rock traveled with the wandering tribes; and, according to *Midrash Num-*

---

19. Cf. *Tg. Onq.* on Num 21:16-20, and Thackeray, *Relation of St. Paul,* 208. It appears that the symbolism of John 7:37-38 is also related to the Feast of Tabernacles and the eschatological rivers flowing out of Jerusalem and the temple. Here the eschatological images of Ezek 47:1-11 and Zech 14:8 are especially important. Ezekiel describes a scene in which water flows from the temple and travels to the east. Wherever the river flows, plants and living creatures flourish. In Zechariah, it is said that "on that day" waters shall flow from Jerusalem, half to the east and half to the west (cf. Zech 13:1). In *m. Sukkah* 4:9 the water libations of the Feast of Tabernacles are described, and in *t. Sukkah* 3:3-11 the eschatological imagery of Ezek 47:1-2 and Zech 14:8 are cited in conjunction with the figure of the well in Num 21:17-18. It is clear that, at least by rabbinic times, the Feast of Tabernacles tradition had come to incorporate both the image of the wilderness rock and the eschatological streams flowing from Jerusalem.

20. See Exod 15:23-25 and *t. Sukkah* 3:11-12. For a brief reconstruction of the well tradition, see Ellis, "Note on 1 Cor 10:4," 53-54.

21. See *Bib. Ant.* 10:7; 11:15; Isa 48:21. Cf. also Driver's trans. in "Notes on Three Passages," 16.

bers, wherever the tabernacle was set up this well/rock settled down in the court of the Tent of Meeting.

In addition, *Targum Onqelos* includes in its rendering of Num 21:18 a reference to the heads of the people, the scribes, who delve the well with their staves (בחוטריהון כרוהא רישי עמא ספריא). By the inclusion of the term "scribe" in the imagery of Num 21:18, the targumist strongly suggests that the digging of the well is a metaphorical reference to the digging of Torah. The concern of the targumist is the scribal interpretation of the law.[22] Not only has the rock of the wilderness tradition come to be associated with the well that follows the wandering Hebrews, but an implicit identification is made between the image of the well and Torah.

This implicit identification is explicit in the *Damascus Rule* 6:3-4: "And they dug the well: 'the well which the princes dug, which the nobles of the people delved with the stave.' The well is the law, and those who dug it were the converts of Israel." In the context of the *Damascus Rule,* Num 21:18 is allegorized in light of the covenanters' perception of the Torah and the requirements of scriptural interpretation.[23] The identification of the well with Torah and the digging of the well with Torah interpretation may in fact have its origin in the etymology of the term בְּאֵר ("well") itself. It is noteworthy that in Deut 1:5 the text states: "Moses undertook to expound (בֵּאֵר) this Torah." The term בֵּאֵר is, of course, related to its cognate בְּאֵר. In 1Q22 2:8 (The Words of Moses) the verbal form of באר appears once again: "[appoint wise men whose] work it shall be to expound (לבאר) [to you and your children] all these words of the law."[24] This cognate verbal link suggests that early in the development of the well tradition the connection between the well, Torah, and Torah interpretation came to expression. Thus, the implicit reference in *Targum Onqelos* to the scribal digging of Torah and the explicit identification of the well and Torah in the *Damascus Rule* appear to be etymologically foreshadowed by the nominal and verbal forms of the root word באר itself.[25]

---

22. Caird, "Descent of Christ," 542-43.

23. P. R. Davies, *The Damascus Covenant: An Interpretation of the "Damascus Document"* (JSOTSup 25; Sheffield: JSOT Press, 1983) 122-24. Cf. also 2:17–3:20 in this document. See also Koch, *Die Schrift als Zeuge des Evangeliums,* 213, n. 60.

24. See the definitions listed for the verbal form of באר in BDB.

25. Verbal forms of באר also occur in Deut 27:8 and Hab 2:2. For nominal forms see, e.g., Gen 21:30; 26:18, 21, 22, 25; 29:2-3; Num 21:16-18; Cant 4:15. See also the Johannine imagery in John 4:14; Rev 7:17; 14:7; 21:6; and CD 19:34.

In rabbinic tradition, the image of the well expands still further. For example, in *b. Avot* 5 it is written that ten things were created at twilight on the eve of the Sabbath, and among them was the mouth of the well. In *b. Ta'anit* 9a the well, which refers to the wilderness rock, was given to Israel on account of the merit of Miriam. It is also interesting to note that in *bar. Avot* 6:1 the person who concerns himself with Torah is likened to a flowing well: "And they reveal to him the secret meanings of the Torah, and he is made as a well that ever gathers force, and like a stream that never ceases."[26] Once again, we find the trope of the well fusing with the image of Torah, or the one who occupies himself with Torah, which then flows forth as an unending stream. That which flows from Torah is likened to the life-giving water that pours forth from the well.[27]

Shortly before Paul, Philo also recounts the image of the wilderness rock. But for him the rock signifies wisdom. In *De legatione ad Gaium* 2.86 Philo writes: "For the flinty 'rock' is the wisdom of God." And in *Quod deterius* 115 he states: "He uses the word rock to express the solid and indestructible wisdom of God, which feeds and nurses and rears to sturdiness all who yearn after imperishable sustenance." The imagery shifts in *De somniis* 2.221-22: "'I stand ever the same immutable, . . . whence showers forth the birth of all that is, whence streams the tide of wisdom.' For I am He 'Who brought the fountain of water from out the steep rock.'" Here wisdom is not identified directly with the rock but appears to be associated with the water that flows from it. And in *De ebrietate* 112 Philo likens wisdom to the well: "Again Moses leads the song at the well, and this time his theme is not only the rout of the passions, but the strength invincible which can win the most beautiful of possessions, wisdom, which he likens to a well. For wisdom lies deep below the surface and gives forth a sweet stream of true nobility for thirsty souls."[28] Philo's application of the rock, the water, and the well to wisdom is predicated on the commonly found association between Torah and wisdom.[29] Wisdom is identified with Torah, and, of course, Torah is also identified with this complex of biblical images.[30]

---

26. Soncino edition. See also *b. Avot Zar* 5b and *Midr. Gen* 41:9; 66:1; 69:5; 84:16; 97:3.

27. See also 1QH 8:7; 8:16; CD 19:34.

28. Cf. *De somniis* 2:271.

29. See, e.g., Sir 24:23 and Bar 4:1.

30. See also the connection between wisdom and Torah in *Midr. Gen* 44:17; *Lev* 11:3; *Num* 10:4. Cf. the important imagery in Wis 10:17-18; 11:4; 16:20-21; 19:7.

We have now established that early in the development of this tradition a number of symbols have come together: the rock, well, Torah, digging the well, and wisdom. In virtually all cases, the implication is clear: something life-giving — water, wisdom, Torah — flows to the people who need to be nourished and sustained. The images in this symbolic world fuse, develop, and are applied in accord with the respective traditions of interpretation. But at the center of this post-biblical interpretive complex stands the symbol of Torah. Torah, often identified with wisdom, signifies the means by which God gives life to the people, just as water from the rock gave them life in the wilderness. Torah stands between God and the people, and it flows with life-giving nourishment. In fact, the breadth of this interpretive tradition indicates that a rich symbolic world has been generated by the association of several biblical texts, and images from these texts have been extended metaphorically to identify the agent of divine nourishment. This symbolic complex echoes through Aramaic and rabbinic traditions, Philo and the Qumran sectaries, the connection between the rock and the well, and perhaps the etymology of the term באר as well. It is a broadly based symbolic world, both temporally and religiously, and it clearly reflects the way Jewish religion was recast at different times and in different quarters. In each case, to partake of the nourishment flowing from the rock, the well, Torah, or wisdom is to partake of the nourishment of God.

Transformation of the Tradition

The association of the rock with the well and the rock with Torah, the identification of wisdom with Torah, and the concept of spiritual drink all combine to form a symbolic constellation that makes possible Paul's connection of the rock and Christ.[31] In the symbolic transformation of the tradition, he has simply substituted Christ for the rock, which as he already knew represented Torah. Thus, as in Rom 10:6-8, Paul christologically re-centered the symbolism by substituting Christ for Torah (the

31. From a tradition-historical point of view, the broadly based character of the symbolism argues for Paul's familiarity with the tradition. On the other hand, Paul himself provides evidence for the way the tradition was developing in first-century Judaism. From a literary and symbolic perspective, however, the important factor is the symbolic culture attested to by the literary evidence and the way it illustrates the character of the Pauline text.

commandment of God in Deut 30:12-14).[32] Christ as the source of spiritual drink has assumed in a figurative sense the role of Torah. For Paul, the messianic Jew, Christ is the means by which God's life-sustaining drink is given to the people. As Philo has understood the prerogatives of Torah in terms of wisdom, Paul has understood them in terms of Christology (cf. 1 Cor 1:24, 30). As the wandering Hebrews drank from the rock that followed them in the wilderness, and as the Jews were nourished by the life-giving waters of Torah, so now, claims Paul, the people partake of the Eucharistic drink of Christ who is identified as the rock of the biblical story.

Unlike in Rom 10:6-7, an identification or equation is expressed here in figurative language: "the rock was Christ." Rom 10:6-8 and 1 Cor 10:4 both indicate, however, that Paul has associated the person of Christ with a scriptural concept (commandment of God) or an object (rock) and has used that imagery to illustrate what he considers to be a contemporary religious truth — namely, that Christ is the manifestation of faith righteousness and that he is the wellspring of spiritual drink. In neither of these texts does Paul elaborate extensively his messianic understanding. He appears to be satisfied in playing on the biblical imagery and in turn using this imagery to develop the respective arguments.

The link between the rock and Christ — as it was between the rock, well, Torah, and wisdom — appears to be grounded in the notion of the wellspring through which God brings forth life to his people. In this interpretive constellation, we see the interplay between the biblical images (rock, well, and water) and the shifting religious symbols that come to be identified with God's sustaining power (Torah and Torah interpretation, wisdom, and Christ). Not only do the scriptural images coalesce and fuse among themselves but the perceived referent of these images also evolves in relation to the shifting symbolic system of the interpreter and the interpreter's tradition. That is what occurred in 1 Cor 10:4, as Paul has come to perceive Christ as the wellspring of heavenly nourishment.[33] In the Eucharist, the people of God drink from this wellspring, and they share in the life-sustaining power of God, which was also poured out upon the people

32. In his reference to Deut 30:12-14 in Rom 10:6-8, Paul has substituted Christ for the commandment of God by explicating three images christologically: "who will go up to heaven," "who will go down into the abyss," and "the word is near you, in your mouth and in your heart." Cf. Bar 3:29-30.

33. Note also the connection with the manna in the wilderness.

in the wilderness of ancient Sinai. Hence, there is a symbolic and functional correspondence between Christ and the rock.

In 10:21, Paul writes: "You cannot drink the cup of the Lord and the cup of demons. You cannot partake of the table of the Lord and the table of demons." The argument against idolatry culminates in this verse, and Christology is clearly the foundation on which the apostle's pastoral counsel rests. To drink from the wellspring of the Lord's cup and to eat from the table — to receive the spiritual nourishment of the Lord — is incompatible with the food and drink of demons. One cannot partake of both: "The cup of blessing which we bless, is it not participation in the blood of Christ? The bread which we break, is it not participation in the body of Christ? . . . Consider Israel according to the flesh, are not those who eat the sacrifices partners in the altar?" (10:16, 18).[34] The reception of spiritual nourishment from the Lord by those who drink his cup and eat from his table implies participation in Christ (cf. 1 Cor 11:23-26). To partake of the food and drink of idols (cf. 10:14, idol worship) implies participation in the demonic, and that is idolatry.[35] This is what differentiates Christ from the idol, God from the demons, and the faithful one from the idolater.

The complexity of 10:14-22 is well known; and though the exegetical issues need not be rehearsed here,[36] the discussion to this point suggests two observations. First, the interpretive context for these verses must not be limited to Hellenistic cult meals or to word studies of κοινωνία. On the contrary, the symbolic world generated by the intertextual character of

34. Cf. the participation language of Rom 6:1-14. In my translations I have rendered the forms of κοινωνία in terms of participation and partner. It should be noted, however, that this term also conveys the implicit sense of communion or commonality. See the discussions of κοινωνία by Willis, *Idol Meat*, 167-81, and Klauck, *Herrenmahl*, 260-62.

35. Compare the continuing discussion in 10:23-33 with the discussion in 8:1-13. Alex Cheung writes: "There is no inconsistency between 1 Corinthians 8 and 1 Cor. 10:1-22. On the contrary, the two passages represent two stages of Paul's argument: not only will eating idol food cause the weak to stumble, but it will also make the Corinthians partners with demons. . . . Paul's position in a nutshell is this: to eat idol food knowingly is to participate in idolatry; therefore, for the sake of the weak and for the sake of yourselves, avoid any food if, and only if, you know that it is idol food." Alex T. Cheung, *Idol Food in Corinth: Jewish Background and Pauline Legacy* (JSNTSup 176; Sheffield: Sheffield Academic Press, 1999) 162.

36. See the arguments by Klauck, *Herrenmahl*, 258-72; Peter J. Tomson, *Paul and the Jewish Law: Halakha in the Letters of the Apostle to the Gentiles* (CRINT 3.1; Assen/Maastricht: Van Gorcum; Minneapolis: Fortress, 1990) 198-202, 208-16; Willis, *Idol Meat*, 165-222.

10:1-13 (10:4 in particular) provides the most immediate and seemingly the most productive context for understanding this text. Second, the symbolic context of which 10:4 is a part argues against reducing Paul's understanding of κοινωνία to a concept of fraternal association. To drink from the Lord's cup and to eat from his table implies for Paul more than a simple association with the Lord and those who represent him. It suggests the reception of spiritual nourishment through an act of ritual participation or communion. However, on the metaphorical level, the distinction between association and communion is not actually drawn.[37] Indeed, as indicated below, the metaphorical language enables Paul to hold both of those elements of κοινωνία together.

Type and Christology

The words "I do not want you to be ignorant, brethren" set the tone for the discussion in 1 Cor 10:1-22 (10:1; cf. 10:14).[38] With these words, the text alerts the reader to the fact that Paul intends to dispel ignorance. But in the design of the text it is not immediately apparent what the reader is to understand. It is not until 10:5 that the significance of the wilderness stories begins to be disclosed, and it focuses on the displeasure of God. All were under the cloud and passed through the sea, all were baptized into Moses in the cloud and in the sea, and all ate spiritual food and drank spiritual drink.[39] Even so, with most of the Israelites God was displeased. The adversative ἀλλά ("but") signals the contrast inherent in this part of the text: being under the cloud, passing through the sea (baptism into Moses), and consumption of spiritual food and drink (10:1b-4) are contrasted with the displeasure of God

---

37. In his review of Willis's book *(Idol Meat)*, L. L. Welborn writes: "Indeed, according to Willis, what the Christian experienced at the Lord's table was not communion with Christ at all, but 'fraternal association,' like his pagan counterparts, distinguished only by its exclusiveness and sense of mutual obligation (pp. 204-222). . . . Yet Paul does not speak of Christians as *koinonoi tou Christou,* as he might have had he wished to describe the relationship between believers assembled at the Lord's table, but of 'participation in the blood of Christ' *(koinonia tou haimatos tou christou)*"; *Critical Review of Books in Religion 1990* (Atlanta: Scholars Press, 1990) 245.

38. Cf. Paul's use of these or similar words in Rom 1:13; 11:25; 1 Cor 12:1; 2 Cor 1:8; and 1 Thess 4:13.

39. See Meeks, "'And Rose Up to Play,'" 65; and Tomson, *Paul and the Jewish Law*, 192.

and the Israelites being thrown down in the wilderness (10:5). The reason for the divine displeasure is still to be disclosed, but a basic contrast or conflict has been established in the text. The insertion of the christological identification in 10:4 also signals that something more is at stake in this contrast than is readily apparent at this stage in the discussion.[40]

Verse 6 is crucial in the literary development of the text. The demonstrative pronoun ταῦτα ("these things") refers back to 10:1b-5 and conjures up images related to the wilderness experience of ancient Israel.[41] But 10:6 is crucial because the conflict focusing on divine displeasure is extended and for the first time in these immediate verses incorporates a temporal distinction between past and present. The linguistic mechanism that Paul employs focuses on the word τύποι ("examples"). "These things" have become "τύποι for us." The significance of the events in the wilderness transcends the pastness of those events. "These things" from the past are τύποι for us in the present. The paraenetic value of the imagery is ready to be exploited.

In 10:6b the reason for the divine displeasure becomes clear: some of them craved evil (ἐπιθυμητὰς κακῶν). To this assertion, the exhortations yet to come in the text are related as examples. Given the transitional character of verse 6 and the lack of a direct scriptural reference, the "craving for evil" is not to be understood as one among other activities that incurred divine displeasure in the wilderness.[42] Rather, the "craving for evil" is better understood as the heading that receives concrete expression in the examples cited in 10:7-10. Thus, the movement of the text is inexorably toward greater clarity regarding what it means that the reader not be ignorant, as well as what it means to incur God's anger. The ethical and paraenetic character of the text develops in tandem with the Israel/church paradigm first signaled in verses 1, 4, and 6.

In verses 7-10, the "craving for evil," the Israel/church configuration, the evidence of Scripture,[43] and exhortation combine to illustrate Israel's

40. For a general discussion of the argument in 1 Cor 8:1–11:1, see Bruce N. Fisk, "Eating Meat Offered to Idols: Corinthian Behavior and Pauline Response in 1 Corinthians 8–10 (A Response to Gordon Fee)," *TrinJ* (n.s.) 10 (1989) 49-70.

41. Meeks writes: "The five positive and the five negative *exempla* are both punctuated and linked with the paraenetic conclusion in verses 12-13 by means of an *inclusio*, verses 6 and 11." Meeks, "'And Rose Up to Play,'" 65.

42. Contrast Meeks, "'And Rose Up to Play,'" 65, 70-71.

43. For the various Old Testament references in 1 Cor 10:1-13, see the expository article by William Baird, "I Corinthians 10:1-13," *Int* 44 (1990) 286-90.

displeasing behavior. Idolatry, immorality, testing the Lord, and grumbling are the four evils enumerated. Each illustration begins with an exhortation (either an imperative or a hortatory subjunctive) not to do as some of the ancient Israelites did. Thus, in each example the paradigmatic quality of ancient Israel for the contemporary Corinthians is symbolically reinforced. In 10:7 the scriptural reference is formally introduced and quoted, and it serves to conjure up images of ancient Israel's idolatry.[44] In the final three examples, the references to scriptural imagery illustrate the consequences of Israel's immorality, testing the Lord, and grumbling. Throughout these four verses, the symbolic and paraenetic linkage between ancient Israel and the church is firmly established. *All* were baptized and partook of spiritual nourishment, but *some* desired evil (illustrated by their idolatry, immorality, testing the Lord, and grumbling). This is the conceptual configuration, established in 10:1-10, which Paul in turn applies to the issue of idolatry in Corinth (10:14-22).

As in 10:6, Paul in 10:11 once again makes the Israel/church figure explicit. "These things" happened to them τυπικῶς ("as an example"), and the demonstrative pronoun clearly refers back to the examples in verses 7-10. In this verse, the force of τυπικῶς relates to ancient Israel.[45] On the other hand, "these things" were written down for our instruction (νουθεσία, in the sense of admonishment), "upon whom the end of the ages has come" (εἰς οὓς τὰ τέλη τῶν αἰώνων κατήντηκεν). The Israel/church trope is clearly maintained in 10:11, but the distinction between the two (Israel and church) also is implicitly acknowledged. The church comprises those "upon whom the end of the ages has come." For the church, "these things" that have been written down have a didactic function, and it is the instructive and admonitory value of "these things" that will be exploited, in order to address the problem of idolatry in Corinth. In the socio-symbolic world of the text, the Israel/church connection intersects the "all"/"some" ("most") distinction, and this symbolic intersec-

---

44. See the argument by Meeks, "'And Rose Up to Play,'" 64-78.

45. The difficulty associated with the translation of τύποι and τυπικῶς stems from the desire (need) to maintain some parity between the two words and at the same time to take into account the fact that the force of τύποι (10:6) is directed toward the church (us) while τυπικῶς (10:11) is directed toward Israel (them). The word "example" is an acceptable rendering (NAB, NRSV), for the word can imply the sense of "type" and "admonishment" in 10:6 and "warning" and "admonishment" in 10:11. This common rendering also maintains some linguistic parity between the two words.

tion becomes the underlying framework for the discussion of idolatry in Corinth.[46]

The closely structured, and perhaps even programmatic, character of the text to this point is interrupted by an exhortation and a word of encouragement in 10:12-13. This encouragement contains three elements: no temptation has overtaken "you" that is not common to human beings; God does not allow you to be tempted beyond your strength; and God provides a way of escape in order that you can endure the temptation.[47] Even if one were to agree that at least part of 10:1-13 forms a literary unit composed prior to its use in the present context,[48] it seems highly doubtful that verses 12-13, as they stand, would have been composed by anyone other than Paul.

The word διόπερ ("for which reason") at the beginning of 10:14 clearly indicates that the implications of the argument to this point are now to be applied to the problem of idol worship and food offered to idols.[49] This introduction is coupled with a direct plea for the beloved ones to flee idol worship and to judge, as sensible people, what Paul says (10:15). In the rhetorical and symbolic strategy of the text, the intersecting coordinates of Israel/church and all/some (most) move, as the circumstances of idolatry in Corinth require, in a decidedly christological direction in 10:16-17. The church participates (κοινωνία) in the body and blood of Christ (v. 16), and because the many partake of the one bread they are one body (v. 17).[50] We who bless the cup of blessing (all/church) and we who break the bread (all/church) participate in the body and blood of Christ. "Because there is one bread, we, many as we are, form one body, for we all partake (all/church) of the one bread."[51] It is in 10:20b-21, when Paul finally exhorts his readers not to be in partnership with demons by drinking the

---

46.
$$\text{All} \underset{\text{Church}}{\overset{\text{Israel}}{\rule{4cm}{0.4pt}}} \text{Some (Most)}$$

47. Baird, "I Corinthians 10:1-13," 289-90.

48. Meeks, "'And Rose Up to Play,'" 65.

49. Barrett refers to διόπερ as an "argumentative conjunction." C. K. Barrett, *A Commentary on the First Epistle to the Corinthians* (HNTC; New York and Evanston: Harper and Row, 1968) 230. Cf. 1 Cor 8:13.

50. Barrett asserts that "common participation" is the correct rendering of κοινωνία. *A Commentary on the First Epistle to the Corinthians*, 231. See note 37 above. The sense of communion and commonality strengthens the cultic and ritual implication of the text.

51. I have followed Barrett's preferred reading of this verse. Barrett, *A Commentary on the First Epistle to the Corinthians*, 233.

cup of demons and eating from the table of demons, that the implicit distinction between all the church and some in the church once again informs the structure of Paul's pastoral paraenesis.

In light of 10:16-17 and the preceding discussion of the wilderness rock,[52] it becomes clear why a sharp distinction between an ecclesiocentric and a christocentric hermeneutic in Paul is problematic, at least in this text.[53] To be sure, Paul does not engage in extensive christological discussions on the basis of Scripture.[54] And he does not involve himself in points of abstract christological development. His Christology and hermeneutic are both contextual and in that sense ecclesiological. And in the case of 1 Corinthians 10, Paul clearly does not enter the discussion with a simple christocentric claim that he wishes to make. But these are not particularly striking observations. More to the point is the fact that Christology and ecclesiology are intimately interconnected for Paul. Indeed, for Paul, Christ as an abstraction manifests himself in the body of the church (e.g., 1 Cor 12:12-27; Rom 12:4-5; and also Eph 4:15-16). From the opposite direc-

---

52. See the discussion above, pp. 154-59.

53. Cf. Hays, *Echoes of Scripture,* 84-87, 121.

54. There is no need for him to use scriptural quotations in this way in his epistles, for the addressees of his letters are already followers of Christ. The apostle, however, is compelled to work out the implications of what it means for both Jews and Gentiles that righteousness is by "faith" and not "works." Almost four out of ten of the apostle's direct quotations are related to justification by faith, being children of the promise, freedom from the law, and in general the relationship between Jews and Gentiles. These Pauline discussions, of course, rest on a messianic presupposition, but they are concerned primarily with faith as the basis of righteousness. Almost one out of four of Paul's quotations deals with ethical or wisdom-related topics, while the remainder of the citations are scattered among a variety of subjects. Only a few biblical citations are directly applied to the figure of Christ. In Rom 9:33, the "stone stumbling" is most likely intended to be understood as referring to Christ; and a few verses further on in 10:6-8 a statement is made about Christ's death and exaltation. Deut 21:23 is quoted in Gal 3:13, and this reference is used to illustrate the statement that Christ has become a curse. This christological interpretation takes a different twist in 3:16 where Christ is identified as the offspring of Abraham. Pss 8:7 and 110:1 are applied christologically in 1 Cor 15:25-27; and in Rom 15:3 the apostle writes: "For Christ did not please himself, but as it is written, 'the reproaches of those who reproached you fell on me.'" This statement also provides the background for the citations in Rom 15:9-12. In that same chapter, the apostle has an indirect reference to Christ in mind when citing Isa 52:15 (15:21). This reference is applied to the situation of Paul's proclamation of the gospel. Finally, the word *deliverer* from Isa 59:20 in Rom 11:26 also appears to refer to Christ. Quotations in Eph 1:20; 1:22; 4:8; 5:31; and Col 3:1 also display explicit christological themes; but apart from these two epistles, the direct citations that have Christ as their referent are confined largely to the examples mentioned.

tion, the church and individual members of the church participate ritually and cultically in Christ (e.g., 1 Cor 10:16-21; 11:23-26; Rom 6:1-11; Gal 3:16; 3:26-29).[55] Thus, the mystical or abstract Christ is indissolubly and dynamically linked to the concrete or social body of Christ, the church, in Paul's hermeneutic. The christological identification in 10:4 establishes the Israel/church configuration literarily and signals that Christology is a crucial element in understanding the nature of idolatry theologically. In that sense, Christology is foundational for Paul's instruction and admonition to the Corinthians.[56] Those who partake of the nourishment of Christ are the body of Christ. For the members of the body of Christ to partake of the food and drink of demons implies an inherent contradiction and strikes a blow against the very body of Christ itself. It is idolatry.[57]

In 10:18, the discussion of idolatry in Corinth relates back to the situation of Israel according to the flesh.[58] Once again, this underscores the

55. Regarding Gal 3:29, Hays writes: "Thus, Gal. 3:29 finally unlocks the riddle of the relation between Paul's ecclesiocentric hermeneutic and his christological convictions. Galatians demonstrates more clearly than any other Pauline letter how these aspects of Paul's thought are complementary rather than contradictory: Paul's understanding of Jesus Christ as the one true heir of the promise to Abraham is the essential theological presupposition for his hermeneutical strategies, though these strategies are not in themselves christocentric" (Echoes of Scripture, 121). As far as this statement goes it is correct, but certain items must be underscored. First, Gal 3:29 ought to be understood in the ritual and baptismal context of 3:27-28. Those who have been baptized into Christ have put on Christ. Second, the ritual context for the statements in Gal 3:16 and 29 tends to blunt the significance of the christocentric/ecclesiocentric distinction. Those who are in Christ are the body of Christ. Third, as far as 1 Cor 10:4 is concerned, the identification of Christ with the rock and the christological identification of Abraham's offspring indicate a common hermeneutical and symbolic impulse to root both Christology and the church in scriptural imagery. The cultic and ritual character of this is especially obvious, as we now see, in 1 Cor 10:14-21. Fourth, Paul's hermeneutic in a given argument may be christocentric, though the point of entry into the discussion is not a narrow christological claim that the apostle wishes to prove. Cf. the language concerning immorality in 1 Cor 6:13-20.

56. See note 45 above.

57. Paul uses symbolism (cup, bread, body, participation in the body of Christ) in order to imagine the connection between the Eucharistic body and the ecclesial body. There is clearly a distinction between the two, but symbolism and metaphor provide Paul with the linguistic means to unite them and to express another aspect of christological reality, as he perceives it.

58. "Israel according to the flesh" in this verse is only in the most remote sense possibly the subject of 10:20a. The emphasis in 10:18 appears to be on the idea of participation. The reference to the altar is used to convey a sense of participation, which in turn relates to

principle of κοινωνία; but in this case Israel according to the flesh supplies the example. This, in turn, raises the question of the reality behind an idol or food offered to idols. As in 8:4, Paul denies that an idol or food offered to an idol is in fact anything. Of course, there are so-called gods in heaven and on earth — many gods and lords — but for us God is one (8:5).[59] Paul firmly maintains that God is one and that the idol in reality is nothing; yet to offer sacrifice to demons and to partake of the food and drink of demons is to participate in the demonic.[60] As Alan Segal remarks: "Though pagan *gods* have no real existence, behind them are *demons* tempting the righteous to destruction."[61] Paul then concludes the immediate discussion with an echo of Deut 32:21: "Shall we provoke the Lord to jealousy? Are we stronger than he?" (1 Cor 10:22).

Christ the Rock

In light of this discussion, what are we to conclude about Paul's identification of Christ with the image of the wilderness rock? Though this identification is not Paul's hermeneutical point of entry into the discussion, it contributes to the rhetorical design of the argument in 10:1-33 in four ways.

First, it serves, along with 10:16-21, to mark symbolically the christological parameters of idolatry. Partaking of the food and drink of idols is contrasted with partaking of the food and drink of Christ. Paul understands idolatry, and perhaps evil generally, in christological terms. Furthermore, in 10:16-17 he clearly implies that idolatry is inimical to the body of Christ, the church.

Second, the connection between the rock and Christ serves to characterize Christ as the agent, indeed symbol, of divine nourishment. This is structurally in line with other Jewish images that view Torah or wisdom as

---

the problems in Corinth rather than to a clear echo of the wilderness stories recounted earlier in the text.

59. Cf. Paul's language in Gal 1:6-7: "to a different gospel, not that there is another [gospel]."

60. Hans Conzelmann, *1 Corinthians: A Commentary on the First Epistle to the Corinthians* (trans. James W. Leitch; Hermeneia; Philadelphia: Fortress, 1975) 173.

61. Alan F. Segal, *Paul the Convert: The Apostolate and Apostasy of Saul the Pharisee* (New Haven and London: Yale University Press, 1990) 230. See also Klauck, *Herrenmahl*, 263-72.

an agent of divine nourishment. It is at Christ's table and through his cup that the church is nourished and sustained. Through the broken bread and the cup of blessing the church participates in the body and blood of Christ. In that sense, the church is the body of Christ. On the other hand, to drink the cup of demons and eat at their table is to partake of the demonic.

Third, the hortatory nature of this text is rooted in *Christ* symbolism, which is enhanced by the identification in 10:4. Paul begins this text: "I do not want you to be ignorant, brethren." Though the ancient Israelites were baptized, ate spiritual food, and drank spiritual drink, most displeased God and were thrown down in the wilderness. Do not be ignorant and do what they did, exhorts Paul. Do not drink the cup of blessing and eat from the Lord's table and yet partake of the food and drink of demons. This is to court the displeasure of God.

Fourth, the christological identification in 10:4 functions as a hermeneutical linchpin in the typology.[62] The metaphorical and functional connection between Christ then and Christ now represents Paul's *as then so now* hermeneutic,[63] and it enhances the connection between idolatry then (Israel) and idolatry now (church).[64] Moreover, the christological identification in 10:4 exhibits a symbolic logic that is born of a rich interpretive tradition based on the image of the wilderness rock. Paul's language of participation in 10:16-21 extends the metaphorical implication of this interpretive tradition, while the identification itself serves to bind together rhetorically the imagery in verses 1-4, 7, 9(?), and 14-22. It is the ritual and christological language in 10:1-22 that contains the peculiar contribution of these verses to the pastoral advice in 10:23-30 and the larger discussion of meat offered to idols and idolatry in 8:1–11:1.

Deuteronomy 32 echoes in the background of 10:1-22, but it is the intrusion of the christological identification in 10:4 and the larger wilderness story that governs the symbolic world of much of this text. Though Paul

---

62. Horsley may be right that in identifying Christ as the rock Paul is not making a major doctrinal statement, but hermeneutically in the context of his pastoral counsel this is more than a side remark or parenthetical statement. Horsley, *1 Corinthians*, 137.

63. If we read *Christ* in 10:9, the metaphorical link with 10:4 is obvious. The textual tradition, however, reflects an understandable concern about the implication that the Hebrews put Christ to the test in the wilderness (hence the readings *Lord* and *God*).

64. Horsley, *1 Corinthians*, 135; and Ben Witherington III, *Conflict and Community in Corinth: A Socio-Rhetorical Commentary on 1 and 2 Corinthians* (Grand Rapids: Eerdmans, 1995) 217.

does not set out in 10:1-22 to establish the christocentric assertion that the rock was Christ, it is precisely this identification that illustrates the convergence of Christology and paraenesis (idolatry) in this discussion. Christology is the crucial factor in the determination of idolatry and in the distinction between *all* and *some*. Likewise, the identification in 10:4 illustrates the convergence of Christology and Pauline hermeneutics. Christ functions as the link between Israel and church, between Scripture (as interpreted by Paul) and the present situation in Corinth. Indeed, the identification of Christ with the wilderness rock virtually jumps out at the reader and intrudes upon the reader's literary consciousness.

Echoes, to continue Richard Hays's metaphor, can be notoriously difficult to control; and, even when they are heard, they are frequently hard to understand. They reverberate here and there, often with little discernible pattern. To focus on 1 Cor 10:4 as a transformed echo of Deuteronomy 32 is, I submit, to focus on the background noise, which is certainly audible in the text. But to minimize or to ignore the material from the wilderness rock story is to ignore the intertextual shout that Paul imposes on the reader and that ultimately serves to shape the literary strategy of the apostle's text.

Equally important to consider in this regard is the distinction between an *allusion* and an *echo* of Scripture. To what extent is Deuteronomy 32 in 1 Cor 10:1-33 an echo and to what extent is it an allusion? This distinction centers on authorial intent and control over the scriptural material. Does Scripture echo through the Pauline text or does Paul exercise control over the scriptural material as he draws it, even in passing, into his own text? The line between an echo and an allusion is certainly subtle and in many cases cannot be drawn with any confidence. Nevertheless, this intertextual distinction is important because it helps to identify the seat of literary control either in the text of Scripture or in the mind of the author (in this case Paul). From a hermeneutical point of view, this also raises the problem of the extent to which a scriptural echo or an echo from the tradition can in fact be used to unlock meaning and theology in the Pauline texts. This needs to be decided in each individual case, but Hays's more general comment is still germane when considering Paul's use of Scripture in this text:

> The vocabulary and cadences of Scripture — particularly of the LXX — are imprinted deeply on Paul's mind, and the great stories of Israel continue to serve for him as a fund of symbols and metaphors that condi-

tion his perception of the world, of God's promised deliverance of his people, and of his own identity and calling. His faith, in short, is one whose articulation is inevitably intertextual in character.[65]

This applies to Paul's use of Scripture, as well as the interpretive material that has grown up around Scripture over time. Scripture is clearly important for Paul, but so is the way Scripture has come to be interpreted.

If the argument developed in these pages is correct, Deuteronomy 32 is certainly a scriptural echo concerning idolatry in 1 Cor 10:1-33, perhaps even an allusion, but it is of modest value in determining the rhetorical character of the Pauline text. The christological identification in 10:4 is a key to the literary strategy of 10:1-33, and it is an important hermeneutical point of entry into the text and the pastoral advice Paul gives the Corinthians. This discussion also raises significant questions about the function of scriptural echoes in the rhetoric of Pauline texts, the role of Christology in Pauline hermeneutics, and the appropriateness of using intertextual echoes to determine the character of Pauline theology.

Conclusion

In conclusion, let me reiterate that I see Paul's use of Scripture as a dynamic work in progress. Despite Paul's passionate tenor, his is a hermeneutic that is open and engaging, not static and closed. Many of the issues that so vexed Paul and over which he struggled so painfully, especially the inclusion of Gentiles into the church, would be ironed out in succeeding generations of the church — and not always successfully in my view. But for all of Paul's rough edges and for all of the conceptual gaps in his reading, even misreading, of Scripture, he was the first Christian theologian to forge a path through many of these perplexing issues. He was an early Christian thinker who explored new theological territory, and as such he was on the very cusp of the church's spread into the Greco-Roman world. He was an interpreter who rethought the Jewish Scriptures and their meaning in the new theological world of an increasingly Gentile church. That is what makes him fascinating to me. And that, too, is what sometimes leaves me shaking my head.

65. Hays, *Echoes of Scripture*, 16.

At important junctures in the church's life, it has often been Paul who has provoked and prodded the church through the voices of reform: Augustine, Luther, Wesley, and Barth, to name but a few. Perhaps Paul still has the capacity to do that as the church now embarks on the twenty-first century. If so, Paul's apostleship will be fulfilled once again in our time, and his words will be once again written also for our sake.

In the Face of the Empire:
Paul's Use of Scripture in the Shorter Epistles

SYLVIA C. KEESMAAT

How do we live in the face of empire? How do we challenge the idolatry of our age? How does Paul draw on his Scriptures to speak to the struggles faced by the Christian communities to whom he was writing? These questions will shape our exploration of Paul's shorter epistles. These letters — Ephesians, Philippians, Colossians, 1 and 2 Thessalonians, and Philemon — range from Paul's supposedly earliest epistle to those seemingly written so late that Paul was dead when he composed them.[1] There is, however, a broad cultural context that links these letters and that also provides the central tradition against which Paul seems to be warning the churches. That context, I suggest, is one of empire.

In recent years, the exploration of Paul's letters in terms of their imperial context has grown by leaps and bounds.[2] I shall, therefore, begin by briefly demonstrating how the language of these epistles provocatively

---

1. Perhaps I should here come clean and confess my judgment that all of these epistles were written by Paul. My exegesis, below, supports such a reading.

2. In addition to those works listed below in relation to the letters we are considering, see Richard A. Horsley, ed., *Paul and Empire: Religion and Power in Roman Imperial Society* (Harrisburg: Trinity Press International, 1997); Richard A. Horsley, ed., *Paul and Politics: Ekklesia, Israel, Imperium, Interpretation: Essays in Honor of Krister Stendahl* (Harrisburg: Trinity Press International, 2000); Dieter Georgi, *Theocracy in Paul's Praxis and Theology* (trans. David E. Green; Minneapolis: Fortress, 1991); and Neil Elliott, *Liberating Paul: The Justice of God and the Politics of the Apostle* (Sheffield: Sheffield Academic Press, 1995).

My thanks to Brian Walsh for reading and commenting critically on this chapter.

challenges the empire in which they were written. I will then move on to a brief consideration of how the imperial reality within which these letters were written resonates with our own cultural reality. Within this broad context of ancient and contemporary empire, I will then explore Paul's quotations of and allusions to the Scriptures of Israel. This exploration will attempt to demonstrate how the context of many of these scriptural allusions resonates with, and provides a challenge to, the dominant imperial ideology that surrounded the early followers of Jesus. In conclusion I will draw some broad implications for our reading of these texts and for the shape of our own communal lives as Christians.

Let me state at the outset that I do not intend to do a detailed source and textual analysis of every reference to Israel's Scriptures in these letters. Such work has been undertaken elsewhere, and I see no need to repeat it.[3] I will, rather, be demonstrating how the passages from Israel's Scriptures to which Paul alludes, or from which he quotes, provide a broad conceptual matrix for Paul's reflections on how to be followers of Jesus, the Messiah of the covenant God. In addition, the wider story of the covenant God in relation to both Israel and the world will be shown to be the underlying narrative to which Paul appeals and which he reinterprets throughout these epistles.

The Imperial Context of Paul's Shorter Epistles

It is becoming increasingly clear from both archaeological evidence and a close reading of the texts themselves that the letters that concern us in this chapter were written to communities in cities with flourishing imperial cults.[4] A prominent temple to Caesar was situated in Ephesus. Philippi en-

---

3. See Christopher D. Stanley, *Paul and the Language of Scripture: Citation Technique in the Pauline Epistles and Contemporary Literature* (Cambridge: Cambridge University Press, 1992); Andrew T. Lincoln, "The Use of the Old Testament in Ephesians," *JSNT* 14 (1982) 16-57; N. T. Wright, "Jesus Christ Is Lord: Philippians 2:5-11," in *The Climax of the Covenant: Christ and Law in Pauline Theology* (Edinburgh: T&T Clark, 1991) 56-98; Stephen G. Brown, "The Intertextuality of Isa 66:17 and 2 Thess 2:7: A Solution for the Restrainer Problem," in *Paul and the Scriptures of Israel* (ed. Craig A. Evans and James A. Sanders; Sheffield: Sheffield Academic Press, 1993) 254-77; and Ivor H. Jones, "Once More, Isaiah 66: The Case of 2 Thessalonians," in *The Old Testament in the New Testament: Essays in Honour of J. L. North* (ed. Steve Moyise; Sheffield: Sheffield Academic Press, 2000) 235-55.

4. On the ubiquity and power of the imperial cult in Asia Minor, see S. R. F. Price, *Rit-*

joyed the status of Roman citizenship as a Roman colony and was properly grateful to Caesar for this benefit.[5] Thessaloniki had been favored with the status of a free city for its loyalty to the emperor.[6] There is an epigraphic recording of a temple to Caesar built during the time of Augustus in Thessaloniki as well as fragments of a statue of Augustus. In addition, Thessalonian coins testify to the widespread presence of the imperial cult.[7] Such evidence is harder to come by for Colossae since it was destroyed in an earthquake between AD 60 and 64; however, the reputation of Colossae in the production of purple cloth for imperial use suggests that the imperial cult would have been practiced in this city as well.[8] In addition, a flourishing temple to the empire existed in the nearest town, Aphrodisias.

This external evidence is supported by the language and imagery of Paul's letters themselves. Paul frequently uses the vocabulary and imagery of the empire and does so in a way that provides a challenge to the empire. Such challenge is often rooted in Paul's allusions to Israel's Scriptures, and hence it will be explicated below. For the purposes of this introductory overview, I will point out a few of the imperial echoes and images without indicating their rhetorical function within the letters.

In an empire celebrated for the bringing of a gospel *(euangelion)* of salvation through the Pax Romana, Paul proclaims another gospel, the gospel of God (1 Thess 2:2, 8, 9) and his Messiah (Phil 1:27; 1 Thess 3:2), a gospel that is growing and bearing fruit in the whole world (Col 1:6) and proclaimed to every creature under heaven (Col 1:23).[9] This is a gospel with a

uals and Power: The Roman Imperial Cult in Asia Minor (Cambridge: Cambridge University Press, 1984).

5. Morna D. Hooker, "The Epistle to the Philippians," in *The New Interpreter's Bible* (Nashville: Abingdon, 2000) 11:469-70.

6. Abraham Smith, "The First Letter to the Thessalonians," in *The New Interpreter's Bible*, 11:677.

7. See J. R. Harrison, "Paul and the Imperial Gospel at Thessaloniki," *JSNT* 25, no. 1 (2002) 71-96, esp. p. 81 for examples and further bibliography.

8. Regarding the earthquake, see Andrew T. Lincoln, "The Letter to the Colossians," in *The New Interpreter's Bible*, 11:580. On the production of purple cloth in Colossae, see Edwin Yamauchi, *The Archaeology of New Testament Cities in Western Asia Minor* (Grand Rapids: Baker Book House, 1980) 157.

9. On the imperial overtones of the language of gospel, see Neil Elliott, "Paul and the Politics of Empire," in Horsley, ed., *Paul and Politics*, 24; Georgi, *Theocracy*, 83; N. T. Wright, "Gospel and Theology in Galatians," in *Gospel in Paul: Studies in Corinthians, Galatians and Romans for Richard N. Longenecker* (ed. L. Ann Jervis and Peter Richardson; Sheffield: Shef-

geographical scope equal to Caesar's. It is a gospel that proclaims a different Savior, the Messiah (Eph 5:23), to whom all things will be subjected (Phil 3:21) and through whom peace is brought to those both far and near, indeed to all of creation (Eph 2:14-17; 6:15; Col 1:20; 2 Thess 3:16).[10]

In addition, there are further imperial references unique to each epistle. In Colossians Paul challenges the ubiquity of imperial images by proclaiming Jesus as the image of the invisible God (Col 1:15), and in language shared with Ephesians he proclaims that Jesus is above all thrones, dominions, rulers, and authorities (Col 1:16; Eph 1:21-23), a clear reference to the throne of Caesar and his dominion, rule, and authority over the whole world. Indeed, all things are under the feet of this Jesus (Eph 1:22), and he is head of the body of the church, not the body politic ruled by Caesar (Eph 1:22; Col 1:18).

In Phil 3:20 Paul baldly states, "but our citizenship *(politeuma)* is in heaven, and from there we are expecting a Savior, the Lord Jesus Christ." The whole sentence is loaded: from the assertion that the citizenship of this Christian community in a Roman colony is not found in Rome, to the expectation of a Savior other than Caesar, who is Lord rather than Caesar.[11]

In 1 Thessalonians, Paul's description of the return of Jesus is rooted in standard imperial language: the *parousia* denotes the coming of an imperial visitor to a city, and the meeting *(apantēsin)* of Jesus in the air echoes the civic welcome accorded to a visiting dignitary or a triumphant ruler.[12] In addition, the words "peace and security" of 1 Thess 5:3 "appear individually on the imperial coinage with monotonous regularity and sum up the protection against external threat offered by Roman power."[13] Similarly, in 2 Thessalonians, the language of *epiphaneia* (manifestation, ap-

---

field Academic Press, 1994) 226-28; Richard A. Horsley, "Paul's Counter-Imperial Gospel: Introduction," in Horsley, ed., *Paul and Empire*, 140-41.

10. On imperial peace, see Klaus Wengst, *The Pax Romana and the Peace of Jesus Christ* (trans. John Bowden; London: SCM, 1987) 8-11; Paul Zanker, *The Power of Images in the Age of Augustus* (trans. Alan Shapiro; Ann Arbor: University of Michigan Press, 1990) 175; Dieter Georgi, "Who Is the True Prophet?" in Horsley, ed., *Paul and Empire*, 42; Helmut Koester, "Imperial Ideology and Paul's Eschatology in 1 Thessalonians," in Horsley, ed., *Paul and Empire*, 162. On "savior" as an official title for rulers in the imperial cult, see Harrison, "Paul and the Imperial Gospel," 87.

11. Further on Philippians as challenge to the empire, see N. T. Wright, "Paul's Gospel and Caesar's Empire," in Horsley, ed., *Paul and Politics*, 160-83.

12. See Harrison, "Paul and the Imperial Gospel," 82-87, for examples.

13. Harrison, "Paul and the Imperial Gospel," 86.

pearance; 2 Thess 2:8) is linked with the appearance of rulers who bring salvation, and the references to grace, peace, and a Savior, as well as the *parousia,* evoke these imperial themes.[14]

Philemon, because of its brevity and specificity, at first glance seems not to reflect such an imperial context, until it is recognized that slavery, the underlying situation of the letter, formed the economic building block for the exploitative economy of the empire. Faithfulness to a social ethic that included slavery was, therefore, faithfulness to the empire. Hence Paul's urging for the release of Philemon was a counter-imperial move at a very fundamental level.[15]

The Imperial Context of North American Christianity

I have taken some pains to outline this context for our investigation because these letters demonstrate a fundamental worldview in which the story of the empire is dominant. Such a worldview is not that far removed from our contemporary context. We, too, live in a political economy that promises peace, like Rome, through the proliferation of violent military action. We, too, live in an empire where the images of corporate success and advertising shape our consciousness and dominate our imagination in ways that promise salvation but in reality enslave us. We, too, live in an empire that relies on the slavery of third-world sweatshops to produce the clothing we so cheaply enjoy.[16] The military promise of Rome to bring peace, the economic exploitation by which Rome maintained control, the domination of the imagination by the images, symbols, and stories of the empire — all find their parallel in our context of military control, economic exploitation of the two-thirds world, and the ubiquity of corporate images and symbols that justify such control by convincing us of the validity of the American (and Canadian) dream.

14. Frederick Danker and Robert Jewett, "Jesus as the Apocalyptic Benefactor in Second Thessalonians," in *The Thessalonian Correspondence* (ed. Raymond F. Collins; Leuven: Leuven University Press, 1990) 486-98.

15. A well-known description that emphasizes the place of slaves, women, and children while drawing a parallel between the household and the state is from Aristotle, *Politics* 1.1260a 9-14.

16. See Naomi Klein, *No Logo — No Space, No Choice, No Jobs: Taking Aim at the Brand Bullies* (Toronto: A. A. Knopf Canada, 2000) 195-229.

In the first century Paul challenged the imperial story by reference to the story of Israel, reinterpreted in the story of Jesus. It may be that in exploring how Paul appeals to these stories we will discover how we, too, can live out of them.

Which Lord? What Gospel? Which Peace?

Ephesians

Ephesians is the most overtly allusive text of the letters we are looking at. Paul's allusions to the Scriptures in Ephesians set up a number of the themes that are central throughout the other epistles under consideration. I will begin with some of the more widely acknowledged allusions and let them set the stage for allusions that I believe are just as prominent but that have not been so widely acknowledged.

Our first text is Eph 1:20-23:

> God put this power to work in Christ when he raised him from the dead and seated him at his right hand in the heavenly places, far above all rule and authority and power and dominion, and above every name that is named, not only in this age but also in the age to come. And he has put all things under his feet and has made him head over all things for the church, which is his body, the fullness of him who fills all in all.[17]

This cluster of verses alludes to two psalms, Ps 8:6 and Ps 110:1, the latter of which is widely used in early Christian documents. Psalm 110 begins this way:

> The Lord says to my lord,
> "Sit at my right hand
> until I make your enemies your footstool."

The royal overtones of the allusion are clear. As Andrew Lincoln points out,

17. All translations are from the New Revised Standard Version unless otherwise noted.

The psalm [110] may well originally have been employed as an enthrone-ment psalm for the king. Its terminology of a session at the right hand had parallels in the ancient near eastern world where the king was often repre-sented as seated next to the tutelary deity of a particular city or nation and where occupying a place on the god's right hand meant that the ruler exer-cised power on behalf of the god and held a place of supreme honor.[18]

In addition, Lincoln observes that throughout the Old Testament the right hand of Yahweh is "represented as the position of favour (Ps 80:18; Jer 22:24), of victory (Ps 20:6; 44:3; 48:10; Isa 41:10) and of power (Exod 15:6; Ps 89:13; Isa 48:13)."[19] Such emphases are prominent within Psalm 110 itself and also in Eph 1:20-23.

The phrase "he has put all things under his feet" from Eph 1:22 could be taken as an allusion to the latter half of Ps 110:1; however, it is actually much closer to Ps 8:6: "you have put all things under his feet" (*panta hypetaxas hypokatō tōn podōn autou*, v. 7 LXX). The effect of this double al-lusion is striking. On the one hand, Psalm 8 is a celebration of humanity as those to whom God has given glory and honor and dominion over all of creation so that all of creation is under their feet, that is, under their rule. The echo then suggests that the Messiah (the Christ of v. 20) is the one whose dominion over all things fulfills what it is to be truly human in the world. (This is, of course, more explicitly demonstrated by Paul in the Ad-amic allusion of Col 1:15, which forms part of the parallel passage to Eph 1:20-23. We will deal with this passage below.) This identification is strengthened in Eph 2:6, where Paul describes how God has "raised us up with Christ and made us sit with him in the heavenly places in Christ Je-sus." The end of this story is like the beginning: humanity, too, is called back to their original rule and calling.

On the other hand, the allusion to Ps 110:1 describes a ruler who is ap-pointed by God to rule over enemies whom God will judge and whose heads he will shatter (vv. 5-6). This is a psalm of victory that celebrates the conquering rule of God's king over his enemies. The situation of this psalm in Ephesians has the effect, therefore, of reinforcing the authoritative rule of the Messiah over all the other rulers, authorities, powers, and dominions of Eph 1:21. In the face of an overwhelming Roman empire that seemed to have

18. Lincoln, "The Use of the OT in Ephesians," 40.
19. Lincoln, "The Use of the OT in Ephesians," 40.

absolute authority, Paul describes the power of God working through Jesus who is above even Roman rule, authority, dominion, and power.

However, the allusion to Psalm 110 not only reinforces this point but also deepens the story line for those with ears to hear. Not only is God's Messiah the true ruler, but God will overthrow all other rulers and subject them to his Messiah. The allusion, therefore, could evoke a violent conquering of enemies. This violence, however, is undermined in Paul's subsequent argument and next scriptural allusion: the proclamation of peace.

The proclamation of peace in Eph 2:14-17 is found in the context of a description of the Ephesian believers when they were estranged from God: they were dead (2:1), following a disobedient ruler and power (2:2); they were children of wrath (2:3), Gentiles by birth, alienated from the commonwealth *(politeias)* of Israel, strangers to the covenant of promise, and without hope (2:12). In Psalm 110 such disobedient Gentiles, alienated from Israel and strangers to the covenant, would have been the recipients of God's judgment. Not so here. In Ephesians, these former enemies are precisely those with whom God has made peace. In this Messiah, what is put to death is not the enemies, but the *hostility* between those far off and those near (Eph 2:13-16), culminating in the peace of v. 17: "So he came and proclaimed peace to you who were far off and peace to those who were near."[20]

We find in this verse an allusion to Isa 57:19. In the context of attacking the unfaithful idolatry of the people, the prophet turns from condemnation to hope: "Build up, build up, prepare the way, remove every obstruction from my people's way" (Isa 57:14). Prepare the way for what? "Peace, peace, to the far and the near, says the Lord; and I will heal them" (Isa 57:19).

The overtones of Isaiah 57, with its emphasis on the idolatry of the people, could not be stronger for those Ephesian Christians, whose former life is described later precisely using the prophetic terminology of idolatry (Eph 4:17-23). However, they now worship a ruler who is part of a different story line — not a story where peace is granted in the Roman manner by means of violent death to the stranger, nor even the story line of Psalm 110 where heads roll to demonstrate the power of a king, but rather the story of a different Messiah, who himself dies that there may be peace.

20. Of course, the empire considered itself the true purveyor of peace; see note 10 above. However, as Pheme Perkins puts it, "Empires may spread a dominant culture or language that forces former enemies to live together in peace. But that is not the new creation in which people are genuinely sisters and brothers in Christ" ("The Letter to the Ephesians," in *The New Interpreter's Bible Commentary*, 11:405).

In addition, the Ephesians passage reflects Isa 52:7, where a messenger brings the good news of peace. In both Eph 2:17 and Isa 52:7, peace *(eirēnēn; eirēnēs)* becomes the object of the proclamation *(euēngelisato, euangelizomenou)*. Isaiah 52 proclaims a word of freedom in the midst of a recollection of captivity. The empires of Egypt and Assyria and the oppression that they inflicted (v. 4) are now challenged by a new gospel, the good news that "your God reigns." The language of Isaiah 52 contains a cluster of words that echo the proclamation to the exiles in Isaiah 40 ("gospel" in Isa 52:7 and 40:9, and Yahweh coming in glory in Isa 52:8 and 40:5), but the imagery here also echoes that of the empire:

> How beautiful upon the mountains
> > are the feet of the messenger who announces a gospel of peace,
> who brings good news,
> > who announces salvation,
> > who says to Zion, "Your God reigns."　　　　　　　(Isa 52:7)

"Peace," "good news," "salvation" — all of these are used by the empire to describe the story of Rome. But the gospel of peace that Paul proclaims is one that challenges the peace of Rome. In evoking Isaiah 52, itself a challenge to Egypt and Assyria, Paul is reminding the Ephesian Christians that their God is one who has a history of challenging oppressive empires with a different peace and another kind of salvation. The world of Isaiah 40 and 52, like the world of the first century, might seem to be dominated by an all-powerful empire, but both Paul and Isaiah bring another word and proclaim another reality: "our God reigns!"

Like Isaiah 52, Ephesians 2 is concerned with allegiance. In a world where allegiance to Rome was ultimate, Paul turns the categories on their head by describing a misplaced allegiance in terms of being aliens and strangers, not to Rome, but to the *politeias* of *Israel*. However, whereas Rome severely judged those who were unfaithful to its *politeias* — and did so by subjecting them to death on a cross — Paul describes a Messiah who makes peace with those who are alien, and who does so by offering himself on such a cross.[21]

---

21. Some have argued that another possible intertext of Eph 2:17 is Isa 9:5. Lincoln gives a number of textual reasons as to why such an allusion is unlikely, although he suggests that subsequent Jewish interpretations of Isa 9:5 may provide the background for Eph 2:17 (Lincoln, "The Use of the OT in Ephesians," 26).

This story line is reinforced in two subsequent allusions in Ephesians. The first is a passage that is concerned with the issue of unity in the community. In Eph 4:8, Paul strikingly paraphrases Ps 68:18:

> When he ascended on high
> he made captivity itself a captive;
> he gave gifts to his people. (Eph 4:8)

> You ascended to the high mount,
> leading captives in your train
> and receiving gifts from people,
> even from those who rebel against the Lord God's abiding there.
> (Ps 68:18)

Like Psalm 110, Psalm 68 is a psalm of conquest. The captives being led are those kings whom God has scattered (vv. 11-14), and as the psalm continues to describe the tribute that kings bring to God, it also describes God's salvation in terms of increasingly violent battle imagery.

The story line of this psalm is not far removed from the story line of Rome, which rejoiced in precisely this kind of festival, where humiliated captives were led in a victory parade while glory and honor were given to Caesar by those subject peoples who had formerly rebelled.[22]

Paul's (mis)quotation of this psalm overturns all such ways of being empire, whether Jewish or Roman, and describes a different Lord and Messiah who made *captivity* a captive (Eph 4:8). That is, no more is captivity the way that enemies are to be treated; no more is servile subjection the order of the day. This Messiah overturns captivity, and instead of receiving tribute as gifts he *gives* gifts (4:8). These gifts are later described this way: "that some would be apostles, some prophets, some evangelists, some pastors and teachers, to equip saints for the work of ministry, for building up the body of Christ" (vv. 11-12). That is, unlike the empire, which seeks to fragment the body with its humiliating festivals, this ruler, this Messiah, is one whose gifts work for unity, for upbuilding, for peace.

Psalm 68 had also been interpreted extensively in rabbinic tradition, becoming associated with Moses' ascension to heaven to receive the Torah

---

22. Price, *Rituals and Power*, 110.

and other heavenly secrets.[23] As a result, Psalm 68 came to be closely associated with Pentecost, which increasingly was the feast that commemorated the law-giving at Sinai.[24] If this is the case, then Paul's citation of Psalm 68 also undermines the law, replacing the gift of Torah, which set Israel apart as a special people before God, with a new set of gifts, which build up a new body, made up of Jew and Gentile, those near and those far off.

Paul's evocation of Psalm 68, therefore, creates a number of resonances for his listeners. On the one hand, they are resonances of God's power and rule over other peoples. But these resonances are undermined by Paul's change of quotation. This results in a subversion of any authority and rule that violently deal in death rather than in building up a new body rooted in peace.

On the other hand, Paul's evocation of Psalm 68 creates resonances of the giving of Torah. And again, the story line of the Torah is undermined, for the gifts of this Messiah are those that create a new humanity drawn from beyond the boundaries of the law.

Such a subversion is again supported in the last allusion that I will explore from Ephesians.[25] As the letter ends with a description of the struggle of this community against the rulers, authorities, cosmic powers, and spiritual forces, Paul evocatively describes the armor of God:

> Stand therefore, and fasten the belt of truth around your waist, and put on the breastplate of righteousness. As shoes for your feet put on whatever will make you ready to proclaim the gospel of peace. With all of these take the shield of faith, with which you will be able to quench all the flaming arrows of the evil one. Take the helmet of salvation, and the sword of the Spirit, which is the word of God. (Eph 6:14-17)

This passage combines various allusions from Isaiah. The first is from Isaiah 11, where the shoot from the stump of Jesse who will be part of a creational restoration is described this way:

23. Lincoln, "The Use of the OT in Ephesians," 19.

24. See Lincoln, "The Use of the OT in Ephesians," 20, for rabbinic and targumic references.

25. Quotations and allusions that are not discussed in this paper are: the allusions to Ezek 16:8-14 in Eph 5:25-27, and to Lev 19:18 in Eph 5:33a; and the quotations of Gen 2:24 in Eph 5:31-32, and Exod 20:12 LXX in Eph 6:2, 3. The suggested allusions to Zech 8:16 and Ps 4:4 in Eph 4:25-26 and Prov 23:31 in Eph 5:18 are to my mind too faint to be warranted.

> Righteousness shall be the belt around his waist,
> and faithfulness the belt around his loins. (Isa 11:5)

This ruler will act for the poor and judge the wicked. His rule will be a sign to other nations that God is glorious and has called his people back from their captivity (vv. 10-16).

Such hope for captive Israel is central in the second allusion, from Isa 52:7:

> How beautiful on the mountains
> are the feet of the messenger who announces peace,
> who brings good news,
> who announces salvation,
> who says to Zion, "Your God reigns."

For Isaiah, the gospel of peace is that, in spite of all appearances to the contrary, God is the one who reigns. These overtones, of course, are central to the message of Ephesians 6.

The last allusion is to Isa 59:17. Israel is unable to practice righteousness or justice, and so God intervenes to enact such justice and righteousness:

> He put on righteousness like a breastplate,
> and a helmet of salvation on his head;
> he put on garments of vengeance for clothing,
> and wrapped himself in fury as a mantle. (Isa 59:17)

All three of these passages announce God's reign; one passage describes the Messiah who brings this reign. All announce salvation, God's peace, good news, and righteousness. Two describe this salvation in terms of judgment on the nations: in Isaiah 11, God's people will swoop down on the Philistines, plunder the people of the east, and put forth their hands against Edom, Moab, and the Ammonites (Isa 11:14); in Isaiah 59, God will deal out wrath and requital to his enemies (Isa 59:18). It is striking, therefore, that while Paul borrows the terminology of these passages he does so in a way that rejects such violent judgment on behalf of God's people. This is most clearly seen in Paul's description of the armor of God in Ephesians 6. Rather than appropriating the imagery of Isa 59:17 in its entirety, Paul stops short. Vengeance and fury are *not* part of the armor of this community. As we have seen, the Ephesian Christians are living out a different story, one that challenges the parameters and assumptions not only of the Roman empire but also of Israel when Israel acts like empire.

Whose Image?

Philippians

Philippians continues this redefinition of the community in the Christ hymn of 2:5-11:

> Let the same mind be in you that was in Christ Jesus,
> who, though he was in the form of God,
> > did not regard equality with God
> > as something to be exploited,
> but emptied himself,
> > taking the form of a slave,
> > being born in human likeness.
> And being found in human form,
> > he humbled himself
> > and became obedient to the point of death —
> > even death on a cross.
>
> Therefore God also highly exalted him
> > and gave him the name
> > that is above every name.
> So that at the name of Jesus
> > every knee should bend,
> > in heaven and on earth and under the earth,
> and every tongue should confess
> > that Jesus Christ is Lord,
> > to the glory of God the Father.

This poem contains both an extended allusion to Adam and an obvious echo of Isa 45:23, both of which challenge the story line of the empire.[26]

26. The following section is dependent on Sylvia Keesmaat, "Crucified Lord or Conquering Savior: Whose Story of Salvation?" *HBT* 26, no. 2 (2004) 73-79.

Although Adam is not explicitly mentioned in Phil 2:5-11, both Morna Hooker and N. T. Wright have convincingly demonstrated that this passage hinges on a contrast between Adam and Jesus.[27] Hooker puts it this way: "To make sense of any parallel with Adam in Philippians, we have to understand Christ to be the 'blueprint' of what Man was *meant* to be, the perfect image of God and reflection of his glory."[28] The question, of course, is, What precisely was humanity *meant* to be? What was the significance of being "in the image of God" and "a reflection of his glory"?

Throughout Israel's history, the language of humanity being created in the image of God carried polemical weight. According to the mythology of Babylon, for instance, humanity was created as a slave people to do the menial labor of the gods. In the face of such a view of humanity, Israel in exile under Babylonian rule told a different story, a story of humanity created not to be slaves but to be the image-bearer of God and to reflect God's glory in their stewardly dominion over the earth (Gen 1:26-28; 2:15).[29]

Similarly, in the Roman empire, where the emperor embodied the glory of the gods and where the images of the emperor dominated public space, this story of humanity as the image of God challenged the imperial ethos. In Israel's telling of the story, the call to image God and to bear God's glory is not limited to the ruler but is applied to all of humanity (see, for instance, Psalm 8). The structure of imperial society, rooted in the superiority of the emperor and of those who were closest to him, was thus undermined by Paul's allusion to Adam.

The role of Adam in Israel's history, however, was not one of unambiguous fulfillment of this calling. Throughout the biblical story, and in rabbinic tradition, Adam (and Israel) lost this glory by worshiping images. As Hooker puts it:

> Paul — like the Rabbis — does not say that man ever lost the image of God. . . . The things which man *did* lose were the glory of God and the dominion over Nature which were associated with that image; and he

27. See Morna D. Hooker, "Philippians 2:6-11," in *From Adam to Christ: Essays on Paul* (Cambridge: Cambridge University Press, 1990) 88-100; Hooker, "Adam *Redivivus*: Philippians 2 Once More," in Moyise, ed., *The Old Testament in the New Testament*, 220-34; Wright, "Jesus Christ Is Lord," 62-90.

28. Hooker, "Adam *Redivivus*," 231.

29. J. Richard Middleton, "The Liberating Image? Interpreting the *Imago Dei* in Context," *CSR* 24 (1994) 8-25.

lost them when he forgot that he himself was *eikōn theou,* and sought to find that *eikōn* elsewhere.[30]

In Philippians 2 these themes come together in a way that not only recalls the story of Adam but also brings that story to its fitting conclusion. Unlike Adam, and all of humanity after him, who had sought to be equal to God (cf. Gen 3:5), Jesus did not see his equality with God as something to be exploited. Rather, in giving up his rights, he was, in the end, the one who finally did fulfill the calling of Adam in ruling over creation and reflecting God's glory in that wise rule. In his own humility he became Lord of all things in heaven and on earth, bringing glory to God the father (Phil 2:10-11).

The whole story line of Phil 2:6-11, therefore, with its echoes of the Adam narrative, sets up Jesus as the one who fulfils the calling to be truly human. And Jesus does so in a way that challenges all the conceptions of humanity held dear by the empire. In an empire held together by a social system that functions by a close adherence to status and social distinction, the story of Jesus is one where the one who is equal to God abandons all the privilege of that rank and becomes a slave who dies the death of the lower classes. This alone would be regarded as the worst kind of folly. But, paradoxically, the result of this giving up of the life of privilege for the death of the oppressed is an exaltation that places Jesus in the same category as Caesar, ruler of the world. Moreover, in proclaiming Jesus as Lord, the claim of Caesar to universal lordship is challenged. As N. T. Wright puts it, "the poem in [Phil 2] has exactly the same shape as some formulaic imperial acclamations; Jesus, not Caesar, has been a servant and is now to be hailed as *kyrios.*"[31]

On the one hand, Paul's echo of Adam in these verses challenges the imperial claim that Caesar is the only legitimate ruler over the world who bears the image and glory of God. This allusion evokes the story of Israel, where all of humanity is called to bear God's image and reflect God's glory in wise rule over the world. On the other hand, by telling the story of Jesus as a fulfillment of the calling of humanity, Paul challenges the rule of

---

30. Morna Hooker, "Adam in Romans 1," in *From Adam to Christ,* 83. I would nuance this slightly by arguing that humanity didn't lose the dominion over nature; but rather, in not bearing the image of God, humanity became unable to faithfully fulfill the calling to have dominion. The result of such a loss of calling is unfruitfulness (see Hosea 4 and Isaiah 24).

31. Wright, "Paul's Gospel and Caesar's Empire," 174.

Caesar in the person of Jesus. And Jesus is a ruler whose Lordship over all of creation is not achieved through the socially acceptable avenues of exploiting status and rank. Rather, his Lordship is the result of subversively abandoning such status and rank in humble obedience. Jesus is the Lord who not only challenges all other *claims* to rule but also challenges all other *paths* to lordship and rule.

The climactic ending to this hymn contains a very strong allusion to Isa 45:23. In Isaiah, this verse is itself the climax of a chapter that asserts that Israel's God is the only God of all the earth.[32] Moreover, God's rule over all the earth is demonstrated in his choosing of Cyrus in order to set the exiles free (45:1, 13). Also central to this chapter is a contrast between idols and gods who are unable to save, on the one hand (45:20), and the Lord, on the other, who is not only the creator of heaven and earth besides whom there is no other (45:5, 6, 14, 18, 21, 22) but also the one who is able to save (45:15, 17, 21, 22). For those with ears to hear, the overtones of Isaiah 45 in Philippians 2 are clear: in Jesus, God has accomplished what was promised of old; in Jesus, the Messiah, the anointed one who is Lord, the old promise has come true. And this promise has come true, not in Cyrus, nor in Rome, but in Jesus, the new Adam, anointed by God.

In the face of the idolatry of the empire, in the face of the worship of Caesar as lord over all the earth, Paul's allusion to Isa 45:23 reinforces the claim that Jesus is Lord, and it does so by evoking texts that proclaim the power of Israel's God over idols who are impotent to save. In the face of the claims of Babylon and even Persia, Isaiah claimed that Yahweh was the only God of heaven and earth before whom all idols are revealed as vanity and before whom every knee shall bow and every tongue swear (Isa 45:23). In the face of Rome, Paul claimed that Jesus was the Lord before whom all status is revealed as irrelevant and before whom every knee should bend in heaven and on earth and under the earth, and whom every tongue should confess (Phil 2:10-11).

However, Paul's evocation of Isa 45:23 also has another effect. As I indicated, Isaiah's confession emphasizes that Yahweh is the only God before whom all will bow. Paul, however, has applied the language of the one true God to Jesus. Not only does the phrase "Jesus is Lord" challenge Caesar's claim to lordship (after all, "Caesar is lord" was the patriotic and safe acclamation, rather like "God bless America"), but "Jesus is Lord" also contains

---

32. Wright, "Jesus Christ Is Lord," 93.

an implicit redefinition of Yahweh as Lord. Wright describes this redefinition vividly:

> The task of the man who would represent Israel and so save the world is a task which, in Old Testament language, is (however paradoxically) reserved for God himself. The final position of the obedient man — set in glorious authority over the world, in fulfillment of Genesis 1:26ff, Psalm 8:4ff and Daniel 7:14 — is one which (according to Isaiah 45) is thoroughly appropriate for God himself. And, to look at the question from the other side, the nature of a human being, that is, the fact that human beings are made in the image of God, means that becoming human is thoroughly appropriate for one who from the beginning was *en morphē theou*.[33]

Here we have two sides of the same coin: Jesus is the one who fulfills the calling and task of Yahweh to save Israel and rule over the world; and in so doing he fulfills the human calling, which was always to image this God. We have here not only a redefinition of what it is to be human but also a redefinition of what it is to be God. Unlike Caesar, deified after his death, who wielded his supposedly god-given rule through violent and oppressive military and economic control, Jesus reveals a God who becomes human, becomes like a slave, and suffers death in order that those over whom he rules might be transformed from humiliation to share in his glory (Phil 3:21). This is not the image of God that the empire portrayed. Jesus, therefore, not only redefined monotheism but also redefined what God-shaped authority actually looks like.

Colossians

These themes are strengthened and intensified in Colossians. Although Colossians contains no overt quotations of Israel's Scriptures, it is rich in allusions that not only appeal to Israel's story but also deepen the critique of empire that we have been exploring so far in these letters. This critique begins in the first ten verses of Colossians 1, which contain two provocative references to bearing fruit:

33. Wright, "Jesus Christ Is Lord," 95.

You have heard of this hope before in the word of truth, the gospel that has come to you. Just as it is bearing fruit *(karpophoroumenon)* and growing in the whole world, so it has been bearing fruit among yourselves from the day you heard it and truly comprehended the grace of God. (vv. 5-6)

For this reason, since the day we heard it, we have not ceased praying for you and asking that you may be filled with the knowledge of God's will in all spiritual wisdom and understanding, so that you may lead lives worthy of the Lord, fully pleasing to him, as you bear fruit *(karpophorountes)* in every good work and as you grow in the knowledge of God. (vv. 9-10)

For the Colossian community, the claim of fruitfulness and fertility was all around them, a claim rooted in the oppressive military might of the empire, in the controlling social structures of the empire, and in the evocative images of lush fertility found on the buildings, statues, and household items that shaped their visual imagination.[34] It was a claim that incessantly called everyone to acknowledge that Rome was the source of abundance, and that in order to participate in that abundance in the midst of scarce resources they needed to be faithful to the empire and the structures, oppressive or not, that made the empire powerful.

This was no new claim. Throughout its history, Israel not only lived in the shadow of empire but also constantly grappled with the claims of empire to be the source of abundance, security, and fertility, whether those claims were made by Egypt, Babylon, Persia, Rome, or even Israel's own rulers.[35] But there was also a counter-testimony with that history, a witness to an alternative social vision that challenged the claims of empire. The fruitfulness of Yahweh, and the fruit that Israel was called to bear, was central to that counter-testimony. In every period of Israel's history and in every genre of its literature, there is a witness to God's fruitful blessing in creation and the practice of a social ethic that images God in redemption and

---

34. See Zanker, *The Power of Images,* 171-79, for descriptions of the link between fruitfulness and military might, as well as the ubiquity of images of fruitfulness.

35. See Genesis 47; Exod 16:3; 1 Kings 4:20-23; 1 Kings 21. On 1 Kings 4:20-23, see Walter Brueggemann, "'Vine and Fig Tree': A Case Study in Imagination and Criticism," in *A Social Reading of the Old Testament: Prophetic Approaches to Israel's Communal Life* (ed. Patrick D. Miller; Minneapolis: Fortress, 1994) 91-110.

care for creation and neighbor. Again and again the two are linked: fertility and fruitfulness in the land, on the one hand, and peace and security, on the other, are rooted in a rejection of the militaristic consumerism of the empire and the social and economic practices that support it. The language of such blessing is the language of fruitfulness (Lev 26:3-6; Isa 5:1-7; Ezek 34:25-31; Mic 4:1-5; Zech 8:1-16).

These themes come to their climax in Jesus. The community that Jesus envisions not only is judged by its fruit but is itself a manifestation of the fruitfulness of Yahweh. At key points in the narrative — some of them foundational, some of them climactic — we meet the metaphors and language of fruitfulness. For instance, the parable of the sower, which sets the stage for all of the other parables, reaches its zenith in those who hear the word and understand it and bear fruit *(karpophorei),* yielding a hundredfold, or sixty, or thirty (Matt 13:23; par. Mark 4:20; Luke 8:15). This is fruit that grows out of being rooted in the word of Jesus. Again, at the end of the Sermon on the Mount (or the Sermon on the Plain, in Luke), Jesus uses the metaphor of a tree being known by its fruit *(karpōn;* Matt 7:16-20; Luke 6:43-45). This is the summation of a long discourse in which Jesus describes the shape of the community that he is calling into being: "Love your enemies, do good to those who hate you, bless those who curse you, pray for those who abuse you" (Luke 6:27-28). By bearing this fruit, the community refuses to engage the empire on its own terms. It refuses to let enemies be enemies, to let debtors be debtors. As the parallel passage in Matthew shows, reconciliation is the fruit of this kingdom (Matt 5:2-26).

By using the language of fruitfulness, with all of its overtones from the story of Israel and the preaching of Jesus, Paul in Colossians is proclaiming a different gospel that bears fruit fundamentally different from the fruit of the empire. This fruit is rooted not in military alliances and in military might, but in the practice of justice and faithfulness, in the following of a Savior who calls his followers to practice a loving and forgiving generosity that undermines the hoarding abundance touted by the empire. For those in Colossae with ears to hear, these scriptural allusions evoke a whole new world and way of life.

An Image That Brings Peace

The poem of Col 1:15-20 brings together almost all of the themes that we have discussed thus far:

> He is the image of the invisible God,
>   firstborn of all creation,
> for in him were created all things,
>   things in heaven and things on earth,
>   things visible and invisible,
> whether thrones or dominions
>   or rulers or powers —
> all things have been created through him and for him.
> He is before all things,
>   and in him all things hold together.
> He is the head of the body, the church,
>   he is the beginning,
> the firstborn from the dead,
>   so that he might come to have first place in everything.
> For in him all the fullness of God was pleased to dwell,
> and through him God was pleased to reconcile to himself all things,
>   whether on earth or in heaven,
> by making peace through the blood of his cross. (author's trans.)

This hymn evokes the same themes that we discussed in Ephesians and Philippians. Once again Paul alludes to the fulfillment of the Adam story — Jesus is the image of God. We have an allusion to the creation of wisdom in Prov 8:22, created as the firstborn of creation. The sweep is cosmic, from creation to new creation. There is also a faint echo of Gen 9:8-17 in this passage, for in Genesis 9 God reaffirms the covenant with all living things, and the phrase "all living things" or "all flesh" is repeated nine times in the Greek text. In Col 1:15-20, the repetition of "all things" or "everything" occurs seven times.[36] By confessing that, in Jesus, God reconciles all of creation to himself, Paul is reaffirming God's most foundational covenantal promise to be faithful to all of creation.

The identification of Jesus with God, and the linking of God's cove-

---

36. Gen 9:10, 11, 12, 15(×3), 16(×2), 17; Col 1:15, 16(×2), 17(×2), 18, 19, 20.

nant promise to creation with the reconciliation of all things in Jesus through the cross, is a clear challenge to the empire. Not only does the language of image evoke Adam, but it also evokes Caesar, whose images were ubiquitous throughout the ancient world both in statues and on coins.[37] The claim that Jesus is above all thrones, dominions, rulers, or powers, like the similar claim in Ephesians, challenges the throne, dominion, rule, and power of Rome. And Jesus' making of peace, not by killing others on the cross, but by offering up himself in sacrificial death, was a powerful challenge to Roman peace, also maintained by the blood of the cross, a death inflicted on those who challenged Rome's rule.

Paul is here asserting the primacy of the story of Jesus over against the story of Rome. This alternative story line, with its proclamation of a different peace, is rooted deeply within the story of Israel. That story, however, is redefined in Jesus, in whom its central character finds expression.

This challenge to the empire is reinforced in Paul's description, in Colossians 2, of a worldview that is attempting to capture the imagination of the Colossian Christians. Paul's description of this worldview, according to Brian Walsh, echoes the scriptural prophetic polemic against idolatry. Perhaps the best way to draw out the parallels is in the form of a chart.

The Colossian Philosophy	Idolatry
1. the philosophy is captivating (Col 2:8)	1. idolatry makes repentance and knowledge of God impossible (Hos 5:4)
2. the philosophy is empty deceit (2:8), and a shadow without substance (2:17)	2. idolatry is worthless, vanity, and nothingness (Isa 44:9; 57:13; Jer 2:5; Pss 97:7; 115:4-7; 135:15-18)
3. the philosophy is a human tradition (2:8), a human way of thinking (2:18), that imposes human commands and teaching (2:20)	3. idols are constructed by human hands (Isa 2:8; 41:6-7; 44:12; Jer 10:1-10; Hos 8:4, 6; 13:2; Hab 2:18; Ps 115:4)
4. the philosophy is puffed up without cause (2:18) and deceives people by employing so-called plausible arguments (2:4, 8)	4. idolatry results in a deluded mind and a fundamental lack of knowledge (Isa 44:18-20; Hos 4:6); an idol is a teacher of lies (Hab 2:18)

37. See Zanker, *The Power of Images*, 33-77.

5. the philosophy is of no value in checking the flesh (2:23)	5. idolatry is impotent, without value, and does not profit (Jer 2:11; Hos 7:16; Isa 45:20; 46:1-2; Hab 2:19; Pss 115:4-7; 135:15-18)
6. the philosophy disqualifies, insists on self-abasement (2:18), and promotes severe treatment of the body (2:23)	6. idolatry is a matter of exchanging glory for shame (Hos 4:7; 7:16; 13:1-3; Jer 2:11; Ps 106:20; Rom 1:23)[38]

Paul's language in these verses evokes the world of the prophetic critique of idolatry, and in so doing his critique of the empire finds a context in larger biblical tradition. For instance, "the proclamation that Christ triumphs over the rulers and authorities on the cross (2:15) is clearly rooted in the prophetic confession that YHWH is Lord and shares glory with no idols (Isa 42:8; 48:11)."[39] These overtones are heightened when they are put in parallel with Col 1:15-20. As we have seen, prophetic critique of idolatry is rooted in the confession that Yahweh, not the idols, is creator of heaven and earth (Isa 40:12-26; 44:9-28; 45:12, 18; Jer 10:11-16; 51:15-19; Pss 115:16; 135:5-7). So also Paul's critique of the philosophy is rooted in the assertion that Jesus is the one through whom and for whom all things were created (Col 1:15-17). The result of such an echo is that Paul's allusions to empire; his assertion that Jesus is the true image, not Caesar; that Jesus is over all thrones, dominions, rulers, and powers; that Jesus is the head in whom all things hold together, not Caesar; and that Jesus is the one in whom the deity dwells — all of these assertions are rooted in the larger biblical narrative of Yahweh as the one who offers a salvation that defeats the captivity, deceitfulness, vanity, shame, and impotence of idols and the empires that image them. For the Colossian Christians, therefore, Paul's allusions to Israel's Scriptures provide an alternative story line that fundamentally challenges the claims of the story of the empire.

---

38. Most of these references are from Brian J. Walsh, "Late/Post Modernity and Idolatry: A Contextual Reading of Colossians 2:8–3:4," *Ex Auditu* 15 (1999) 8-9. Notice that Isaiah 45 and 57 were discussed above.

39. Walsh, "Late/Post Modernity and Idolatry," 9.

Whose Judgment? What Salvation?

1 Thessalonians

Colossians is permeated with allusions to the beginning of the story; in the Thessalonian correspondence we find reference to the story's end. I will focus first on the controversial passage of 1 Thess 4:13–5:11, which describes the coming of the Lord.[40] Various Old Testament passages have been suggested as the background for the imagery of this passage. Suggestions range from the Sinai theophany, where we find the juxtaposition of a trumpet and of clouds, to the story of Jacob's ladder (Gen 28:10-17), where we find angels descending from and ascending to heaven. While some of the imagery may be similar in these passages, it seems that a little more conceptual affinity is needed for the allusion to have plausibility.[41]

One passage where such affinity is found is, of course, Dan 7:13-14. This passage was recalled frequently in first-century appeals for God to bring salvation. In Daniel 7, the Son of Man comes with the clouds of heaven and receives dominion, glory, and kingship so that all peoples, nations, and languages should serve him. The coming of such a figure in Daniel was, of course, a direct challenge to the Babylonian empire, under which the people suffered in exile. Hence if Paul is alluding to Daniel, he is evoking the powerful image of God coming in salvation to defeat one empire, and he is doing so to confront the claims of another.

Paul's language in Thessalonians powerfully subverts the rhetoric of empire. As we noted above, *parousia* (advent or coming, 1 Thess 4:15), *epiphaneia* (manifestation or appearance, 2 Thess 2:8), *apantēsis* (meet, 1 Thess 4:17), *eirēnē kai asphaleia* (peace and security, 1 Thess 5:3), and *sōtēria* (salvation, 1 Thess 5:8) are all terms that not only find their roots in Jewish apocalyptic writing but also are technical terms for the coming of a ruler to a city *(parousia)*, the manifestation of the ruler who brings salvation *(epiphaneia, sōtēria)*, the civic delegation who met and accompanied a ruler back into the city *(apantēsis)*, and imperial propaganda for peace and

---

40. The following section is dependent on Keesmaat, "Crucified Lord or Conquering Savior," 89-92.

41. It seems more likely that the overwhelming background for these images is not found in the Old Testament, but rather in the Gospels, particularly Matt 24:27, 31; 25:5; Mark 13:35-37; Luke 21:34-36.

security *(eirēnē kai asphaleia)*.[42] In the context of the larger background of the apocalyptic vision of Daniel 7, itself a promise of vindication in the face of Babylon and the suffering it had produced, Paul deliberately uses language that evokes another empire, Rome. In so doing, he recalls the eventual defeat of pagan empires that is promised in Israel's Scriptures and effectively makes these promises the ground of hope for the Christians in Thessaloniki, suffering at the hands of Rome.

Such hope is strengthened in Paul's allusion to Isa 59:17 in 1 Thess 5:8. As we saw above, Paul quite explicitly echoes Isa 59:17 in Eph 6:14-16. Here the allusion is fainter: "but since we belong to the day, let us be sober, and put on the breastplate of faith and love, and for a helmet the hope of salvation" (1 Thess 5:8). Paul has replaced "put on the breastplate of righteousness" *(enedusato dikaiosunēn hōs thōraka)* with "put on the breastplate of faith and love" *(endusamenoi thōraka pisteōs kai agapēs)*, and "a helmet of salvation" *(perikephalaian sōtēriou)* is replaced with "a helmet of the hope of salvation" *(perikephalaian elpida sōtērias)*. The context of these verses is an assurance of the vindication of the community. Wrath will come like a thief in the night upon those who belong to the darkness, those who chant the imperial slogans of peace and security; but for those who belong to the day, salvation and life are the result of this coming. In Isaiah 59, Yahweh has seen that there is no one to intervene and save (v. 16), and so he dons the garments of not only righteousness and salvation but also vengeance and fury (v. 17). This context of judgment is echoed in 1 Thessalonians 5. However, as in Ephesians 6, now it is the *community* that dons the breastplate and helmet. And for their battle, faith and love become the breastplate that protects their heart, and the hope of salvation protects their heads. As for the garments of vengeance and fury, these are not the appropriate clothing of the community at all: "see that none of you repays evil for evil" says Paul a few sentences later (1 Thess 5:15).

This echo of Isa 59:17, by recalling a promise of salvation and judgment, roots the story of the Thessalonian Christians in the larger story of Israel. In that story God promised judgment on the unfaithful and deceitful who chanted the slogans of "peace, peace" in the midst of injustice and oppression (Jer 6:14; 8:11; Ezek 13:10). So also the Thessalonians hope for salva-

---

42. Harrison, "Paul and the Imperial Gospel," 82-87; Koester, "Imperial Ideology and Paul's Eschatology in 1 Thessalonians," 158-62; Smith, "The First Letter to the Thessalonians," 677.

tion in the face of an empire that has reduced peace and security to the vocabulary of ideology. In the midst of their oppression they have hope that God will come again as he has in the past, to grant salvation. The counterpoint of the passage also makes clear what this salvation is from. In an empire that promised peaceful salvation but that in reality inflicted violence and oppression,[43] the Thessalonian Christians are to hope in a salvation that comes from another Lord, Jesus the Messiah. The extensive use of *kyrios* in Thessalonians emphasizes this challenge to the empire.[44] This challenge, and this note of apocalyptic judgment, continues in 2 Thessalonians.

2 Thessalonians

The apocalyptic imagery of 1 Thessalonians is continued in this second epistle. A number of scholars have explored Isaiah 66 as the background of 2 Thess 1:1–2:12.[45] In that passage, the judgment of God is meted out on those who are unfaithful, both within and without Israel. It is a cosmic vision, ending with the new heaven and the new earth, a place of nourishment and peace. However, the last verses of the chapter are ones of judgment. Such a vision of apocalyptic judgment is not, of course, alien to either 1 or 2 Thessalonians. These are churches that are suffering extensive persecution, and hence both letters are filled with lengthy critique of the empire and pointed judgment upon their persecutors, both Jewish and Gentile.

43. Frederick Danker and Robert Jewett point out that the term "salvation" was used as a way to speak of a benefactor. Of course, Caesar, as the ultimate benefactor, was also the most prominent savior; see Danker and Jewett, "Jesus as the Apocalyptic Benefactor in Second Thessalonians," 490. Harrison notes that *sōtēr* was an official title for sovereigns in the Hellenistic ruler cult and the Roman imperial cultus ("Paul and the Imperial Gospel at Thessaloniki," 87).

44. *kyrios* occurs in 1 Thessalonians in the following places: 1 Thess 1:3, 6, 8; 2:15, 19; 3:8, 11, 12, 13; 4:1, 2, 6, 15(x2), 16, 17; 5:2, 9, 12, 23, 27, 28. See Harrison, "Paul and the Imperial Gospel at Thessaloniki," 78. Adolf Deissmann, *Light from the Ancient East: The New Testament Illustrated by Recently Discovered Texts of the Graeco-Roman World* (trans. Lionel R. M. Strachan; New York and London: Harper and Brothers, 1934) 353, also points out that "in the time of the most important of St Paul's letters, the number of examples suddenly rushes up tremendously . . . the statistics are quite striking; everywhere, down to the remotest village, the officials called Nero kyrios." I owe this reference to my student, Joel Black.

45. Most recently, Brown, "The Intertextuality of Isa 66:17 and 2 Thess 2:7," 254-77; Jones, "Once More, Isaiah 66," 235-55.

I would like to suggest that 2 Thess 1:1–2:12 also draws very broadly on scriptural traditions that affirm God's faithfulness to the righteous and that appeal to God's judgment on the unrighteous and the lawless. Such traditions are found both in Isaiah and in the Psalms. One of the most striking echoes is found in 2 Thess 1:9: "They will suffer the punishment of eternal destruction, separated from the presence of the Lord and from the glory of his might" *(apo prosōpou tou kyriou kai apo tēs doxēs tēs ischuos autou)*. The verse echoes a repeated refrain from Isaiah 2: "And now enter into the rock and hide in the earth from before the fear of the Lord and the glory of his might *(apo tēs doxēs tēs ischuos autou)*, when he rises up to break apart the earth" (Isa 2:10, 19, 20). This passage is a passage of judgment against Israel's idolatry. In that context, the people will enter into the rock and hide in the earth in order to escape the glory of the Lord's might. Conversely, in Thessalonians, those who oppress the Thessalonian Christians will not hide from the glory of the Lord's might but will rather be excluded from it.

More prominent in this passage are echoes of a number of psalms that characterize the wicked as those who do lawless deeds *(anomian)* and characterize rulers as "lawless rulers" *(thronos anomias;* Ps 93:4, 16, 20, 23 LXX). For example, Psalm 94 (93 LXX) calls upon God as a God of vengeance to judge the wicked (vv. 1, 2), themes developed by Paul in 2 Thess 1:8. Similarly, the catena of psalms that Paul quotes in Rom 3:10-18 depicts the wicked as the ones who do acts of lawlessness, or who are lawless (Pss 5:4 [5:5 LXX]; 14:4 [13:4 LXX]; 36:2-4, 12 [35:3-5, 13 LXX]). Strikingly, these lawless ones (often translated "evil doers") and their lawless works (often translated as "evil deeds") are closely linked in these psalms with deception and a lack of truth. These themes are also present in 2 Thess 2:10, where Paul describes the lawless one in terms of wicked deception.

Whether or not the Thessalonians would have identified the lawless one with a specific person such as the figure from Dan 11:36-38, who also pays no respect to other gods (Dan 11:37; cf. 2 Thess 2:4), or Pompey, or Gaius Caligula,[46] Paul's description of him using the language of lawlessness has deep resonances in the literature of the Psalms, particularly those psalms that contrast God's judgment of the wicked with God's faithfulness to the oppressed. In addition, the assertion in Psalm 94 that God is not allied with lawless rulers provides a context that associates lawlessness with the ruling powers, whoever they might be. Hence Paul's echoes here serve

---

46. See Smith, "The First Letter to the Thessalonians," 759.

to reassure the persecuted Thessalonian Christians that the empire in which they find themselves is no different from that of the psalmist, who also suffered at the hands of lawlessness and lawless rulers. And like the psalmist, who confidently expected God's salvation in the face of such oppression, the Thessalonian Christians can also rest confidently in God's promise for vindication.

The longing for vindication raises the question of how we read these texts of judgment, especially in light of the message of reconciliation and peace that was central to Ephesians and Colossians. First, let us remember that such texts of apocalyptic judgment are born out of situations of intense persecution and suffering. These are not people in power who are advocating violence against those whom they oppress; these are the oppressed. Second, let us note what these texts do *not* say. Neither of these epistles calls upon the community to take up arms, to resist their oppressors violently, to give an eye for an eye. These are apocalyptic texts that call upon *God* to defeat the powers that perpetuate the persecution they are suffering. Such vengeance, such defeat of evil, such defeat of injustice is in the hands of God, who will finally establish a kingdom of righteousness, justice, and peace, not by violently defeating the human enemies of his people, but by defeating the great power of evil, Satan. Even in the apocalyptically charged 1 Thessalonians, the only battledress is the breastplate of faith and love and the helmet of the hope of salvation (5:8).

An Embodied Story

The cosmic vision that is found in the above epistles must come to expression in the lives of particular communities in the empire. I would like to focus on two final allusions in Colossians and Philemon in order to demonstrate how the calling to live out of a liberating story alternative to the hegemonic narrative of the empire was manifest in the life of the early church.

Philemon

Let us look first at Philemon. There are no overt quotations and no overt allusions to any texts from the Scriptures of Israel in the letter to

Philemon. However, the subject of slavery was central both in the biblical story and in the Roman empire. In this letter Paul is, in a roundabout way, urging Philemon to set Onesimus, his slave, free. "I preferred to do nothing without your consent," he writes, "in order that your good deed might be voluntary and not something forced" (v. 14). Later Paul concludes, pointedly, "Confident of your obedience, I am writing to you, knowing that you will do *even more* than I say" (v. 21; italics added). The "more" than he says, is, of course, granting Onesimus his freedom. And here we meet the central narrative theme of Israel's Scriptures. Freedom from slavery is at the heart of the exodus, in which God freed Israel from slavery. This act of liberation became the basis for numerous laws, particularly the laws of the Sabbath year when slaves were set free (Deuteronomy 15), and the laws of Jubilee, when slaves were not only freed but also given back their inheritance of land (Leviticus 25). It is in the context of such a narrative, such a story of freedom from slavery, that Paul places the freedom that Jesus accomplishes for the early Christian community.[47] It is no wonder, then, that in the letter to Philemon Paul calls for the fundamental shape of that story to be reflected in the life of the early church.

Colossians

An allusion to this story can also be discerned in the letter to the Colossians. There, in the infamous household code, Paul tells slaves that from the Lord they will receive the inheritance (Col 3:24). In Israel's story, slaves receive their inheritance in the year of Jubilee, when their land is returned to them and they are freed to return to it as well (Lev 25). This allusion to Jubilee has the effect of recalling that story into the middle of Paul's injunctions here, raising the challenge of Jubilee at the heart of a passage on slavery. That, along with Paul's other rhetorical strategies in this passage, has the effect of undermining the structure of the household code in which this language occurs.[48] Since slavery was one of the economic building blocks of the empire, this allusion has the effect of calling into question

47. See Sylvia C. Keesmaat, *Paul and His Story: Reinterpreting the Exodus Tradition* (Sheffield: Sheffield Academic Press, 1999).

48. Further on this, see Brian J. Walsh and Sylvia C. Keesmaat, *Colossians Remixed: Subvertng the Empire* (Downers Grove: InterVarsity, 2004) chap. 11.

SYLVIA C. KEESMAAT

the economic basis of the whole imperial system, with its oppressive reliance on slave labor.

Reading Our Story

As we have seen, the whole of the biblical narrative is evoked by Paul in such a way that the story of Israel challenges the story of the empire. The calling of humanity to image God and not the idols of imperial rule, the call to image a Messiah who brings peace rather than violence, the reminder that the destiny of this world is in the end in the hands of God and a crucified Messiah, not the hands of a Roman ruler — all of these provide an alternative story and alternative praxis in the face of empire. Moreover, as we have seen, underlying this alternative story is the story of a people who have left the practice of idolatry in order to be image bearers of the one true God and his Son, Jesus. Such idolatry, and the imperial structures it is rooted in, is challenged at every point, from the creation narrative, where humanity is proclaimed the true and only image of God, to the end of the story, where God's coming will judge the idolatrous practices of the wicked. In the middle of the story we meet Jesus, the one who redefines exactly what the image of God is and at whose coming the rulers of the world will finally be judged for their oppression of the righteous. In addition, however, the story of Jesus not only subverts the story of the empire but also subverts the story of Israel when Israel acts like an empire. In the end, Jesus is the true image of God who shows us how to be truly human; his death on a cross finally brings true reconciliation and peace; and his coming in glory will bring salvation and vindication to those who serve him.

Like the Christian communities to whom Paul addressed these letters, we, too, live in an empire whose violence and oppression are rooted in idolatry. None understand this better than those who experience the promises of the empire for what they are: as captivating, deceitful, and impotent. So Chilean theologian Pablo Richard writes:

> We live in a profoundly idolatrous world — economically, socially, politically, culturo-ideologically, and religiously. We live crushed under the idols of an oppressive and unjust system. To live the demands of faith in this context is not simply a "pious" or personal act; it necessarily entails

a radical confrontation with that system. Idolatry is a question of politics and a question of faith.[49]

Just as the prophets linked the worship of idols to unjust economic practices, we can see the evidence of idolatry in the unjust social and economic practices of globalized capitalism. The consumer materialism of North American culture bears all the characteristics of idolatry: the economy bestows on us our ultimate value; it provides a solution to the basic puzzles of life; it gives us meaning by making us producers or consumers; it has its cathedrals disguised as malls; and it is aggressively evangelistic via television, advertising, and the Internet.[50] This system enslaves our imagination and requires sacrifices that demand the death of our children, the children of the two-thirds world, and the creation itself. And global capitalism has a power that is all the more insidious because it is not recognized as a religion.[51]

> Globalization isn't just an aggressive stage in the history of capitalism. It is a religious movement of previously unheard of proportions. Progress is its underlying myth, unlimited economic growth its foundational faith, the shopping mall (physical or online) its place of worship, consumerism its overriding image, "I'll have a big Mac and fries" its ritual of initiation, and global domination its ultimate goal.[52]

But there is more than the economic aspect of the idolatry that has captivated our world. The prophets are strenuous in their denunciations of Israel's reliance on military alliances for security. Israel is to be the people that relies only on Yahweh, that takes as gift the security and abundance that Yahweh has to offer. And instead, the text makes clear, Israel shows that it is faithless by putting confidence in military alliances (Isa 30:1-7;

---

49. Pablo Richard, "Biblical Theology of Confrontation with Idols," in *The Idols of Death and the God of Life* (trans. Barbara E. Campbell and Bonnie Shepard; Maryknoll, NY: Orbis, 1983) 24.

50. See Brian Rosner, "Soul Idolatry: Greed as Idolatry in the Bible," *Ex Auditu* 15 (1999) 82-83.

51. See Harvey Cox, "The Market as God: Living in the New Dispensation," *Atlantic Monthly* 283, no. 3 (March 1999).

52. Brian Walsh, "Will You Have Fries with that Faith?" *The Varsity* 120, no. 41 (March 7, 2000) 10.

Amos 8:4-10; Psalm 146). It isn't a far stretch to look at the current military industrial complex and recent military actions that are necessary to maintain the North American lifestyle and hegemony in the world and realize that the judgment extends to us as well. We look for peace and security in military might, rather than in the God who proclaimed that swords should be pounded into tools for tending the garden (Isaiah 2 and Micah 4) and a Savior who broke down the dividing wall of hostility and brought peace through his death on the cross (Eph 2:11-21; Col 1:20). The only weapons we are called to bear are truth, righteousness, the gospel of peace, faith and love, the hope of salvation, and the word of God (Eph 6:14-17; 1 Thess 5:8).

Our own imperial context, then, falls under the judgment not only of the prophets but also of Jesus and of Paul. Can we learn strategies for responding to our own reality from this ancient text? At the most basic level, Paul shows us how our rootedness in the story of Israel and the story of Jesus provides us with an alternative vision to that of the empire. Our story subverts the propaganda of our empire by telling the story of a Messiah who brings peace through suffering love rather than through military action. Our story subverts the idolatry of the empire by proclaiming Jesus as the image of what it is to be truly human, rather than the images of idolized beauty and corporate power that shape our culture. Our story, with its judgment on idolatrous economic and military practices, provides us with the language and symbolism for judging a military industrial complex that is so deeply bred in our bones that we find it hard to imagine that there may be another way of living in the world. Our story demonstrates that any alternative vision that proclaims God's shalom for good life on this earth must begin with the shaping of covenantal alternative economic and political communities here and now in our own local contexts. Our story demonstrates, in the recollection of the Jubilee year and Paul's urging of Philemon to free the slave Onesimus, that our covenantal communities should embody economic and political practices that proclaim freedom to the slave. And, most fundamentally, our story proclaims the reality that our God reigns — not corporations, nor military might, nor the siren call of a consumer culture. In acknowledging that rule, perhaps our lives will also be shaped by the truth, justice, faithfulness, peace, and salvation that form the clothing of the follower of Jesus (Eph 6:14-17).

Job as Exemplar in the Epistle of James

KURT ANDERS RICHARDSON

The testing of Job, the story of his physical suffering, and the verbal opposition of his friends convey a bleakness without relief not unlike that expressed by William Butler Yeats in his poem "The Second Coming":

> Things fall apart; the center cannot hold;
> Mere anarchy is loosed upon the world . . .
> The best lack all conviction, while the worst
> Are full of passionate intensity.

For Job, the center that did not hold was not his family, his friends, or even his own faith, but his God. Conventional wisdom is challenged in the book, and only a special kind of prophetic faithfulness will be able to endure. And yet this portrayal of the faithful under trial attracted the author of James[1] as exemplary from the Old Testament.

The singular mention of Job in the whole of the New Testament[2] by

---

1. The curious question of how Ἰάκωβος becomes "James" and not "Jacob" is explored by Luke Timothy Johnson. The English "James" is derived from the Old French "Jaimes," which is related to the Spanish "Jaime" and Italian "Giacomo," both of which appear to be derived from the Vulgar Latin "Jacomus," a "softening" of the Latin "Jacobus," which transliterates the Greek and Hebrew. Thus, we actually have the "Epistle of Jacob" — not an apocryphal/pseudepigraphical text but one that resonates with Old Testament references to the Patriarch (cf. Gen 25:26; Exod 3:6, 15; Isa 40:27; Mic 2:12). See Luke Timothy Johnson, *The Letter of James* (New York: Doubleday, 1995) 93.

2. Although Paul in 1 Cor 3:19 cites Job 5:13 with these words: "For the wisdom of this world is foolishness with God. For it is written, 'He catches the wise in their craftiness.'"

the epistle of James has something of a parallel in the Old Testament in Ezekiel's prophecy. Job is numbered among the truly great prophets of God, alongside Noah and Daniel, in Ezek 14:14, 20, and alongside Abraham, Rahab, and Elijah in James 5:11, part of the "closing statement" of the epistle.[3] In Sir 49:9, in the well-known catalog of the faithful, Job is also included together with the prophet Ezekiel (cf. *T. Abr* 15:10 and esp. *T. Job* 1:2; 4:5-6; 27:3-10; 39:11-13).[4] Each of these references points to the person of Job as prophet, while the book that bears his name is classified among the canon's wisdom texts. Job appears to be recognized, then, as something of a sapiential prophet. Job is named among the great, and so it is not altogether surprising that he should appear among the exemplars of James. The approach of this paper will be (1) to review the kind of sapiential prophet Job's book portrays him to be, (2) to analyze his role in James, and (3) to offer some conclusions that present the complementarity of Job's prophetic wisdom with the wisdom of Job extolled throughout James.

A couple of initial assumptions are in order. The possibility of Job appearing as he does so uniquely in the text of James can be attributed to the special way in which James recapitulates and reinterprets the major dimensions of Old Testament religion: law, prophecy, and wisdom.[5] The text of Job presents him as a type of faithful personage who embodies the virtues James wishes to teach. Indeed, James appears to have the text of Job in mind as he makes reference to Job. There is some question regarding this. Davids, affected by Cantinat's questioning of whether the canonical Old Testament actually presents Job as patient, quickly concludes that it "appears certain, therefore, that James is citing Job, not from the canonical record, but from the expanded traditions which the community had heard such as the one which is recorded in Test. Job."[6] Putting aside the fact that the passages cited have to do with Job's need to voice his complaint, not a calling upon God to reverse his fortunes — this clearly would indicate his lack of patience — Davids quickly moves to reasons for preferring the apocryphal book as James's source. But no direct reference to the *Testament of Job* is detectable in James. Indeed, as if not persuaded himself,

---

3. Peter H. Davids, *The Epistle of James* (Grand Rapids: Eerdmans, 1982) 181.
4. Sir 49:9: "For God also mentioned Job who held fast to all the ways of justice."
5. Johnson, *James*, 29.
6. Davids, *James*, 187.

Davids finally asserts that while "it is unlikely that James had read the extant Greek Test. Job, it is certain that such narratives were common in his period."[7] This last statement is obviously the case, but what he thinks is "certain" is hardly so. Later in this paper, I will point out the greater likelihood that James did have the canonical Job in mind.

Job as Sapiential Prophet

In Job,[8] the virtues of the man are presented programmatically at the very beginning of the book, first by the author (1:1), then by God himself (1:8) within the council of heaven, among the בְּנֵי הָאֱלֹהִים, "sons of God."[9] Although some traditions of interpretation render the image of Job ambiguous at best, the text of Job reports the integrity of Job and God's pleasure with him (27:5; 31:6). The "problem of Job" is that God allows the *appearance of extreme displeasure to befall Job*. Rather straightforwardly, it is הַשָּׂטָן, the "Satan"[10] or the Accuser, who, having listened to the boast of God concerning his unique servant Job (not unlike exemplary Noah, who enjoyed God's singular favor; Gen 6:8-9), proposes a test to determine whether or not Job's piety is genuine and therefore to see whether God's esteem is justified.

The Satan speaks quite literally from the "devil's advocate" position. The text of Job presents God as a king holding court. Satan, one among the "sons of God," has that peculiar role of rhetorical contradiction for the purpose of putting a king's statements and judgments to the test in order that he either should avoid error or perceive undetected dangers in thought and will. On the other hand, even if the pronouncements of the king are wholly justified, certainly testing the limits of virtue is worthy of one so accomplished in it. If we wonder how such a being can be part of

---

7. Davids, *James*, 187.

8. I take the narrative type of Job to reflect the "conflict dialogue," as argued by James Crenshaw, "Wisdom," in *Old Testament Form Criticism* (ed. John Hayes; San Antonio: Trinity University, 1974) 228.

9. Or angels; cf. Job 38:7; 1 Kings 22:19.

10. "Satan" is derived from a term meaning "to obstruct" or "to oppose," with the sense of "one who plays the adversary" (cf. Num 22:22; 1 Sam 29:4; Ps 109:6; 1 Chron 21:1; Zech 3:1; cf. also Rev 12:10); thus he is "the Adversary" and yet is a functionary of the divine court.

God's "court of advisors," we should consider the later declaration of Job regarding all the heavenly beings: "God puts no trust even in his holy ones, and the heavens are not clean in his sight" (15:15).

Job is presented as virtuous in a unique sense, his righteousness outshining that of many righteous (1:8; 2:3). Indeed, in the very first verse of the book he is said to be תָּם "perfect" or "blameless" and יָשָׁר "upright." The source of this estimation is the fundamental holiness of the man whose heart וִירֵא "fears" God and who consequently acts by וְסָר "turning away" from evil. His extraordinary virtue is matched with his extraordinary wealth, which his children apparently enjoy more than he does, but he enjoys his God most of all and intercedes constantly on behalf of his merrymaking children. "Rising up early" (1:5), every week he performs sacrifice for his beloved children. As a result, he is universally recognized as righteous both by God and by his contemporaries (1:8).

A dual perspective is evident in the first two chapters of Job. The text presents the events in the royal council of the divine and also those in Job's life, intending to show not merely the fate of the human under the hand of the divine but also the appropriate response of the human to divine decision. There is no indication that God had a particular interest in testing Job. This is important, since it can help us to focus precisely on that which triggers the suggestion of testing: the boasts of God. Indeed, two boasts immediately precede the two severe tests that Satan is allowed to impose upon Job. God claims that Job is incomparable in his righteousness, repeating the claim of the author that Job fears God and turns away from evil (1:1, 8). In this respect, since the text so straightforwardly instructs the reader as to one of the reasons why the righteous suffer, God's judgment is put to the test by their testing. Satan offers the contrary judgment that Job is motivated only by his earthly benefits to perform his acts of righteousness. In other words, his friendship with God is based only in Job's personal sense of well-being. Satan does not bring any evidence against Job and thus is arguing simply from his experience of roaming the world. He takes the position of adversary against the contention of God and the practice of Job that Job performs sacrifices with a pure heart. He is perhaps a confirming voice to God that he should indeed be regretful that he had made humanity. Job is an inconvenient counter-example to what Satan probably regarded as a nearly perfect argument based upon nearly universal wickedness. God does not question the appropriateness of the test but believes that Job will endure.

The calamities begin, but with respect to the source and agency of those calamities the text is ambiguous. The Satan invites God to "stretch out *your* hand" to "touch" or destroy Job's property and people, with the hypothesis that "he will curse you to your face" (1:11). God consents to the test but declares, "only do not stretch out *your* hand against him," meaning taking his bodily life. God declares to Satan that all but Job's life is "in your power" (1:12), and the result is a personal holocaust for Job: everything and everyone but Job and his wife are destroyed. In the next round of the testing, Job's afflictions will all but slay him. For God and the Satan, there will be no question of divine injustice, but neither can Job be proven to be false. Job passes the simple but consequential test to determine whether his integrity depends upon the benefits of heaven.

And Job retains his integrity: "until I die I will not put away my integrity from me" (27:5; cf. 2:3; 31:6). By the end of the book, God does not find fault with Job or contradict anything he has spoken — Job is a truthful prophet. Instead, God calls upon Job to perform the intercessory work of a prophet whose prayers sanction the sacrifices of sinners (e.g., 1 Sam 15:10-23; 16:1-5). Finally, Job is blessed with prosperity double that of his "pre-tribulational" condition and dies at an advanced age. Interestingly, the short narrative of Job's "afterlife" is post-sacrificial: his brothers and sisters "showed him sympathy and comforted him for all the evil that the Lord had brought upon him" (42:11). This is perhaps the best link with James. The important thing for James, however, was to refute any direct connection between testing and judgment.

What, then, is the canonical book's lesson about Job's suffering? I would contend that it is the prophetic faithfulness of one subjected to non-judgmental suffering. The key text for discerning this is found in Job 2:3, where God strikes Job "for no reason" (לְבַלְּעוֹ חִנָּם) — almost as the wicked strike the innocent. Job is extolled as a blamelessly virtuous man, but then God declares three things in his address to the Satan: (a) Job "still persists in his integrity," (b) "you incited me against him," (c) "to destroy him for no reason." The first statement credits Job's virtue to Job along with his determination to hold fast to his piety. The second statement clarifies any question of God having caused the suffering, although Satan "incited" (מוּת) him to act against Job. The third declaration makes a connection with the first, validating Job's self-testimony as to his integrity and offering a kind of divine confession that the power to take Job's life has almost finished Job.

The phrase "for no reason" can also be translated "without cause," and it finds particular meaning in legal contexts where false witnesses have indicted the innocent (cf. 1 Sam 19:5; 25:31; 1 Kings 2:31; Job 22:6; Pss 35:7; 119:161; Prov 1:11; 3:30; 24:28). Indeed, the Satan had asked God, "Does Job fear God for nothing?" (1:9). Job himself declares: "For he crushes me with a tempest, and multiplies my wounds without cause" (9:17). God does not claim to be justified in causing Job's suffering. The larger statement of 2:3 is a rebuke to Satan, but God has nevertheless complied with the incitement. Of course, Job's sufferings are not limited to physical pain; it is psychological as well. His friends recognize the evil that has befallen Job, but their search of wisdom requires them to blame him. Time and again Job must defend himself against accusations of being in the wrong (6:24, 29, 30; 19:3, 6; 21:27; 32:3; 34:10; 36:23; 40:8). Tragically, any effort he makes to do so is taken as further evidence against him.

In the end, God reminds Job that he humbles the proud (40:6-14). But in this case he has humbled the humble — in order to make Job perfect? "In all this Job did not sin or charge God with wrongdoing" (1:22; cf. 2:10) in what he said. His self-defense was not faulty at the point of personal righteousness. Job is not privy to the council where the debate took place over his integrity; indeed, that case has already been decided. Job's endurance was God's proof against the Satan's hypothesis that piety and prosperity are mutually interdependent.[11] And certainly the counsel of Job's friends had turned into a new form of testing: incessant exposure to accusations of justifiable suffering. So God comes to Job to contend with these accusations on behalf of his own honor but also on behalf of the rightness of his servant Job. God claims his noble prerogatives of majesty, superior knowledge, and power. It is clear by God's response to Job when he quotes God and attempts to correct himself as one who has spoken in ignorance in 42:3: "'Who is this that hides counsel without knowledge?' Therefore I have uttered what I did not understand, things too wonderful for me, which I did not know," that God had simply wanted Job to remember his greatness and the latter's humble position.

But ultimately, the book of Job, along with Ecclesiastes, is part of what could be called the "minority report" within the wisdom literature of the Old Testament: the benefits of wisdom do not always correlate with experience in an inequitable world. "Job himself serves as a vivid case study that refutes any rigid application" of the doctrine of retribution. "Perhaps

11. David J. A. Clines, *Job 1–20* (WBC; Dallas: Word Books, 1989) 28ff.

Job should be viewed as one of the first hammer swings at the monolith of punitive suffering."[12] The purpose of Job's suffering seems obscure, although he states in 23:10, "But he knows the way that I take; when he has tested me, I shall come out like gold." The outcome of this journey of suffering will be pure treasure.

Analyzing Job's Role in James

This relation is particularly interesting in terms of the way biblical wisdom demonstrates itself according to a number of common features and expressions. Since James uniquely references Job, the exploration of these parallels will enrich our reading of the Jacobean passage.[13] As to how James possibly perceived Job, Laws points to the rabbinic tradition, which saw him as a proselyte, a convert from idolatry, just as Abraham (2:21) and Rahab (2:25), the other exemplars of the epistle, were. Indeed, even Elijah (5:17) was a prophet sent to the Gentiles (cf. Luke 4:25ff.).[14] The final section in which the reference to Job appears is counsel to those who are to be encouraged by the examples of the prophets and especially by Job, who comforted the poor during his life and exemplified "consummate patience."[15] And yet what they face now at the hands of the rich will be reversed for both parties in the judgment (5:5-8).

Job's role is that of an exemplar[16] (ὑπόδειγμα), one to imitate, to emulate. Job is the one mentioned together with all the prophets. James declares:

> Indeed we call blessed those who showed endurance. You have heard of the endurance of Job, and you have seen the purpose of the Lord, how the Lord is compassionate and merciful. (5:11)[17]

---

12. N. Clayton Croy, *Hebrews 12:1-13 in Its Rhetorical, Religious, and Philosophical Context* (Cambridge: Cambridge University Press, 1998) 96-97.

13. I am especially indebted to the outstanding and exhaustive work by Theresia Hainthaler, *"Von der Ausdauer Ijobs habt ihr gehört" (Jak 5:11): Zur Bedeutung des Buches Ijob im Neuen Testament* (Frankfurt am Main: Lang, 1988).

14. Sophie Laws, *The Epistle of James* (Peabody, MA: Hendrickson, 1980) 215-16.

15. Davids, *James,* 181.

16. Cf. Richard Bauckham, *James* (New York: Routledge, 1999) 56-57.

17. Unless otherwise indicated, the NRSV is employed throughout.

The context of this statement is James's intense warning against the rich whose judgment is imminent (5:1-6) — perhaps not unlike the judgment that would have befallen Job's friends, who, if they are in error in their speech regarding God, would be in error in their actions toward the believing poor who happen to be God's elect as favored subjects of his love and generosity (2:5).[18] James's more immediate context of 5:7-11 contains the exhortation to wait patiently in order to "strengthen your heart" (στηρίξατε τὰς καρδίας ὑμῶν). The exhortation to patience (μακροθυμήσατε) is, in all likelihood, in the face of suffering at the hands of the rich, who have oppressed some of them to the point of causing debilitation and death.[19] As Johnson points out, the use of the verb ὑπομένω (5:11) most often implies passivity in the waiting,[20] which implies dependence upon divine action rather than one's own (Pss 24:3; 32:20; Prov 20:9c; Mic 7:7; Isa 40:31; et al.). It is used in the LXX of Job frequently with the sense "endure" (Job 6:11; 9:4; 14:14; 15:31; 17:13; 22:21). Later in our Joban passage (James 5:11) "those who endure" (τὴν ὑπομονὴν) will utilize the more frequent term (Matt 10:22; Mark 13:13; Luke 8:15; 21:19; Rom 2:7; 5:3; 8:25; 15:4; 1 Cor 13:7; 1 Thess 1:3; 2 Thess 1:4; 1 Pet 2:20; et al.). The sense of this word and its cognates also reflects a passive stance, usually with regard to a superior. But the former term can also refer to God's *long-suffering* (Rom 2:4; 9:22; 1 Tim 1:16; 1 Pet 3:20; 2 Pet 3:9, 15). Patience in the face of suffering is the focus, and James wants his addressees to "take the prophets" as their models of the same. Job is the exemplary sapiential prophet who endures, patient in his suffering.

The makarism[21] (cf. 1:12) for those who suffer in faith is reinforced by the example of those the community calls "blessed" (μακαρίζομεν). The relation to the concluding beatitude of Jesus, comparing his disciples with the prophets persecuted by their own people, also comes to mind (Matt 5:11-12). The implication, of course, is that every believer who faithfully endures will be blessed and honored by the Lord. Connecting with the makarism of 1:12, "endurance" (ὑπομονή) is used to show how closely related the example of

18. The wider context, 4:11–5:11, is comprised of three eschatological proclamations of warning and exhortation, each introduced by ἀδελφοί and how they should face the extremely difficult conditions of poverty; cf. David Hutchinson Edgar, *Has God Not Chosen the Poor? The Social Setting of the Epistle of James* (Sheffield: Sheffield Academic Press, 2001) 197-209.

19. This is the second imperative after that in v. 1 directed against the πλούσιοι but now directed toward the ἀδελφοί.

20. Johnson, *James*, 312.

21. Blessing, beatitude, from μακάριος, e.g., Matt 5:3-12.

Job is to the purpose of the entire letter. But one should also mention that this term might properly be considered the guiding theme of the book of Job.[22] This is certainly how the apocryphal book *Testament of Job* presents it: endurance along with mercy virtually typifies Job's life.[23] Indeed, makarisms are employed only in this early cluster of verses in James 1:12, 25.

The term "end" (τέλος) also only appears (along with its cognates) in 1:4, 17, 25; 3:2; 5:11. As such, patience becomes the proof of faith, since it cannot be practiced without faith and, indeed, is the means by which faith is strengthened. The ground for this blessing is that the suffering is part of God's purpose for the believer. This is explicated rather more fully in Hebrews 12, where God has the prerogative of a father who tests the loyalty of his son and heir and simultaneously instills discipline. Indeed, the author of Hebrews explains the motive: God disciplines us for our good, "in order that we may share his holiness" (12:10). Although the context has been oriented toward a disciplining in this life, the eschatological emerges with this reference to sharing in God's holiness.

Much in James's exhortation revolves around the nearness of the Lord in his coming. "Parousia" is something of a technical term in James for the coming of Jesus (cf. 1 Thess 2:19; 3:13; 4:15; 5:23; 2 Thess 2:1; 2 Pet 1:16). His coming as judge makes him the opponent of the rich from the previous verses. This judgment, which brings about both the end of the schemes of the rich and the reward of the patient, here is likened not to a crown of life (James 5:7) but to a farmer's fruit. Just as the word is a seed implanted in the believer (1:21), mixed with deeds, here it grows up to bear "precious" (τίμιον) fruit. In this case, the work is waiting; and Job waited, enduring his condition, until the Lord delivered him.

But the theme of our context is determined by the twice-repeated verb for patience (μακροθυμέω). The virtue of patience manifests itself in "strengthening the heart" (v. 8), a virtual synonym for patience, not grumbling against one another (cf. 4:11-12) — the second imperative of the section — but following the example of the prophets, particularly of Job. Those who are patient, who endure non-judgmental suffering — that is, testing at the hand of the Lord — who accept his purpose, experience both his compassion and mercy, as well as the "crown of life" in the perfecting of their faith (cf. 1:12).

22. Hainthaler, *Ijob*, 319.
23. Cf. Laws, *James*, 215.

This leads us, then, to consider the nature of "testing" (πειρασμός) in James 1:2. The question is whether the use of πειράζω in vv. 13-15, where one is led into sin by one's own evil desires, might have the same sense. But God is not the source of this second type of testing since God tempts no one to sin. The first usage then entails something like suffering, tribulation, or persecution (cf. Acts 20:19; 1 Pet 1:6; 4:12; 2 Pet 2:9; also Sir 2:1-6, which for some is the nearer context for James). But none of these alone fully describes the divine role implied — indeed, the overriding divine purpose indicated by "testing of faith" (τὸ δοκίμιον . . . τῆς πίστεως). Instead of one's own internal temptations, these tests come from outside the believer and the believing community. Indeed, the joy of such testing, indicative of divine care and election, is a not infrequent notion in the New Testament. What is poverty, after all, but a kind of suffering in the overwhelming number of human cases, imposed from outside, and yet a condition of special favor and election in God's sight? Hence the powerful rhetorical and theological question of the following chapter: "Did not God elect the poor of the world to be rich in faith?" (2:5).

The patience that is developed through testing, then, is the principle illustrated by the life of Job. Indeed, it will be proven that he is the man he is. The only thing that Job will prove to have lacked is (a) the severest testing of his faith and (b) the silence prompted only by the Lord speaking, which brings about the end of his speaking. Indeed, the matter of speech in James and in Job is strikingly significant. Although the friends of Job are even incensed by Job's speaking about God, they are the ones who will be judged to have spoken falsely, while God declares that Job has spoken rightly of him (Job 42:7). With these words the voice of God vindicates the life of his servant — a title that James has taken for himself (James 1:1). Then v. 12 brings to completion what James has introduced about non-judgmental divine testing in vv. 2-4, which will give way to the more negatively construed type that leads to sin if unchecked. But this verse introduces the eschatological dimension. Of course, the following verses do imply a kind of testing that is accomplished not by spiritual celebration but by spiritual warfare against a commission of sin.

Thus, the "crown of life" is extended to all who are patient in the face of trial, who "love God" and have discovered the power of faith and love in patience. This crown of life is promised (ἐπηγγείλατο) according to several passages in the New Testament (particularly Rev 2:10; also 3:11; 4:4, 10; 6:2;

9:7; 12:1; 14:14; 1 Cor 9:25; Phil 4:1; et al);.[24] it is a comprehensive significa-
tion of Christ's assurances to believers.

Finally, James 5:11 presents Job as the one whose exemplary endurance is derived from direct references in Job 1:21 and 2:10. The LXX of Job
intensifies the sense of patient submission to God's purpose whereby humility and patience are appropriate attitudes.[25] The key is that James has
appropriated fully the sense of endurance of the Old Testament book: endurance is the response to an external catastrophe that has befallen the believer according to the plan of God to test the believer's faith. Of course,
the catastrophic aspect of the testing gives way to other external tests,
namely conflict with friends. This conflict, including conflict with God,
comes to predominate the sense of testing throughout the book (cf. Job
13:14-16; 14:13-15; 16:18-21; 19:25-27). All Job can do in the face of his contrary friends is not to yield to them and to utter his complaint to God. Of
course the "wise" (cf. James 3:13) friends of Job believe they have detected
in him a self-justifying "wisdom" (James 3:15) and are certain of his fault
before God — that his sufferings are judgmental signs of divine displeasure. Job is prepared to have God slay him — he has rued the day of his
birth anyway — and at least then he would have the chance to justify himself before God (Job 13:15). But Job demonstrates his readiness for complete patience if God will but explain the suffering (14:14). In 16:18-21 there
is a change from Job challenging God to his complaint as one stricken by
God, and his patience is demonstrated in that in his sleeplessness he looks
constantly to God (16:21). Finally, his faith intensifies yet further with the
knowledge that his Redeemer lives and with his longing to see God (19:25-
27). He endures to the point where God reveals himself to him (42:2-6).

The testing of Job produced patience, and therefore he is the example (ὑπόδειγμα) that James claims him to be (5:10). God blessed Job in the
end. As Hainthaler asserts, Job is not merely the example of endurance, as
someone who merely waits out the period of tribulation; rather, he is an
example of patience (ὑπομονή — twice in James 5:11 in reference to this
virtue and to Job's exemplarity by no usage of blessing, μακροθυμέω), since
he is also exemplary as a witness to his own faith in God. As such, it is gen-

24. By comparison, cf. the fascinating "crown of boasting" (στέφανος καυχήσεως) of
1 Thess 2:19; "crown of righteousness" (δικαιοσύνης στέφανος) of 2 Tim 4:8; and "crown of
glory" (δόξης στέφανον) of 1 Pet 5:4.
25. Hainthaler, *Ijob*, 321.

uine faith.[26] Genuineness of faith is important to James (1:21; 2:10), but in Job's case it is determined not by an act of mercy but by an act of true patience shown in his use of speech in bearing witness to God. Mere endurance would not have produced the fruit of Job's lips for which the Lord commends him as his servant (Job 42:7). Indeed, Job appears to have served God in his debilitation with the one instrument he had left: his voice (recalling the Lord's one condition as Satan smites Job; 2:6).

The role of speech is important in Job as well as in James. James extols the one who is able to control the tongue, for he considers such control the link to all impulses of the body and indeed a sign of that believer's perfection (3:2). At this point one should also wish to claim that James had real familiarity with the book of Job, actually citing it in 5:2 (cf. Job 13:28).[27] The attention of the book of Job to Job's purity of speech is conspicuous:

Job again took up his discourse and said:
"As God lives, who has taken away my right,
    and the Almighty, who has made my soul bitter,
as long as my breath is in me
    and the spirit of God is in my nostrils,
my lips will not speak falsehood,
    and my tongue will not utter deceit.
Far be it from me to say that you are right;
    until I die I will not put away my integrity from me.
I hold fast my righteousness, and will not let it go;
    my heart does not reproach me for any of my days." (27:1-6)

By the end of Job's testing these words will be justified. But as is typical of the book of Job, the extent of his righteousness is already declared at the beginning. In spite of the immense losses and suffering that have befallen Job, the writer declares in 2:10: "in all this Job did not sin with his lips."

In fact, there has been some question as to whether Job in fact does sin in his speech.[28] He is certainly accused of something just short of blas-

26. Hainthaler, *Ijob*, 323.

27. Hainthaler, *Ijob*, 324, who also cites Clement of Alexandria's and Augustine's similar estimations of James.

28. Cf. William R. Baker, *Personal Speech-Ethics in the Epistle of James* (Tübingen: Mohr, 1995) 192-94.

phemy by his friends, in spite of 1:22 and his rejection of this sin to his wife in 2:10. But Job figures this out, so to speak, relatively early in the dialogues. He is aware that his position and possible defense are weak in comparison to God's strength. As he states in 9:14-21,

> How then can I answer him,
>   choosing my words with him?
> Though I am innocent, I cannot answer him;
>   I must appeal for mercy to my accuser.
> If I summoned him and he answered me,
>   I do not believe that he would listen to my voice.
> For he crushes me with a tempest,
>   and multiplies my wounds without cause;
> he will not let me get my breath,
>   but fills me with bitterness.
> If it is a contest of strength, he is the strong one!
>   If it is a matter of justice, who can summon him?
> Though I am innocent, my own mouth would condemn me;
>   though I am blameless, he would prove me perverse.
> I am blameless; I do not know myself;
>   I loathe my life.

Interestingly, this is a prediction of the outcome of the testing of Job. God will finally reveal himself, will claim superior strength and skill. Job will shut himself up, knowing that he is blameless and yet loathing his life in 40:1-2, 5-6.

Let us look more closely at "patience" (ὑπομονή) in terms of its relation both to Job and to James.[29] This term occurs only once in the LXX of Job in 14:19 (although Aquila, the great translator reacting to Christian appropriations of the LXX by producing a fresh translation, ca. 128 CE, will include 4:6; 6:8; 17:15). Interestingly, the term often used in Greek with which ὑπομονή competes is ἐλπίς ("hope"). The friends of Job make the connection between righteousness and hope by suggesting that if Job makes right with the Lord there is still hope, but without this, Job's destiny is doubtful (cf. 8:11-13, 14-20). Hainthaler works out this relation between the terms in the LXX of Job in the following way. The most significant He-

---

27. Following Hainthaler's excursus, *Ijob*, 324-29.

brew term is תִּקְוָה, which gets translated ἐλπίς when Job is being confronted with his contrary friends (Job 4:6; 7:6; 8:13; 11:18; 11:20; 27:8), but also gets translated with ὑπομονή/ὑπομένω. And yet it is clear, at least in a couple of instances, that the best translation of ὑπομονή would be "hope" (14:14; 17:15) in the context of tribulation and where the religious sense is prominent, particularly of resurrection in the first text. But primarily the term means to "stand firm" (9:4; 33:5; 41:3), "remain" (8:15; 15:31; 20:26; 22:21) — each with a strong sense of "waiting" and "enduring" more than "hoping." Job's faith is maximally tested, but it will lead to the true knowledge of God. The moment of revelation is not that for which Job had hoped, but it is the reality that brings an end to his speaking. The words of Job truly come to an end, but his devout actions continue as the double blessings of God come upon him.

Behind this text (James 5:11) likely stands Job 1:21-22; 42:10-17. In 1:21-22, the context is anthropological in that the human being is born without possessions, naked, and comes to death in the same way (cf. 1 Tim 6:7). The verse takes theological and liturgical shape as praise to God for his grace, certainly, but also for his inscrutability. The utter dependency of the human being upon God at all times and under all circumstances is the singular emphasis.[30] In 42:10-17, just as Job had praised the Lord in his misery, now the Lord blesses him afresh and more intensively than before the testing. Together with James 5:11, the virtues of Job (devotion and uprightness) and God (mercy and love) find resonance. They abide in a reconciled relation that existed before but has been made more profound by the confirmation of God's faith in Job. His sacrificing is over, and he receives blessings at the hands of friends and family alike.

James's Perfect Man and the Exemplarity of Job

James's citation of Job is curious because of its uniqueness in the New Testament, but one does not have to go very far for an explanation. The rich figure prominently in James's framework as those who murderously defraud their workers, who are the source of envy among believers, and who take them to court. But James is aware that there are righteous rich who must learn to "rejoice in their debasement" (1:10). Job is the exemplar of

30. Hainthaler, *Ijob*, 316-17.

this; after all his book opens with "this man was the greatest of all the people of the east" (Job 1:3). In spite of a rather easy exegesis rendering the rich as outsiders in James, Job serves as an example of righteousness and of faithfulness simultaneously. When we consider Job's self-pronouncement in Job 29:1-17, it is easy to understand how some regard James as having this Old Testament book primarily in mind:

> Job again took up his discourse and said:
> "O that I were as in the months of old,
>   as in the days when God watched over me;
> when his lamp shone over my head,
>   and by his light I walked through darkness;
> when I was in my prime,
>   when the friendship of God was upon my tent;
> when the Almighty was still with me,
>   when my children were around me;
> when my steps were washed with milk,
>   and the rock poured out for me streams of oil!
> When I went out to the gate of the city,
>   when I took my seat in the square,
> the young men saw me and withdrew,
>   and the aged rose up and stood;
> the nobles refrained from talking,
>   and laid their hands on their mouths;
> the voices of princes were hushed,
>   and their tongues stuck to the roof of their mouths.
> When the ear heard, it commended me,
>   and when the eye saw, it approved;
> because I delivered the poor who cried,
>   and the orphan who had no helper.
> The blessing of the wretched came upon me,
>   and I caused the widow's heart to sing for joy.
> I put on righteousness, and it clothed me;
>   my justice was like a robe and a turban.
> I was eyes to the blind,
>   and feet to the lame.
> I was a father to the needy,
>   and I championed the cause of the stranger.

I broke the fangs of the unrighteous,
    and made them drop their prey from their teeth."

Themes such as "friendship of God," care for the poor and the widow, and zeal for righteousness make Job an example of James's perfect man, who appears in the context of controlled speech in 3:2: "Anyone who makes no mistakes in speaking is perfect, able to keep the whole body in check." And of course Job is extolled by his author as one who did not sin in all his speaking.

What Job must go through is a final acquisition of the virtue of patience, which can come only by testing through suffering. Job is an exemplar of endurance in the face of non-judgmental testing. Unlike Hebrews 12, which uses the analogy of a father disciplining and chastising erring children, James uses the example of Job, who was tested but not chastised. This is a remarkable example, since James can find a great deal of fault in his double-minded addressees. But he refrains from making the connection. Do they want to be like the rich? Then they will fall under the "judgment without mercy" that they are destined to endure without repentance. James's testing (τὸ δοκίμιον) is not a disciplining or a chastising, but a process of proving and strengthening for future experiences so that wisdom will endow the believer with the perfecting gift of patience, ὑπομονή. Becoming one who lives by this gift has an active effect, even though the believer herself is rather passively enduring the non-judgmental suffering, in that patience "perfects" the believer, "so that you might be mature and complete, lacking in nothing" (James 1:4). Patience is an agency all its own, an agent of holistic formation that, when it is done working, makes the believer free from lack.

James also seems to have in mind the turning point at which Job declares, "I know that you can do all things, and that no purpose of yours can be thwarted" (Job 42:2). Although the sense of τέλος in James follows the expected sense of completeness (1:17, 25; 3:2), it is used in 5:11 for divine "purpose" in terms of "end."[31] In this way James resonates with Job at the point of his last words in his face-to-face encounter with God and the ending of his testing.

31. Although Laws, *James*, 216, sides with the translation "end," she is aware that Job's end is not eschatological according to the text. But James's orientation to the eschaton precludes this sense of τέλος; better to side with "purpose" relative to the nature of trials and exemplary faith as seen at the beginning and throughout the epistle.

A few further connections should be mentioned: (1) From the standpoint of righteousness and salvation, James appears to be nearly quoting in 5:2, "your clothes are moth-eaten," from Job 13:28, "like a garment that is moth-eaten." James's viewpoint is an apocalyptic orientation in view of the demise of the unjust rich whose wealth consumes them, and Job's statement comes out of the prophetic context of complaint against the rich. In the latter case, it is the once-rich Job himself who observes his own wasting flesh. (2) From the perspective of the transitory, James 1:11b, "It is the same way with the rich; in the midst of a busy life, they will wither away," quotes the well-known Isa 40:7 but seems to have resonance also with Job 14:2, "he comes up like a flower and withers." The fading flower stands for the perishing glory of human nature (Isaiah) and specifically of the rich in James. Indeed, as part of the *exordium* of James, it represents part of his main teaching: "It may be that James interprets Job as an example of reversal of status . . . : those who endure humiliation are exalted by God in the end."[32] Although Job and Isaiah are focused primarily upon human nature, Job can speak specifically of the scoffers in this sense in 24:24. (3) In terms of testing in suffering, James's use of "patience," ὑπομονή, particularly in the unique reference to Job in 5:11, indicates active endurance, steadfastness, and constancy. This endurance is a matter of one's own faith in God, and Job's has been tested to the limits of the mind, heart, body, and soul. It is quite possible, then, that with the words "the patience of Job" in 5:11, James has the entire book of Job in mind.[33] Indeed, to read this verse concerning the "endurance of Job and its sequel is to have a complete and self contained example for James's argument."[34] If we understand the speeches of Job as a special case of patient endurance against erroneous speech, then the other virtuous dimensions of Job's life have their full complement. Although Job's body has become the locus of divine testing, precisely because he has kept his tongue in check his faith is perfected.

32. Bauckham, *James*, 216, n. 38.
33. Hainthaler, *Ijob*, 337-38.
34. Laws, *James*, 217.

The Use of Scripture in the Pastoral and General Epistles and the Book of Revelation

Andreas J. Köstenberger

Introduction

In the allotted space it is virtually impossible to do justice to the topic of the use of Scripture in the Pastoral and General Epistles as well as the book of Revelation. The task becomes only slightly more manageable when one realizes that there are no OT references in Titus and virtually none in the Johannine epistles. So how does one eat an elephant? As the joke goes, "one bite at a time." In the Pastorals, which will be dealt with first, OT references are limited to a few clustered passages. James's thought is clearly steeped in Israel's Scriptures, and hence one finds frequent scriptural echoes or allusions, yet explicit OT references are limited to a manageable number of instances.

The story is different with Hebrews. All I can hope is to lay out the basic structure of the argument of the unknown author, which is intricately related to OT Scripture. The epistle of Jude, too, draws significantly on the OT, though it does so in a rather different fashion. Again, space permits only laying out the logic underlying Jude's use of the OT in the context of the structure of his book as a whole. After dealing with instances of the use of the OT in 1 Peter (which are most pronounced in the first three chapters of the book, particularly chapter 2), I will discuss 2 Peter in relation to Jude, on whom 2 Peter 2 is likely dependent. The essay concludes with a summary treatment of Revelation.

The Pastorals

Paul's use of the OT in his four longer and six shorter epistles has already been considered. It remains to investigate his use of the OT in the Pastorals.[1] Overall, references to the OT are comparatively infrequent. In 1 Timothy, there are essentially two clusters of references: 1 Tim 2:13-15 (related to the role of women in the church) and 5:17-19 (on the question of remuneration of preaching and teaching elders).[2] In 2 Timothy, Paul cites or alludes to Scripture in 2:19 and 3:8. Beyond this, there is the significant global reference to "inspired Scripture" in 2 Tim 3:16. No OT reference is found in Titus.[3] We will briefly investigate each significant OT reference in 1 and 2 Timothy in the order of occurrence.

1 Timothy

The first major cluster of references in Paul's first letter to Timothy is found in the context of his injunction that women not teach or exercise authority over men in the church (1 Tim 2:12). Paul adduces two reasons — both taken from the OT — for this ruling: Adam's creation prior to Eve (1 Tim 2:13; cf. 1 Cor 11:8-9); and the scenario of the fall (Genesis 3; cf. 2 Cor 11:3). There is also a possible allusion to Gen 3:15 or 16 in 1 Tim 2:15. What concerns us here is not Paul's actual teaching or the (difficult) exegesis of this passage but questions related to Paul's use of the OT in this instance.[4] As in other cases, the primary reason for Paul's invoking the OT seems to be the intended rhetorical and persuasive effect this reference would have on the reader. By making a pronouncement, not in his own name, but in

---

1. For a defense of the Pauline authorship of the Pastorals (plus further bibliography) see my forthcoming commentary on 1 Timothy, 2 Timothy, and Titus in the Expositor's Bible Commentary series (rev. ed.; Grand Rapids: Zondervan).

2. Note also the allusions to the Decalogue in 1:9-10 (on which see my forthcoming EBC contribution) and the allusion to Isa 52:5 in 6:1.

3. See D. Moody Smith, "The Pauline Literature," in *It Is Written: Scripture Citing Scripture* (ed. D. A. Carson and H. G. M. Williamson; Cambridge: Cambridge University Press, 1988) 272, who lists 1 Tim 5:18 and 2 Tim 2:19.

4. On the exegesis of 1 Tim 2:9-15, see esp. Andreas J. Köstenberger and Thomas R. Schreiner, eds., *Women in the Church: An Analysis and Application of 1 Timothy 2:9-15* (2nd ed.; Grand Rapids: Baker, 2005).

material continuity with the OT, the apostle clearly expected to increase the likelihood that his readers would accept his teaching as authoritative, since the authority of the OT was widely recognized already, while his teaching was yet in the process of being evaluated.

In the case of 1 Tim 2:13, Paul's statement is a result of a straightforward reading of the Genesis 2 narrative. There it is plainly stated that God first created Adam and then Eve (Gen 2:7, 18-22). Contrary to some recent scholars who claim that Genesis 2 is "poetic narrative" and the sequence of creation is not to be taken literally,[5] Paul quite clearly took Genesis 2 literally. Some dismiss this as Paul's succumbing to "traditional rabbinic teaching." Jewett goes so far as to allege that the apostle is here dependent on "incorrect" rabbinic teaching.[6] Scanzoni and Hardesty claim that such a "traditional rabbinic (and one might add 'Christian') understanding . . . is not supported by the text."[7]

More recently, William Webb has proposed that Paul's argument from primogeniture in 1 Tim 2:13 is cultural and thus not permanently valid.[8] More likely, the apostle here appeals to human origins, which is a more profound ground of appeal than a mere primogeniture argument.[9] To put it differently, Paul's argument in 1 Tim 2:13 is not the mere analog to "Esau was born first, then Jacob." Rather, Paul judges the order of creation in Genesis 2 to be theologically significant for the way in which the Creator intends the man and the woman to relate to each other. Hence the apostle does not conceive of his teaching on the male-female relationship as novel or creative. His only innovation (if this is the appropriate term to use) consists in his application of the Genesis 2 paradigm (which has implications for marriage and the family; see esp. Gen 2:18, 20) to the church, which is later in the same epistle identified as "God's household" (1 Tim 3:15; see also 1 Tim 3:4-5, 12).

---

5. So Virginia Ramey Mollenkott, *Women, Men, and the Bible* (rev. ed.; New York: Crossroad, 1988 [1977]) 83. Mollenkott says, "Paul's argument is . . . belied by the poetic nature of the [Genesis] narrative," and "if we insist on upholding the validity of Paul's reasoning process, we are going to have serious problems."

6. Paul K. Jewett, *Man as Male and Female* (Grand Rapids: Eerdmans, 1975) 119.

7. Letha Scanzoni and Nancy Hardesty, *All We're Meant to Be* (Waco, TX: Word, 1974) 28.

8. William J. Webb, *Slaves, Women and Homosexuals* (Downers Grove: InterVarsity, 2001) 134-45 (see also 236-37).

9. Jimmy Agan, "Review of *Slaves, Women & Homosexuals* by William J. Webb," *Presbyterion* 29, no. 1 (2003) 51.

What about 1 Tim 2:14? It is noteworthy that Paul grounds his injunction in 1 Tim 2:12, not in one, but in two OT passages. What is more, these are sequentially related. First Timothy 2:13 reflects Paul's reading of Genesis 2, while 1 Tim 2:14 refers to Genesis 3. This makes his rationale and his claim to scriptural authority all the more sweeping and comprehensive. One might add that this is true regardless of precisely how one interprets Paul's rationale in 1 Tim 2:14.

In addition, a good case can be made that Paul in 1 Tim 2:15 alludes to the fall narrative in the following fashion. First Timothy 2:14 indicates that Eve, "the woman," fell into sin. However understood, this, according to Paul, serves as one of two reasons for his injunction that women not teach or exercise authority over men in the church in 1 Tim 2:12. The logical connection between 1 Tim 2:14 and 15 very likely becomes the question, "If the woman fell into sin at the fall, how can women [in Paul's and any other day] then be preserved from the tempter?" Paul's answer in 1 Tim 2:15 involves women's attending to their domestic and familial responsibilities.[10]

Hence Paul grounds his injunction regarding women teaching and/or exercising authority in the church profoundly in the foundational Genesis creation narrative (i.e., Genesis 2–3). One might also note that the fact that Paul grounds his injunction in creation as well as in the fall seems to contradict the notion, advanced by biblical feminists, that male headship is solely a function of the fall.

The next appeal to Scripture is found in 1 Tim 5:17-18, where the topic is the remuneration ("double honor") of preaching and teaching elders (cf. 1 Tim 3:1-7, esp. vv. 2 and 4; see also 4:13). Apparently, the necessity of remuneration of elders was not yet universally recognized, hence Paul senses a need to make his case. Possibly, the apostle saw the inadequate remuneration of elders as the cause of other problems in the church, though this is subject to conjecture. In support, Paul cites "Scripture" *(graphē)*, a rare term in the Pastorals, as part of the introductory formula "the Scripture says."[11] The quotation is taken from Deut 25:4 LXX (also cited by Paul in 1 Cor 9:9): "Do not muzzle the ox while it is treading out the grain." Strung together with this Old Testament quota-

---

10. For this interpretation, see my essay "Ascertaining Women's God-Ordained Roles: An Interpretation of 1 Timothy 2:15," *BBR* 7 (1997) 107-44.

11. This is the only instance of *graphē* in 1 Timothy; the term occurs once in 2 Timothy (3:16); it is not found in Titus.

tion is a second statement: "The worker deserves his wages" (Luke 10:7// Matt 10:10; cf. *Did.* 13:1).

Remarkably, Jesus' words are placed side by side with OT Scripture (though it is possible that only the first quotation is explicitly identified as such). The fact that the wording of Jesus' saying is identical to the version preserved in Luke indicates that the latter was likely Paul's source (cf. 1 Cor 11:24-25; Luke 22:19-20).[12] Those lacking the background to comprehend the OT saying (the ox was allowed an occasional bite as it treaded out corn) will understand the principle in Jesus' plain words, an illustration taken from everyday life. Anyone who works ought to be paid, including those who labor in the church (cf. 1 Thess 5:12). While the apostle himself regularly chose to forego remuneration (1 Cor 9:12, 15; 1 Thess 2:6-9), he insists that workers in the church are entitled to being paid. The following verse (1 Tim 5:19), pertaining to accepting accusations against elders, involves a clear allusion to the OT principle requiring two or three witnesses (see Deut 19:15; cf. Matt 18:16; 2 Cor 13:1).

In assessing the OT quotations and allusions in 1 Timothy, one notes that virtually all of them have parallels in other Pauline writings: 1 Tim 2:13-15 in 1 Cor 11:8-9; 1 Tim 5:17-18 in 1 Cor 9:9; and 1 Tim 5:19 in 2 Cor 13:1. This suggests that, while the apostle did not draw on the OT with great frequency in his first epistle to Timothy, he occasionally saw fit to use scriptural passages that he had used in previous correspondence and that formed part of his repertoire and argumentation. One also notes that in both major instances of Paul's use of the OT in 1 Timothy the apostle quotes or alludes to, not one, but two passages, employing a two-pronged approach to grounding his ruling on a given issue in the Scriptures.

2 Timothy

The first cluster of OT references in 2 Timothy is found in 2:19. In the context of warning against false teachers (including Hymenaeus and Philetus), Paul first cites Num 16:5, "The Lord knows those who are his,"[13] and then

12. So George W. Knight, *The Pastoral Epistles* (NIGTC; Grand Rapids: Eerdmans, 1992) 233-34. For a list of possibilities, see I. H. Marshall, *The Pastoral Epistles* (ICC; Edinburgh: T&T Clark, 1999) 616.

13. The citation is from the LXX, but Paul corrects the LXX rendering of the Hebrew *YHWH* with *ho theos*, replacing it with *ho kurios*.

provides a conflated allusion to another set of OT passages: "Everyone who confesses the name of the Lord must turn away from wickedness."[14] As in 1 Timothy, the apostle cites two OT passages to make his point. Of particular interest is the introductory formula: "Nevertheless, God's solid foundation stands firm, sealed with this inscription." The terms "solid foundation," "stands firm," and "sealed" all highlight the unshakable nature of the truths of Scripture invoked by Paul. His primary reference is to God's knowledge and sovereignty, and the need of Paul and other believers to base their Christian confession on true repentance and a corresponding lifestyle.

The two foundational truths asserted by Paul are as follows. First, despite growing defections and the resulting disillusionment, God is not deceived: he has known those who are his all along (Num 16:5). Hence one thing is clear: Hymenaeus, Philetus, and their company do not belong to God's people. Chained and nearing the end of his life, the apostle draws comfort from the sovereign omniscience of God. Second, just as the people of Israel in the wilderness needed to distance themselves from Korah's rebellion, the Ephesian believers ought to separate themselves from the false teachers (Num 16:26). Truth and error must not be allowed to coexist. Interestingly, Paul's dual appeal to Scripture is found in the center of a section (2 Tim 2:14-26) that also features several other illustrations — such as that of the workman in 2:15 or that of the large house in 2:20-21 — and metaphors (esp. gangrene in 2:17).

The other noteworthy instance of Paul's reference to Scripture in 2 Timothy is found in 3:8, where the apostle alludes to the references to Egypt's magicians in the book of Exodus (cf. Exod 7:11, 22; 9:11), also in the context of warning against false teachers. Paul here draws on extra-biblical information regarding the identity of the Egyptian magicians opposing Moses (CD 5:19; Pliny, *Nat. Hist.* 30.2.11 [77 CE]; *Tg. Ps.-Jon.* to Exod 7:11-12), and he likens the false teachers to Jannes and Jambres, men who opposed the truth. Similar to Jude, the apostle employs typology, linking OT

---

14. The phrase "who confesses the name of the Lord" is found in several places in the LXX (Lev 24:16; Isa 26:13; Jer 20:9). As Marshall, *Pastoral Epistles*, 758, notes (with reference to an unpublished M.Th. thesis by T. G. Larson), most scholars favor Isa 26:13 as a source text, though the verbal parallelism with Lev 24:16 is actually closer. If so, the quotation does not summon believers to refrain from evil but rather urges the false teachers to mend their ways. The wording of the phrase "turn away from wickedness" is closest to the citation of Ps 6:9 in Luke 13:27 (so rightly Marshall), though the context is different.

figures with contemporary persons. Just as the attacks against Moses, God's servant, were unsuccessful, so the heretics will not prevail against Timothy.

Beyond this, there is the significant global reference to Scripture as "inspired and useful for teaching, rebuking, correction and training in righteousness" in 2 Tim 3:16. As in 2:15, Scripture is presented as the primary tool for ministry for the person of God, and the development of workmanlike skill in handling it is urged. It is interesting that Paul here elevates Scripture as the supreme instrument in the preacher's toolbox but that, at least in the Pastorals, he himself uses it rather sparingly. The apostle does, however, draw on Scripture very significantly in his longer and shorter epistles, as James Aageson's and Sylvia Keesmaat's essays in the present volume demonstrate.

The term "inspired" or "God-breathed" is likely a Pauline coinage,[15] but the concept of the creative, life-giving breath of God and the image of the word of God as "breathed" by God have deep OT roots.[16] The notion of inspiration is not foreign to the OT (Num 24:2; Hos 9:7). Moreover, because it has God as its source, Scripture is "useful" in a variety of ways (cf. Rom 15:4; 1 Cor 10:11). Once again, the message is consistent with Pauline teaching elsewhere (Eph 2:8-10). Proper Christian training must be grounded in Scripture; it must be thorough, including both instruction and correction; and it is not merely for a person's own edification or intellectual stimulation but is equipment for ministry to others.

The references in 2 Tim 2:19 and 3:16, then, provide a fitting conclusion to the discussion of Paul's use of and stance toward Scripture. Clearly he viewed the Scriptures as both divinely inspired and profitable for teaching and training in righteous living (positive use) and (negatively) for rebuke and correction. Those in charge of the church must draw preeminently on Scripture as they encourage believers and refute the error of false teachers. Beyond this, the apostle adduces specific Scripture passages in his pronouncements regarding the role of women in the church, the payment of teaching elders, and God's sovereignty over false teachers.

---

15. Subsequent references include Ps.-Phoc. 129; *Sib. Or.* 5.308, 407 (c. 90-130).

16. See Genesis 1–2; Ps 33:6; Isa 42:5. Cf. M. R. Austin, "How Biblical Is 'the Inspiration of Scripture?'" *ExpTim* 93 (1981) 77-79.

The General Epistles

We will briefly survey the use of the OT in the General Epistles in the order James, Hebrews, Jude, 1–2 Peter, and 1–3 John. In deviation from the canonical order, James is treated first because it represents a fairly early instance of Jewish Christianity. Jude is treated prior to 1–2 Peter because it likely served as a *Vorlage* for 2 Peter 2. Otherwise the canonical order is kept.[17]

James

While much of James's thought is steeped in OT Scripture, there are only a few specific references to the OT. The first major cluster of references is found in 2:8-12, where the command to love one's neighbor as oneself is called "the royal law" (2:8) and it is said that believers will be judged by the "law of liberty" (2:12; cf. 1:25: "the perfect law, the law of liberty").[18] While no one can keep the whole law (2:10-13), works must nonetheless accompany faith. James cites Abraham as a scriptural example of one who showed his faith by what he did (and Rahab is offered as a secondary example, 2:25). The patriarch did not merely provide a verbal confession of belief in God; he offered up his son Isaac. Thus Gen 15:6 was fulfilled, which says that "Abraham believed God, and it was credited to him as righteousness."[19]

This is a very interesting instance of James's reading of the OT Scriptures. In the context of Gen 15:6, Abram, distressed about his lack of a son to fulfill God's promise to him, has a vision of the Lord, who reiterates his promise of a son. He shows Abram the starry sky and promises offspring as abundant as those stars. Then follows the statement regarding Abraham's faith in God's (reiterated) promise of a son. Only later in Genesis does one find the narrative regarding Abraham's offering of Isaac (Genesis 22), which is followed by a reiteration of God's promises to Abraham (Gen 22:16-18; cf. Gen 12:1-3). While at first God's promise to Abraham appears

---

17. Cf. R. Bauckham, "James, 1 and 2 Peter, Jude," in Carson and Williamson, eds., *It Is Written*, 303-17, who follows the order Jude, James, 1 Peter, 2 Peter.

18. See Bauckham, "James, 1 and 2 Peter, Jude," 308-9, with further reference to L. T. Johnson, "The Use of Leviticus 19 in the Letter of James," *JBL* 101 (1982) 391-401, who shows that Lev 19:12-18 furnishes the backdrop to James's entire epistle.

19. For a treatment of this passage against its ancient backdrop, see Bauckham, "James, 1 and 2 Peter, Jude," 306-7.

to be unconditional, the subsequent narrative reveals that it is predicated upon Abraham's obedient faith in action (e.g., Gen 22:16: "because you have done this").

While it therefore appears at first that James does not do justice to the immediate context of Gen 15:6 — in which no reference to Abraham's obedient action is found — a closer look reveals that James interprets the Genesis narrative pertaining to Abraham holistically, rightly concluding that faith and obedience cannot be separated. This is apparent from the very beginning, as when God's initial promise to Abraham in Gen 12:1-3 is immediately followed by a record of Abraham's obedient action in response (Gen 12:4). Over against those among his readers who sought to divorce faith from works, James, in effect, argues that what God has joined together let no man put asunder. Faith and works are two sides of the same coin.[20]

The only other formal citations of Scripture in the epistle of James are the cluster of references to the OT theme of God's jealousy in 4:5 and to Prov 3:34 in James 4:6. Regarding the former, it is interesting to note that the words cited as "Scripture" in 4:5 do not closely reproduce any one OT text. One may therefore surmise that a more global and thematic reference is at work here (cf., e.g., Exod 20:5; 34:14; Zech 8:2).[21] Separating oneself from the unbelieving world, however, requires God's gracious enablement. Receiving this grace, in turn, calls for humility, which occasions James's citation of Prov 3:34. James elaborates on this need for humility in 4:7-10. The fact that Prov 3:34 is also cited in 1 Pet 5:5 suggests that this passage was commonly used in the early church to stress the need for humility.

Space does not permit me to engage in detail the numerous OT allusive references in the book of James: the twelve tribes scattered among the nations (1:1); true religion consisting in looking after orphans and widows (1:27); the need to control one's tongue (3:1-12) and the supreme value of wisdom (3:13-18); the examples of Job (5:10-11, treated by Kurt Richardson in an essay included in this volume) and Elijah (5:17-18).[22] While formal ci-

20. For a very brief comparison of Paul and James, see my essay "Diversity and Unity in the New Testament," in *Biblical Theology: Retrospect and Prospect* (ed. Scott J. Hafemann; Downers Grove: InterVarsity, 2002) 152-53.

21. Cf. Douglas J. Moo, *The Letter of James* (TNTC; Grand Rapids: Eerdmans, 1985) 146. A similar dynamic can be observed in John 7:37-39.

22. Regarding James's use of OT figures as ethical and religious paradigms and his treatment of the Mosaic law, see Bauckham, "James, 1 and 2 Peter, Jude," 306-9.

tations are relatively rare in James, the entire epistle is flavored by scriptural principles, imagery, and exemplars. Coupled with the relative paucity of references to the Lord Jesus Christ (but see 2:1), this renders James the prime example of early Jewish Christianity in the NT canon.

Hebrews

It is clearly impossible in the space allotted to provide a full treatment of the use of the OT in the book of Hebrews. A few programmatic comments must suffice. With regard to the epistle's setting, we may note that while the author is unknown, the setting can be reconstructed to some extent: certain people are shrinking away from formal association with their fellow believers in light of mounting persecution (e.g., 10:25). The author encourages those believers to persevere, asserting the superiority of Christ and the new covenant he instituted over the old covenant system. Retreating back to Judaism is not a legitimate option, and rejecting God's final revelation in his Son (1:2) will be met with certain judgment (e.g., 2:3).

To this end the author invokes the OT Scriptures to argue for the Son's superiority over the angels, stringing together several OT references in 1:5-13 (Ps 2:7; 2 Sam 7:14; Pss 97:7; 104:4; 45:6; Isa 61:1, 3; Ps 102:25, 26; Isa 51:6; Ps 110:1) and in 2:6-8 (Ps 8:4-6). The cumulative impression created by this long string of OT references is that the author has ample scriptural support for his contention that Jesus is superior to the angels (despite the fact that the Son was briefly and temporarily humbled as a man, 2:9-18).

In 3:1, Jesus is identified as the Apostle and High Priest of our confession (even though it is not until later, beginning in chapter 5, that the theme of Christ's high priesthood is taken up more fully) and said to have been faithful over God's house — not as a servant, as Moses was, but as a Son (3:2-6). In the following section (3:7–4:11) the author provides a midrash-style Christian exposition of Psalm 95. This psalm, in turn, recalls the disobedience of wilderness Israel and urges the Israelites in the psalmist's day not to harden their hearts, lest they fail to enter God's rest. The author's argument picks up on the time gap between the original events recorded in the Pentateuch and the psalmist's exhortation, noting that the relevance of God's message to wilderness Israel was not limited to this group of people but was reiterated at a later juncture of salvation history (e.g., 4:7).

From this the author draws the conclusion that God's original exhortation is not limited even to the psalmist's day but continues to be relevant for his own contemporary audience "today." The rest promised to God's people was not realized when Joshua led Israel into the Promised Land, the author concludes, or David would not have reiterated God's exhortation centuries later. Hence it remains for God's people to enter into God's rest (that is, heaven). Thus the author wants his audience to learn the lesson wilderness Israel failed to learn: that entering into God's rest requires faith, rather than unbelief, in God's promises. In their day, this involved faith, not only in God, but in God's final revelation in his Son (1:2).

In chapter 5, then, the author of Hebrews turns more fully to an exposition of the unique high priesthood of Christ. After reiterating the quotation of Ps 2:7 in 1:5 (5:5), he cites the reference to the eternal priesthood of Melchizedek in Ps 110:4 (5:6; note the inclusion with 7:17, 21) and provides an exposition of this enigmatic OT figure (Gen 14:18-20) with reference to Christ.[23] The major purpose of the author's drawing on Melchizedek seems to be his desire to point to the existence of a type of priesthood attested in the OT other than the Levitical one that epitomized the regulations of the old covenant system. Thus the author is able to assert the superiority of the high priesthood of Christ over that of the Levitical code. Jesus' priesthood is permanent (7:24), and he offered up himself (7:27) once for all (10:10).

Another example of the author's careful reading of the OT in addition to Psalms 95 and 110 is his references to Jeremiah 31, which frame the section from 8:8 to 10:17. From the use of the term "new" covenant in this (and only this) OT passage, the author infers that the Mosaic covenant was destined to become obsolete once this new covenant envisioned by the prophet had been instituted (8:13), and he maintains that in Christ this time has now arrived. The importance of Jeremiah 31 for the author's argument can be gauged from the fact that the quotation of Jer 31:31-34 in Heb 8:8-12 is the longest OT quotation in the entire NT. The crucial implication drawn from the institution of the new covenant in Christ is that the readers must hold fast to their confession without wavering (10:23).

23. For a discussion of possible points of contact between Hebrews and the Qumran literature (esp. 11QMelch.), see A. T. Hanson, "Hebrews," in Carson and Williamson, eds., *It Is Written*, 296-97, though his theory is doubtful "that Hebrews saw Melchizedek as an appearance of the pre-existent Son, but did not have the scope or perhaps the nerve to say so" (p. 296).

In support of this contention, the author embarks on a tour through the OT Scriptures in order to demonstrate that faith characterized God's people throughout salvation history. Abel, Enoch, Noah, Abraham, Sarah, Isaac, Jacob, Joseph, Moses, Rahab, Gideon, Barak, Samson, Jephthah, David, Samuel, and the prophets are all cited as examples (chap. 11). However, it is on none of those examples, making up "a great cloud of witnesses," that his readers ultimately ought to fix their eyes; it is none other than Jesus himself, who "for the joy set before him endured the cross, despising the shame" (12:2). Suffering is interpreted as God's instrument by which he disciplines his children (12:5-11, citing Prov 3:11-12). The followers of Jesus, who suffered in order to sanctify his people through his blood, ought to be willing to suffer ostracism with him (13:12-13), for theirs is an expectation of a "lasting city" (13:14) — namely, Mount Zion, the heavenly Jerusalem — and the company of myriads of angels, God the judge of all people, the spirits of the righteous made perfect, and Jesus, the mediator of a new covenant (12:22-24).

Only a brief sketch of the use of the OT in Hebrews could be given here. The sustained use of the OT in this NT book shows how the author sought to engage his audience — "Hebrews" — on their own terms, that is, through Israel's Scriptures, seeking to demonstrate from those same Scriptures the superiority of Christ, his priesthood, and his new covenant, and the need for faith in God's Son.

Jude

The epistle of Jude is directed against false itinerant teachers who had infiltrated the church and preached a gospel that perverted the grace of God into a license for immorality (v. 4).[24] The danger was acute in that those heretics participated in the congregation's *agapē* meals (v. 12) and actively sought to proselytize among its members (vv. 22-23). In his refutation of and warning against these false teachers, Jude draws significantly on the OT Scriptures. Within the concentric (chiastic) structure of his epistle, Jude follows a pattern of interpretation that involves the citation of a given text (or types) followed by his midrashic exposition of this text with reference to the false teachers. The structure of the letter can be laid out as follows:

---

24. Concerning the relationship between Jude and 2 Peter 2, see the discussion under 2 Peter below.

A. Greeting (1-2) *Agapētoi*
B. Occasion (3-4) *Hypomnēsai de hymas boulomai*
C. Reminder (5-7) *Homoiōs mentoi kai houtoi*
D. The False Teachers (8-13) *Prophēteusen de kai toutois*
D′. Quotation from *1 Enoch* (14-16) *Hymeis de, agapētoi, mnēsthēte ton rhēmatōn*
C′. Reminder (17-19) *Hymeis de, agapētoi*
B′. Exhortation (20-23)
A′. Doxology

Within this structure, one can diagram Jude's utilization of and commentary on certain texts:[25]

Verse	Text	Verse	Midrash
5-7	#1 Three OT types	8-10	*Homoiōs mentoi kai houtoi*[26]
11	#2 Three more OT types	12-13	*Houtoi eisin*[27]
14-15	#3 *1 Enoch* 1:9	16	*Houtoi eisin*
17-18	#4 Apostolic prophecy	19	*Houtoi eisin*

As can be seen from the diagrams above, verses 5-7 (elaborated upon in 8-16) and 17-19 are labeled as "reminders," while 8-13 and 14-16 correspond to each other in the body of the letter. The transitions between the respective *Vorlage* texts and the midrashic expositions are characterized by two stylistic elements: verb tense forms and the term *houtoi*. All verb tenses in the texts are in the aorist or future, while all verbs in the commentary sections are in the present tense. Beyond this, texts and midrashic portions are tied together by link words: *asebeis/asebeia* (4, 15, 18); *blasphēmein/ blasphēmia* (8, 9, 10); *planē/planētēs* (11, 13); *zophos . . . tērein* (6, 13).[28]

The logic underlying the midrashic portions is as follows: (1) the sins committed by the false teachers are analogous to the sins of their OT coun-

---

25. Cf. Bauckham, "James, 1 and 2 Peter, Jude," 303-4.

26. In addition, there is an allusion to the pseudepigraphical work *Assumption of Moses* in v. 9. Note that Jude 10, too, begins with *houtoi*. For a detailed discussion, see Richard Bauckham, *Jude, 2 Peter* (WBC; Waco: Word, 1983) 65-76.

27. Bauckham, "James, 1 and 2 Peter, Jude," 304-5 (with further bibliographic references), notes that, similar to vv. 8-10, the commentary in vv. 12-13 includes secondary allusions (he cites Ezek 34:2; Prov 25:14; Isa 57:20; *1 En.* 80:6).

28. For a more detailed list, see Bauckham, "James, 1 and 2 Peter, Jude," 305-6.

terparts; (2) for this reason their condemnation will likewise correspond to the judgment visited upon the OT types. This is demonstrated for the entire salvation-historical period: from OT times to the Second Temple period and to apostolic times. The references to the OT in vv. 5-7 and 11 each involve three types: wilderness Israel (Num 14:29-30), the fallen angels, and Sodom and Gomorrah (Gen 19:24-25); and Cain (Gen 4:3-8), Balaam (Num 31:16), and the sons of Korah (Numbers 16) respectively. The order is not salvation-historical but topical.

Jude's midrashic method evinces a certain affinity with the *pesher* exegesis practiced at Qumran. Characteristic of both is the conviction that the OT texts constitute eschatological prophecies that are applied by the interpreter to the situation prevailing in his own contemporary community. Also represented at Qumran are thematic pesharim (4QFlor; 11QMelch). Yet Qumran did not use apocryphal texts or oral Christian prophecies. Typological scriptural interpretation is absent as well. Jude, on the other hand, "applies Scripture to the last days not only as prophecy, but also as typology, in which the events of redemptive history are seen to foreshadow the eschatological events."[29]

1 Peter

Peter's first epistle is designed to strengthen believers in the face of imminent suffering by reminding them of the eternal nature of their inheritance and of the ephemeral nature of their suffering. The apostle seeks to help his readers to understand their calling in the midst of an unbelieving, even hostile, world along the lines of God's old covenant people. They are to focus on Christ's example in suffering and to promote godly relationships among believers. The first major theological theme of Peter's use of the OT in his first epistle is that he applies OT language referring to Israel freely to the church (esp. in chaps. 1–2):

- believers are the elect, the diaspora, God's chosen ones (1:1-2);
- they are the final recipients of the message of the OT prophets (1:10-12);
- they are to be holy as God is holy (1:16; citing Lev 19:2);

29. Bauckham, *Jude, 2 Peter,* 5.

- the word of the Lord is identified with the apostolic gospel (1:24-25; a *pesher*-style argument from Isa 40:6-8);[30]
- they have tasted that the Lord is good (2:3, alluding to Ps 34:8);
- as those established in Christ (2:6-8; citing Isa 28:16 LXX; Ps 118:22;[31] Isa 8:14), they are God's people chosen to declare his praises (Isa 43:20-21 LXX), a royal priesthood[32] and a holy nation (Exod 19:6 LXX); in the language of Hosea, those who once were not a people had now become the people of God; those who had not received mercy, now had received mercy (2:10; cf. Hos 2:23; cf. 1:6, 9; 2:1).[33]

Significantly, the NT people of God are presented as a "spiritual house," a "holy priesthood bringing spiritual sacrifices." God's people are built up as a holy temple, whereby the temple is now the community of believers rather than the physical structure of the building. As Bauckham has shown, 1 Pet 2:4-10 resembles Jude 4-19 in its midrashic style and use of source texts:[34]

30. In this quotation Peter generally reproduces the Hebrew and Greek text, except that he adds the word "as"; refers to "glory" rather than "grace, loveliness"; renders "withers away" as "fallen off"; and replaces "word of God" with "word of the Lord."

31. Interestingly, Peter is shown to refer to the same passage (Ps 118:22) in his speech to the Sanhedrin in Acts 4:11.

32. "Royal priesthood" follows the LXX in its reversal of the MT, "priestly kingdom." The present passage is a shaky basis for the doctrine of the priesthood of all believers (note the corporate noun "priesthood," focusing on the collective rather than the individual aspect), for, just as in OT Israel not every Israelite served as priest (this was reserved for the tribe of Levi) but Israel as a nation served as a mediatorial (i.e., "priestly") kingdom mediating God's presence to the surrounding nations, so the NT church is corporately set up as a mediatorial entity (a "priesthood") in order to declare the message of our glorious God to the unbelieving world (1 Pet 2:9b alluding to Isa 43:21 LXX). The notion of the "priesthood of all believers" has been classically formulated by Luther, who claimed, "Every shoemaker can be a priest of God" (cited in David F. Wright, "Priesthood of All Believers," in *New Dictionary of Theology* [ed. Sinclair B. Ferguson, David F. Wright, and J. I. Packer; Downers Grove: InterVarsity, 1988] 532), over against Roman Catholic teaching regarding a special priestly class. However, it appears that neither Exod 19:6 nor 1 Pet 2:9 is adequate to support the notion that the NT teaches a "priesthood of all believers," especially since the book of Hebrews clearly indicates the obliteration of the OT priestly system through the once-for-all sacrifice of Christ, who holds a unique and eternal high priesthood.

33. Note that Isa 28:16 is referred to also by Paul in Rom 9:33 and Eph 2:20; Ps 118:22 is referred to by Jesus in Matt 21:42, Peter in Acts 4:11, and Paul in Rom 9:33; and Hos 2:23 is cited by Paul in Rom 9:25.

34. Bauckham, "James, 1 and 2 Peter, Jude," 310.

Verses	Texts	Verses	Texts
4-5	Introduction	6-10	Midrash
4a	Jesus the chosen stone	6-8a	The chosen stone: Texts 1-3
5b	Believers God's chosen people	9-10b	The chosen people: Texts 4-6

As Bauckham notes, the introduction in 1 Pet 2:4-5 already signals the subsequently cited portions of Scripture. The texts for the midrash can be diagrammed as follows:

> 6b+7a Text 1 (Isa 28:16) + interpretation 9 Text 4 (Isa 43:20-21) + Text 5 (Exod 19:5-6)
>
> 7b+c Interpretation + Text 2 (Ps 118:22) conflated, then Text 4 expanded
>
> 8a+b Text 3 (Isa 8:14) + interpretation 10 Text 6 (Hos 2:23) paraphrased (cf. 1:6, 9; 2:1)[35]

The second major theological theme illustrated by way of reference to the Hebrew Scriptures by Peter is that of Jesus as an example of righteous suffering. In 1 Pet 2:18-25 (esp. vv. 21-25), Christ is presented as an example of suffering for what is right. This is done by a midrashic exposition of Isa 52:13–53:12:

- in 2:22, Peter cites Isa 53:9 (the Servant committed no sin, no deceit was found in his mouth);
- in 2:23, Peter alludes to Isa 53:7 (the Servant did not revile in return);
- in 2:24, Peter alludes to Isa 53:4, 5 (the Servant bore our sins; by his wounds we are healed);
- in 2:25, Peter alludes to Isa 53:6 (we all like sheep went astray).

Again, Peter does not follow the textual order but comments from his source text as his argument requires.

Third, the apostle follows up on believers' need to follow Christ's example in suffering righteously by further references to the Hebrew Scriptures in the third chapter of his epistle. First Peter 3:10-12 features a citation of Ps 34:12-16 (LXX with minor rephrasing; note already the allusion to Ps

---

35. See Bauckham, "James, 1 and 2 Peter, Jude," 311, for a list of catchwords that link the texts, similar to Jude 4-19 (see above).

34:8 in 1 Peter 2:3).[36] This is followed in 1 Pet 3:14 with a citation from Isa 8:12-13 (cf. the quotation of Isa 8:14 in 1 Pet 2:8 noted above). The fact that both citations are from previously cited texts (Psalm 34; Isaiah 8) makes clear that Peter was steeped in OT thought and used specific OT texts as his point of departure as he applied these to his contemporary context.

Interestingly, he does not cite his source text for his notoriously difficult statement in 1 Pet 3:19-20 that Christ "went and preached to the spirits in prison who disobeyed long ago when God waited patiently in the days of Noah while the ark was being built." Peter continues, "In it only a few people, eight in all, were saved through water, and this water symbolizes baptism that now saves you also . . . by the resurrection of Jesus Christ" (1 Pet 3:20-21). Possibly Peter's reference involves traditions surrounding the interpretation of Gen 6:4. While Peter's source for this information is unknown, the following reconstruction of his message seems plausible:

- Christ died for sins once for all; he was put to death in the body (1 Pet 3:18);
- he was made alive by the Spirit (the resurrection; 3:19);
- subsequent to the resurrection, he proclaimed his triumph to those demonic spirits held in Hades who had disobeyed in the days of Noah (the so-called "descent into Hades"; 3:19-20; note also the reference to the flood in 2 Pet 3:6);
- finally, Christ ascended into heaven and was seated at God's right hand, with all angels subject to him (3:22).

Peter's interpretation of the salvation of Noah and his family through the waters of the flood with reference to believers being saved through the waters of baptism is typological, whereby the flood waters constitute the type and the waters of baptism represent the antitype. Just as Noah and his family were not saved literally by water but through the water on account of their faith in God, so baptism is not the ground but merely the vehicle of believers' salvation in Christ.

Peter concludes with two citations from the book of Proverbs. In 4:18

36. See also the allusion to Ps 34:15 in Heb 12:14. Bauckham, "James, 1 and 2 Peter, Jude," 312-13, notes the chiastic structure of 1 Pet 3:8-11. He also observes that in 2:3-4 the allusions to Psalm 34 serve to link 2:4-10 to what precedes and that 2:3-4 make it clear that the author read the psalm christologically, identifying *kyrios* with Christ and possibly intending the *pesher*-like word play *chrēstos* (= *Christos*) *ho kyrios*. Hence *kyrios* in 3:12 is also Christ (see also 1:25).

he refers to Prov 11:31 LXX, and in 5:5 he cites Prov 3:34 LXX (also cited in James 4:6; see above). As Bauckham notes, the latter passage occurs in the context of a cluster of parallels with James 4, which seems to suggest a common paraenetic tradition.[37]

2 Peter

The only formal citation of the OT in Peter's second epistle is likewise from the book of Proverbs. Second Peter 2:22 quotes Prov 26:11, "A dog returns to its vomit," as an illustration of the fate of the false teachers. While much of the second chapter of Peter's second epistle likely represents an adaptation of the epistle of Jude, Peter added this quotation from Proverbs to Jude's description. Beyond this formal citation there are several additional references to Israel's Scriptures. The reference to the inspiration of the prophetic Scriptures in 2 Pet 1:19-21 bears some resemblance to 1 Pet 1:10-12. The reference to the flood in 2 Pet 3:6 resembles 1 Pet 3:19-21.[38]

A comparison between Jude and 2 Peter 2 (both of which contain several OT allusions) reveals numerous parallels between those two passages, which makes it probable that a direct literary relationship exists between these two documents. Apart from verbal parallels, both documents follow a very similar sequence of argument:

Jude 4-19	2 Peter 2:1–3:3
wilderness	Israel
angels	angels
	Noah
Sodom and Gomorrah	Sodom and Gomorrah
	Lot
archangel Michael	[archangel Michael]
Cain	
Balaam	Balaam
Korah	

37. Bauckham, "James, 1 and 2 Peter, Jude," 312.

38. The context of the flood reference in 2 Pet 3:6 seems to be a rather unique false teaching in Peter's day, which denied the reality of the universal flood in Noah's day owing to the belief that God does not intervene in human history (2 Pet 3:4). Hence these false teachers denied the future reality of Christ's return as well.

Hence Jude and Peter concur in the basic story line: angels — Sodom and Gomorrah — [archangel Michael] — Balaam. Two major changes are apparent. Negatively, Peter omits reference to apocryphal material. Neither the *Assumption of Moses* (Jude 9) nor *1 Enoch* (Jude 14-15) is featured. The possible reason for this is the uncertain canonical status of these documents among Peter's readers. On the positive side, Peter replaces the negative examples of Cain and Korah with the positive examples of Noah and Lot. This balances out his presentation. Rather than being entirely negative in his denunciation of false teachers, as is Jude, Peter balances negative examples (angels, Sodom and Gomorrah, and Balaam) with positive ones (Noah and Lot).

As Bauckham notes, the flood and the destruction of Sodom and Gomorrah were "the classic illustrations of God's discriminatory judgment, in which the righteous, however few, are spared."[39] In the case of the flood, the righteous man was Noah; in the case of Sodom and Gomorrah, the righteous man was Lot. Their situation as righteous people in the midst of an unbelieving, godless world and their righteous suffering suited them as paradigms for Peter's readers in that their situation was similar (cf. the treatment of 1 Peter above). Hence "Noah and Lot are types of faithful Christians who hope for deliverance at the parousia (2:9a), but meantime must live righteously in the midst of an evil society doomed to judgment."[40] As Bauckham notes, it is interesting that in his accounts of Noah and Lot the author does not focus on their deliverance but on their righteous lives in the midst of their evil contemporaries.[41]

What is more, Peter so reworked Jude that now the argument follows a chronological order. While this falls short of certainty, it seems probable that the direction of the changes went from Jude to Peter rather than vice versa. All things being equal, it is more likely that Peter balanced out his presentation and added positive examples than that Jude negativized Peter's portrayal by excluding all positive characters and adding more negative ones; it is more likely that Peter omitted reference to apocryphal material than that Jude added it; and it is more likely that Peter reworked Jude's material so that it reflected a salvation-historical order than that Jude so

---

39. Bauckham, "James, 1 and 2 Peter, Jude," 314.

40. Bauckham, "James, 1 and 2 Peter, Jude," 314.

41. For the haggadic traditions surrounding Noah and Lot, see Bauckham, "James, 1 and 2 Peter, Jude," 314-15.

rearranged Peter that his presentation did not. If the above reconstruction is correct, 2 Pet 2:1–3:3 is not original with Peter but reflects an adaptation of the material found in Jude 4-19.

1–3 John

The solitary OT reference in the Johannine epistles is the reference to Cain as the paradigmatic example of hatred of one's brother in 1 John 3:12. Lack of love for one's fellow person is thus presented as a major characteristic of the world. Otherwise, John does not invoke Israel's Scriptures in his epistles, presumably because the heresy with which he was confronted was christological (the issue was the denial or confession of the Son, 1 John 2:22-23), and so his refutation necessitated a christological rationale rather than citation of the Hebrew Scriptures.

The Book of Revelation

The book of Revelation is replete with allusions to the OT. Counts vary, but most detect close to four hundred OT references in the book, which would be an average of almost twenty per chapter or almost one per verse.[42] There are references to the Pentateuch, Judges, 1–2 Samuel, 1–2 Kings, the Psalms, Proverbs, the Song of Solomon, Job, and major and minor prophets. About half of the references are from the Psalms, Isaiah, Ezekiel, and Daniel. The highest proportion of allusions in Revelation in relation to a book's length is from Daniel, particularly Daniel 7; the greatest number of actual allusions is from Isaiah.

The non-formal character of OT references in Revelation makes textual identification more difficult. It is also difficult to determine whether or not the author refers to a given text consciously or subconsciously. There are also many conflations of texts; at times as many as four, five, or six different passages are merged into one picture.[43] In some cases, we may

42. G. Beale, "Revelation," in Carson and Williamson, eds., *It Is Written*, 333, n. 1, notes that the UBS[3] count is 394, while the NA[26] counts 635 references. I am indebted to Beale's presentation for the following treatment.

43. Examples of this procedure include the depictions of Christ in 1:12-20, of God on the throne in 4:1-11, or of the diabolical beast in 13:1-8.

be dealing with a mind saturated with OT Scripture. At least in the case of the clearer OT references in his work, there seems to be reason to believe that the author intentionally refers to scriptural material.[44] In any case, owing to the composite nature of many of the OT references in Revelation, the evocative power of its images is greater than the sum of its component parts.

As Beale notes, it is important to determine whether the visions depicted in the book have an experiential basis (as the book itself seems to claim) or whether we are here dealing primarily with a literary work.[45] The entire book consists of the description of four visions, each of which is clearly marked by the introductory phrase "in the Spirit" (1:10; 4:2; 17:3; 21:10). These visions are presented within an epistolary framework as addressed to seven churches in Asia Minor (Rev 1:4; 2–3). Much of the material seems to be prophetic in nature (1:3; 22:18-19), dealing with both the seer's contemporary situation (that is, end-of-first-century Rome) and the prospect of end-time events centering around God's judgment, Christ's return, and the final state.

At the heart of the message of the book seems to be the typological identification of Rome (with its empire cult and its persecution of Christians) with Babylon (the historical power responsible for Israel being taken into exile). This typological framework is then extended into the future to point to a future personage called the "antichrist," who will embody some of the same characteristics typical of earlier oppressors and persecutors of God's people. Within this framework John presents his theodicy vindicating God's righteousness, which appears to be in question owing to the suffering faced by believers.

One major device found in Revelation is using OT antecedents as a theological lens through which later events are understood and presented. The trumpets and bowls in Rev 8:6-12 and 16:1-9, for example, draw on the pattern of the plagues preceding the exodus, though these images are creatively reworked and reapplied. One also finds frequent instances of reapplication, such as from God to Christ or from Israel to the church.[46]

---

44. So rightly Beale, "Revelation," 321.

45. In my judgment, only the former seems to do full justice to the inherent claims in the book itself. Studying Revelation exclusively from the vantage point of literary analysis therefore seems to be reductionistic.

46. For the former, see, e.g., Rev 4–5; for the latter, see, e.g., the references to Exod 19:6 in Rev 1:6 and 5:10.

However, as Beale rightly notes, changes of applications do not necessarily indicate a disregard for the OT context.[47] Overall, Christ serves as the hermeneutical key, and the OT provides the salvation-historical backdrop against which the apocalyptic visions in the book are to be understood.

Beale notes the following uses of the OT in Revelation:

- the use of segments of OT Scripture as literary prototypes (e.g., the use of Daniel, esp. chaps. 2 and 7, in Revelation 1, 4–5, 13, and 17; the use of Ezekiel in Revelation 4; 5; 6:1-8; 6:12–7:1; 7:2-8; 8:1-5; 14:6-12; 17:1-6; 18:9-24; 20:7-10; 21:22; and the use of exodus plagues in Rev 8:6-12; 16:1-9);
- the thematic use of the OT (Daniel's "abomination of desolation"; the divine warrior; the earthquake motif; the "day of the Lord"; hymns and liturgical motifs);
- the analogical use of the OT (judgment theophanies; tribulation and persecution of God's people; seductive, idolatrous teaching; divine protection; victorious battle of God's people over the enemy; apostasy; and the divine Spirit as the power for God's people);
- the universalization of the OT to stress redemptive fulfillment (e.g., the application of Exod 19:6 to the church in Rev 1:6 and 5:10; the use of Zech 12:10 in Rev 1:7);
- possible indirect fulfillment uses of the OT (e.g., Rev 1:1 cf. Dan 2:28-29, 45; Rev 22:10 cf. Dan 12:4, 9; Rev 1:13-14 cf. Dan 7:13);
- the inverted use of the OT to stress irony (e.g., Rev 3:9 cf. Isa 45:14; 49:23; 60:14; Rev 5:9 cf. Dan 7:14); and
- the stylistic use of OT language (the author's attempt to reproduce semitic idioms in his use of the Greek language).

An interesting case study of the use of the OT in the book of Revelation is the use of Zech 12:10b-14 in Rev 1:7. The comparison between the OT *Vorlage*, "And they shall look upon me whom they have pierced and shall mourn for him" (MT; the LXX has "because they have danced derisively" in the place of "whom they have pierced"), and Rev 1:7, "And every eye will see him, even those who pierced him; and all the peoples of the earth will mourn because of him," reveals the following pattern of changes:

47. Beale, "Revelation," 322: "this is not a logically necessary deduction." Note also Beale's distinction between literary and historical context on p. 323.

- John universalizes the subject of "look" and "mourn"; the OT *Vorlage* (MT = LXX) has "house of David and inhabitants of Jerusalem"; John speaks of "every eye" and "all the peoples of the earth";
- John changes the first-person object of "look" to the third person; people no longer look at "me," that is, Yahweh (Zech 12:4), but on "him," that is, Jesus;
- John changes the relative pronoun from accusative to nominative, thus emphasizing the subject rather than the object.

Hence John in Rev 1:7, in keeping with the universal scope and messianic nature of Zechariah 12–14, transforms Zech 12:10-14 in order to show the fulfillment of the Abrahamic blessing of the nations through the suffering and reigning messianic seed.

Conclusion

The above survey of the ways in which the OT is used vividly demonstrates the remarkable variety in which the NT writers used Israel's Scriptures. In some books references to the OT were found to be virtually absent (Titus, 1–3 John). On the other end of the spectrum, the books treated in the present survey also include the two NT documents in whose thought the OT is perhaps most central (Hebrews, Revelation), though Hebrews focuses more on typology and conceptual patterns while Revelation is more allusive and evocative in its apocalyptic images. Paul's two letters to Timothy contain a comparatively small number of OT references that are clustered around specific issues addressed by the apostle. Of the remaining writings, James as an exemplar of early Jewish Christianity was found to be steeped in OT thought (though his explicit quotations are more limited), while Jude and the two Petrine epistles are predominantly midrashic in their use of the OT.

The variety in the ways in which the OT is used in the Pastoral and General Epistles and in the book of Revelation reflects the variety of scriptural uses in the larger Jewish world of the first century of the common era. It appears that the use of the OT by a given NT writer depended upon a variety of factors, which included the type of polemic in which he wished to engage, his own command of Scripture and the scriptural literacy prevalent among his audience, his genre of writing, and other factors. The theological application, too, displays a considerable scope. In some instances the use of the OT is christologically constrained (Hebrews, Revelation); in other instances the typological substructure at work is ecclesiological in a general (1 Pet 2:4-10) or more specific sense (1 Tim 2:13-15), or designed to indicate the imminent judgment of false teachers in keeping with God's judgment of the immoral and rebellious in Israel's past history (Jude 4-19; 2 Peter 2). Another frequent pattern of usage entails that of referring to OT characters as exemplars of conduct worth emulating (the "hall of faith" in Hebrews 11 or the references to Abraham, Rahab, the prophets, Job, and Elijah in the book of James).

Examples could be multiplied. We close with the realization that the NT writers, by their varied use of the OT in their writings, bear witness to the unity between the history of Israel, the coming of Christ, and the history of the early church. This consciousness of the salvation-historical connectedness of God's people of all times provided a common, fertile ground for the argumentation of the different writers of the NT. Whether the need of the moment was to demonstrate the superiority of Christ over the OT priesthood and sacrificial system; to denounce false teachers who had turned God's grace into licentiousness; to ground one's ecclesiastical adjudication on various issues in authoritative tradition; to provide an illustration, analogy, or exemplar; or to give expression to one's visionary experiences, Israel's Scriptures provided the quarry from which the raw materials could be taken.

To require the NT writers to be slavish in their adherence to the OT or to limit them to one particular type of usage or pattern would be inappropriate. Not only did some of the above-mentioned factors set certain parameters for their OT usage, but as authors they were free to work with their raw material, the Scriptures, as a potter works with his clay, shaping and reshaping it to mold it into the form he desires for the product he chooses to create. This is not to minimize the role of the divine Spirit in the process. It is to stress, however, that the Scriptures provided a quarry rather than a straitjacket, a wide open field rather than a prison, for the NT writers as they formulated their message. Understanding the various text types of the source texts is of some importance, as is a proper appreciation of the literary contexts. Most important, however, is the apprehension of the theological message of the NT writers, including those places where it is enhanced or adorned by their use of the OT.

It seems fitting to conclude this essay with Paul's words in 2 Cor 3:16-

18, where the apostle uses an OT reference to describe the glorious present condition and future destiny that are ours as believers in Jesus the Messiah: "But whenever anyone turns to the Lord, the veil is taken away. Now the Lord is the Spirit, and where the Spirit of the Lord is, there is freedom. And we, who with unveiled faces all reflect the Lord's glory, are being transformed into his likeness with ever-increasing glory, which comes from the Lord, who is the Spirit."

Hearing the Old Testament in the New:
A Response

ANDREAS J. KÖSTENBERGER

It is a distinct honor to have participated in this colloquium and to respond to these excellent papers. I am humbled by the vast array of subjects covered and look forward to further fruitful dialogue. One essay that ought to be required reading for a discussion such as this is Stanley Porter's "The Use of the Old Testament in the New Testament: A Brief Comment on Method and Terminology."[1] In this essay, Porter laments and documents the terminological confusion surrounding the use of such terms as "quotation," "allusion," "echo," and "intertextuality." Porter contends that "the criteria for determining and labeling the use of Old Testament and related texts in the New Testament are far from being resolved and even further from providing objective tests."[2] While research continues unabated, many do not define their terms, and those who do fail to provide the kinds of definitions necessary.

Porter closes with three recommendations: (1) know the goal of one's investigation; (2) define one's categories and then apply them rigorously; and (3) adopt an author- rather than audience-centered approach to studying the use of the Old Testament in the New. Regarding defining

---

1. In *Early Christian Interpretation of the Scriptures of Israel: Investigations and Proposals* (ed. C. A. Evans and J. A. Sanders; JSNTSup 148; Sheffield: Sheffield Academic Press, 1997) 79-96.
2. Porter, "Use of the OT in the NT," 88.

The following paper represents an edited version of the response I gave at the actual colloquium. In some cases presenters have subsequently modified their papers.

one's categories, Porter suggests using "explicit or direct quotation or citation" in terms of "formal correspondence with actual words found in antecedent texts." An "allusion" (or "echo") may be defined as "the nonformal invocation by an author of a text (or person, event, etc.) that the author could reasonably have been expected to know."[3] It is armed with this set of definitions that I set out to respond briefly to these papers.

"The Use of the Old Testament in the New Testament as a Rhetorical Device: A Methodological Proposal"

In the opening paper, Dennis Stamps has argued the thesis that the use of the OT in the NT takes place not primarily in an inner-Jewish context but within a clash of cultures, so that the key question is "how the diverse ways the NT uses the OT are persuasive in that collision of cultures." His initial survey of methodological issues discusses the question under the three rubrics of terminology, hermeneutics, and theology.

Stamps first deals with the knotty question of how to refer to the "OT" as used by the New and settles on "Jewish sacred writings" as the best designation. He says that the canonical boundaries were not fixed at the time the NT was written, but the concept of sacred writings was well established. Citation is defined as any quotation, however many words, which has verbal correspondence with the textual tradition; reference is any way in which the NT writers invoke the Jewish sacred writers, whether by a quotation or by naming a character or event or by referring to a theme, etc. Stamps likes the categorization of OT references by R. T. France (though France does not define his categories): verbatim quotations with or without introductory formulae; clear verbal allusions; clear references without verbal allusions; possible verbal allusions; and possible references without verbal allusions.

Stamps points out that first-century Judaism was by no means monolithic, which has important implications for the use of the OT in the NT in that different Jewish communities varied in their use of their sacred writings. Especially since Stamps earlier refers to the importance of considering the "communal context" of the NT documents in assessing how this may have impacted their use of OT texts, I wonder whether this may also affect issues of canon. While there may not have been a universally

3. Porter, "Use of the OT in the NT," 95.

agreed upon canon in first-century Judaism, is it possible that the different Jewish communities each had canons that served as authoritative bases for their lives and practice? I will return to this point when I deal with Timothy McLay's paper below.

Stamps next addresses the issue of whether to adopt an author- or an audience-oriented perspective in studying the use of the OT in the NT. He says determining the author's intent is slippery but legitimate, though in the end unnecessary. Determining the level of audience understanding is judged to be virtually impossible, though Stamps holds out some hope for using the construct of the "ideal reader or hearer." I wonder how these judgments square with Stanley Porter's conclusions in the aforementioned article. Stamps sprinkles references to Porter throughout his essay, but there may be some variance in their views. This seems to be the case particularly with Stamps's focus on studying the *effects* of the use of the OT in the NT on the readers. How does this accord with Porter's advocacy of an author-oriented perspective? This may call for further resolution and may be the subject of fruitful discussion.

Stamps proceeds to point out that Christians were innovative in their use of the Jewish sacred Scriptures and that there are differences between different Christian writers or communities in the way these Scriptures are interpreted. He also raises the interesting question of how or whether the historical development of Christianity influenced the way the OT was used by different NT authors. In his discussion of intertextuality, Stamps notes that studying the use of the OT in the NT is more complex than merely determining the transfer of meaning; among other things, some social and cultural baggage gets attached to some texts (with reference to the work of V. K. Robbins). Echoing Porter's concerns, Stamps calls for more precision in defining one's terms and in declaring one's hermeneutical concerns and theological perspective.

Stamps's real burden comes to the fore in part two of his paper, the NT use of the OT as rhetorical device. Here Stamps makes a case, first, for understanding the use of the OT in the NT as a rhetorical device, and, second, for focusing on the Hellenistic context in which much of the writing of the NT took place. Overall, he makes this two-part case in a measured, well-qualified sense, which will likely, at least to a certain extent, appease those who are reluctant to follow Stamps all the way owing to their conviction that the Jewish background is primary. I will return to this issue in the conclusion below.

After a brief survey of key early Greek writers, Stamps defines rhetoric as "the ways and means employed in a text to persuade and the intended effect(s) of those ways and means." Stamps first briefly discusses the way in which the use of authoritative tradition in first-century Jewish and early Christian writings may be viewed in terms of persuasion. This includes Philo, the rabbinic or Pharisaic tradition, and the Dead Sea Scrolls. In each case, the OT is used in an intra-communitarian and extra-communitarian sense (my terms). The group's interpretation serves to validate the truthfulness of its community ethos among its members (intra-community) and to convince others of the truthfulness of the group's beliefs (extra-community).

Stamps proceeds to point out that in Greco-Roman writings, too, quoting respected authors gave weight to one's argument. Here he draws both on primary quotations and on the work of Christopher Stanley. I would like to interject at this point that I am not convinced that the parallels adduced here are complete. Stanley says that both the Homeric texts and the sacred Jewish writings functioned as primordial texts and exercised formative influence on communal life and thought. That may be so, but did they do that in exactly the same way? Does it make any difference that one group of writings may fall in the category of myth while the other includes significant portions of historical narrative? To consider another parallel adduced by Christopher Stanley (and seconded by Stamps), "[b]oth texts [Homer and the OT] were cited in argumentation as authoritative for both the author and the audience." But were they considered authoritative in exactly the same way? It occurs to me that "authoritative" may have meant something different in the respective contexts (similar to "inspiration"). These are but two examples of what may be a more endemic problem with putting Greco-Roman rhetoric and the use of the OT in the NT on the same level.

The next topic of discussion is early Christian writings and Hellenistic culture. Stamps concludes that "[i]t may be helpful to begin to see the NT as part of this clash of cultures and its writings as part of the persuasive agenda of the post-NT writers." Paul's argument that justification by faith precedes the law, Stamps argues, may be persuasive, not so much because it employs some form of Jewish exegetical practice, but because it corresponds to a Hellenistic concern to establish truth in that which is most ancient. I would like to see more discussion on this. Stamps himself acknowledges the need for more work in this area. One wonders particularly about how proselytes would have understood the NT writers' use of the OT.

Stamps's paper closes with a brief discussion of how we hear the OT in the NT today. I will limit my remarks to respond to one comment Stamps makes regarding the stance that "the meaning that is intended for the hearer today is the one that was intended in the original context." Stamps says that, regardless of the merits of such an argument, "the use and impact of the Bible in modern society and culture cannot be limited to that interpretative stance *because the majority of modern hearers or readers are not able to excavate that meaning, nor do they wish to.*" My question is, granted that many modern readers are unable or unwilling to excavate the originally intended meaning, could the lack of ability and/or willingness to excavate that meaning not limit the impact of Scripture on those individuals? In my view it certainly does. Why else devise a curriculum to teach our students the biblical languages and exegetical skills so that they may in turn impart this skill to people in their congregations if not to remedy the problem of lack of ability? And as far as lack of desire to excavate the originally intended meaning is concerned, are we to excuse and accept that lack of desire by capitulating to it and by devising a method that accommodates it? The argument, at least the way it is put by Stamps, strikes me as unduly pragmatic. If this kind of reasoning were to prevail, I submit that it would have radical implications for theological education, to go no further.

To conclude my response to Stamps's paper, I think he has made his case about as well as it can be made. If I am correct that his burden is actually twofold, first, to commend an understanding of the NT's use of the OT as a rhetorical device, and, second, to make a case for considering the Hellenistic context, I would find the first argument more persuasive than the second. I have long felt that the rhetorical dimension of the NT's use of the OT has been unduly neglected and underrated. Clearly, it seems to me, the answer to the question, "Why does, say, Paul cite the OT in a given instance as opposed to just stating his own view on the subject?" involves the issue of persuasion. Since the Jewish sacred writings were already considered authoritative by many in Paul's audience, if the apostle could show that his teaching was consistent with, and in further application of, these writings, he would considerably increase the likelihood of his teaching being accepted by many in his audience (cf., e.g., 1 Tim 2:13).

Regarding the second element, however, more discussion is needed. I believe what is needed now is not so much an advocacy paper for considering the Hellenistic background as a weighing of Jewish exegetical practices and Greco-Roman rhetorical conventions as to their possible influence on a given NT writer's argument in a particular instance (such as the Pauline teaching on justification by faith). I may raise one further overall concern. Stamps correctly notes that, while most NT authors were Christian Jews, most NT documents originated not in Palestine but in the larger Greco-Roman world; hence one should give more attention to the Hellenistic environment, including rhetoric, in studying the NT writers' use of the OT.

However, if Stanley Porter is correct in his call for an author-oriented approach to the study of the NT's use of the OT (and I think he is), and by Stamps's own acknowledgment most NT authors were Christian Jews, would it not follow that one might expect these authors in many instances to have followed Jewish conventions for citation, allusion, etc., rather than Greco-Roman ones in their use of the OT? It seems that Stamps's emphasis on Hellenistic rhetoric is a function of his more reader-oriented approach (note his emphasis on "effect"); if one focuses on the author instead, one may very well continue to look primarily to Jewish models. If this observation is correct, one's openness to seeing the NT writers draw on persuasive methods influenced by Greco-Roman rhetoric in their use of the OT will depend at least to some extent on one's overall approach to studying the use of the OT in the NT, whether author- or audience-oriented, and it is this question that then would need more discussion.

Specifically, if Knowles and Porter are correct that Matthew and Luke in their use of the OT significantly draw on Jesus, and Jesus was a Palestinian Jew, then what are the implications of this for seeing Hellenistic rhetoric as a backdrop? Did Jesus — in Palestine, in the 30s CE — then draw on Greco-Roman rhetoric? Or would Stamps argue that this entered into the NT document only on the level of contextualization at the time of writing of, say, Matthew or Luke? Even there, however, I am not sure that at least Knowles and Porter found significant alteration between Jesus' use of the OT and that of the evangelists. After all, Gospels are primarily about Jesus, and Jesus was a Palestinian Jew ministering in the 30s CE, which would seem to pose certain limits for Hellenistic influence (even though I am well aware of Hengel's study).

Another test case would be Peter's use of the OT in his speech at Pentecost in Acts 2 (treated by Porter). How influenced by Greco-Roman rhetoric was Peter in his Pentecost address? Or how much of a factor was it as Luke recorded it? Again, one wonders if Peter, a Jew, speaking in Jerusalem to a largely Jewish audience (Acts 2:14, 22-23), would have drawn significantly on Hellenistic rhetoric. Perhaps Stamps's case shows more promise with regard to the NT epistles, though even there one should note that Paul was a rabbinically trained Jew, and if an author-oriented approach is taken one would expect Paul's use of the OT in many ways to reflect his Jewishness and rabbinic training.

"Biblical Texts and the Scriptures for the New Testament Church"

The paper by R. Timothy McLay is a fitting application of the cautions registered in Stanley Porter's above-mentioned essay in that it defines important terms such as "canon" and "Scripture" at the outset and in that the goal of McLay's investigation is carefully delimited as dealing with the questions of how we know that the NT writer was citing the OT/Hebrew Bible and what versions the NT writers were using. McLay points out that the concept of canon presupposes the existence of Scripture, a set of writings recognized by a faith community as authoritative for its faith and practice. McLay's first important conclusion pertains to the OT canon. Citing Sundberg, he contends that there was no unanimity regarding the OT canon's precise extent in the first century of the Christian period. From this lack of consensus McLay infers that though "there were texts of Scriptures" there was "no sense of a canon during the early church era."

However, this seems to me to be a rather disjunctive way of putting things. It is one thing to note that not everyone agreed on the precise delimitation of the OT canon; it is quite another to say that because there was no perfect unanimity on the subject there was "no sense of canon" during the early church altogether. In fact, as far as I know there is currently no consensus on this issue. If there is any agreement at this point it is that the conventional hypotheses — the Alexandrian theory (which holds to a restricted Palestinian and a more extensive Alexandrian canon) and the three-phase theory (which postulates the canonization of the Pentateuch in the fifth century, of the Prophets toward the end of the third century BCE, and of the Writings toward the end of the first century CE) — are, if not untenable, at least in serious need of revision and refinement. Positively, there seems to be a degree of gridlock between two schools of thought, one holding that the church's sense of canon went from uncertainty to certainty (J. Barr, J. Barton, L. M. McDonald) and the other that the movement was in the opposite direction, from certainty to uncertainty, with the canon having been closed in the middle of the second century BCE (R. Beckwith, M. Coogan, E. E. Ellis). If anything, the second view seems to be gaining ground.[4] McLay seems to follow McDonald and others who hold the first view. My purpose here is simply to remind us that there are viewpoints other than that represented by McLay that are held by reputed scholars.

In his discussion of the issue, McLay does not mention Jesus' reference to the period "from the blood of Abel to the blood of Zechariah" (cf. 2 Chron 24:20-22) in Luke 11:50-51//Matt 23:35, which has featured prominently in the debate. While different interpretations are possible, this dual set of references would seem to need to be taken into account in the present context. The passages have conventionally been interpreted to imply, if not a definitive list of OT canonical books, at least the existence of a canon that started with Genesis and ended with Chronicles.[5] This, it is argued, would explain why Jesus chose Zechariah (ca. 800 BCE) as his endpoint, a prophet who was not the last to die a martyr's death *chronologically,* though he would have been the last *canonically* if the Jewish canon in Jesus' day (or at least the canon Jesus and others presupposed) indeed concluded with the book of Chronicles.

In his recent article, which seems to concur with the thrust of McLay's argument, H. G. L. Peels has questioned whether Luke 11:51//Matt 23:35 is suited to function as a "crown witness" for the traditional view. According to Peels, the murders of Abel and Zechariah are unique in the OT in that they, and they alone, combine the violent murder of an innocent person who is dedicated to God with the cry for divine retribution (Gen 4:10; cf. Heb 11:4; 1 John 3:12; 2 Chron 24:22). When Jesus invokes these two figures in his discourse against the Pharisees and scribes, he therefore evokes this entire history of righteous, innocent martyrdom. For this reason Peels contends that "Jesus' words . . . would have sounded exactly the same if the narrative of Zechariah's death had occurred in the book of

---

4. See the survey and footnotes in H. G. L. Peels, "The Blood 'from Abel to Zechariah' (Matthew 23,35; Luke 11,50f.) and the Canon of the Old Testament," *ZAW* 113 (2001) 584-85.

5. Cf. Peels, "The Blood 'from Abel to Zechariah,'" 586, n. 8, who refers to the virtually unanimous verdict of NT scholarship on this subject.

Kings or in the Psalms," so that Luke 11:51 cannot bear the weight of serving as proof text for an early closing of the canon.

Peels's argument does serve as a helpful corrective of the traditional view, whose exegetical basis has often been overstated. However, it seems that the very evidence Peels cites can be used against him. Peels himself closes his essay by pointing the way forward to an investigation of the following questions: "Does the canon of the Old Testament itself deliver signals of an intended closure? Was there a purposeful final redaction not only of the individual books but also of the books of the Old Testament as a whole? Is it possible to trace the 'redactional glue' between the different sections of the canon?"[6] Yet Peels fails to consider the possibility that the presence of Abel and Zechariah at the beginning and the end of a possible OT canon would constitute a very suggestive instance of redactional *inclusio,* providing respective bookends that could envelop OT history fueled by a messianic dynamic. While not entirely in conventional terms, this would give new impetus to the traditional interpretation of Luke 11:51.

Moreover, the possibility should not be too quickly dismissed that Jesus in Luke 24:44 witnessed to a two- or threefold division of the Law, the Prophets, and the Writings (or at least the Psalms). In any case, returning to McLay's contention that there was "no sense of a canon during the early church era," it seems important to distinguish between the canon as being permanently fixed and agreed upon by all sides and the existence of a "sense of canon," at least in certain circles, whether or not there was universal unanimity regarding a specific list of books.[7] As John Sailhamer noted in an important response to a paper by Lee McDonald at an annual Institute of Biblical Research meeting a few years ago, it is certainly possible (if not likely) that there existed at least several canons that functioned authoritatively for their respective communities.[8] Thus the Sadducees would have had one agreed-upon set of books they considered authoritative, while the Pharisees might have had another. On a different note, I wonder about McLay's argument that the notion of inspiration was a "further implication" of the notion of a list of scriptural books that necessi-

6. Peels, "The Blood 'from Abel to Zechariah,'" 600-601.

7. Cf. Peels, "The Blood 'from Abel to Zechariah,'" 583, n. 1, who notes that, while the term "canon" was applied to the Bible only in the fourth century CE, "[t]his does not mean that this notion of canonicity was lacking in earlier times and centuries."

8. Unpublished response, Annual Meeting of the Institute for Biblical Research, November 19, 1994.

tated the preservation of these texts. Was inspiration merely a *further implication* of the notion of canonicity or a *foundational conviction* that provided a self-authenticating witness to the Scriptures' revelatory character? I suspect that McLay and I would answer this question differently.[9]

McLay concludes not only that there was no agreement as to the precise extent of the OT and NT canon in the early centuries of the common era but that there "are a wide variety of textual variants, ranging from single words or morphemes to whole sentences and paragraphs" in comparing the ancient texts for any book of Scripture. McLay then proceeds to provide an unusually incisive treatment of Heb 1:6 and various antecedent texts, such as OG Deut 32:44, 4QDeut^q 32:43, the MT of Deut 32:43, and Odes 2:43.[10] My only comment here is that McLay does not seem to consider to any significant extent the possibility that the Odes (which he dates ca. 100) borrow from Hebrews, in which case they would not constitute an independent witness but be derivative of Heb 1:6.[11]

During the course of his discussion, McLay enunciates the important principle that "the NT citations should be evaluated as witnesses to alternative biblical texts where their readings differ from the known witnesses." In a footnote he adds the important qualification that the methodology of citation by NT writers constitutes another significant factor to consider. He concludes that the OG, 4QDeut^q, MT, and Odes 2:43/Heb 1:6 "represent four separate and distinct ways that the biblical text was transmitted and that they all were regarded as Scripture." Apart from the just-noted assumption that Odes 2:43 and Heb 1:6 represent independent witnesses, however, this seems to give inadequate consideration to the issue of citation method in this specific instance. McLay does not seem to allow here for the possibility of intentional alterations that do not amount to "corruptions" or "errors."

One final word is in order regarding McLay's choice of Heb 1:6 as his paradigm passage. He says the "choice is not random," but he does not say why the passage was chosen, though one surmises that he regards the pas-

9. For the sake of documenting the history of discussion I retain this original response, though McLay subsequently removed the statement from his essay.

10. However, McLay does not provide his own reconstruction of the likely original Hebrew text.

11. At one point McLay suggests that "if the author of Hebrews was citing from Odes, then the Odes were understood to be Scripture." But since McLay dates the Odes ca. 100, this would require Hebrews to be written after 100, which is held by few.

sage as typical of the state of affairs at large. The very least that can be said here is that McLay's paper itself does not furnish substantiation of such an implied claim. Most readers who are aware of similar instances elsewhere will probably agree that this does not provide an isolated instance. Nevertheless, even if McLay's analysis of his chosen passage is on target (and I believe that in many ways it is), this still would not necessarily mean that he has thereby drawn more broadly valid conclusions about issues of canon, textual transmission, and the NT use of antecedent Scripture.

"Scripture, History, Messiah: Scriptural Fulfillment and the Fullness of Time in Matthew's Gospel"

Michael Knowles's paper starts out, creatively, with a characterization of Matthew's Gospel in the language of T. S. Eliot: a coherent whole held together by a single, unifying vision depicting "[b]oth a new world/And the old made explicit, understood." Matthew, the scribe, brought forth from his treasure store both "old" (Second Temple Judaism) and "new" (the hope of redemption fulfilled in Jesus the Messiah). Knowles observes that Matthew prefers introducing his scriptural citations with a formula including the word "fulfill" *(plēroō)*, while Jesus' quotations usually involve the use of the formula "It is written" *(gegraptai)* or the rhetorical question, "Have you not read?" While Matthean scholarship has often focused on the former, Knowles helpfully elucidates the latter, contending that Matthew's method and interpretation of the OT are grounded in that of Jesus.

Let me raise a couple of specific minor points at this juncture. First, Knowles notes that in Matt 11:10 Jesus employs a combined citation of Exod 23:20 and Mal 3:1. He proceeds to note that, hence, *Matthew* "shares with other Jews the fundamental conviction that all of Scripture speaks with one voice." Since it is actually *Jesus* to whom the citation is attributed in the Gospel, should one not say that *Jesus* shared with other Jews that fundamental conviction, rather than merely Matthew? Later Knowles comments on the use of "it is written" by the chief priests and scribes in regard to Mic 5:1-3, asserting that this represents the one "uniquely Matthean use" of this particular formula. But if the statement is placed in the mouths of the chief priests and scribes, why not say that it is they who used the formula rather than labeling this a "uniquely Matthean use," especially since it would be the only instance of such a use by the evangelist?

Knowles's discussion of Jesus' use of the formula "Have you not read?" is very perceptive, even intriguing. The only thing that perhaps could be brought out more clearly, if I am correct in this, is that the question also serves as a (not-so-subtle) rebuke of Jesus' opponents. *Of course* they have read and are familiar with the Scripture passages adduced by Jesus. Yet Jesus' point is that, even though they are familiar with those passages, they have failed to discern and take to heart their true meaning. For this Jesus' opponents are rebuked — they should have done so, but they did not. If they had, they would agree with his interpretation of those passages. At the very least, Jesus' pointed way of wording his argument personally engages his hearers and challenges them to go back to Scripture to see whether or not Jesus' interpretation is correct.[12]

From his treatment of Matthew's (and Jesus') explicit scriptural citations and a brief discussion of less explicit references, Knowles distills one basic principle governing the use of Scripture in Matthew's Gospel: Matthew's interpretation of Scripture with reference *to* the Messiah is ultimately based on interpretations of Scripture *by* the Messiah. Because of his messianic focus, for Matthew Scripture is "not only foundationally authoritative but also univocal in its prophetic testimony." This elucidation of various lines of continuity between prophetic testimony and their fulfillment in Jesus the Messiah, which he considers a form of "actualizing" or "accommodational" interpretation, Knowles calls "messianic exegesis." It may be noted that Knowles does not deal with possible critical objections to assuming that Matthew's representation of Jesus' use of Scripture is accurate. It would also be interesting to know how Knowles conceives of the implications of this principle for the contemporary use of the OT.

In dealing with Matthew's fulfillment quotations, Knowles has an interesting way of resolving the difficulty of determining the OT reference of 2:23: "He will be called a Nazorean." Maintaining that "the main point of Matthew's citation is not simply that Scripture points toward and finds its fulfillment in the events of contemporary history, but moreover that messianic history itself dictates what Scripture must mean," Knowles turns the issue on its head, stating that it is a historical fact that the Messiah did live in Nazareth, so "[i]f this is what happened, that is what Scripture *must* mean:

---

12. Perhaps this is what Knowles means when he says that the challenge "places ultimate responsibility for proper interpretation firmly upon the reader." How could it be otherwise?

finding an exact text to match the facts was, it would appear, of secondary importance." I would argue that it is at least equally likely that the evangelist did see scriptural warrant for the Messiah's dwelling in Nazareth (whether or not we can agree on the primary passage he might have had in mind) and that he did find some typology at work that may not be as apparent to those further removed from his day and interpretive culture. Later in his paper Knowles states that in this instance "the historical necessity of validating Jesus' residence in Nazareth takes precedence over exegetical precision."[13] Would it not be better to acknowledge the possibility that the difficulty here might lie, not with the evangelist's "exegetical precision" (as tempting as it might be to conclude this), but with the contemporary interpreter's ability to decode this difficult instance of the NT's referring to the OT?

Knowles proceeds to cite several examples where "it is the Messiah's life that clarifies the meaning of Scripture, even to the point of implying that the true intent of key texts remains hidden apart from him." Space does not permit detailed engagement of his treatment of individual passages, but his statement of the overall principle is helpful. What it shows is that, not only did Jesus possess authority to interpret Scripture, but so did Matthew (and by implication the other evangelists and NT writers). Indeed, it is hard to see how the straightforward application of a grammatical-historical method would lead one to the kinds of exegetical conclusions at which Matthew arrived regarding the OT texts in question that he interpreted messianically. Just as for Paul it was the realization that Jesus was indeed the promised Messiah that unlocked the meaning of Scripture for him, "the events of Jesus' life unlock for Matthew the intended meaning of Scripture — a meaning that would (presumably) never have emerged had the Messiah's advent not revealed it." Hence it is not that first-century Jews should have been expected to be able to put together the various pieces of the OT puzzle regarding the Messiah and to recognize Jesus as such the moment he arrived on the scene. Rather, they had to be open to consider Jesus' claims in light of his words and works and be willing to go back to Scripture to see whether the Scriptures could be read in a way that they could be seen to find their fulfillment in Jesus the Messiah.

From an investigation of the varied use of Scripture in Matthew 21,

---

13. Knowles reworded this statement subsequent to the colloquium as follows: "the historical necessity of *affirming* Jesus' residence in Nazareth takes precedence over *literal or literalistic exegesis*" (changed wording in italics).

Knowles draws the following conclusions: (1) Scripture forms the backdrop of both Jesus' teaching and the events of his life, without distinction; (2) Matthew does not prefer one type of reference over another: textual and typological allusions and explicit formulae with direct quotations of Scripture are all juxtaposed; and (3) Matthew's method implies little or no apologetic intent. By way of brief assessment, the first conclusion seems clearly borne out by the data; the second one seems to be true for Matthew 21 and perhaps for the Gospel overall, but there does seem to be a preponderance of fulfillment quotations in Matthew 1–4 rather than the picture of multiplicity of references postulated by Knowles; the third conclusion I find unobjectionable, but I suspect that others who make more of the influence of Matthew's contemporary situation on the writing of his Gospel will probably differ.

Knowles notes that, once Matthew had reached the conclusion that Jesus was the Messiah to whom Scripture pointed, "the reverse process would have increasingly taken over: the life and teaching of Jesus became the key to illuminating all the mysteries of the biblical text, a living, more immediate 'canon' against which to assess the meaning of the written text." This is very well put, as long as one is not asked to imply that allowing Jesus' life and teaching to illuminate the written text meant necessarily to commit "exegetical imprecision" (or worse).[14] I think Paul Miller in his essay on John makes a similar point, namely that John did not read the OT apart from Jesus and in fact elevated openness to future (or present) divine revelation as an essential prerequisite to understanding and faith. Remarkably, such openness to read and reread Scripture in light of the new divine revelation in Jesus was found also in Matthew the scribe.

"The Beginning of the Good News and the Fulfillment of Scripture in the Gospel of Mark"

As Craig Evans notes at the outset of his excellent paper, the extent and significance of the use of the OT in Mark have often been underestimated.[15]

---

14. But note now Knowles's reworded statement (referred to in the previous footnote) where "exegetical precision" has been changed to "literal or literalistic exegesis."

15. For instance, Mark's use of the OT is not given its due in Morna Hooker's essay on this topic in *It Is Written: Scripture Citing Scripture; Essays in Honour of Barnabas Lindars*

As Evans demonstrates, Mark quotes frequently from both the Law and the Prophets and cites or alludes to Scripture at key points in his narrative. What is more, Peter O'Brien and I have found that Mark's Gospel evinces a "demonstrable and sustained" "grounding of Jesus' mission in Old Testament conceptualities." While references to the Abrahamic promise are absent, Mark draws repeatedly on the Psalms' portrayal of the circumstances surrounding the Messiah's death and on Isaiah's depiction of the Jewish rejection of the Messiah.[16]

The following theme clusters are rooted firmly in the OT:

1. the ministry of John the Baptist;[17]
2. Jesus' rejection by the Jews;[18]
3. Jesus' confrontation with the Jewish leaders on topics such as the temple,[19] the law,[20] and Jesus' Davidic sonship;[21]
4. Jesus' sufferings and death on the cross;[22] and
5. the second coming.[23]

What this list of theme clusters demonstrates is that, not only does Mark repeatedly cite or allude to the OT, but Mark's entire christological

---

(ed. D. A. Carson and H. G. M. Williamson; Cambridge: Cambridge University Press, 1988), where in a mere nine pages only citations from and allusions to the Pentateuch are discussed and there is little sustained theological exploration.

16. Andreas J. Köstenberger and Peter T. O'Brien, *Salvation to the Ends of the Earth: A Biblical Theology of Mission* (NSBT; Leicester: Apollos/Downers Grove: InterVarsity, 2001) 81-82.

17. See Mark 1:2-3 (citing Isa 40:3 and Mal 3:1). Cf. the extended account of the Baptist's end in 6:14-29, and 9:11-12 (alluding to Mal 4:5-6).

18. See Mark 4:12 (citing Isa 6:9-10; cf. Mark 8:18); 7:6-7 (citing Isa 29:13 LXX); 12:1, 10-11 (citing Isa 5:1-2 and Ps 118:22-23).

19. Mark 11:17 (citing Isa 56:7 and Jer 7:11).

20. See Mark 2:23-28 (alluding to 1 Sam 21:1-6 and 2 Sam 15:35); 7:10; 10:19; 12:19, 26 (cf. Exod 3:2, 6, 15, 16; 20:12; Deut 5:17; 25:5); 10:4-8 (cf. Deut 24:1, 3; Gen 1:27; 2:24).

21. Mark 12:36 (citing Ps 110:1; cf. Mark 14:62; 16:19).

22. See Mark 9:12 (alluding to Psalm 22 and Isa 53:3; cf. Mark 10:45; 14:60-61; 15:4-5); 14:34 (alluding to Pss 42:5, 11; 43:5). Substantiated from the OT are also the following: (1) Judas's betrayal (Mark 14:18, citing Ps 41:9); (2) the scattering of Jesus' followers (Mark 14:27, 50, alluding to Zech 13:7); (3) the soldiers' casting of lots for Jesus' garments (Mark 15:24, citing Ps 22:18); and (4) the sponge of vinegar (Mark 15:36, quoting Ps 69:21).

23. Mark 13:14, 19, 24-26 (citing or referring to Dan 7:13-14; 9:27; 11:31; 12:1, 11, and other OT apocalyptic passages).

presentation is set self-consciously within an OT framework. In this Mark reflects the pervasive convictions of the early Christians and ultimately Jesus' own messianic self-consciousness (not to speak of that of John the Baptist). Remarkably, this is the case despite Mark's predominantly Gentile readership. As Stanley Porter has shown in his essay in the present volume, Luke's Gospel, too, though primarily addressing a Gentile audience, is thoroughly grounded in an OT framework.

The purpose of these brief remarks related to Mark's use of the OT in general at the outset of my response to Craig Evans's paper is twofold: first, I want to show that Mark's use of the OT is both pervasive and sustained rather than merely superficial and sporadic; second, I would argue that the primary (Gentile) audience of a particular Gospel does not necessarily influence a given evangelist's use of the OT to the extent that he refrains from grounding his presentation of Jesus in OT conceptualities merely because his audience may not be (thoroughly) familiar with it. Perhaps Richard Bauckham's influential volume arguing for a less restrictive approach to conceiving of the Gospel audiences is important here.[24]

These things said, I turn to Evans's provocative and original hypothesis that Mark wrote to challenge the contemporary notion that Vespasian was the fulfillment of prophecy and the world's savior. My response is essentially threefold.

First, it should be noted that Evans's argument is predicated on a late, post–CE 70 dating, not only of Mark, but since he holds to Markan priority, also of Matthew and Luke. Some may be reluctant to accept Evans's argument owing to their view on Synoptic relationships and the dating of one or several of the Synoptic Gospels.

Second, even if Evans's thesis is granted for the sake of the argument, the question arises, how pervasive was the effect of Mark's alleged purpose on the entire Gospel? In other words, does the Roman background merely constitute Mark's point of departure, or does it provide the backdrop for Mark's use of the OT throughout his Gospel? In his oral response to questioning at the colloquium, Evans seemed to back away a bit from arguing the latter and appeared to move in the direction of the former. Clearly, one should not make more of Mark's contemporary (Roman) context than is warranted.

24. Richard Bauckham, ed., *The Gospels for All Christians: Rethinking the Gospel Audiences* (Grand Rapids: Eerdmans, 1997).

In light of the above-listed matrix of OT themes in which Mark's portrait of Jesus is grounded, one wonders whether the Roman context adduced by Evans is large and significant enough to warrant making it the major occasion for writing and the determinative christological trigger for Mark. It seems more possible that the wording of the Gospel opening, "The beginning of the gospel about Jesus Christ, the Son of God," reflects an allusion to the contemporary Roman scene laid out by Evans. This, however, would function on the level of contextualization, rather than affecting the foundational theological formulation of Mark's Christology. Perhaps the Gospel was essentially completed when the heading was added.

The third issue pertaining to Evans's proposal relates to its verifiability. Evans has adduced some fairly impressive parallels, but the question remains how conclusive these parallels will be judged to be by other scholars in the field. After all, not all apparent parallels may turn out to be true and relevant parallels once investigated.[25] Will Evans be able to convince other Markan scholars of the viability of his thesis? The question here is not just whether his proposal is possible or plausible; will Markan scholarship conclude that Evans's construal is probable or even compelling? It will be interesting to see how other Markan scholars respond to Evans's provocative thesis.

"Scripture Justifies Mission:
The Use of the Old Testament in Luke-Acts"

I turn to Stanley Porter's fine paper on the use of the OT in Luke-Acts. There is little (if anything) that I disagree with in this essay, but perhaps I can further underscore the significance of Porter's findings by supplying a few insights of my own. To briefly summarize the main lines of Porter's argument, he defends at the outset the "apologetic proof from prophecy" approach to Luke-Acts and shows that objections to this consensus view cannot be sustained. He views Luke-Acts as a two-volume work written by Luke. In keeping with Porter's above-noted endorsement of an author-centered approach, he judges the use of the OT in this work to reflect Luke's authorial intentions, specifically his chosen way of portraying Jesus

---

25. Cf. Samuel Sandmel, "Parallelomania," *JBL* 81 (1962) 1-13.

and the mission of the early church. Beyond this, in a particularly commendable feature of his essay, Porter considers the question how the use of the OT in Luke-Acts reflects, not merely Luke's, but also Jesus' use of the OT, and he comes to positive conclusions.

Porter specifically focuses on one key event described early in each book in which Scripture is central: Jesus' inaugural address in the synagogue at Nazareth in Luke 4:18-19, with its use of Isa 61:1-2; and Peter's Pentecost address in Jerusalem in Acts 2, referring to Joel 2:28-32; Pss 16:8-11; 110:1.[26] I might add that the reference to Isaiah 61 in Luke 4:18-19 stands out all the more as Luke's use of the OT otherwise differs little from that of Matthew and Mark, but only he includes the present reference. The passage portrays a figure that combines four personages — the final eschatological prophet, the Messiah, the suffering servant, and a royal ruler — to which Porter adds the notion of a veiled reference to Jesus' divinity. Importantly, Porter sees this to reflect not only Luke's theology but Jesus' own self-conscious appropriation of the Hebrew Scriptures. Jesus fulfills OT prophecy and as the Spirit-anointed Messiah provides universal salvation.

These themes are further developed in the second key text, Acts 2, through the use of additional OT references. Joel 2:28-32 speaks of the pouring out of God's Spirit on all people, the occurrence of a variety of eschatological signs, and the extension of salvation to all those who call on the name of the Lord. Jesus' resurrection and his being made both Lord and Messiah fulfill the Davidic prophecies of Pss 16:8-11 and 110:1. Throughout, Porter deals with the significance of differences in wording between the OT texts and their use in Luke-Acts, but his primary contribution lies in demonstrating that using the OT for Luke was not merely one of several authorial devices but an integral part of his hermeneutic. As Porter notes, "the notion of fulfillment of scriptural texts seen as prophetically uttered is a fundamental hermeneutical principle in Luke-Acts." I would add that this is all the more significant as Luke in all likelihood was a Gentile writing predominantly to Gentiles.

I would like to supplement Porter's essay in several ways. First, to take Porter's argument one step further, I would argue that not only do

---

26. Many have recognized the pivotal nature of Luke 4:18-19 in the Gospel. Köstenberger and O'Brien, *Salvation to the Ends of the Earth*, 115, call it "programmatic"; R. R. Menzies, *Empowered for Witness: The Spirit in Luke-Acts* (JPTSS 6; Sheffield: Sheffield Academic Press, 1994) 145, speaks of Luke 4:16-30 as "the cornerstone of Luke's entire theological program." See also the literature cited in Köstenberger and O'Brien on p. 115, n. 18.

Luke and Acts signal important emphases in the two respective *openings* of these books by their use of the Hebrew Scriptures, but the same dynamic is at work in their respective *endings*.[27] The Gospel closes on the striking, programmatic note of the resurrected Jesus pointing out to the two disciples on the road to Emmaus that "everything written about me in the law of Moses, the prophets, and the psalms must be fulfilled" (24:44). Luke continues,

> Then he opened their minds to understand the scriptures, and he said to them, "Thus it is written, that the Messiah is to suffer and to rise from the dead on the third day, and that repentance and forgiveness of sins is to be proclaimed in his name to all nations, beginning from Jerusalem. You are witnesses of these things. And see, I am sending upon you what my Father promised; so stay here in the city until you have been clothed with power from on high." (24:45-49)

Not only does the Gospel thus end with a very significant reference to Scripture — and Scripture in its totality as referring to Jesus as Messiah at that — but this reference at the end of the Gospel anticipates the opening of the book of Acts, which narrates the disciples' waiting in Jerusalem until the outpouring of the Spirit and their subsequent bearing witness, "beginning at Jerusalem," to all nations.[28]

Equally significant and programmatic is the concluding OT reference in the book of Acts, where Paul is shown to quote Isa 6:9-10 to the Jewish leaders in Rome in order to ground the extension of gospel preaching to the Gentiles theologically in the Hebrew Scriptures.[29] Hence Luke's hermeneutic of allowing Scripture to carry forward his theological message, be it through the words of Jesus (Luke 4:18-19; 24:45-49), Peter (Acts 2), or the apostle Paul (Acts 28:26-27), encompasses not merely the *beginnings* of the two works that make up his composite work but also their *conclusions*. This, of course, does not alter the theological foci detected by Por-

27. This insight was triggered by reading John Sailhamer's unpublished response to Lee McDonald at the annual meeting of the Institute for Biblical Research, November 19, 1994.

28. For a sustained treatment of the "Lukan Great Commission," see Köstenberger and O'Brien, *Salvation to the Ends of the Earth*, 123-27.

29. Note the equally strategic placement of a reference to Isa 6:10 in John 12:40 at the end of the first major half of John's Gospel.

ter: the mission and identity of Jesus in Luke's Gospel, and the extension of universal salvation in the book of Acts.

Second, the early key passages on which Porter focuses do not occur in a vacuum but follow on the heels of a carefully crafted matrix of OT references that provide a framework for these more extended scriptural citations. The angel's announcement to Mary focuses on the Davidic promise (Luke 1:32-33; cf. 1:27; 2 Sam 7:12-13); Mary's song includes a climactic reference to the Abrahamic covenant (Luke 1:55); Zechariah combines references to David (1:69) and Abraham (1:73); Simeon's song, finally, invokes the reference to the suffering servant serving as a "light for revelation to the Gentiles" in Isa 49:6 (2:32). There are also several possible allusions to the exodus (1:51, 71). Thus, when Luke narrates Jesus' inaugural address in the synagogue at Nazareth, he has already established a matrix of scriptural fulfillment that spans from Abraham, the exodus, and David to Isaiah's suffering servant, and it is on that servant that the emphasis squarely falls in Luke 4:18-19. Hence the reference to Isa 61:1-2 in the latter passage does not come as a surprise to the alert reader of the Gospel but harks back and elaborates on a web of references earlier in the Gospel.

Third, there are other major motifs involving the OT found at the beginning of both Luke's Gospel and the book of Acts. The promise of Israel's restoration is mentioned in both Mary's and Zechariah's songs (Luke 1:54, 68) and is also alluded to in the narratives regarding Simeon (who had been waiting for "the consolation of Israel," 2:25) and Anna (2:38). The same restoration of Israel is also referred to at the beginning of Acts in 1:6 (cf. 3:19). Importantly, however, salvation is shown in both places to extend beyond Israel to the Gentiles. This universality of salvation is a second, related theme that is mentioned both at the beginning of Luke's Gospel and in the book of Acts, again involving scriptural expectations. In Luke, this is found in more incipient terms (2:32; cf. Isa 49:6); in Acts the universal scope of the gospel is considerably more overt from the start (1:8, cf. Isa 49:6; 2:21, cf. Joel 2:32).[30] Significantly, this universal mission takes place through the instrumentality of Jesus (in Luke) and of the apostles (in Acts) as God's appointed witnesses (Acts 1:8; cf. Luke 24:48).

---

30. For a treatment of Acts 1:8 in light of its OT background and its function in the book of Acts, see Köstenberger and O'Brien, *Salvation to the Ends of the Earth*, 130-31.

"'They Saw His Glory and Spoke of Him': The Gospel of John and the Old Testament"

At the very outset of his interesting paper, Paul Miller states as his concern the question of how John used Scripture in his presentation of Jesus the Messiah. It is always difficult to fault someone for not doing something he never declares to be part of his purpose, but for my part I would have liked to see Miller include also the dimension of Jesus' own use of the OT (similar to the way this is done in Knowles's and Porter's papers).[31] If Matthew's use of the OT is dependent on Jesus (Knowles's thesis), and if Luke accurately reflects Jesus' use (Porter), the question arises whether or not this is true also for John. Miller's lack of consideration of Jesus' use of the OT is, of course, in keeping with the trend in Johannine scholarship to bracket consideration of Jesus out of the equation, because John is considered to be more theologically oriented than the Synoptics and the historical accuracy of John's portrait of Jesus is consequently questioned. I am not implying that this is the reason why Miller chose not to deal with Jesus' use of the OT. In any case, I would have liked to see him include Jesus in the scope of his discussion.

But let me now turn to Miller's actual paper with its focus on John's use of the OT.[32] As to text, he notes that John is eclectic, quoting often (but not always) from the Greek. Miller rightly points out that, in John's use of the OT, function determined form, which frequently led the evangelist to alter or adapt the wording. (I would have liked to see this important insight play a more prominent part also in Timothy McLay's paper, which I critiqued above.) As to method, John used techniques he inherited and adapted from Jewish Scripture study. Miller mentions both midrash and *pesher* as the orbit within which John interpreted OT passages, specifically those that fit a promise and fulfillment pattern concerning the Messiah. As to introductory formulae, John resembles Matthew, with the added twist that he uses these formulae as a major structural device. By his consistent use of "it is written" or "as the Scripture says" in the first half and of "in order to fulfill" from 12:38 onward, the evangelist marks off the second half of the Gospel, beginning in 12:37, from the first half, which narrates Jesus'

---

31. See my "Jesus as Rabbi in the Fourth Gospel," *BBR* 8 (1998) 97-128.

32. If the present response is more extensive than the responses to the other papers, this reflects my interest in the subject and the need to test Miller's hypothesis in some detail in order to determine its validity.

public ministry to the Jews. Miller detects in this subtle switch of formulae a corresponding shift in the function of Scripture in the Gospel. In the first half, Scripture serves as "a kind of sign" anticipating Jesus' passion and resurrection; chapters 13-20 narrate the fulfillment. As Miller notes,

> Once the chain of events leading to the crucifixion is set in motion, the role of Scripture changes. Scripture does not only point to Jesus but is fulfilled in two senses: first, its meaning is fully disclosed in Christ; and secondly, it is completed, superseded, and even replaced by the living words of Jesus. The true meaning of Scripture cannot be found within the text itself, but only in its fulfillment in Jesus and in the sending of the Spirit.

Hence John's use of the OT is much more than merely a question of which antecedent texts he uses or which method of appropriation is chosen by the evangelist; John's use of Scripture is a crucial part and vehicle of his christological vision. (In this finding Miller concurs with Porter, who detected a similarly programmatic function of Scripture in Luke-Acts.) What is more, by fulfilling Scripture, Jesus in his words and works becomes the new paradigm that sets the standard for future generations of disciples. A study of John's explicit quotations by itself would be grossly inadequate in order to grasp his use of Scripture. (This echoes Porter's argument in his earlier essay that a study of the OT in the NT must consider *all* of the available evidence.)[33] At best such citations may serve as windows to some of the broader themes upon which John draws in order to articulate his own christological vision.

Thus we have come all the way from text, method, and introductory formulae to biblical theology and hermeneutics. As C. K. Barrett pointed out over fifty years ago, for John the OT served as a comprehensive framework for his articulation of the new revelation in and through Christ. This calls, not for atomistic, rigid, or merely technical analysis, but for holistic and spiritual understanding. If John's christological vision involving the OT was the result of years of spiritual and theological maturation and sustained reflection on the significance of Christ, the understanding of this vision requires no less spiritual and theological maturation on the part of the interpreter. What we need is not only the tools but also the heart and mind of a spiritually discerning disciple.

33. Porter, "Use of the OT in the NT," 89.

Miller proceeds by recasting the issue. The question is not really so much, how does John use Scripture? but, for John, what *was* Scripture? As Miller rightly notes, more is involved here than that John considered Scripture to be inspired and authoritative. Demonstrably, John's understanding of the relation of Scripture to Christ is distinctive. While the hermeneutics underlying the Synoptists' use of the OT seem to be more implicit and traditional, John's hermeneutic (similar to Paul's) appears to be more explicit and creative. At the heart of Miller's essay is his formulation of the hermeneutic underlying John's use of Scripture: "*Scripture is the enduring record of those who saw the activity of the divine Logos prior to its appearance in Jesus and then testified to what they had seen.*" Jesus, the Word made flesh, was revealed in pre-incarnate fashion, as it were, to Moses and the prophets. Hence the unity of the Scriptures is christologically founded.

What is more, John is interested not so much in the *text* of Scripture as in the *act of seeing* that gave rise to the text. Miller alludes to the importance of "seeing" in this Gospel with reference to the work of Craig Evans on the use of Isa 6:9-10 in John 12:39-40 and of A. T. Hanson and G. L. Phillips. While I would not want to diminish the importance of "seeing" in John's Gospel — to the contrary, I would have liked Miller to provide a more extensive discussion of passages such as John 9:39-41 — the crucial climactic statement in John 20:29, where Jesus pronounces a blessing on those, unlike Thomas, "who have not seen and yet have believed" (NIV), would need to be given full weight.[34] This pronouncement is widely — and I think rightly — interpreted as relativizing the place of "seeing" in a person's faith (somewhat akin to Paul's statement in 2 Cor 5:7 that he lives "by faith, not by sight") and as indicating a transition from the period of Jesus' earthly ministry to the apostolic period where others would believe on the basis of the disciples' word (17:20; cf. 15:27).

This relativization of the value of "seeing" at the end of John's Gospel comports with the relative value assigned by the evangelist to Jesus' "signs," which serve as temporary aids to believing and as christological windows that often prove insufficient to evoke faith in those who see them (see esp. 12:37; cf. 4:48). For this reason it seems hard, in light of 20:29, to maintain

34. I am not sure that Miller's statement that John in 20:29 does not sharply distinguish "between two mutually contradictory phenomena" but merely cautions against those "who would stop short of the full vision of faith" does justice to the wording of the text in question. ". . . not seen and yet" *(mē, adversative kai)* does seem to indicate a contrast; and not only that, it arguably constitutes the contrast to which the entire narrative builds.

in an unqualified sense (as Miller does, with reference to Evans) that "'vision' is the predominant metaphor in John for the knowledge of Jesus that comes by faith." Perhaps it would be more accurate to say that "vision" is the predominant metaphor for how people in the OT prior to Jesus' coming came to know God. Yet it seems that, according to John (as well as Paul; cf. Rom 10:17), people ought to believe in Jesus on the basis of the apostolic testimony regarding Christ, apart from (physical) seeing. Also, I am not sure that all of John's uses of Scripture (such as John 10:36) can be made to fit under the rubric of Miller's definition. I wonder if subsuming everything under "seeing Christ in the OT" is running the risk of reductionism.

In the rest of his paper, Miller (following Hengel) looks at four "paradigmatic figures" in John's Gospel — Abraham, Moses, Isaiah, and John the Baptist — as he pursues his thesis that John interpreted Scripture through the twin themes of *vision* and *witness*. In the remainder of my response, I will seek to evaluate the validity of this thesis in light of the stated emphases in the respective texts of John's Gospel. With regard to John the Baptist, Miller's thesis seems to be plainly borne out in that the Baptist declares in 1:34, "I have seen and I testify that this is the Son of God." Regarding Miller's treatment of the Baptist, I will comment only on his assertion that the Baptist is "not directly tied to the Scriptures of Israel." What about Isa 40:3 in John 1:23, where the Baptist invokes the reference to "a voice of one crying in the wilderness"? Does this not tie the Baptist to OT Scripture?

Concerning Abraham, Jesus maintained that he "saw [my day] and was glad" (8:56; though Miller's assertion that "Abraham's worthiness derived from his insight into the ways of the Logos" would seem to require further substantiation). Here Miller, while briefly touching on the original polemic between Jesus and the Jewish leadership, in his commentary on 8:56 focuses on Jewish tradition regarding Abraham. I would add that more important is the way in which the evangelist brings out the dynamic of the original argument. At stake is, as Miller notes, the Jewish claim of descendance from Abraham. While this was doubtless true physically, Jesus seeks to show that, spiritually, such a claim ought to have involved a faith component as well, since Abraham was open to divine revelation. Hence the Jewish claim of Abrahamic descendancy is unmasked as presumption, for it is not accompanied by this same Abrahamic quality of faith. Thus Abraham became one of Jesus' crown witnesses rather than the basis for Jewish religious complacency and presumption. I would argue that, while "seeing" does in fact occur at the climactic point in 8:56, it is not the predominant motif in the pericope. Rather, the primary issue is that of true *believing*:

- in 8:30, it is said that many (of the Jews, v. 22) came to believe in Jesus;
- in 8:31, Jesus addresses those who had believed and urges continual belief as the proof of true discipleship;
- the following interchange reveals that the Jews' faith in 8:30 was in fact inadequate, and hence these people did not meet the criterion of continual faith stipulated by Jesus in 8:31.

This seems to tie in with the well-known emphasis on believing in the entire Gospel (as is illustrated by the ninety-eight instances of *pisteuein*), including the prologue (1:12) and the purpose statement (20:30-31).[35] Now, how does Abraham figure in this controversy? It appears that he, unlike the Jewish leaders in Jesus' day, did show continual faith by taking the long view of looking forward to Jesus' coming, which is adumbrated in 8:56 by the expression "seeing Jesus' day." If I am correct, it is believing, more than seeing, that is emphasized here, which would be in keeping with Jesus' statement in 20:29 and the purpose statement in 20:30-31. One final point regarding the reference to Abraham in John 8:56: while he is said to have "seen" Jesus' day, there is no word regarding his testifying; it is simply said that "he was glad." (The implication here is that Abraham saw Jesus' day by faith and was glad; Jesus' Jewish opponents should be equally glad rather than oppose him.) Should this lack of "witnessing" terminology be noted by Miller, since he uses Abraham as a paradigm for "seeing *and* testifying"?

But what about Isaiah? According to the evangelist, he "saw his [Jesus'?] glory and he spoke of him" (12:41). The context for this assertion is the concluding indictment of Jewish unbelief in 12:37ff. Contrary to the notion that this unbelief *obstructed* God's plans, John affirms that it in fact *fulfilled* them, and in support of this rather startling assertion (how could Israel's rejection of the Messiah be willed by God?) John cites two passages from Isaiah, Isa 53:1 and 6:9-10.

The first quotation seems to serve the purpose of showing that Jewish unbelief was already massive during the period of Isaiah's preaching.

---

35. It is also interesting to note that this would comport well with Paul's emphasis on Abraham as "the believer" (e.g., Rom 4:9-25, esp. 4:19-25; Gal 3:6-29, esp. 3:6-9). See also Heb 11:8-12.

The implied answer to the prophet's question, "Lord, who has believed our report? And to whom has the arm of the Lord been revealed?" is "No one," or at least, "Very few." In keeping with John's theodicy, then, this constitutes scriptural proof that massive Jewish unbelief in light of genuine divine revelation is found typologically already at earlier strategic points in salvation history; hence the Jews' intransigence to Jesus' claims follows earlier typological precedent.

Second, Isa 6:10 is cited to show that human unbelief is said in that passage to be the ultimate result, not of human willful rejection and obduracy, but of divine hardening. Both points — that massive Jewish unbelief when faced with genuine divine revelation is not unprecedented, and that human willful rejection is ultimately the result of divine hardening — combine to form John's crucial theological point at the end of his first major section, which deals with Jesus' (largely unsuccessful) ministry to the Jews, namely, that both things are true at the same time. The Jews at large, represented by their leaders, did reject Jesus' messianic claim; and Jesus nonetheless is who he claimed to be — and all of this is in keeping with the message of the very Scriptures that the Jews invoked to make their case against Jesus. Hence Scripture serves as the grounds on which the argument concerning the legitimacy of Jesus is waged, and its message is shown to bear out *Jesus' and John's* contentions, not that of the Jews in Jesus', John's, or any other day.

Let me make a few points regarding this pericope in relation to Miller's presentation. First, as in the previous pericope, a case can be made that believing, more than seeing, is the major theme. In 12:37, it is said that the Jews were not *believing* in Jesus; this is followed by the first quotation from Isaiah in 12:38, where the prophet asks the question, "Lord, who has *believed* our report?" In the next verse, 12:39, it is said that "For this reason they *could not believe*," with the clear emphasis being on "could not," addressing the theodicy question mentioned above. To make this point, the second quotation from Isaiah is adduced, which finally does mention "seeing." Even there, though, it seems that "seeing with their eyes" is linked with "perceiving with their heart," only the combination of which leads to conversion and healing. Heart perception, in turn, is very close to "believing" as opposed to mere physical seeing. Then follows the evangelist's explanatory gloss regarding Isaiah "seeing his glory" and "speaking of him," which like the earlier reference to Abraham presents Isaiah as more open to genuine divine revelation than his Jewish compatriots (very likely involving an allusion to Isa 53:12, per Craig Evans as followed by Miller). But in 12:42-43, again, the emphasis is squarely on *believing,* or rather *not* believing, which is followed by Jesus' final indictment of Jewish unbelief in 12:44ff.

At least on a verbal level, then, there are two references to seeing in 12:37-44 (i.e., 12:40 and 41), one of which (12:40) is negative, while there are at least six references (seven, if "perceiving with their heart" is counted), and one in virtually every verse, to believing. For this reason I would argue that care must be taken not to sacrifice John's demonstrable verbal message (which seems to focus on believing or not believing) for an attractive larger hypothesis (which centers on seeing and testifying). On a related note, as Miller himself notes, John's method of using Scripture is complex. I would argue that we should try to do justice to his method in its complexity rather than run the risk of distorting it by unilaterally focusing on one aspect at the partial exclusion of others. For the Isaiah passage, this would include the theodicy, typology, and other thematic and literary aspects of John's message. Doing justice to the complexity of John's use of Scripture in this and other passages therefore calls for detailed analysis of each aspect of John's method, plus analysis of how the various aspects are interrelated.

The last figure discussed by Miller is Moses. A few comments must suffice.

First, on a minor note, is it overstating the point at least slightly to say that "Moses permeates the entire Johannine portrait of Jesus"?

Second, while it is true that "Jesus supersedes and replaces Moses as the decisive bearer of revelation" and thus in a sense "establishes an entirely new paradigm of revelation," is this all that needs to be said? Don Carson and others have inferred from the absence of a Greek adversative in 1:17 that John (unlike Paul) did not antithetically relate the law and Jesus Christ.[36] Carson, in commenting on Matt 5:17, has also shown that the Jews' major shortcoming was that they treated the law *qua lex* and thus missed the law's prophetic function pointing to Jesus.[37] Hence would it not be more accurate to say that for John the relationship between divine

36. D. A. Carson, *The Gospel according to John* (PNTC; Grand Rapids: Eerdmans, 1991) 132.

37. D. A. Carson, "Matthew," in *Expositor's Bible Commentary* 8 (Grand Rapids: Zondervan, 1984) 140-47; cf. Carson, *Gospel according to John,* 133-34.

revelation in the law and divine revelation in and through Jesus also contains an element of continuity, even typology, so that God is shown to act consistently throughout salvation history? Without denying Miller's point, perhaps it is important to supplement it by this additional qualification.

Third, in relation to Miller's paradigm of "vision and witness," where in John is it said that Moses saw God or Jesus, and is this John's emphasis? In the context of 1:17, in 1:18, the converse seems to be stated: no one (one surmises that this includes Moses) has seen God at any time. In 1:45, reference is made to "him of whom Moses in the law and also the prophets wrote." Miller describes this as Moses "seeing God" and as apprehending the glory of the Logos and witnessing to him. It should be pointed out, however, that there is no mention of Moses "seeing" in this or any other text in John, only of him "writing." Would this not indicate an emphasis on the written product, the Scriptures, rather than on the preceding act of seeing?

In fact, Moses' experience of seeing would seem to be largely irrelevant to John's audience; no one questioned his credentials. The more important question by far was whether or not the written product, the Scriptures, were to be read with an openness toward the possibility that they might accommodate the notion of Jesus being the Messiah (or even support it) or as essentially closed and as an end in themselves. Moving on to the major passage in John involving Moses, 5:39-47, there is no mention of Moses *seeing*, only of Moses *writing* about Jesus (5:46-47). The focus is on the Scriptures as the written text, not on any preceding vision of the preincarnate Jesus. Moreover, as in the case of Abraham, *believing* (or the lack thereof) is the declared emphasis in the Johannine text: "For if you *believed* Moses, you would *believe* me. . . . But if you do not *believe* his writings, how will you *believe* my words?"

To sum up. Of the four figures adduced as proof for Miller's thesis of vision/witness, John the Baptist is said to do both; Moses is said to have written, which is tantamount to bearing witness, though there is no mention of Moses seeing; Abraham is said to have seen Jesus' day, though there is no mention of Abraham bearing witness; and Isaiah is said to have both seen his glory and to have spoken of him. Overall, therefore, textual support for the thesis does not seem to be overwhelming. This is not to dispute the merits of the vision/witness proposal, just to put into perspective its paradigmatic status and to suggest a reformulation. Rather than the act of seeing followed by the bearing of witness, perhaps it might be more accurate to say that John's hermeneutic of Scripture involves an emphasis on openness toward divine revelation at whatever stage of salvation history individuals find themselves.

Abraham, Moses, Isaiah, and John the Baptist, each at his respective juncture of the history of salvation, were responsive to this divine revelation and open to what the future might hold, whether or not the revelation was narrowly christological and whether or not they fully understood the implications of that revelation. One might therefore speak of *the quality of openness and spiritual receptivity to divine revelation, followed by a willingness to act on that revelation in obedience and witness.* It is Jesus' challenge, and continues to be the challenge of John's Gospel, that those at later junctures of salvation history — be it the Jewish leadership in Jesus' day, John's audience in their day, or readers of John's Gospel ever since — ought to maintain a stance of openness toward divine revelation. If they do so, it is Jesus' and John's conviction that they will draw the proper conclusion regarding the identity of Jesus — that he is indeed the Christ, the Son of God — and that they will believe and witness to what they have come to know.

One final comment. I would have thought that a paper focusing on John's use of the OT might give central attention to John's "signs" concept. As I have tried to show elsewhere, "signs" are a key structural component in the Fourth Gospel and clearly involve OT antecedent theology, surrounding both Moses and the exodus and later prophetic literature.[38] Jesus called what he did "works"; John selected certain of Jesus' works, labeled them "signs," and drew attention to these works' symbolic significance as pointing to Jesus as Messiah. That he did so methodically is beyond question; also central is the role of "signs" in the concluding statement in 12:37ff. and the purpose statement in 20:30-31, not to speak of the two signs in Cana serving as a framing device for Jesus' first major ministry cycle in chapters 2–4 (cf. 2:11; 4:54). Theologically, too, the signs are highly significant, playing a key part in John's Gospel both negatively in his theodicy over against Jewish unbelief (12:37ff.) and positively in serving as aids to faith for believers (20:30-31; cf. 2:11; 10:38; 14:11). Especially since here one can neatly distinguish between Jesus' use of the OT and the evangelist's (only the latter uses the term "signs" in this Gospel, with the exception of 4:48), this would seem to serve as an ideal subject for the

38. See my article "The Seventh Johannine Sign: A Study in John's Christology," *BBR* 5 (1995) 87-103.

study of John's use of the OT involving larger theological and hermeneutical considerations.[39]

"Written Also for Our Sake: Paul's Use of Scripture in the Four Major Epistles, with a Study of 1 Corinthians 10"

James Aageson's oral remarks were concerned with intertextuality and inner biblical exegesis in Paul's major epistles and the problem of scriptural echoes as set forth in Richard Hays's *Echoes of Scripture in the Letters of Paul.* A later written paper (combined with his original, oral presentation and included in the present volume) develops these issues in detail in the case of 1 Cor 10:1-22. On the basis of passages such as Rom 4:23-24, Gal 4:29, and 1 Cor 9:10, Aageson contends that the Scriptures are written also for our sake. For Paul, the OT was not merely "an authoritative record" but "a sacred realm" that revealed the "very structure of righteousness according to faith," not merely "a static source of authority to be mined at will" but "a well-spring of . . . life-giving nourishment." Scripture was not just text, and interpretation not just discerning textual meaning; it involved "generating a sense of God's purpose for the world and its redemption."

In this, Paul operated with a christological presupposition rooted in his Damascus road experience, which led to conclusions that proved confounding to many of his Jewish contemporaries. Paul's promise-fulfillment framework is seen in passages such as Rom 1:1-2, Rom 3:21, and 1 Cor 15:3-4, which indicate Paul's belief that the gospel was "promised beforehand," "attested by," and "in accordance with" the OT, without his feeling a need to cite specific scriptural passages to substantiate this claim. Yet, Aageson says, "by and large Paul does not use direct scriptural quotations to establish his Christology, let alone to prove that Jesus is the Christ." According to Aageson, this contrasts with Luke's portrayal of Paul in Acts (e.g., 17:2-3; 28:23) where Paul is shown to prove *from the Scriptures* that Jesus is the Christ. Here I would argue that a better way to resolve this apparent discrepancy lies close at hand. To be sure, Paul rarely cites Scripture to establish his Christology or to prove that Jesus is the Christ in his *letters,*

---

39. Miller did add a section with the title "Is Scripture a 'Sign'?" to his final essay, arguing that Scripture has a "sign-like" quality to it, but when I called for a treatment of "signs" in relation to John's use of the OT, this is not what I had in mind.

but he did not have to: the believers already had embraced this conviction. The instances cited by Aageson in the book of Acts, on the other hand, deal with Paul's *missionary preaching,* where the apostle very much engaged in this kind of scriptural proof, since this was precisely what his non-Christian audience required in order to be persuaded by Paul's message.

In what follows, Aageson resolves the question of whether we ought to seek to reproduce Paul's hermeneutic or scriptural exegesis in our day by claiming that, not only is this not possible (owing to our different context), but it is not even desirable because it would be "a violation of our own responsibility to come to the texts of Scripture, Paul's letters included, as interpretive agents who take our contexts as seriously as Paul took his own." At this point in Aageson's paper, in my view, he moves from a more descriptive to a more speculative mode, and I must confess that I part company with him at that juncture in some significant ways, which I will seek to summarize briefly in the following remarks.

At times Aageson seems to present alternatives in unduly dichotomous ways, such as when he maintains that "scriptural interpretation ought not (perhaps cannot) be reduced to a *mere task of trying to discover meaning in the texts of Scripture.* . . . . Rather, it is a generative and creative task that is invariably open-ended" (emphasis added). Is there no middle ground here? Can one not try to discover scriptural meaning *first* and *then* seek to determine how that meaning applies to one's own situation?

Aageson himself seems to sense that some of his readers might be reluctant to follow him here, since he here speaks of "the risk of entering into a post-modern interpretive house of mirrors," but he is undaunted, adding that just as "Paul's reading of Scripture added yet one more element to the rich tradition of post-biblical interpretation," so "our readings of Scripture will do similarly." Personally, I find this statement astounding. Is there really no difference between Paul and us? What about his regular assertion of his apostleship at the outset of his letters? This seems to imply a certain status of authority that resists the type of interpretive leveling suggested by Aageson. Aageson adds that "to seek to do otherwise may simply render the texts mechanical, archaic, and lifeless." He does say "may," but does it have to? Again, a certain stereotype is conjured up that seems to slant the direction of the discussion Aageson's way, without, in my view, allowing for a middle ground, such as that one may engage Paul's argument both with a view toward understanding the apostle's context in his day and a view toward determining the significance of Paul's argument for one's own contemporary situation *without* doing so in a "mechanical, archaic, and lifeless" fashion.

Later in his paper, Aageson elaborates further that the church ought not merely to repeat Paul's thinking on a given issue but rather should understand that "Paul invites each theological generation into the question anew" — and come to conclusions different than Paul? This seems to be the implications of Aageson's statement, and, indeed, he proceeds to state that "Paul did not pronounce the final word" on the subject of Israel and the church in Romans 9–11 but rather "prompted and contributed to the church's ongoing conversation on the subject." Paul got the conversation started and made his contribution, but we must not feel bound by his conclusions and pronouncements. For my part, I find it difficult to square this assertion with, for example, Paul calling the teaching of the Judaizers "a different gospel" that is really "no gospel at all" in Gal 1:6-7, with the robust defense of his apostleship in 2 Corinthians 10–13 or his claim to unique insight into the divine *mystērion* of Gentile inclusion into the church on equal terms with the Jews in Eph 3:2-11 and other places.[40]

What does it mean for Paul's apostleship to "be fulfilled once again in our time," as Aageson puts it? Is there nothing foundational about Paul's salvation-historical role? It seems hard to deny this in light of Paul's own claims to apostleship. And what about Aageson's contention that Paul does not merely have "rough edges" and "conceptual gaps" in his use of Scripture, but that one can detect "even misreading" of Scripture on Paul's part (though Aageson does not elaborate on this point)? Reading Paul's letters, one does not get the impression that Paul saw himself merely as starting the conversation and as voicing his own humble opinion. Rather, his writings by and large exude the confidence that, by the grace of God and owing to his apostolic commission, Paul settled certain controversial issues, such as Gentile participation in the church on equal terms with Jews, once and for all.

For this reason I cannot follow Aageson here. If Paul's contribution is merely a start, but may actually misread Scripture, then what does that do to our view of Scripture? Scripture would not be authoritative but merely serve as a starting point for our own theological reflection. This would also

---

40. Cf. Richard B. Hays, *Echoes of Scripture in the Letters of Paul* (New Haven: Yale University Press, 1989) 180-83, who answers both questions, "Are Paul's specific interpretations of Scripture materially normative?" and "Are Paul's interpretive methods formally exemplary?" in the affirmative.

leave a vacuum of authority in that it would be unclear on what basis a given interpretation would be superior to any other. It is one thing to say that Paul wrestled with difficult issues that defied easy resolution or that he humbly acknowledged his own limitations in understanding divine mysteries, as he does in Rom 11:33-36, and quite another to maintain that Paul misread Scripture and that we must find theological solutions on our own. Paul's argument need not be given in the form of a "systematic theology" or a "polished theological treatise" to convey his apostolic authority. For these and other reasons, I submit that there are other ways to conceive of Scripture having been written "also for our sake" than to substitute our own reading of Scripture for that of the biblical writers.[41]

Let me now turn to Aageson's comments on 1 Cor 10:1-22 in which he challenges Richard Hays's claim that Paul is reading the wilderness story through the lens of Deuteronomy 32. Aageson contends that it is rather the images and ideas provoked by the wilderness rock tradition in the history of Jewish interpretation that shape Paul's christological identification of Christ as the rock in 1 Cor 10:4. Hays focuses on "background noise"; Aageson pays attention to the "intertextual shout that Paul imposes on the reader and that ultimately serves to shape the literary strategy of the apostle's text." Limited space does not permit an adjudication of this controversy. I do question whether reducing the role of Deuteronomy 32 in relation to 1 Corinthians 10 to "background noise" is adequate. I also wonder whether the intertextual trajectory presented by Aageson can be demonstrated to have served the determinative function in Paul's argument in 1 Corinthians 10 as Aageson contends. At the same time, I concur that more attention should be given to the baptismal and Eucharistic allusions in the text.

---

41. In an oral response following the presentation of this paper, Aageson contended that to the contemporary reader there seem to be instances where Paul misreads the OT. However, as I pointed out in response, a distinction ought to be made between the *appearance* of such a misreading and an *actual* misreading of the OT in Paul. It is my contention that, while the former may be present, the latter is doubtful. Aageson countered by saying that this is too "Christian" a reading of Paul, to which I pleaded guilty. I do read Paul as a Christian (how could I do otherwise?), as does Aageson, but I deny that this necessarily has a negative effect on my ability to understand Paul's use of Scripture. There is nothing wrong with giving Paul the benefit of a doubt or with being open to the possibility that the problem in a given instance of Paul's use of the OT is, not Paul's reading (or misreading) of the OT, but my limited ability to understand it.

Overall, it seems to me that more weight ought to be assigned to the context of 1 Corinthians 10 in the epistle. As is commonly acknowledged, chapters 7–16 contain Paul's responses to various questions posed by the Corinthians. The topic addressed in chapters 8–11 is that of the Corinthians' participation in idolatrous worship in the context of their eating of food that had been sacrificed to idols in the pagan temples. While the apostle acknowledges the non-reality of pagan gods, he advocates considerateness and a judicious, responsible use of one's Christian freedom and knowledge rather than flaunting one's superior insight, which would be unloving and divisive.

In chapter 9 Paul uses himself as an example. As an apostle, he is willing to relinquish his own rights, focusing on gospel essentials instead. Otherwise, he might be disqualified (1 Cor 9:27). In this context, then, he adduces the example (1 Cor 10:6, 11) of the ancient Israelites, who partook of the spiritual nourishment provided by God (the rock in the wilderness representing — that is, typologically foreshadowing — Christ), but committed idolatry nonetheless. This serves to illustrate the contemporary danger: that the Corinthians participate in the Lord's Supper but also partake of idolatrous practices.

The Israelites' example thus serves as a salvation-historical reference point for the apostle's warning against pride. One's spiritual privileges may become someone else's downfall. Hence the bottom line in 1 Cor 10:14 is this: flee from idolatry. Similar to the recipients of the epistle to the Hebrews, a choice is required from the Corinthians. They cannot have one foot in the church and another in their pagan surroundings. On a practical level, Paul's solution is, therefore, that the Corinthians may partake of food offered to idols where such does not violate anyone's conscience; where it does, they ought to refrain (10:23-30). Everything should be done to the glory of God and for the furtherance of the gospel; in this the Corinthians should follow the apostle's example (10:31–11:1).

In light of the embeddedness of 1 Cor 10:1-22 in its literary context, then, it seems possible to miss the forest for the trees and to make too much of the question of what constituted the *Vorlage* or antecedent trajectory for Paul's discussion. While this is an important question, even more important is Paul's theological message. Hence the critical issue to be understood is the way in which the OT background adduced by Paul serves as an example for the Corinthians' contemporary situation. In this context, Paul points the way forward by presenting himself as the model to follow.

Not questions of intertextuality but the theological issues raised and adjudicated by the apostle should occupy one's primary attention.

"In the Face of the Empire: Paul's Use of Scripture in the Shorter Epistles"

In her treatment of Paul's use of the OT in his shorter epistles (Ephesians, Philippians, Colossians, 1 and 2 Thessalonians, and Philemon), Sylvia Keesmaat utilizes a narrative approach in order to show that the story of the covenant God in relation to both Israel and the world provides a wider conceptual matrix for Paul's reflections on how to be followers of Jesus, the Messiah of the covenant God. She identifies empire, and specifically the flourishing imperial cults, as the primary point of reference. In his apologetic against the empire, Paul frequently employs the vocabulary and imagery of the empire, and his challenge of the imperial cults is regularly and significantly couched in his allusion to Israel's Scriptures.

Ephesians is interpreted against the backdrop of the *pax Romana*, where Rome, too, made peace by blood of the cross — by crucifying the followers of Jesus — and of Roman victory parades, which would later issue in coins proclaiming *Judea capta*. Paul's purpose is identified as subversion of Roman imperial power by the message of salvation in Jesus Christ. Philippians, in the celebrated Christ-hymn of 2:5-11, sets forth how Jesus, not the Roman emperor, is to be hailed as *kyrios*. In Colossians, specifically in Col 1:15-20, Keesmaat plausibly detects a "faint echo" of Gen 9:8-17, one of several instances where Paul is seen to assert the primacy of the story of Jesus over that of Rome; and this alternative story line, with its proclamation of a different kind of peace, is in turn found to be rooted deeply within the story of Israel.

Keesmaat finds similar OT echoes in the Thessalonian correspondence and in the epistle to Philemon. Of particular interest is the fact that Keesmaat in her reading of Philemon discerns repeated not-so-subtle hints on Paul's part that he wants Philemon to free Onesimus, his slave turned fellow Christian. This seems to cast doubt on William Webb's recently set forth "trajectory hermeneutic" (or, as he calls it, "movement-of-the-redemptive-spirit hermeneutic"), which rests to a significant extent on the contention that Paul had not yet come to a clear understanding that slavery was wrong. In the way Paul evokes Israel's story to challenge that of

Rome, Keesmaat finds an important paradigm for contemporary Christians. We, too, must learn to subvert the story of our empire with its consumer culture, powerful corporations, and military might.

While not everyone will see all the allusions or echoes Keesmaat detects in the shorter Pauline letters, and while some may judge her narrative approach to be in need of supplementation by other exegetical strategies, I found her treatment of Paul's use of the OT both suggestive and intriguing. She has made a good case for Paul's use of the OT to challenge the Roman empire. She does not offer any explanation as to why Paul would use the *OT* to engage the empire rather than doing so in some other way. This would be an interesting subject for further discussion. On a note of caution, it may be helpful to guard against the danger of a reductionism that interprets everything in these letters against the imperial paradigm set forth by Keesmaat. Rather than being Paul's *only* strategy, using Israel's story to critique that of Rome may more properly be considered to be one of several major strategies employed by the apostle in his use of the OT in these letters.

On a much more minor note, some readers may differ politically with Keesmaat's repeated negative allusions to the United States' recent military interventions in Afghanistan and Iraq.

"Job as Exemplar in the Epistle of James"

Kurt Richardson's paper is remarkable already in the skill he shows in writing a close to twenty-page, erudite paper on one or two verses of Scripture (James 5:10-11). But then, a recent writer managed to write an entire monograph on James 5:11![42] The paper focuses on a biblical writer's reference, not to specific texts of Scripture, but to a person mentioned prominently in the OT — Job. Notably, this is the only reference to the person of Job in the entire NT. After providing an insightful discussion of the kind of sapiential prophet Job's book portrays him to be, Richardson turns to an analysis of Job's role in James.

For James, "Job is the exemplary sapiential prophet who endures, pa-

---

42. Theresia Hainthaler, *"Von der Ausdauer Ijobs habt ihr gehört"* (Jak 5:11). *Zur Bedeutung des Buches Ijob im Neuen Testament* (Frankfurt am Main: Peter Lang, 1998); cited by Richardson in n. 13ff.

tient in his suffering." In context, the reference is probably to the suffering endured by the poor at the hands of the rich (James 5:1-6). Patience denotes waiting upon God rather than taking matters into one's own hands. Richardson notes that the connection of the present passage with the makarism of 1:12 shows how closely related the example of Job is to the purpose of the entire letter. He also notes the connection with the final beatitude of Jesus in Matt 5:11-12. Patience, in turn, serves as the proof of faith (James 1:3, 4, 12), for without faith there can be no true endurance. Those who accept God's purpose of suffering will witness at the Lord's return both the judgment of the rich and the reward of those who endured. This is summed up in the rhetorical question of 2:5: "Did not God choose the poor of this world to be rich in faith and heirs of the kingdom which he promised to those who love him?"

Richardson shows how James does not merely refer to Job in a general manner; he has appropriated fully the sense of *hypomonē* in this OT book: "endurance is the response to an external catastrophe that has befallen the believer according to the plan of God to test the believer's faith." Not only was Job patient in the face of unjust suffering; in the end he was blessed by God. Moreover, Job's patience proved that his faith was genuine. Richardson notes that Job and James also share a common emphasis on speech. James extols the virtue of controlling one's tongue (James 3:2); Job's book testifies that "[i]n all this Job did not sin with his lips" (Job 2:10; cf. 9:14-21). In the end, James notes that the Lord was shown to be full of compassion and mercy (James 5:11; cf. Job 42:10-17).[43] Hence endurance in suffering is shown to result in greater blessing and a deeper sense of God's mercy and compassion.

Richardson concludes that Job serves as a fitting exemplar for James in that, while there were many unrighteous rich who exploited the poor, there were also some righteous rich who must "glory in their humiliation" (1:10), and it is with regard to those *righteous rich* that Job serves as an exemplar (Richardson cites Job 29:1-17). As Richardson rightly notes, this defies an oversimplified reading of James as casting the rich as outsiders. Richardson proceeds to reiterate that "Job is an exemplar of endurance in the face of non-judgmental testing." Unlike Hebrews 12, this testing is not a disciplining and chastising, but a process of strengthening for future expe-

43. Richardson helpfully notes the connection between James 5:11 and the final turning point in Job, where likewise God's purpose is mentioned (Job 42:2).

riences, so that wisdom will teach the believer patience. According to James, the result of endurance is the perfection of one's faith (1:4). James's is an apocalyptic orientation that points to the transitory nature of wealth (1:11b; cf. Isa 40:7; Job 14:2).

Richardson's paper is a fascinating case study of the use of the OT by a NT writer that focuses, not on one or several individual passages of a book of Scripture, but on the message of that book in its entirety. In essence, it is as if Job himself has come to personify the virtue of endurance under suffering. Hence Job as a person transcends individual passages in the book of Job as an almost legendary character to whom reference can be made without citing specific passages. At the same time, Richardson has shown how James's appropriation of the book of Job is anything but glib, and, to the contrary, how James has grasped the essential message of the book, in a way that is similar, I might add, to how one might grasp the moral of one of Aesop's fables or the major point (or points) of one of Jesus' parables.

I have but one additional comment to make. A certain dissonance emerges at the very end of Richardson's paper when Job is cited as an exemplar of two things: (1) the righteous rich; and (2) endurance in the face of non-judgmental testing. On the face of it, these two aspects seem to be contradictory, since there is no necessary relation between being rich and enduring suffering. In fact, the opposite appears to be the case. The rich, because of their wealth, are typically the ones who impose suffering on the poor rather than being the victims of suffering. I believe that it is precisely at the intersection and resolution of these two paradoxical aspects of Job's exemplary function that one arrives at a deeper understanding of James's appropriation of Job. I submit that it is not merely as a *righteous rich* person that Job serves as an exemplar but as a righteous rich person *who endured non-judgmental testing.*

In this life the rich often are able to avoid suffering. This is where the asset of their wealth turns into a major liability. For their wealth provides the rich with a means of insulating themselves from suffering and often renders them perpetrators of injustice in this life, until they die and face God's judgment or until Christ returns; then they are themselves subject to judgment, yet now it is too late for them to humble themselves. Job is different precisely in that he, while wealthy, allowed himself to be humbled in this life and was willing to endure such suffering. He thus allowed God's judgment to do its work on him still during his earthly lifetime and thus was able to experience God's blessing beyond the suffering. By implication, any other rich person willing to be humbled in such a way will likewise experience God's blessing.

Yet, perhaps even more important, in the context of James 5:10-11 Job in fact serves as an example for the poor (not rich) who endure abuse by the rich. Job, the wealthy-turned-pauper, in his endurance serves as an example even for those who were never (as he was) wealthy in the first place. There is a certain lack of parallelism in this analogy in that Job endured the loss of wealth and responded well, while the poor in James's audience never had to cope with such a loss. Yet the major point of the analogy stands nonetheless: Job, in his experience of the loss of wealth, and James's hearers, in their experience of exploitation by the rich, require endurance, even though the connection between Job's initial and eventual wealth and James's audience's experience of abuse by the wealthy is not perfectly analogous. Thus the common denominator may be found not so much in the circumstances of Job and James's hearers as in their common experience "that the Lord is full of compassion and mercy" (James 5:11).

Conclusion

It is my conviction that the papers offered in this Bingham colloquium volume make an important contribution to the ongoing discussion of the complex and multifaceted issues surrounding the NT use of the OT. Dennis Stamps has made an important case for looking at this issue in terms of rhetoric and its effect of persuasion. Timothy McLay has provided us with a well-argued test case of one use of Scripture in the NT, which demonstrates that matters are much more complicated and difficult to adjudicate than is often recognized, even by scholars. Michael Knowles has advanced discussion of Matthew's use of the OT by distinguishing between Matthew's and Jesus' use (complete with different introductory formulae) and by making a plausible case that Matthew's "messianic exegesis" was grounded in Jesus' own reading of Scripture. Craig Evans has set forth the original and provocative thesis that Mark wrote to challenge the contemporary notion that Vespasian was the fulfillment of prophecy and the world's savior. Stanley Porter has shown that the use of Scripture in Luke-Acts was not merely a proof-texting enterprise but part of Luke's fundamental hermeneutic.

In a very interesting and thought-provoking contribution, Paul

Miller has suggested that John's use of the OT focused on Scripture as a witness by those who saw the pre-incarnate Jesus in terms of "vision/witness." In salvation-historical order, this would include Abraham, Moses, Isaiah, and John the Baptist. While I have suggested certain modifications of Miller's thesis and noted that John's "signs" theology would also merit significant attention, Miller's treatment is suggestive at many points and is sure to make a major contribution to the study of John's use of the OT. James Aageson has made a bold case for the interpretive responsibility and privilege of the contemporary reader of Scripture, suggesting that, since Scripture is "written also for our sake," we must read Scripture for ourselves and come to our own conclusion regarding its significance for us today. While I have begged to differ with him at these points, clearly the last word has not been spoken, and others will have to take up this important issue. Sylvia Keesmaat has shown, convincingly in my opinion, how Paul's use of the OT in the shorter epistles was significantly shaped by his effort to contextualize his message in his Greco-Roman surroundings.

Kurt Richardson, last but not least, has contributed a fine study on Job as exemplar in James. Job, as a well-known OT figure, is cited in James's epistle as an exemplar of faithfulness in non-judgmental suffering, particularly for those readers who suffered exploitation at the hands of the rich in James's day.

While the conference papers covered a vast area of topics, it is probably inevitable that certain lacunae were left. My essay, prepared subsequent to the conference on the Pastorals, General Epistles, and Revelation, is designed to close some of this gap. Research on these and other topics will no doubt continue, and I believe scholarship stands in the debt of the scholars who participated in this Bingham colloquium.

Index of Modern Authors

Clark, H. H., 34, 35
Clarke, A. D., 108
Clines, D. J. A., 218
Collins, J., 57
Collins, R. F., 186
Conzelmann, H., 105, 177
Coogan, M., 262
Cook, E. M., 92
Cox, H., 211
Cranfield, C. E. B., 87
Crenshaw, J., 215
Cross, F. L., 135, 164
Cross, F. M., 56
Croy, N. C., 219

Dahl, N., 105
Danker, F., 186, 206
Davids, P. H., 214, 215, 219
Davies, W. D., 62, 63, 65, 67, 73-75
De Boer, M. C., 144
Deissmann, A., 206
Dittenberger, W., 93
Dockery, D. S., 21
Dodd, C. H., 18, 19, 131, 139, 153
Doeve, W., 164
Draisma, S., 19
Driver, S. R., 164, 165
Droge, A. J., 31
Dunn, J. D. G., 31, 124, 137
Dupont, J., 105, 124
Dwyer, T., 86

Edgar, D. H., 220
Ehrenberg, V., 93
Ehrhardt, A., 106
Ehrman, B., 55
Eliot, T. S., 59, 60, 70, 265
Elliott, N., 182, 184
Ellis, E. E., 40, 70, 114, 129-31, 133, 152, 164, 165, 262
Eltester, W., 105, 110, 113
Enns, P., 14
Evans, C. A., 9, 11, 14, 15, 25, 27, 29, 41, 97, 101, 104-6, 108, 110-15, 125, 126, 128,

130, 135, 140, 183, 255, 269, 277, 278, 281
Evans, C. F., 12, 27

Ferguson, S. B., 244
Fernández Marcos, N., 57
Fewell, D. N., 19
Fields, W. W., 55
Fischel, H. A., 26
Fish, S. E., 17
Fishbane, M., 14, 55, 57, 71, 153
Fishwick, D., 94
Fisk, B. N., 172
Fitzmyer, J. A., 100
Fling, P., 47, 57
Fortna, R. T., 133
Foster, P., 60
France, R. T., 12, 13, 15, 256
Franklin, E., 106, 107
Funk, R. W., 102

Gaebelein, F. E., 117
García Martínez, F., 101, 113
Georgi, D., 182, 185
Gerrig, R. R., 34, 35
Glasson, T. F., 133, 143
Green, J. B., 10, 12, 24, 125
Greer, R. A., 14
Guelich, R. A., 102
Gundry, R. H., 13, 15, 73, 75, 79, 87

Haag, E., 57
Haenchen, E., 121
Hafemann, S. J., 238
Hainthaler, T., 219, 221, 223-26, 229, 290
Hanson, A. T., 21, 137, 138, 240, 277
Hardesty, N., 232
Harnack, A., 31
Harris, J. R., 152
Harrison, J. R., 184, 185, 205
Hartin, P. J., 11
Hatch, E., 31
Hatina, T. R., 86
Hay, D., 66

Index of Ancient Sources

13:14	62	28:17	82	10:4	85
13:23	200	28:18-20	82	10:6-8	77
13:35	74, 77	28:20	82	10:6-7	84
13:52	61			10:19	84, 269
15:7-9	77	**Mark**		10:45	269
15:7	147	1–8:26	102	10:52	96
16	62	1:1	94	11	79
18:16	77, 234	1:2-3	85, 269	11:9-10	85
19:4-5	64, 77	1:2	62, 63, 76, 84, 85,	11:12-14	79, 97
19:7	147		95, 102	11:17	63, 77, 269
21	65, 79, 267	1:3	74, 76, 85, 102	11:17a	85
21:2	78	1:10	85	11:17b	85
21:4-5	77, 78	1:11	85	11:20-21	79
21:5	73, 74	1:14-15	103	11:20	97
21:9	65, 79	1:17	66	12:1-9	79
21:13	63, 77, 79	1:41	96	12:1	85, 269
21:14	75, 79	1:44	147	12:10-11	65, 77, 79, 85,
21:15	65, 79	2	62		269
21:16	65, 77	2:5	96	12:19	269
21:18-21	79	2:23-28	85, 269	12:26	64, 77, 84, 147,
21:33-41	79	2:25-26	64, 76		269
21:42	65, 77, 79, 244	4:11	74	12:29-31	84
21:43	79	4:11-12	85, 86, 139	12:36	66, 77, 85, 148,
22:24	147	4:12	77, 85, 269		269
22:31-32	64, 77	4:20	200	13	87
22:31	65	4:29	85	13:2	87, 96
22:43	148	5:34	96	13:13	220
22:44	66, 77	6:1-6	110, 116	13:14	85, 269
23:35	262	6:14-29	269	13:18	87
24:27	204	6:34	84	13:19	269
24:30	66, 77	6:56	96	13:24-26	269
24:31	204	7:6-7	85, 269	13:26	66, 77, 85
25:5	204	7:6	77, 147	13:35-37	204
26:24	63, 77	7:10	84, 147, 269	14:1	85
26:31	63, 77	7:33	96	14:18	85, 269
26:32	82	8:17-18	139	14:21	63, 77
26:54	72, 77	8:18	85, 269	14:24	85, 86
26:56	62, 72, 77	9:7	85	14:27	63, 77, 85, 86,
26:64	66, 77	9:11-12	269		269
27:9-10	75, 77	9:12	85, 269	14:29	77
28:7	82	9:48	85	14:34	85, 269
28:8	82	10:3	147	14:49	62, 72
28:10	82	10:4-8	269	14:50	269